DEGREES OF FREEDOM

DEGREES OF FREEDOM

LOUISIANA AND
CUBA AFTER SLAVERY

Rebecca J. Scott

*For Emmet Eichacker,
with very best wishes,
Rebecca Scott
January 2006*

THE BELKNAP PRESS OF
HARVARD UNIVERSITY PRESS
Cambridge, Massachusetts
London, England
2005

Library of Congress Cataloging-in-Publication Data

Scott, Rebecca J. (Rebecca Jarvis), 1950–
Degrees of freedom : Louisiana and Cuba after slavery / Rebecca J. Scott.
p.   cm.
Includes bibliographical references and index.
ISBN 0-674-01932-6 (alk. paper)
1. African Americans—Civil rights—Louisiana—History.   2. Citizenship—
Louisiana—History.   3. Slaves—Emancipation—Louisiana.   4. Sugar growing—
Social aspects—Louisiana—History.   5. Louisiana—Race relations.   6. Blacks—
Civil rights—Cuba—History.   7. Citizenship—Cuba—History.   8. Slaves—
Emancipation—Cuba.   9. Sugar growing—Social aspects—Cuba—History.
10. Cuba—Race relations.   I. Title.

E185.93.L6S29 2005
323.1196'07291'09034—dc22   2005047035

To the memory of Tomás Pérez y Pérez

Contents

Maps

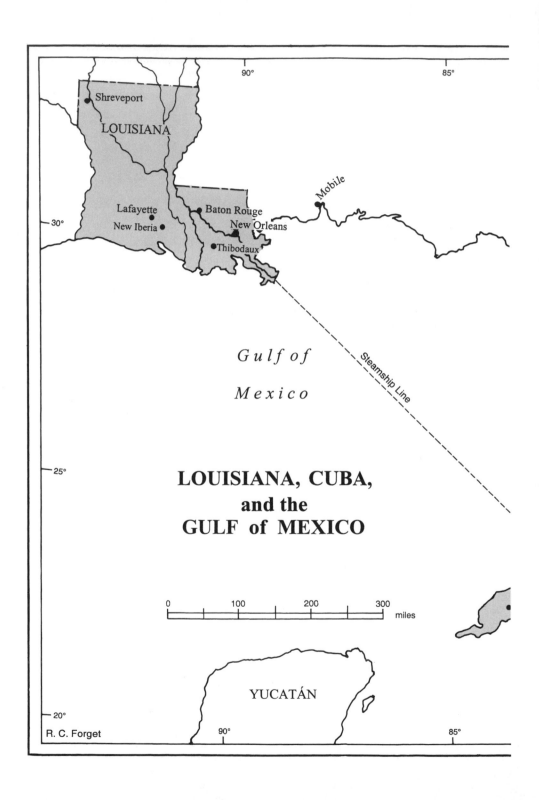

Gulf of

Mexico

Steamship Line

**LOUISIANA, CUBA,
and the
GULF of MEXICO**

LOUISIANA

Shreveport

Lafayette
New Iberia

Baton Rouge
New Orleans
Thibodaux

Mobile

YUCATÁN

R. C. Forget

0   100   200   300
miles

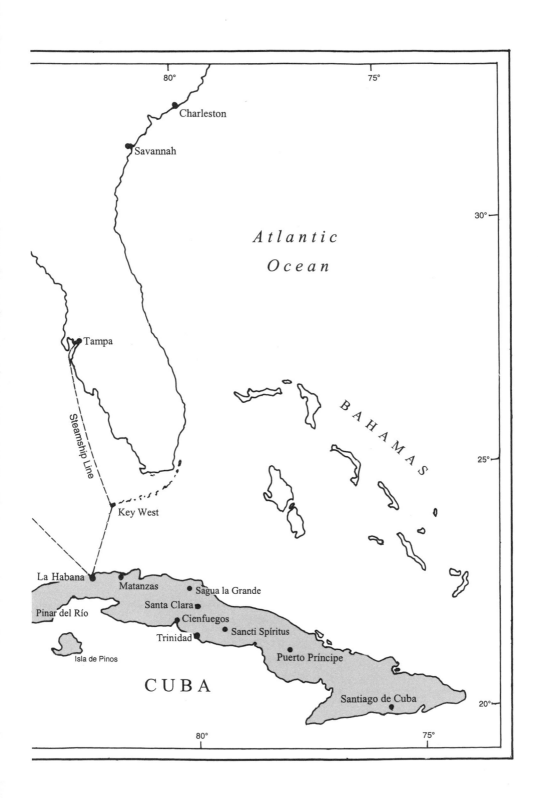

80°

75°

● Charleston

● Savannah

*Atlantic
Ocean*

B A H A M A S

30°

25°

● Tampa

Steamship Line

● Key West

La Habana ●
Matanzas ●
● Sagua la Grande

Santa Clara ●

Pinar del Río

● Cienfuegos

● Sancti Spíritus

Trinidad ●

Isla de Pinos

● Puerto Príncipe

C U B A

● Santiago de Cuba

20°

80°

75°

DEGREES OF
FREEDOM

Introduction

AT THE MIDPOINT OF THE NINETEENTH CENTURY, THE PLANTATION production of sugar in both Louisiana and Cuba rested on the enslaved labor of tens of thousands of men and women of African descent. On both sides of the Gulf of Mexico slaves planted, hoed, cut, lifted, and hauled the sugar cane. On through the night work crews kept the mills grinding and the kettles boiling to turn the cane juice into crystals. It seemed that there would be no end to constraint and exertion.

Yet in the second half of the nineteenth century each of these slave systems was destroyed by war and by the upheaval and legislation that followed war. At this moment, when the two economies faced enormous challenges, former slaves stepped forcefully onto the public scene. As soldiers, laborers, and traders, as farmers and activists, they sought to win and then give durable meaning to their freedom. The place of black and white workers within the sugar economy, and the conditions of their encounters with each other, proved to be a crucial element in a struggle in which labor and politics were inextricably linked. There is, in effect, no convincing way to isolate something called "race relations" from the specific ways in which black labor was employed in the countryside and power was reallocated in the polity. People did not live their "race" separate from their work or their politics.

Planters and merchants in Havana and New Orleans, part of the same intertwined Atlantic world, kept a close eye on each other. A record-breaking harvest in Cuba could mean lowered profits in Louisiana; a new tariff in the United States could be a blow to Cuban producers. At the same time, the Caribbean and the Gulf of Mexico opened the way to the circulation of people, information, and ideas. Political activists in New Orleans and Havana often knew of each other's campaigns and tribulations.

Louisiana and Cuba were for each other nearby possible worlds, evolving differently and embodying alternatives hidden at home but visible abroad. The stories of Louisiana and Cuba also overlapped and intersected, making comparison a matter of daily experience. Men and women from each society could begin to see what freedom had come to mean on the other shore, with all that this might suggest about their own future. More ominously, each could see some of the forces working against them, though such forces operated quite differently on either side of the Gulf of Mexico.

In the summer of 1884, for example, the exiled Cuban rebel leaders Antonio Maceo and Máximo Gómez took a steamship from San Pedro Sula, Honduras, to New Orleans. Maceo, born into a free family of color in Santiago, Cuba, and Gómez, born into a white family in the Dominican Republic, were both veterans and symbols of the armed struggle for Cuban independence that had begun in 1868. They were traveling together to the United States to build morale among Cuban exiles and to raise money for the next attempt. They arrived in New Orleans on August 9 and moved with their families into a rented house at 227 St. Phillip, in the neighborhood of Faubourg Tremé, a few blocks from Perseverance Masonic Hall and a few more from Economy Hall, longstanding places of sociability and politics for people of color. Two decades after the end of slavery in Louisiana, New Orleans was paradoxically a bastion of white supremacy in politics and a fertile ground for cross-racial organizing in the public sphere, particularly in the dockworkers' unions and among civil rights activists. Although it was not the

norm for a white family and a family of color to rent a house together, Faubourg
Tremé was as likely a place as any to be able to breach the state's increasingly rigid
color line.[1]

In the 1880s Antonio Maceo was known in the greater Caribbean as a man of
color who combined a commitment to slave emancipation and racial equality with
a genius for military leadership and an implacable hostility to Spanish colonial
rule. In New Orleans, however, he and Gómez seem to have lived discreetly, leaving their families in Faubourg Tremé while they traveled to Florida and New York
to address Cuban exiles. After a visit to Mexico to seek diplomatic support,
Maceo left New Orleans in 1885, the plans for an immediate renewal of armed
struggle abandoned. Along with his brother José and the black Cuban veteran
Agustín Cebreco, he spent much of 1887 supporting himself by building houses
on contract with the Panama Canal Company, and then moved on to Costa Rica.[2]

In 1895 Maceo and Gómez returned to Cuba and led a stunning rebel invasion
from the east to the west of the island. That spring, a group of Louisiana activists
put the news of the Cuban rebels' military exploits on the front page of their New
Orleans newspaper, *The Crusader*. These members of what they called the Citizens'
Committee were in the midst of organizing Homer Plessy's Supreme Court challenge to Louisiana's racial segregation, but they did not fail to follow the progress
of Maceo's campaign in Cuba.[3]

These crossings and recrossings of the Gulf of Mexico—the soldier Antonio
Maceo's journeying from Cuba to New Orleans, and the *Crusader*'s invocation of a
broadly Caribbean political community—suggest something of the geographic
scope of the postemancipation struggle for freedom and citizenship. By February
of 1898, when the explosion of the U.S. battleship *Maine* in Havana harbor moved
the United States toward intervention in the Cuban war against Spanish rule, the
possibility of linking the fate of Cuba to that of Louisiana became even more apparent. Pierre Carmouche, a blacksmith from Donaldsonville, Louisiana, and a
vocal supporter of the Plessy challenge, wrote to the U.S. secretary of war to offer his services and those of 250 other "colored Americans, on short notice, in the
defence of our country, at home or abroad." In July, a few months after the entry
of the United States into the Cuban war, Carmouche was mustered into a regi-

ment of U.S. Volunteers and commissioned first lieutenant. Thousands of black Louisianians lined the sidewalks of New Orleans on August 17 as the regiments marched to the docks and boarded the troop transport for Santiago, Cuba.[4]

After a few weeks in Santiago, Carmouche and the men of the Ninth Volunteers took the train across the Boniato Ridge to the town of San Luis, which they were to garrison while the terms of peace between Spain and the United States were being negotiated. This was Antonio Maceo's home territory, and his family still lived in the neighborhood. But Maceo had died in the struggle, and it was his former comrade General Agustín Cebreco whose rebel soldiers held the countryside around San Luis, watching and wondering what the U.S. military intervention and occupation of Cuba would bring. Cuban observers were by no means convinced that the U.S. Ninth Volunteers actually constituted a contribution to what Pierre Carmouche had envisioned as "Cuba libre and the success of Maceo."[5]

Maceo's trip to the United States and Carmouche's to Cuba were each a means to an end, an effort to gain rights at home by going farther afield in pursuit of alliances and respect. Maceo had hoped to find the freedom to organize in order to renew a military struggle. Carmouche hoped to prove his community's patriotism and valor to a broad North American public in the face of crushing defeats for equal rights at home in Louisiana. Maceo's initial goal of Cuban independence from Spain was accomplished after his death, though his larger vision of racial confraternity was far harder to achieve. Carmouche's goal of civil rights and respect was thwarted at every turn. Carmouche himself left Louisiana in despair and ended his days working as a janitor in Detroit, Michigan.

The book that follows is a comparative history which, along the way, turns into something else. Its initial chapters build on the historical tradition of the comparative study of slavery and emancipation. They explore two worlds of sugar plantations and their neighboring farms and towns, tracing the achievement of freedom and the exercise of political voice. The second half of the book, however, moves into a different register, as the stories become intertwined rather than juxtaposed, and several of the dramatis personae begin to meet one another.

The comparative framework itself has a history as a mode of analysis. Faced with the panorama of segregation, black disfranchisement, and racialized violence in the American South, historians in the post—World War II era asked whether the legacies of slavery had perhaps played themselves out differently elsewhere.[6] Soldiers, travelers, journalists, activists, and novelists had long commented on the different social meanings of color in the United States and Latin America, but such observations were hard to interpret rigorously. Practices found in Latin America, for example, could be attributed to "Latin culture" or Catholic doctrine, to different states of economic development or different experiences of emancipation. Moreover, appearances of difference could themselves be deceiving. Seemingly more flexible racial etiquettes might disguise a reality of dichotomies and discrimination. But recognizing that things were different elsewhere did make the racial order of the U.S. South seem less natural and less timeless, and invited the development of theories and interpretations to explain the difference.

This book differs from most earlier works in that it takes the construction of postemancipation society, rather than slavery or race relations, as the subject for comparison.[7] It also moves back and forth across different scales of observation, seeking to understand the structural constraints under which individuals and groups operated after the end of slavery, and the role their actions had in modifying those constraints. Tracing the story of the meanings of freedom requires particular attention to method and moment. It would be foolhardy to generalize about the lives of the several hundred thousand men, women, and children spread across the largest island in the Caribbean or about their counterparts in the entire state of Louisiana. An alternative is to plunge into microhistory, seeking insight into historical dynamics by reconstructing local events and the social networks in which they unfold. Microhistory has costs, however, since observations bounded by the limitations of a single plantation or neighborhood can be disproportionately shaped by the idiosyncrasies of individuals, terrain, or circumstances.

One strategy for resolving this problem is to employ a zoom lens, shifting the magnification and the focal point in order to seek out patterns of individual behavior without losing sight of the ways in which these are framed by a broader economy and polity. For much of the Cuban portion of this study, the panoramic view encompasses the central province of Santa Clara, a region where small-scale agriculture persisted alongside a massive sugar industry. The south coast district of Cienfuegos, where sugar production had expanded rapidly from midcentury onward, provides a closer view of the world of cane. And at intervals, two adjacent plantations in a single Cienfuegos neighborhood—Soledad and Santa Rosalía—come into focus as struggles for authority take the form of a shouting match between an administrator and an enslaved woman, or a brawl at a country store. By moving back and forth between these levels, one can tell a story in which names and faces emerge, while situating the actions of individuals within larger structures of production and political organization.[8]

Louisiana's world of cane was largely confined to the state's southern parishes, with their commercial gaze trained on New Orleans. The city and its surrounding sugar zone thus provide an appropriate panorama. Labor organizing, White League repression, and electoral mobilization can be seen in particular detail by narrowing the aperture and focusing on the bayou parishes west of the city, where these dramas were played out with particular intensity. Individual towns and plantations sometimes become the point of reference, as in the spring of 1898 when Pierre Carmouche climbed on his horse in Donaldsonville and rode along the river and the bayou to convince his fellow black citizens in places like Smoke Bend and Belle Alliance that their futures and their principles would be well served by joining him in volunteering to serve in the war in Cuba.[9]

I have borrowed the title *Degrees of Freedom* from the physicists, who speak of the "degrees of freedom" of a dynamically evolving system. These are the number of independent dimensions along which one must specify values for each of the component elements in order to specify fully the state of the entire system at a given moment. Statisticians use the same phrase to capture the process by which, as values for different elements of a system are fixed on each of its dimensions, the range of possibilities for the total state of the system narrows. The application of the concept to social processes is of course metaphorical—but it helps to convey the way in which two broadly similar systems can evolve over time into dramatically different end states. Close scrutiny of that evolution concentrates our attention on the dimensions along which key variations occur. Even if initial conditions are comparable, and even though the processes of change themselves can be seen to be governed by causation against a similar background, evolution over time possesses certain genuine degrees of freedom.[10]

Detailed comparative study permits an exploration of structures and choices as they became manifest in actual space and time. Such comparison helps us to spot countercurrents as well as the dominant themes, and to avoid romanticizing or demonizing on the basis of individual events or features. A racially exclusive system may inadvertently create space for fragile cross-racial alliances, like those that persisted on the New Orleans waterfront and reemerged in Louisiana politics in the 1890s. A more inclusive political system makes room for more durable alliances, but the state may nonetheless employ racialized violence, as occurred in Cuba in 1912. Examining the points of similarity and variation between two systems enables us to see the tensions within each, while investigating the sources of their variance from each other.

The tightly linked contests for citizenship carried out at the end the nineteenth century and into the start of the twentieth in Cuba and Louisiana found contrasting constitutional expression, which in turn shaped future possibilities long beyond the immediate postemancipation period. In 1898 African Americans in Louisiana faced disfranchisement in a new state constitution, and in 1901 Cubans reached toward a guarantee of universal manhood suffrage in a new national constitution. For former slaves and their descendants, however, no resolution was ever definitive, and each racial order still contained glimpses of its opposite. Rural workers in Louisiana saw their electoral rights denied, but activists in New Orleans sought through mutual-aid associations and judicial challenge to restore some of these rights and to allocate new resources to former slaves. Male rural workers in Cuba saw their electoral rights affirmed, but their mobilization could at times still be portrayed by their enemies as the resurgence of a "black peril." Negotiating and protecting the space for political and collective action remained a perpetual challenge in both places.

As the twentieth century opened, these two nearby possible worlds had traveled paths that revealed not only the different degrees of social and political freedom for the individuals within them, but also degrees of freedom in the evolution of societies after slavery more generally. When Bárbara Pérez, a laundress born into slavery on the Santa Teresa plantation in central Cuba, read the newspaper aloud to her neighbors in the 1890s, her audience was one of sugar workers and artisans of African, Spanish, Cuban, and Chinese descent. For her listeners in the foothills town of Arimao, cross-racial social alliances had begun to take shape in their workplaces and in the anticolonial movement. When in those same years Junius Bailey, a teacher and school principal born into slavery in rural Louisiana, spoke to teachers and students in the bayou parishes, his audience was largely confined to people of color, and their life prospects lay in the deep shadow cast by disfranchisement and legal segregation. Bailey had participated in, and his listeners had lived through, the massive cross-racial sugar strikes of 1887, and some of them had likely witnessed the recruitment in nearby Ascension Parish in 1898 of a company of black soldiers for Cuba. But the Knights of Labor had been expelled from the sugar parishes, and Company L of the Ninth Volunteers returned from Cuba physically weakened and politically pushed aside.

Defeat was not the same thing as submission or the obliteration of memory, however. At the beginning of the twentieth century, the Creole activist Rodolphe Desdunes of New Orleans reflected back on the despair that swept through his community following the Supreme Court's devastating refusal of their claims to public respect in *Plessy v. Ferguson* and the Louisiana legislature's imposition of further legislative humiliations on people of color. Desdunes disagreed, he wrote, with those who counseled prudent silence. "We believe that it is nevertheless more noble and worthy to fight than to show oneself passive and resigned. Absolute submission increases the oppressor's power and creates doubts about the sentiments of the oppressed." These were not just brave words, emerging from a Romantic republican rhetorical tradition. Desdunes also spoke with a sense of limits gained from the hard experience of the New Orleans activists in the *Plessy* case who had felt, in his bitter words, "the satisfaction of forcing the hand of the U.S. government, by acting through the offices of one of its own constitutive branches."[11]

The memoir by Rodolphe Desdunes was published in 1911, quietly, by a French-language press in Montreal. In Louisiana itself, the space for the discussion of civic and political equality had narrowed almost to the vanishing point. In Cuba in that same year, the space for discussion was still quite open, and different groups of activists debated whether the best strategy for asserting their full rights lay through the labor movement, the political parties, or a racially specific mobilization. With universal manhood suffrage enacted into law, some Cubans of color raised the question of proportional representation and of a right to a fair share of elective and appointive offices. When an Independent Party of Color mounted an armed protest on behalf of these demands in the eastern province of Oriente, however, the state reacted with furious repression. The ideal of a transracial Cuban citizenship survived this confrontation, but was weakened. Over the next decades, activists would renew the struggle to restore its potential.

Historical comparison, in its simplest form, involves a juxtaposition of different outcomes and a search for the most powerful explanatory variables. But in digging out structures and stories I have found that there is no stopping point, no moment when the multiple forms of human action emerge clearly as distinct "variables," or the outcomes announce themselves as final outcomes. Though frustrating to the scholar, this indeterminacy was perhaps all to the good for the historical actors. They lived their lives in perpetual tension between their aspirations and what was possible under the circumstances. Traces of their actions, moreover, are not just hidden in the archives, awaiting discovery by an assiduous researcher. Living memory holds them as well. In the spring of 1998 I presented a paper entitled "Reclaiming Gregoria's Mule" at a small conference in the provincial archives of Cienfuegos, Cuba. A member of the audience suggested that I might find it interesting to talk with his grandfather, Tomás Pérez y Pérez. Tomás Pérez, it turned out, had known the former slave Ciriaco Quesada, the veteran of the 1895 Cuban War of Independence who succeeded in 1899 in forcing the administrator of the Santa Rosalía plantation to relinquish the mule in question. "Ciriaco was a tall man, quite thin," he recalled.[12]

As I listened to Tomás Pérez speak, the microhistory of Santa Rosalía began to take on weight and volume. Then, in 2002, a librarian in Michigan informed me that a great-grand-nephew of the Louisiana soldier Pierre Carmouche now worked as an attorney in Detroit. Over coffee, Leroy Soles and I traded photocopies, his of the family letters, mine of the Carmouche pension file. He recalled seeing on his grandmother's wall the portrait of Pierre Carmouche in uniform, a sword at his side.

In the pages that follow, Bárbara Pérez, Ciriaco Quesada, Pierre Carmouche, and others will at intervals appear as carriers of the history I am trying to narrate.

Voices from the past are difficult to capture. But individuals' actions, and the memory of those actions, can speak just as loudly as their words. For in the effort to give meaning and substance to their own freedom, they helped to redefine the boundaries of freedom itself and shaped the world of those who would follow them.

CHAPTER ONE

Two Worlds of Cane

1803–1860

> *. . . fields of sugar cane had once crept like an open secret across the land.*
>
> George Lamming, *In the Castle of My Skin*

IN CENTRAL CUBA IT SPREAD UP ALONG THE RIVERS, IN SOUTH LOUISIANA it came down the bayous. Cane covered the land, as in George Lamming's Barbados, like an open secret. The hot, noisy business of sugar production was accompanied by the acrid smell of burned cane and the sweet odor of boiling cane juice, by the sound of the rolling mill and of boys yelling at mules or at oxen, by the tension of breakdowns and the omnipresence of coercion and intimidation. Men with capital laid their hands on men and women with neither capital nor legal freedom, and together they changed the landscape. The cane planted, weeded, cut, and ground by slaves became sugar sold by planters, who in turn bought more slaves and sold more sugar.

In Louisiana, the improvisations of the agricultural system under French and Spanish rule gave way after the U.S. Purchase of 1803 to a more rigorous calculus of profitability, as thousands of new forced migrants were brought into the world of large-scale sugar production. In the Lafourche basin to the west of the Mississippi River, cane cultivation expanded rapidly in the aftermath of the War of 1812. Farmers and entrepreneurs of various backgrounds took the initiative: Creoles who traced their ancestry to France, Acadians descended from the French-speaking settlers who found refuge in Louisiana after their expulsion from Nova Scotia, Anglo-Americans recently arrived in the region. Louisiana's most successful planters were soon men of vast wealth.[1]

By midcentury, some 1,500 sugar plantations were arrayed along the Mississippi River and its bayous. An 1858 map conveys their geography: sugar properties appear as ribbons of land, varying in width, each fronting on the river or the bayou. The high land of the natural levees serves as a thoroughfare joining estates to each other and linking them to nearby towns, while the backswamps define the interior edge of successful planting. As the alluvial land slopes back from the levee, it often becomes too low to be drained and planted in sugar. The characteristic shape of a Louisiana sugar plantation thus reflects the pattern of land and water of the lower Mississippi Valley, the lineaments of French and Spanish land grants, and the prevailing technologies of drainage and transportation.[2]

Slavery on Louisiana sugar plantations acquired a particular reputation for hardship and torment as planters tried to extract exhausting, coordinated, and precise labor from men and women holding hoes and cane knives.[3] In 1860 the fourteen leading sugar parishes of Louisiana held 116,000 slaves and produced about 87,000 metric tons of sugar, along with cotton and corn. Some of this sugar was sold to be consumed directly; the rest went to be further refined elsewhere. The feverish activity of a sugar plantation consumed fuel, energy, and lives, while the New Orleans slave market fed the region with slaves brought south from the older plantation areas. The six bayou parishes on which this book often focuses—Lafourche, Terrebonne, Assumption, Ascension, St. Mary, and St. Martin—together held about 49,000 slaves and produced 47,000 metric tons of sugar in the 1860 season.[4]

Even in the sugar parishes, only a fraction of the total acreage was suitable for planting in cane. There were also fields of corn, sweet potatoes, and potatoes, and the year's labor was divided between producing sugar and raising foodstuffs for those who produced sugar. Vast swamplands at the far edge of each property were a buffer and a resource, a point of intersection between the residents of the plantation and the moss-gatherers and woodcutters who inhabited the wetlands. There too lay the *brulés,* burned-over ridges of sandy soil where the poor, many of

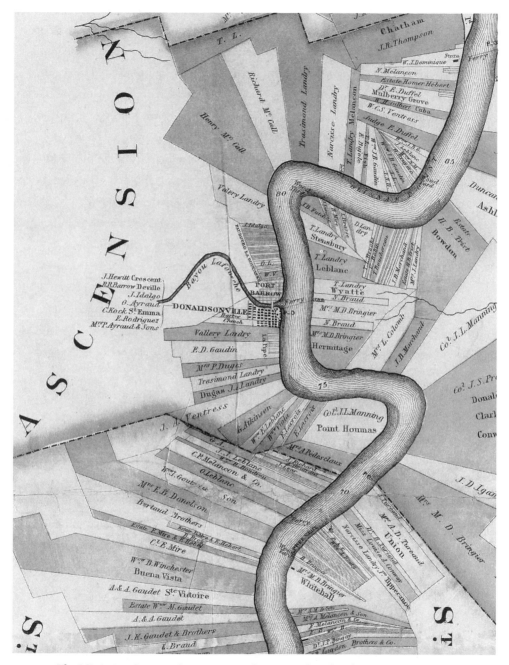

The Mississippi River at the junction with Bayou Lafourche, showing sugar plantations and other landholdings along the river in Ascension Parish, 1858.

them Acadians or Canary Islanders, lived off of small plantings of corn.[5] "Back of the plantation" thus designated a diverse terrain of poverty, but also of freedom, and when enslaved workers fled, it was usually to the mosquito-infested lowlands, crawling with alligators. Angry when a new overseer forced him to work by the clock rather than by the task, for example, the cooper Octave Johnson escaped to the swamps, four miles behind the plantation house of his owner. During 1861 and 1862 Johnson and his runaway companions stole animals from the plantation, traded surreptitiously with those still held in slave quarters, and struggled to elude the dogs sent to track them by Eugène Jardeau, "master of hounds."[6]

Within and alongside the plantations, the interstices between cane plantings also provided some possibility for free families and slaves to cultivate food crops. Two parallel systems of smallholding coexisted there, one of small-scale free owners, renters, and squatters, including poor whites and occasional free people of color, and another of slave cultivators working within customary arrangements that allowed them to grow vegetables and staples and to raise poultry. The land the slaves used included kitchen gardens, close to the quarters, and "Negro grounds," located somewhat farther away.[7]

The complex geography of the lower Mississippi Valley was matched by an equally complex social structure. Situated at a variety of indeterminate points between masters and slaves were Louisiana's free people of color, numbering almost 19,000 in 1860. Many of these families were descended from early French, Spanish, and African settlers, augmented by exiles and migrants from Haiti and Cuba, and by newly manumitted slaves. The 1803 Treaty of Cession following the Louisiana Purchase had recognized a formal claim to citizenship by this community, but President Thomas Jefferson quickly backed off on that promise. Newly arriving refugees from the French and Spanish West Indies often brought an equally robust sense of their claims as citizens, but they too found themselves thwarted by the increasingly exclusionary behavior of white Louisianans and the categorical refusal of the federal government to accord them the rights they thought they deserved.[8]

The parents of Rodolphe Lucien Desdunes, the historian of the Creole community of color, were Henriette Gaillard from Cuba and Jérémie Desdunes, a wheelwright from Haiti. Along with other young people born in the 1840s,

Rodolphe Desdunes came of age in a society in which, as he later wrote, "slavery was the pivot around which everything revolved." In the face of slavery's dominance, members of the free community of color built several remarkable educational and philanthropic institutions that encouraged a broadly Caribbean and Atlantic perspective, drawing inspiration from their variety of experiences elsewhere. In one school the children filled their copybooks with imagined letters to kin in Haiti and Mexico. As Desdunes and others matured, they chafed at the humiliations imposed on them. The most radical among them looked toward the example of Haiti's early abolition of slavery, as well as the fusion of republicanism, Christianity, and social activism in France's 1830 and 1848 revolutions.[9]

Networks of trade and family linked some urban free people of color to the backcountry and the smaller towns along the river and bayous. Eulalie Mandeville, the free colored half-sister of the white entrepreneur Bernard Marigny, for example, developed a small dairy operation on a plot of land near the river. She moved to New Orleans and went on to accumulate a fortune as a retailer (*pacotilleuse*) by sending free and slave vendors out into the countryside with wares to sell. Her *marchandes* were said to have traveled upriver to Donaldsonville and overland to Atakapas in the west, building on her substantial line of credit to weave together a web of capital and consumption. Living in an informal but lifelong union with a white man, Eugène Macarty, Eulalie Mandeville continued to lay claim to her own money and her own reputation and was able to withstand a lawsuit brought by Macarty's kin after his death. Her fortune remained intact, and her children carried on with their father's surname and their mother's racial identity.[10]

Other families of color rooted in New Orleans sent tendrils out into the countryside, generating complex genealogies. In November of 1803, the free *mulato* Juan Bautista Pedro, natural son of a free black woman and an "unknown father," married the free *mulata* María, legitimate daughter of Carlos Dupart and Carlota Belair. The witnesses at the ceremony included the free black man Noël Carrier, captain of the black militia of New Orleans, the free *mulato* Mauricio Populus, and the free black man Magloire Durand. In 1820 the couple named their son Pierre Carmouche et Dupart, following the Spanish style in giving him surnames from his father and mother. Pierre Carmouche in turn moved up the river to Donaldsonville, and took as his spouse Adèle Colomb, born a slave on an Ascension Parish sugar plantation and manumitted along with her mother and her siblings in 1846.[11]

In the sugar country, however, the space for free people of color was narrow indeed. In 1860 Ascension Parish held 7,376 slaves, but counted only 168 free people of color. In Lafourche Parish the figures were 6,395 slaves, 149 free. A few niches existed for a free man of color to work as a blacksmith or a small farmer, or for a woman to plant a garden, but rural south Louisiana was emphatically a slave society.[12]

In the decades that preceded the Civil War, Louisiana's legislators systematically tightened the constraints on people of African descent, slave and free, rural and urban. It became more and more difficult to replicate the manumission achieved by Adèle Colomb in Ascension Parish in 1846, or the ability to live in a free union with a white man and own property in her own name defended by Eulalie Mandeville. The free population of color in New Orleans fell in size between 1840 and 1850, and in 1857 the Louisiana legislature prohibited all future manumissions.[13]

The squeezing out of free people of color translated into isolation and diminished hopes for those held as slaves. The rural Louisiana into which the northern free man Solomon Northup was flung by kidnapping in the 1840s already had the feel of a prison camp, from which it took him years to escape, and his eloquent narrative of captivity conveys vivid images of flight and recapture.[14] By 1860 Louisiana law was implacable in its hostility to the very existence of free persons of color, and fierce with regard to fugitives. Although individual masters still found ways to free occasional favored slaves, the freedom thus gained was hemmed about with dangers.

Across the Gulf of Mexico, on the island of Cuba, a comparably brutal system of slavery in sugar had become equally entrenched. Building upon a substantial trading history in cattle, tobacco, and coffee, planters established modern sugarmills, initially around the transportation facilities and infrastructure of Havana, then out into the wide flatlands of adjacent Matanzas. Separate beachheads were established farther east at the city of Trinidad on the south coast and at Sagua on the north.

The institution of slavery had existed in Cuba for centuries, but it surged forward at the end of the eighteenth century as planters aggressively expanded their use of the land and of a captive labor force.[15]

By the 1830s entrepreneurs who had accumulated capital in the core areas pushed a railway out from Havana, and over the next decades they built lines connecting Sagua la Grande and the city of Santa Clara to the southern port of Cienfuegos. Railways expanded the range of sugar growing by drastically reducing the cost of shipping. By the early 1860s, what would later become the central province of Santa Clara held the largest number of mills on the island, and was second in total production only to the wide savannas of Matanzas. Planters from the now fading southern city of Trinidad had established new mills around the vast bay of Cienfuegos, whose fertile river valleys provided easy transportation to the newly developed port.[16]

Of the 69,000 slaves who were counted in the central region of Cuba in 1862, the majority lived on the more than four hundred sugar plantations. Bringing in a harvest of 145,000 metric tons of sugar in 1860, the sugar industry on these newly opened lands showed greater dynamism than the older areas. The districts of Sagua la Grande on its north coast and Cienfuegos on the south coast held dozens of highly mechanized mills, producing in that year 46,000 tons of sugar in Sagua and 43,000 in Cienfuegos. Each thus produced nearly as much sugar as Louisiana's six bayou parishes combined.[17]

The Cuban agricultural landscape was quite different from that of Louisiana. Landholding had evolved gradually from the early and expansive municipal grants of grazing rights, through the scattered private sale of the most accessible lands suitable for sugar, and then to an increase in formal surveying and private purchase. The shadows of the designations of the original *hatos* and *corrales*, each a circular grant designed for grazing, show through many nineteenth-century maps, but they are largely supplanted by new holdings. The cultivable flatlands in Cienfuegos, for example, were by the 1860s dotted with *ingenios*, as the field-and-sugarmill complexes were called. These properties were not the neat rectangles of Louisiana, however, but irregular polygons defined by an array of cane fields and woodlands. River frontage was handy for transportation, but did not define the shape of the property. At the center of each plantation was the *batey*, an indigenous term denoting a clearing, in this case the open space in front of the sugarmill, with its towering chimney. The largest plantations had slave barracks, the smaller ones a village of *bohíos*, palm-thatch huts. Although sloping or stony land was less suitable for cane than the flat valley floor, most plantations faced no firm boundary to cultivation comparable to the swamps of Louisiana. In times of high sugar prices, they were likely to expand acreage onto marginal lands, contracting it again when prices fell.

Cane, however, had come relatively late to a Cuban landscape already shaped by generations of growers of tobacco, coffee, and food crops, as well as small- and large-scale cattle raising. Each plantation blurred at the edges into a scatter of small towns, small farms, and ill-defined crown land. A multiplicity of niches and interstices allowed for subsistence cultivation, stock raising, and market gardening by nonslaveholding free people. Around Cienfuegos, for example, a swath of tobacco farms along the Arimao River dated back to the early colonial era, and much of the land in the foothills of the Trinidad mountains was still unclaimed. The institution of slavery, moreover, dated back three centuries on the island and had been through several cycles of expansion and retrenchment. Economic decline had often loosened the bounds of control, indirectly facilitating manumission and self-purchase by slaves, thus bringing a flow of individuals out of the category of slave and into the category of free. The resulting free population of color held its own numerically, even when the expansion of sugar cultivation brought large-scale legal and illegal imports of slaves. This made enslavement no less onerous for those subjected to it, but it shaped almost everything about the society outside the plantation's boundaries.

Centuries of settlement, intermixture, migration, and manumission had yielded a thoroughly heterogeneous countryside, and in much of central Cuba the plantations themselves were geographically still overshadowed by the spaces between them. Tens of thousands of free families categorized as white, black, or *mulato* cultivated small farms across the hills and minor valleys. All told, in 1862 the central area counted some 42,000 free people of color, at a time when the region held 69,000 slaves and 6,000 Chinese indentured workers. The area's white population in the same years was counted at 163,000.[18]

Any use of color terms from census records, of course, can be misleading. In

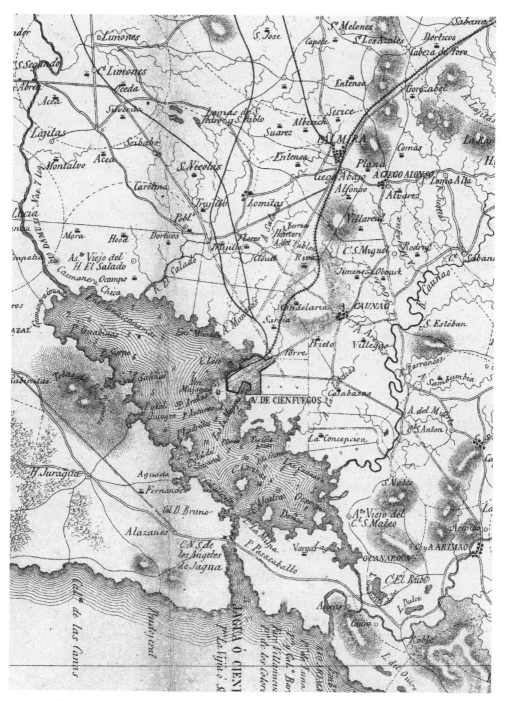

The countryside around the bay of Cienfuegos, Cuba, ca. 1875. The early circular grants for grazing are visible, as well as the later sugar plantations, marked with the symbol ⬛.

daily life, attributions of color, self-identifications, and the social significance of perceived color could all shift with a shift in context, and were sometimes disputed and even litigated. The demographic contrast between central Cuba and southern Louisiana was nonetheless as sharp as the geographic. In Louisiana's bayou parishes the population designated as being of color outnumbered the white by 1.6 to 1, and within the population of color slaves outnumbered free persons by a staggering 46 to 1. In central Cuba, by contrast, the reverse was true: whites outnumbered people of color by 1.5 to 1. Moreover, within the population of color slaves outnumbered free people by only 1.6 to 1. Even those ratios varied according to crop mix and geography. The prosperous sugar-producing jurisdiction of Cienfuegos in 1861 held one free person of color for every two slaves, while in the adjacent district of Trinidad their numbers were nearly equal. In the hill town of La Sierra, which lived on stock raising and small-scale farming, all three groups were roughly equal in number: 201 residents were counted as white, 150 as free people of color, and 214 as slaves. The rural district of Arimao, which held both small farms and several major sugar plantations, listed 1,488 slaves, 1,182 whites, and 401 free people of color.[19] The overall pattern was clear: in central Cuba, every enslaved person would have occasion to encounter many other people of color who were free, often living close by and performing similar work.

Louisiana and Cuba both moved to the annual rhythm of the same crop, constrained equally by the botany of cane. But their work and planting cycles were quite different. The matching heat and humidity of Cuban and Louisiana summers mask a crucial difference in their winters. Frost could hit Louisiana in November or December, with devastating consequences. Low temperatures halted growth before the cane plant had matured, and frost followed by thaw risked spoiling the cane. While Cuban plantations had the luxury of allowing cane to follow an eighteen-month growth cycle, and the cane produced new "ratoon" growth from the old roots after the harvest year after year, Louisiana's growers were held within a tight schedule, forced to cut after eleven months, and to replant every few years. When low temperatures threatened, they had to calculate whether to order workers to cut prematurely and "windrow" the cane, laying it on the ground and covering it in hopes of both retaining its sucrose until milling time and sustaining the viability of the seed cane. Producing sugar profitably in this environment required a high degree of labor discipline and endless calculation by managers. Observers and participants alike commented on the systematic, difficult, and exacting labor performed by the enslaved workers of Louisiana's sugar plantations, although they often commented as well on the excitement of the harvest season itself.[20]

In central Cuba, the enterprise of sugar planting was not threatened by annual frost or by the risk of a breach in the levees and flood—though on rare occasions hurricanes could destroy immense acreage in a few hours. Cuba's rainfall and temperature were ideally suited to cane, and the land itself generally required no ditching for drainage. The spread of cane cultivation came at the expense of the island's forests and would eventually wear out the fertility of the land. But in the 1860s the enterprise still looked very promising. Cuban planters could revel in the size of the crops they produced, and nowhere were they more buoyant than in the central region later designated as the province of Santa Clara, where advances in output both permitted and then required new advances in processing.

Unlike most of Louisiana's sugar country, Cuba's plantation frontiers still offered spaces in which a free person of color might even aspire to wealth. As Eulalie Mandeville's children came of age in New Orleans, three of them chose to move from Louisiana to Cuba to try their hand at coffee growing. Over several years, they lost large sums of money attempting to establish plantations in the vicinity of Santiago de Cuba in the east. Their gamble failed, and they ended up back in New Orleans. They were nonetheless correct in thinking that the slave system around which life revolved in Cuba was one that allowed a relatively large role for free people of color, particularly in the eastern coffee regions and in the mixed-farming areas of the center.[21]

The larger world of the Caribbean and the Gulf of Mexico was an exceptionally mobile one. Eulalie Mandeville's partner, Eugène Macarty, had come from France to Louisiana; their natural children went from Louisiana to Cuba and back again; Rodolphe Desdunes's parents came from Cuba and Haiti to New Orleans. What was true of free people of color was also true of planters. Anglo-American, French, Spanish, and Acadian accents could be found among Louisiana planters, and their names convey something of the linguistic and cultural diversity of the region: in Terrebonne Parish, the family of William Minor presided over South-down and Hollywood plantations, while J. J. Piedra called his estate Isla de Cuba. In Ascension Parish, just outside of Donaldsonville, plantations owned by Trasimond Landry alternated with those of John and Richard McCall.[22]

In central Cuba the promise of wealth from investment in sugar drew entrepreneurs from an even wider range than in Louisiana. Again, a sample of names hints at the story: in 1860 Doña María del Rosario Aloy de Sarría, from a distinguished Cuban Creole family, owned the Soledad plantation, which would later pass into the hands of the Bostonian Edwin Atkins. The elegant Carolina plantation belonged to William Stewart, from Philadelphia. The queen of Spain was an investor in the Santa Susana plantation, through a company called La Gran Azucarera. Cubans of Basque origin named Apezteguía owned Constancia, and the Basque Agustín Goytisolo built innovative light rail lines on his estate called San Agustín, and then moved back to Spain and settled in Catalonia. Elías Ponvert, whose roots were in Haiti, ran Hormiguero plantation, and the Venezuelan-born Terry family bought up one sugar property after another in the southern part of the island. Central Cuba's sugar elite was thus distinctly cosmopolitan, and its wealthiest members turned their plantations into showcases of architecture, landscaping, and industrial investment.[23]

The ancestors of the enslaved men and women of Cuba and Louisiana who made all this investment productive had themselves come from various points in the Atlantic world. By 1860 the great majority of Louisiana's slaves were born in the Americas, though often not in Louisiana. In the bayou country, a few elderly survivors of the Middle Passage labored alongside men and women who had been sold downriver from Missouri, or brought from other states to the north and east of Louisiana, and a small number of slaves smuggled in from Africa via Cuba. (When, after the Civil War, national citizenship became possible for men and women of color, Yarrow Williams came forward in Terrebonne Parish to swear that he was "a native of Africa that he is 105 years of age and emigrated to the United States of America in the year 1818." He received citizenship.)[24]

The legal closing of the transatlantic slave trade to the United States after 1807 had led to a steady decline in the proportion of African-born slaves and an increase in the numbers who were either imported from the Upper South or born in Louisiana. New Orleans was home to a vigorous interstate market in slaves, fu-eled by the demands of the sugar industry. In 1859–1861, the sugar planter Rich-ard Pugh from Lafourche Parish, for example, bought slaves from Tennessee, South Carolina, Missouri, Florida, and Kentucky.[25] Although the Louisiana slave population had thus shifted from African- to American-born, the severe disease environment, demanding working conditions, and unbalanced sex ratio of the sugar parishes had long kept demographic growth among slaves low or negative. By the 1850s, however, the influx of slaves from outside had begun to slacken, making it more likely that family structures would develop and that slave commu-nities would achieve a more stable form. In 1860 most Louisiana slaves apparently lived in nuclear families rather than in single-person units. This development helped to buffer some of the cruelties of slavery, but could not insulate slaves from sale and abuse.[26]

In central Cuba, where the contraband transatlantic slave trade was still in full operation in the 1850s and continued at least as late as 1867, the proportion of African-born slaves in the population was much higher. On the western side of the bay of Cienfuegos, for example, Tomás Terry's Caridad de Juraguá plantation cultivated a modest 12 *caballerías* of land (about 400 acres), but held a massive slave barracks. It was easy to infer—and difficult to prove—that cargoes of Afri-can slaves were landed on the shore, transported to the barracks for a period of acclimation, and then sold as if long part of the workforce. Despite the formal il-legality of the trade, planters in central Cuba were accustomed to buying African slaves without fear of confiscation. The African ethnonyms used on the Santa Rosalía plantation—Donato Lucumí, Alejandro Congo, Manuel Gangá—give the game away. Even today, Caridad Quesada recalls listening in her childhood to sto-ries told by the strong-willed Má Rita, who had come as a young girl on an illegal slave ship from Africa.[27]

The Santa Rosalía plantation itself had been built on a hillside between the Arimao and the Caunao rivers by a cooper from the Canary Islands named José Quesada. By 1860 he owned some 190 slaves, among them a young woman named Andrea who would later take the surname Quesada and devote much of her energy to defying those who tried to control her. The adjacent Soledad plan-tation, owned by the Albis/Sarría family, also held more than a hundred slaves, most of whom would eventually take the surname Sarría. A few miles further toward the city of Trinidad, Sebastián Pérez Galdós, brother of the famous Spanish novelist Benito Pérez Galdós, had built an estate called Santa Teresa.[28]

Even within the relatively closed world of the plantation, opportunities occasionally emerged for the acquisition of skills that could open up new possibilities. On the occasion of his niece's birthday, Sebastián Pérez Galdós had moved the slave named Bárbara from the fields into the house to serve her. As Bárbara Pérez later recounted the story, one day when the mail arrived at the house there was no one else to receive it. She took the packet from the postman, opened it, and tried to decipher a newspaper she found inside. Suddenly the young mistress walked in and Bárbara braced for punishment, folding the paper up and bending her head. The niece, however, told her that there was no reason to beg pardon. If Bárbara wanted to learn to read, she would teach her, as long as she didn't tell anyone. They worked together, and Bárbara acquired a skill that she would exercise for the rest of her life, in private and to a wider public. Though still closely linked to her uncles and other kin who worked in the fields, Bárbara Pérez had taken a decisive step away from one of the bonds of slavery.[29]

Those who remained in the fields continued to chafe at those bonds. In both Louisiana and Cuba, the world of sugar production was marked by a marriage of disciplined field labor and sophisticated mill equipment. A mid-nineteenth-century sugar plantation was a factory in the field, drawing a portion of the rural population into the rhythms and risks of a fully industrialized processing operation. Planters boasted of their investments in steam-powered equipment and their increasing yields. A few of Louisiana's most prosperous and enterprising planters moved on to the use of vacuum pans rather than open kettles for processing the juice, and many more of their counterparts in Cuba had already taken that step. But the grinding, boiling, clarifying, and crystallizing of sugar remained an immensely loud and exacting operation, and for the long weeks of the harvest the mill filled the environs with sound and smoke and drama. The human effort involved was outsized, from putting arms at risk in the face of the huge grinders to the hoisting of thousand-pound hogsheads or two-hundred-pound bags of sugar. Slaves built the wealth of their owners by risking life, health, and limb. Both parties to the transaction knew it, and modern scholars have confirmed it. Sugar production was a deadly serious business, and it translated into high rates of mortality and injury.[30]

The northern free man of color Solomon Northup, after his kidnapping and sale into slavery, was hired out to work for three successive years on a Louisiana sugar plantation in the late 1840s. His subsequent detailed description of the work routine conveys both the pressure of labor in the cane and the accomplishment of achieving the position of lead cutter in a gang of between fifty and one hundred slaves. He also worked in the mill, which he described as an "immense brick building." An external steam boiler supplied power to an "endless carrier" of chain and wood, which the slave children fed with cane headed for the "two great iron rollers, between two and three feet in diameter and six or eight feet in length."[31]

Comparable equipment could be found on medium-sized Cuban estates, but by midcentury the largest Cuban mills were housed in vast multistory factories. The imposing Constancia plantation, located in the Cienfuegos district, employed hundreds of slaves and produced 1,484 metric tons of sugar in the 1860 harvest. A bit to the north, José Suárez Argudín's Angelita shipped 2,208 tons out of the port of Sagua la Grande. But Santa Susana beat them all with a modern Derosne apparatus to increase yields, and produced 2,240 tons. The interior of Santa Susana's boiling house looked rather like a modern chemical factory.[32]

The barracks of a fully mechanized Cuban sugar plantation might at times resemble a prison in their imposition of constraint and appearance of isolation. But in truth there was no way of isolating Cuban slaves from the wider world. Not only had African-born slaves like Má Rita survived the Middle Passage, but others had come westward to the expanding estates of the Cienfuegos region from the nearby district of Trinidad or the distant eastern province of Santiago. Each of these transitions broke up kin groups and communities, served as an occasion for new communication, and could stimulate renewed resistance. Once resettled, enslaved men and women would find in the surrounding countryside evidence of the possibility of black freedom.

In central Cuba the interplay of free, enslaved, and semi-enslaved (including indentured Chinese workers) was almost continuous. More important than the raw numbers were the circumstances of those people of color who were free: most

The boiling house of the Santa Susana sugar plantation, Cienfuegos, Cuba, around 1856.

lived in the countryside as renters, owners, or squatters, or worked as artisans on plantations and in town. Their social world overlapped with that of their neighbors counted as white and with that of slaves hired out to cut wood or sent to sell goods in the market. In these encounters, the distinction between slave and free might be an occasion for conversation, for challenge, for mockery, or for solidarity. But whatever the subtext of such communications, the likely result was further chafing at the bonds of slavery—and further ingenuity in finding ways out.

In southern Louisiana as well, the dichotomy of white and black, free and slave, was challenged by free people of color cultivating small farms, working as artisans, or operating as tradesmen and tradeswomen. But the free population of color was largely concentrated not in the countryside but in the city of New Orleans, where they worked as craftsmen and in small-scale commerce. Among them were an impressive cadre of sophisticated Creole intellectuals of African descent, some of whom earned a living as artisans. The philanthropist Arthur Esteves, for example, worked as a sail maker; the poet Nicol Riquet was a cigar maker; the mathematics teacher Basile Crokere was at the same time a cabinet maker.[33] Upriver, the medium-sized crossroads town of Donaldsonville held only a few dozen free people of color, including Pierre Carmouche, his wife, Adèle Colomb, and, after 1861, their son, Pierre Lacroix Carmouche. They cultivated a reputation for respectability and sought to make the best of a precarious situation.

Much has been made of the presumed elitism of Louisiana's free people of color, and some were themselves the owners of slaves. However, there was often only one degree of family separation between slaves and free people in the same locale, and formal ownership of slaves by free people of color was at times simply a mechanism for circumventing the state's increasingly harsh laws against manumission. There was material here for pragmatic alliances as well as social divisions, and the social distinctions themselves might shift rapidly under changed circumstances.[34]

Such lateral ties provided little protection against the force of the market, however, and the presumption of slavery shadowed those of African descent. The young Pierre Landry, son of an Ascension Parish planter and a slave woman, was raised as if free by Pierre Bouziac and his wife, Zaides, a local free couple of color. But upon the death of his father, the thirteen-year-old Pierre Landry was remanded back into slavery and sold to the sugar planter M. S. Bringier to settle up the estate.[35]

Louisiana and Cuba, in sum, shared markets, technologies, and a bedrock reliance on a coercive labor system marked by brutality. To be a slave on a sugar plantation in Cuba or in Louisiana was to be pushed to labor at the limit of one's endurance, and to be ever haunted by the threat of sale. It was not primarily at the heart of the plantation that these two slave systems differed, but at the edges. In Cuba, slaves might daily see kin and neighbors of color who were free and even propertied, as well as Chinese contract laborers who worked at the same tasks but under different rules. It was possible to imagine such neighbors as allies or, more immediately, as partners. On Soledad plantation, for example, the Chinese workman Pastor Pelayo joined with the slave woman named Wenceslaa Sarría, constituted a family, and had several children, founding a lineage whose descendants identify themselves as Cubans of African and Chinese ancestry.[36] Some slaves in rural Louisiana, by contrast, would live their whole lives without ever seeing a black man or woman who was legally free. And to the extent that they heard of the actions of the state government in Baton Rouge in the 1850s, the news was all bad: further restraints on manumission and heightened control of slaves.

While a slave in Cuba might more easily than a slave in Louisiana envision attaining his or her own individual freedom, in both societies slavery itself looked nearly invincible in the 1850s. Spain's colonial rule in Cuba provided an armed force and an administrative apparatus designed to sustain the legal structures that enabled one group of human beings to hold another group of human beings as property. The fragile legal rights Spain granted to slaves—of which the most important was the right to gradual self-purchase—were barely discernible in the countryside, although they were frequently invoked in the cities.[37] In Louisiana, what legal rights had once been accorded to slaves had been aggressively rolled back in both city and country, and even the master's own right to free his slave would be almost entirely blocked after 1857.[38] The slave in Louisiana was not only a "person with a price" but a being whose very right to have rights had been squeezed almost to the vanishing point. A customary privilege to cultivate a garden, perhaps and sometimes. But rights, almost never.

In the 1860s, however, both the bayou parishes of Louisiana and the valleys of central Cuba were rocked and changed forever by two military conflicts that exploded into the North Atlantic world: Civil War in the United States, and anticolonial insurgency in Cuba. Systems of slavery that had withstood slave revolts and financial crises, elite rivalries and market uncertainties, now faced the challenge of military mobilization on their own territory. Moreover, the possibility of the complete abolition of slavery moved abruptly onto the national agenda, pushed forward by activists, soldiers, and slaves themselves.

The plantations of southern Louisiana were exceptionally vulnerable to the tumult of war. When the Union navy captured New Orleans in 1862, it opened the region to the advance of Union soldiers. Even those planters whose political sympathies lay with the Whigs, and who had opposed secession, dreaded the arrival of troops whose presence would "demoralize" the enslaved workforce. Bringing the discussion of emancipation home to the quarters in the presence of contending military forces and a weakened state could trigger a breakdown of the social relations on which the institution of slavery rested. And although federal authorities themselves equivocated on the future of slavery, the free population of color in New Orleans was waiting in the wings, its most vocal members armed with a resolute French-inflected ideology of immediate abolition and universal manhood suffrage.

The U.S. Civil War hit slavery in Cuba as well, for it hastened the end of the contraband transatlantic slave trade that had provisioned Cuban plantations. The withdrawal of U.S. ships and capital, combined with a British blockade of ports in West Africa, began to choke off the supply of new slaves to Cuba's still-expanding sugar industry.[39] Moreover, the sectional conflict in the United States raised the possibility that economic and technological progress, which most Cuban planters avidly sought, might come to be generally seen as incompatible with slavery, an institution to which they still clung. The continued flourishing of slaveholding in the United States through the 1850s had provided reassuring evidence for the Cuban elite that in a "modern" nation prosperity could be achieved alongside the holding of property in men and women. But Cuban planters now had only to look as far as Louisiana to see that the entire edifice could be brought down in short order. Equally important, beginning in 1868, Cuban slaves in eastern and central districts like Cienfuegos had only to look as far as the settlements of insurgents and outlaws in the hills to see that the structures of power and authority that sustained their enslavement were under attack. The arc of history was beginning to bend their way.

CHAPTER TWO

Building Citizenship

Louisiana, 1862–1873

*In spite of the efforts of the Chief of the Bureau of Freedmen, the
negroes persist in thinking that a division of property will be made
for their benefit. Incendiary speeches on the part of designing men
impress these ignorant people with the most exaggerated notions of
their rights and privileges.*

New Orleans Daily Crescent, November 18, 1865

As the sectional crisis exploded in 1860–61, Louisiana's political
class followed the rest of the southern states into secession, despite the long-
standing Whig sympathies of many sugar planters. The collapse of the Whig
Party, which had supported duties on imported sugar, left such men politically
homeless, and in the end their commitment to slavery, it seemed, was deeper than
their commitment to the Union. But from the moment of the capture of New
Orleans by Union forces on April 29, 1862, slavery in Louisiana was mortally
threatened. Although Union general Benjamin Butler thought first not of the
slaves but of the bonanza that would come from seizing the cotton and sugar those
slaves had just produced, de facto emancipation quickly ran ahead of federal policy. Slaves took to the roads and rivers in hopes of leaving captivity behind, or
downed tools and challenged their alleged owners to figure out how to make
chattel bondage work in the absence of masters' control of state authority. Refugees from the rural districts made their way to federal camps and forts, seeking
security and offering their services.[1]

Union forces soon prepared to extend their control out into the countryside.

The same watercourses and railroad lines that had made it easy for planters to ship sugar out now enabled troops to sweep in. General Butler exulted to Secretary of War Edwin Stanton in November of 1862: "I have moved Brigadier-General Weitzel into the La Fourche country and have taken possession of the richest portion of Louisiana. Thousands of hogsheads of sugar of the value of at least a million of dollars ought at once to pass into the hands of the United States, together with much other property."[2]

Legally, that "other property" still encompassed enslaved laborers. But in the tumult of invasion legality hardly determined power relations. Already in July of 1862 Welman Pugh, the son of the owner of Woodlawn plantation, had reported "a perfect stampede of the negroes" on several plantations, and Union officers near New Orleans reported the arrival of thousands of "contrabands," a term used by Butler for the slaves of disloyal southerners.[3] No one knew quite how to reconcile the Union's cautious, abstract antislavery policy with the concrete refusal of black men and women to submit to bondage itself. Federal officials initially attempted to stabilize the labor situation without resolving the larger issue. Like their counterparts in the white leadership in the Cuban independence movement a few years later, they imagined that their progressive intentions and their attacks on enemy slaveowners would suffice to persuade slaves that general emancipation itself could wait.

President Abraham Lincoln's preliminary Emancipation Proclamation in September 1862 seemed to promise more, but Butler's replacement, Major General Nathaniel Banks, hastened to remind anyone who would listen that the proclamation did not actually call for emancipation in areas then under Union control: "It is manifest that the changes suggested therein and which may hereafter be established do not take effect within this State on the 1st of January proximo nor at any precise period which can now be designated, and I call upon all persons—soldiers, citizens, or slaves—to observe this material and important fact, and to govern themselves accordingly." In the final text of the Proclamation delivered on January 1, 1863, thirteen Union-occupied Louisiana parishes, including Terrebonne and Lafourche, were explicitly exempted, a reflection of Lincoln's hesitancy on emancipation itself and of his reluctance to alienate Louisiana slaveholders who might yet be persuaded to cooperate with Union occupation.[4]

SABINE   93°

RAPIDES   AVOYELLES

Red R.

TEXAS

Sabine River

Calcasieu

POINTE COUPEE

ST. LANDRY

Atchafalaya

IBERVILLE

CALCASIEU

Lafayette
LAFAYETTE

St. Martinville
ST. MARTIN

Bayou Teche

Sabine Lake

VERMILLION

ST. MARY
Franklin

Vermillion Bay

SOUTHERN LOUISIANA
ca. 1864

Gulf of Mexico

R. C. Forget   93°   92°

The news of emancipation was more powerful than the details of its withholding. General Banks was reduced to trying to block the circulation of information and to prevent contact between black soldiers and the communities from which they had come: "Soldiers enrolled in the regiments of Native Guards will not be allowed for the present to visit the localities of their enlistment nor will visitors be received unnecessarily in their camps." Toward the end of Banks's desperate and confused decree, he gave the game away, acknowledging that violence and

war would surely end slavery: "We may control the incidents of the contest, but we cannot circumvent or defeat the end. It will be left us only to assuage the horrors of internecine conflict and to procrastinate the processes of transition."[5]

Such procrastination seemed initially to favor the interests of slaveowners, even if federal officers were increasingly unwilling to enforce prerogatives claimed under the formal name of slavery. The long tradition of Whig and Unionist sympathies among Louisiana planters made it possible for some of them to argue that

they were loyal citizens who should be left in peace and allowed to command labor under intermediate wartime arrangements. For their benefit, Banks's General
Order No. 12 of late January 1863 set up a highly constraining system of just-
barely "free" labor. The major newspaper of Lafourche Parish, *La Sentinelle de
Thibodaux,* expressed a willingness to take Banks at his word concerning the continuity of labor control. Its writers observed wryly that "wise men do what they
can when they cannot do what they wish" ("Les hommes sages font ce qu'ils
peuvent quand ils ne peuvent pas faire ce qu'ils veulent"). They proposed that
a committee of lawyers and slaveholders draw up lists of slaves in order to
strengthen the claims of owners.[6]

But it was too late. The promise of freedom was strong, and Union camps were
close. Peter Yawyer, a soldier from New York stationed near Thibodaux in January of 1863, wrote to his brother that "a good many thousand acres of sugar cane"
would "rot on the ground this season for the want of hands to gather it." Yawyer's
sympathies appear to have lain with the white residents of the parish, whom he
described as "very peaceable," "most all French," and "heartily sick of the war." But
his explanation for the impasse was lucid: "The negroes concluded that they had
worked for nothing long enough."[7]

As in other areas of the South under Union occupation, ambiguous formula-
tions of the rights and duties of "free laborers" brought endless conflict between
employers and those who had been their slaves. Administrators and workers
tugged and hauled over the choice of overseers, the right to garden plots, and the
pace of work in the fields. On Southdown plantation in Terrebonne, for example,
laborers insisted on gathering their own corn before turning to the cutting, stack-
ing, and covering of cane to protect it from frost. In a time of scarcity and uncertain markets, with the authority of masters undermined by the federal presence,
subsistence took priority. As the contests continued, federal authorities adjusted
official policy on labor, cutting and trimming to meet the competing demands of
ideology and expediency.[8]

Alexandre DeClouet of St. Martin Parish kept a memorandum book that conveyed the vicissitudes of attempting to maintain control of slaves on the edges of
the war zone. DeClouet believed himself to own 247 slaves as of May 1863. But
he noted that 192 of them were "partis avec les yankis"—gone with the Yan-

kees—leaving only 55. Sixty-five were then captured by Confederate forces at Berwick Bay, restoring his total to 120. But 54 departed in August. His final total: just 66 of the original 247 slaves remained under his apparent control.[9]

General Banks's determination to "procrastinate the processes of transition" foundered on the rocks of planter intransigence, slave initiatives, and his own growing need to recruit black soldiers. By January of 1864 Banks acknowledged that the laws and provisions of the state constitution pertaining to slavery were now "inoperative and void," and in September a Louisiana state Constitutional Convention assembled under Unionist auspices made abolition official.[10] But no one knew what legal structures would succeed the now abolished ownership of property in men and women, or whether a widespread reallocation of other forms of property would ensue.

The initiatives of free men of color in New Orleans, combined with growing military necessity, continued to push the uncertain Union high command toward increasing recruitment of black soldiers, though many federal officials still balked at the thought of officers of African descent. Black refugees from the plantations were among the first recruits to the new Union regiments, where they initially served under volunteers like Charles Sauvenet, from the free population of color. The recruitment of African American soldiers strengthened a pattern of collaboration and communication between the city and the countryside that would be repeated at crucial moments in struggles over freedom during the next forty years. For all the social distance between them, darker-skinned rural sugar workers and lighter-skinned town-dwelling men of some property found a terrain of alliance. A long-free man of color later put it bluntly in a conversation with a visiting northerner: "We have no rights which we can reckon safe while the same are denied to the fieldhands on the sugar plantations."[11]

Union soldiers often encouraged black runaways to volunteer for service on the spot, with or without the formality of a recruiting officer.[12] Other former slaves were conscripted. When all was said and done, Louisiana contributed more black soldiers to the Union army than any other state—some 24,000, nearly one in every three of the state's black male population aged eighteen to forty-five. Thousands of these men were from rural parishes, and their departure to fight for the Union removed crucial manpower from the estates at the same time that it involved their families in the drama of wartime service. Additional men and women served the Union army in various capacities, but never saw their names added to the rolls. Pierre Carmouche senior of Donaldsonville, for example, was thought by his family to have enlisted, though his widow was later rebuffed when she sought a pension.[13]

When planters fled the Union advance or withdrew from their rural properties in the face of turmoil, former slaves often sought to cultivate the land on their own, with an emphasis on consumable crops. During 1864 free activists of color from New Orleans collaborated with occupation authorities to establish "labor companies" that could take responsibility for abandoned plantations. In theory, former slaves working under free men of color would share revenues and prove the virtues of free labor. For a time this strategy helped to raise hopes and fend off starvation. But although some Treasury Department officials were willing to cooperate, their long-term goal remained the restoration of export production, often through the leasing of plantations to northerners eager to become "new masters."[14]

As alternative arrangements for managing plantations became feasible, federal officials scaled back the experiments in collective cultivation that had been undertaken by the "labor companies." Freedpeople who had been in the companies were indignant at the withdrawal of a system that had granted them significant autonomy and apprehensive about what would emerge next. Those who had continued to work on planter-run estates pushed to make sure that promised wages would actually be paid. On Woodlawn plantation the laborers were reported in April 1864 to be "discontented and turbulent."[15]

The end of the war brought formal peace, but no end to struggle. After the assassination of President Lincoln in April of 1865, the divided authority and "sense of drift" in occupied Louisiana gave way to frank counterrevolution under President Andrew Johnson. Unionists eager to build an all-white state government that incorporated Democrats and former Confederates outflanked activists of color and other radical Republicans who sought to establish a cross-racial electorate. Although the ratification of the Thirteenth Amendment in December of 1865 ensured that slavery was gone for good, the question of the structure of work, authority, and access to resources remained altogether up in the air. Congress had established the Freedmen's Bureau to oversee the transition to free labor, and had given the bureau authority to lease confiscated lands to freedpeople, but planters moved to reclaim land and block such initiatives. Some echoes of the earlier "labor companies" persisted. In April 1866 the Freedmen's Bureau agent in Terrebonne Parish reported that Orange Grove plantation was leased by "William James (colored)," and worked by a force of thirty-nine men, thirty-six women, and eleven children, accompanied by fifty-seven dependent children. The agent clarified: "the balance of the negroes on this place partners with him in the hiring and working of it. This place is rented for three years to the Freedmen. Wm. James is the head man." But by July of 1866, a new agent reported routinely that the Orange Grove estate was under the authority of one A. Verrette, and that forty-one hands were working under contract for rations, clothing, quarters, fuel, and wages. William James had vanished from the record.[16]

Gradually the lines of a new free labor system began emerging in the sugar sector, to become dominant over the next years. Planters who had held on to or regained their sugar properties were generally "averse to leasing land to the freedmen," frustrating former slaves' desire to work for themselves. Moreover, employers' insistence on controlling wage laborers directly often made for unhappy relationships. Both planters and agents of the Freedmen's Bureau sought to encourage annual wage labor contracts, though former slaves were quick to see the disadvantages of arrangements that deferred their compensation to a year-end settlement in which they could easily be shortchanged. In the long run, workers' insistence on being paid at least every month would prevail.[17]

Black soldiers who had arrived with the occupation forces, along with local Union veterans who remained in Louisiana after demobilization, communicated frequently with the freedpeople, impressing them with what one newspaper described as an "exalted idea of their own importance."[18] Officials of the Freedmen's Bureau made varying estimates of the impact of the soldiers, some emphasizing their orderly and disciplined habits as a good example to other workers, others charging that they had "erroneous and incongruous notions of liberty" and were thus a bad influence. On balance, such veterans seem to have been a force for assertions of the right to mobility, prompt recompense, and voice—a set of goals that might indeed strike local officials as "incongruous" with the prevailing regime of free labor constrained by annual contracts.[19]

Each January workers negotiated the renewal of their labor contracts, and wages slowly climbed. Like the earlier process of military recruitment, these end-of-year negotiations revealed the web of connections between town and countryside, and the importance of communication across plantation and parish lines. One agent near New Orleans reported in January of 1866: "the freedmen are delaying to make a permanent contract in expectation of orders from the Bureau compelling the planters to hire labor and pay for it at the rate of fifty cents per hour, this idea originated probably among freedmen working on the levee in the city who have recently been 'striking' for the aforesaid wages."[20] In Terrebonne Parish during the same month the local agent regretted that he could file no monthly report on the number of freedmen on each plantation: having recently received their final pay from the previous year's contract, workers showed a disposition "to look around and see where they can get the best wages before entering into new ones."[21]

Although wartime measures had raised hopes of a general land reform, the federal government soon retreated from the prospect of confiscation and redistribution of property, except for a scanty and poorly administered allocation of public land under the Southern Homestead Act. Former slaves nonetheless tried to build on old customs, implicit reciprocities, and their new bargaining position as wage laborers to try to gain a foothold on the land. Louisiana had long had a vigorous internal provisioning economy, resting on slaves' customary entitlements to garden plots and to the right to raise small livestock. After emancipation, those who were now free tried to claim new prerogatives emerging from old entitlements.[22] Even the most ill-tempered masters might end up conceding the point. On Good Friday, 1867, the son of Alexandre DeClouet of St. Martin Parish complained bitterly that the freedpeople declined to work, "being too pious to violate such holiness *by work,* but not too much so to go and harpoon fish in the high water." But a week later he noted without further ado, "Gave the negroes their land this evening."[23] This entry presumably referred to "Negro grounds" that would be theirs to plant in staples and vegetables. Such garden plots held at the discretion of the former master were a far cry from the forty-acre leaseholds envisioned in the bill establishing the Freedmen's Bureau, however, and provided a modicum of subsistence rather than anything resembling security.

Planters' refusal to allow former slaves to rent or purchase additional land had a double set of consequences: immediate hardship for those moving into freedom, and a long-term segmenting of the rural workforce. Class position thus continued to map closely onto color categories: "sugar worker" was associated with blackness and former slave status, "farmer" with whiteness and a birthright to freedom. In mixed-farming parishes like Terrebonne, it had long been common to find a few landless or smallholding white Acadian men working as day laborers on the plantations during grinding season, and a few families of color held plots of marginal land deep in the bayous.[24] But throughout the sugar parishes the great majority of the year-round workforce in the cane fields had been and continued to be composed of black men and women born in Louisiana.[25] Despite postwar experiments and periodic exhortations, the sugar fields did not draw or hold a significant number of immigrants from overseas, and those who did come tended to seek anything but labor in the cane. The seasonal demand for additional labor was more commonly met by hiring black workers from the northern parishes or from nearby states, along with a few white men for work in tasks ancillary to the all-black hoeing and cutting gangs.[26]

At every turn, the reconstruction of labor relations became entwined with the emerging debate over the definition and prerogatives of citizenship. Agitation in favor of black suffrage had been going on for several years, propelled by the increasingly radical *New Orleans Tribune,* established by Creoles of color, and its allies among local Republicans. On November 4, 1865, a coalition called the Friends of Universal Suffrage, rebaptized the "Republican Party of Louisiana," demonstrated its strength by running a "voluntary" election among black and white citizens, alongside the lily-white official elections. With an impressive if unauthorized turnout, participants in the voluntary election sent white northern veteran Henry Clay Warmoth to Washington as a "territorial" delegate to argue their case before Congress.[27]

Nationally, the midterm elections of 1866 gave a very substantial congressional majority to the Republican Party and opened the way for what looked to be a new resolution of the question of suffrage. The Reconstruction Acts, passed over a presidential veto in March of 1867, placed Louisiana in a newly formed Fifth Military District. Beginning in the late spring of 1867, the commander of the district was to supervise voter registration in preparation for elections for delegates to a state Constitutional Convention. By a congressional order that was subject to innumerable interpretations and reinterpretations, men were eligible to register to vote without restriction by color, though disloyalty to the Union during the war could disqualify.[28]

In Lafourche Parish it fell to R. Chandler, a captain in the Thirteenth Infantry, to certify the registration of the eligible voters who presented themselves. Remarkably, Chandler's "Last Revised Registry List" survived the tumult of Louisiana history and came to rest in the state archives. It does not at first glance yield up any secrets, though it does have an unmistakable Louisiana flavor, running alphabetically from Henry Anderson and P. A. Aucoin to Louis Zozelle and Louis Zeringue. It is a list of some 2,868 numbered names, without further detail, divided by letters of the alphabet, and then by the order in which these prospective electors registered. But if one peers at it long enough, with the scene at a registrar's desk in mind and names from subsequent militia lists and judicial cases and contested elections rattling in one's ears, the list begins to hint at the dynamics of electoral mobilization.[29]

The first man with a name beginning with the letter C who presented himself was Oscar Cosier, almost certainly the man recorded elsewhere as Oscar Crozier, mulatto, owner of a modest sugar farm. The third under the letter M is W. H. Murrill (elsewhere Murrell), an African American minister from South Carolina via New Jersey, now working with the new schools for freed children. Both would soon become prominent in parish politics, and remain so throughout Reconstruction.[30]

As registration continued, additional activists of various tendencies picked up their papers. Although elsewhere in the state some white Democrats boycotted the election process, here H. H. Michelet, the Democrat at whose store polling had taken place in the all-white 1866 elections, stepped up quickly to be counted, probably on the same day as his bitter rival W. H. Murrell. Louis Benjamin, almost certainly the schoolteacher of color born in Maine who appears elsewhere as Benjamin Lewis, was number 484. Nelson Taylor, a black field laborer, logged in late but still in time to be counted as number 2,124. Each took a place in the newly expanded spaces of politics and debate.[31]

Black Union veterans were particularly quick to seize the suffrage. Joseph Brown had served in the Seventy-fifth U.S. Infantry (Colored) from November of 1862 to November of 1865, ending the war as a sergeant. Samuel Anderson and George Anderson had served in the Seventy-eighth Colored Infantry up to January 6, 1866, presumably staying on in the occupation forces. They were both among the first 250 men to register in Lafourche Parish. The list of voters who were veterans of the Eighty-fourth Colored Infantry alone was impressive, including Isaac Taylor, Edward Fletcher, Adolphus Martin, and George Washington, all of whom signed up to vote in the first groups of registrants.[32]

As the summer wore on, it also became clear that the federal government was not going to bar Confederate veterans from voting. Thus among the second thousand registrants appeared Taylor Beattie, the former Confederate officer and owner of Orange Grove plantation. Beattie would later make a reentry into politics as a Republican. Many men with Acadian or Creole surnames also signed up: Delphin Babin was number 2,319, and five men with the surname Naquin— Zenon, Lovincy, Eugene, Odressy, and Emile—were among the last to register.

When it came time to vote, the parish had a substantial electorate with a cross-racial and cross-ethnic composition. It is difficult to estimate the impact of the temporary disfranchisement of certain whites judged to have been disloyal. This provision would shortly be lifted, and its effect seems to have been partially counteracted by the prolonged registration process, which had afforded considerable time for white men of various backgrounds to make their way onto the lists. In the state as a whole, a significant fraction of white men of voting age either could not register or did not vote. But the Lafourche list suggests that white Democrats there were holding on to a place in the electoral sphere, even if doing so required submitting to rules established by a Republican Congress and local Union officers. Politics in the bayou parishes continued to be a contested affair.[33]

Elections for the new Constitutional Convention took place across the state in late September 1867. Republicans won in nearly every district, and roughly half of the ninety-eight seats went to candidates of some African ancestry. The bayou

sugar parishes provided an important cadre of men of color, reflecting both En-
glish- and French-speaking constituencies. Lafourche Parish sent William Murrell,
the black pastor, and also sent a white northern officer from the Seventy-fifth U.S.
colored infantry. Terrebonne sent Ulgar Dupart and Frederick Marie, the first a
man of color and the second an immigrant from France. St. Mary sent J. B.
Esnard, of mixed ancestry, and a white man named A. J. Demarest. Ascension
sent P. F. Valfroit and Milton Morris, both men of color. St. Martin sent the black
veteran Sosthène L. Snaer and a white physician named John Vandergriff.[34] In November these men convened with their colleagues from across the state to help
produce a remarkable draft constitution under which the state would, in theory,
consolidate the rule of law in freedom.

The drafting process showed the influence of the prior Afro-Creole political
tradition, with its roots in France and Haiti, as well as of the Declaration of Independence, the U.S. Constitution, and the immediate politics of Reconstruction.
Francophone artisans and small property-holders of color had provided the leadership of the first units of black Union soldiers a few years earlier, undertaking to
lead companies that included black English-speaking workmen from outside the
city. Although many of these officers had been forced to resign by the unrelenting
hostility of General Banks, this group continued through the pages of the *New Orleans Tribune* to advocate an alliance of urban activists and rural voters. For the
radicals who had succeeded in edging out a conciliatory faction of white Republicans, the 1867–68 Constitutional Convention provided an opportunity to advance
a long-standing commitment to equal rights while also proposing practical measures that might expand the freedom of former slaves.[35]

The draft Louisiana Constitution phrased its guarantees in an explicit, expansive, and positive language of rights. Instead of the oblique language of "equal protection of the laws" hammered out in the U.S. Congress as it formulated the
Fourteenth Amendment, or the later Fifteenth Amendment's indirect stipulation
that access to the vote could not be "abridged" by the states on explicit grounds of
race, Louisiana's new Bill of Rights held that all citizens of the state should enjoy
"the same civil, political and public rights and privileges, and be subject to the
same pains and penalties." Along with the bold claim of civil and political rights,
this concept of public rights was a crucial one, echoed and clarified in an explicit

Selected delegates to the 1868 Louisiana Constitutional Convention. The new state constitution held that all citizens were to enjoy "the same civil, political and public rights and privileges, and be subject to the same pains and penalties."

prohibition of racial discrimination on public conveyances and in places of "public resort," or what we would now term public accommodations. This document became a touchstone of political commitment for activists, fusing their claim to political voice with an insistence on public respect.[36]

From the point of view of some of the more conservative members of the convention, such public rights were either incoherent, ill-advised, or anathema. When the phrase was introduced, Representative William H. Cooley of Pointe Coupée, a white lawyer and former slaveholder, refused to endorse it, remonstrating that "I cannot understand the idea of a private individual exercising public rights." W. Jasper Blackburn of Claiborne Parish, an editor from Arkansas, opined that the people of Louisiana were not ready for civil rights either. In the final debate, a group of conservatives charged that in the draft Bill of Rights, "social equality is attempted to be enforced, and the right of citizens to control their own property is attempted to be taken from them." The white physician Thomas P. Harrison simply sputtered that in his opinion, "the whole plan of reconstruction is agrarian and adverse to Christian civilization."[37] On this occasion, however, their reluctance would be overridden, and the broadly universalist language remained in the text.

The phrase "civil, political and public rights" in the final draft thus evoked the juridical equality implied by civil rights, the exercise of voice and electoral power embodied in political rights, and the standing in the public sphere that was glossed as public rights. Article 13 spelled out some of the components of "public rights and privileges":

All persons shall enjoy equal rights and privileges upon any conveyance of a public character; and all places of business, or of public resort, or for which a license is required by either State, parish or municipal authority, shall be deemed places of a public character, and shall be opened to the accommodation and patronage of all persons, without distinction or discrimination on account of race or color.[38]

This insistence on such public rights had its roots in a keen recognition of the shaming intent of separate streetcars, alongside a memory of the multiple humiliations heaped on free people of color in the years prior to the Civil War. The at-

tack by the New Orleans police force on a political convention in 1866, moreover, heightened the importance of the right of assembly. But the commitment to
public rights reflected an even deeper and more radical insistence on the moral
equality of all human beings, whether as part of the body of Christ or as members
of a secular community owing each other respect. The roots of such a commitment lay in a combination of Christianity with French and American revolutionary ideologies, sometimes accompanied by an acknowledgment of the Haitian
struggle and the republican creed of the 1848 Revolution in France. The radical
Louisiana activist coalition of 1868 thus refused the very concept of special privileges based on color, opposed "any idea of systematic subjection," and denied that
former masters had a political *droit de seigneur* over former slaves. As Rodolphe
Desduncs later phrased it, these men of principle would not consent to their own
humiliation.[39]

The draft state constitution granted suffrage to all men who had been resident
in the state for a year, and in the parish for ten days, except for those explicitly
disfranchised for crime or sedition by the constitution itself. The coalition behind
a broad suffrage spoke not only to abstract principle but also to Republican Party
interests, and to the need of former slaves in the countryside for political voice to
counteract the reassertion of mastery by their former owners. Some of the ideological energy behind this language came directly from the urban community of
francophone free people of color. But these urbanites were now also in political
dialogue with their counterparts from the rural parishes, as well as with their
English-speaking neighbors and with newcomers to the state like the Reverend
Murrell and Milton Morris.[40]

It was harder to build a coalition around measures with an explicit class content. Frederick Marie, one of the representatives from Terrebonne, proposed "an
ordinance for the relief of laborers" that would double the taxes on uncultivated
lands in order to push plantation owners to sell or lease lands to rural workers.
Edouard Tinchant urged a similar surcharge, combined with a five-year tax ex-
emption for those holding fewer than sixty acres. Marie further proposed that the
legislature be charged with acting at its first regular session to "secure the rights
and privileges of laborers upon the crops they assist in making, that said crops can
never be disposed of, or removed, before said laborers are fully paid the amount

due them by their employers." Frederick Marie seems to have been a "red Republican," born in France, with notably bold ideas. Many members of the assembly,
however, were reluctant to use the constitution to shape land policy in this way.
They refused to back the radical activists in such social legislation, and on this
they prevailed.[41]

The formal guarantees of rights thus stayed in, and the major economic measures stayed out. But the sweeping assertions of civil, political, and public rights
were in themselves enough to horrify the state's conservatives. Indeed, even as
they drafted the document, the more radical delegates seem to have realized that
the language they were introducing would encounter hostility and might well be
reversed by a later legislature. With a certain prescience, Representative P. F.
Valfroit, a propertyless black schoolteacher from Terrebonne, proposed unsuc-
cessfully that the convention resolve that no legislative body be able to amend the
constitution or call another convention for a period of seventy years. The fantasy
of securing civil rights in the state of Louisiana by fiat through the year 1938,
however, fit neither with political realities nor with familiar rules of legislative
practice.[42]

When the final draft constitution was presented to the electorate, planters and
other anxious defenders of racial hierarchy wanted none of it. The ratification
elections of April 1868 were a wild, freewheeling battle that conservatives characterized as white versus black. Laborers left the fields to cast their votes, and in
the end the constitution carried the day, 66,152 to 48,739. The constitution thus
went into effect, functioning as the state's fundamental document for the next
eleven years. But the radical coalition that had drafted it was already being edged
out by the exuberant Republican Henry Clay Warmoth, who showed an increasing inclination for compromise and for genteel white domination. In the same
April election Warmoth won the governorship easily, and took office in July of
1868.[43]

Decades later, Rodolphe Desdunes recalled the 1868 constitution as one might
remember a beautiful child who had died young, and he evoked with pride the
role of the men he called Creoles in bringing it into being: "they voted for universal suffrage, they permitted interracial marriage, they recognized the civil and po-

litical rights of citizens without distinction of color or previous condition. In other words, they enlarged the scope of civil privileges of all races, instead of restricting it."[44] Despite their inability to maintain a political majority, the authors of the document had written a text whose vision of public rights would inform the initiatives of several generations of Louisiana activists.

Within the framework of this document, the sugar parishes proved over the next decade to be propitious terrain for mobilization, electoral and otherwise. Small boats glided up and down the bayous. Individuals made their way on foot or on horseback along the levees. This was ideal territory for getting organized and staying in touch, between plantation and plantation, and between town and country. Activists in New Orleans knew activists in Thibodaux and Donaldsonville, who in turn were in touch with people in the countryside. The social distance between a fieldworker in Ascension Parish and an editorialist for the *Tribune* could be traversed by an artisan who labored on a local plantation but read the New Orleans paper, or by a voter like the schoolteacher Benjamin Lewis, who moved back and forth between different spheres of action.

The social geography of the sugar region bore little resemblance to cotton country, where sharecroppers' cabins often stood alone. Most sugar plantations lodged significant numbers of former slaves in face-to-face rows of cabins, often with a central chimney and a "gallery" or porch out front. The density of settlement and the predominance of wage labor as opposed to sharecropping helped to focus economic grievances on matters of wages and working conditions that affected large groups of workers. The continued use of gang labor, though exhausting in its physical exigencies, provided workers with the possibility of strength in collective action. Plantations, moreover, could provide a degree of community protection for an activist that would be hard to manage on an isolated farm.[45]

The former slave John J. Moore, for example, returned to St. Mary Parish after the war and took up work hoeing cane on George Cleveland's plantation. He began organizing Republican clubs on various plantations and was pleased to report considerable success. It did not take long for a group of white men to come to the Cleveland plantation to make inquiries. Hiding under a bed, Moore heard them try to coax information on his whereabouts from one of his fellow Republicans.

As Moore later recalled it before a congressional committee, the men admonished his colleague Fred, whom he had appointed head of the Republican Club on the Cleveland plantation, in the following terms:

> Now, Fred, there is but one way that you niggers can live here with us, and that is to let politics die. Leave them alone; you cannot live with us, and live and work and vote against our interests. All that you get and all that you have comes from us and by us; and now if you do not let politics alone you will get killed here. It is white peoples' business; the business of negroes is to go into the fields and work, and we will pay you.

Upon hearing this argument, Moore later added dryly, "I thought then that I had a very poor chance there." But in practice, Moore kept on organizing. The "civil, political and public rights" asserted in the new state constitution were costly to exercise, but activists like Moore responded with defiance rather than with deference.[46]

Under the new regime, some local courts began to enforce the legal priority of the laborers' wage claims, circumventing planters' reluctance to settle demands for back pay until they had met other obligations. In the majority black, strongly Republican parish of Terrebonne, the parish court issued a judgment in 1869 against the owner of Caillou Grove plantation. He was ordered to recognize the workmen's "first privilege as laborer" and to sell his crop to pay $143 to David Thomas, $140 to Sephio Cook, $140 to Willis Jones, and so forth. The powerful tool of the laborers' lien could give workers a first crack at the uncertain profits of sugar planting, before other creditors took their share. Exercising it, however, required that freedpeople get a fair hearing in the local courts, which in turn required maintaining the judicial standing and public respect that conservatives were bent on denying them.[47]

With access to courts now a possibility, former slaves were quick to see the importance of the terms of a written contract and the importance of their signatures on these documents. William H. Minor of Terrebonne chronicled the reluctance of former slaves to submit to his terms: "Negroes still refuse to sign contract other persons are offering higher wages and the right to keep stock." In the days that followed, however, Minor was able to persuade some workers to sign, and by early February he was shipping sugar to Natchez. The following year he tried to create some additional competition for the former slaves, hiring "eighteen white men from the city," apparently Germans. But the very next day he reported that seven of the white men had left, without "any good reason for so doing." The next month he noted that "Mr William has recd fifty four Chinamen. They are large stout looking men."[48]

Throughout 1869 and 1870, as former slaves held out for higher and more regular wages, planters in the bayou country pondered new sources of laborers. Perhaps they should send a representative to Europe? Or maybe just to Virginia? At a meeting in Houma, Mr. B. F. Smith remonstrated, "What security had he that hands brought out by him and for him would remain with him?" It seemed clear to Mr. Smith that "such a state of things ought not to be." But it was. Workers could leave; they could bargain; they could even choose to move to the newly formed, securely Republican Grant Parish in the northern part of the state, where entrepreneurs invited them to leave wage labor behind and rent land.[49]

Perhaps most important, workers could vote. On Southdown plantation, the plantation journal for November 7, 1870, noted, "No work today. All hands gone to vote." The results were soon clear: "Cutting cane today and hauling wood. The Rads carried the Parish by about 415 votes!"[50] Terrebonne Parish had gone Republican again. Meanwhile, nearby St. Mary Parish sent the former slave and intrepid organizer John J. Moore to the state House of Representatives. Assumption sent George Washington; Ascension returned Milton Morris; and Lafourche sent John Nelson. In all, thirty-six men of color were elected to the House. They included the musician Eugène V. Macarty, who used his rich baritone to speak in public assemblies on questions of rights and liberties.[51]

Organization and voting by black fieldhands remained dangerous, and the physical security of those who undertook these projects depended to a considerable extent on Republican rule of the state, backed up by the presence of federal troops. Through the early 1870s white-supremacist leagues, clubs, and "rifle companies" proliferated, portraying themselves as the legitimate representatives of the people. The Republican leadership was faced with a dramatic "crisis of legitimacy" among many white voters.[52] In an effort to defend his regime while reaching out to conservatives, Governor Warmoth appointed former Confederate general James Longstreet, now a Republican and a proponent of sectional reconciliation, to the post of Adjutant General of Militia. By the time of the 1870 election, Longstreet commanded an assortment of Irish immigrants, urban men of color, and former Confederate soldiers. Die-hards among the Democrats, however, saw the appointment merely as evidence of Longstreet's perfidy, and anathematized the state forces as a "negro militia."[53]

To the statewide Republican Party, the militia were an instrument for holding on to power and deterring terror by violently antiblack groups like the Knights of the White Camelia. For black communities, militia members were also poten- tially an element in the community's capacity for self-defense, the armed guaran- tee that black Republicans would not simply be shot by indignant white Demo- crats. But the very image of a black militia could be used by the conservative press in the rural parishes to evoke images of violence and a world turned upside down. And in the time it took for troops or militia to arrive from New Orleans, any- thing could happen.

It is all the more impressive that black public officials were as bold as they were. Thomas A. Cage, born a slave in Terrebonne Parish, returned there after acquiring an education in the North and served as assessor, justice of the peace, and tax collector. William H. Keyes, a man of color elected to parish office, car- ried out public auctions "in front of the brick building at Houma, occupied by the parish officers, (there being no Court House in the parish)." Despite inadequate infrastructure, Republican spirits in Terrebonne may have been kept high in part by collaboration with the members of the Fire Company of neighboring Thibodaux, who in June of 1867 invited one and all to a "Fête Champêtre," which seems to have been the francophone equivalent of a barbecue.[54]

As the 1872 elections approached, however, the contradictions of Republican rule in Louisiana had become fully manifest. Fewer than five hundred federal troops, under the command of the reluctant William H. Emory, were present in the entire state, a force altogether insufficient to prevent intimidation of Republi- can voters. Rivalry between the political parties and among factions at the top was mirrored in struggles among different groups at the parish level, including in- creasing efforts by local white notables to intimidate Republican officeholders and

their black supporters. The outcome of the election for governor was itself ambiguous, complete with two inaugurations of rival contenders.[55]

During the year that followed, the power of Republican governor William Pitt
Kellogg eroded, and the apparent results of local elections were by no means
definitive. In Lafourche Parish, for example, a dispute flared over the results of
the elections for sheriff, recorder, clerk, and parish judge. The parish seat of
Thibodaux had itself become bitterly contested ground, with competing parties,
public officials, and associations. The white-run *Thibodaux Sentinel* reported scorn-
fully in May of 1873 that there was a "secret society" in town, to which only "pure
blooded radicals" and people of color were admitted, and which was characterized by initiation rites of a "pronounced indecency."[56] The Reverend William
Murrell, Sr., of the Methodist Episcopal Church, feared violence, particularly
from a group of "bulldozers" (white vigilantes) who were rumored to be on their
way from Texas. A contingent of Metropolitan Police came out from New Orleans to keep the peace, and perhaps at the same time to install the Republican
contenders, but they were greeted with derision and passive resistance by the
town's white notables. Further sarcasm was heaped on the Reverend Murrell by
the *Thibodaux Sentinel,* which ridiculed his stove-pipe hat and gold-headed cane,
mocked the way he parted his hair, and accused him of cowardice. The vulnerability of Republican activists in such circumstances was stark. In response to a request to guarantee Murrell's safety, the sheriff simply replied, "No. I can guarantee no man's lives, I can not stand watch over any man." The Metropolitan Police
soon returned to New Orleans, leaving Murrell on his own.[57]

Relentless white hostility encouraged close collaboration between black officeholders and their rural constituents. The African American working poor and
the "aspiring class" lived close together in Terrebonne and Lafourche, and there
were many Union veterans among them.[58] Republican activism in the bayou parishes, moreover, seems to have been characterized by relatively few divisions between freeborn and freed, or between northern- and southern-born. Those who
served as county commissioners (called police jurors in Louisiana) shared experiences, interests, and anxieties with their constituents; they were willing to spend
long hours pondering questions of hogs, mules, and the need for fences, alongside
the usual issues of patronage and politics.[59] Responding to the widespread prior-

ity placed by freedpeople on education, activists like T. A. Cage and W. H. Keyes from Terrebonne, and Taylor Nelson and the Reverend Murrell from Lafourche also served on the local school boards.[60]

Household number 135 of the Third Ward of Lafourche Parish illustrates this compression of what might otherwise be construed as a class hierarchy. The census enumerator took William E. Kerr, age thirty-seven, white, born in Connecticut, to be the head of the household, and listed his occupation as "retired United States soldier." Next appeared Tench Goodly, age twenty-two, a black boatman born in Louisiana. Then came Taylor and Mary Nelson, he a black farm laborer born in Mississippi, she a black woman born in Louisiana, now occupied in "keeping house." Last was Benjamin H. Lewis, age thirty-one, mulatto, born in the state of Maine, who taught school in the Second Ward of neighboring Terrebonne Parish.[61] In 1872 Lewis shared with Mary Ann Clay the responsibility for teaching seventy-five male and forty-one female children. His supervisor would later judge him a "faithful, hard working teacher" and term the Nichols School "among the best in the Parish." Like other northern-born teachers of color in schools in the Reconstruction South, Benjamin Lewis was on the front lines of the interlinked struggle for education, respect, and the right to exercise political voice.[62]

Through the early spring of 1873, the Democratic newspaper in Thibodaux kept up its campaign of scorn directed at black activists, particularly those affiliated with the "Benevolent Society of Thibodaux," of which William Murrell was apparently president. Black service in the military also seemed to rankle, and the *Sentinel* reported to its readers that "the colored woman Lolotte Plummer" had recently returned from New Orleans with "two hundred and sixty odd dollars for services of her deceased husband as a soldier in the Federal Army." But on no subject was the *Sentinel* more bitter than that of the militia and the Metropolitan Police, the instruments by which Republican governors tried to contain white vigilantism and dispense patronage. These multiracial militarized emblems of the new order elicited its utter contempt.[63]

Over the course of 1873, members of the Republican majority in the Louisiana General Assembly took one step after another to try to consolidate their base. After urging the U.S. Congress to enact legislation "that will insure all classes of citizens their full rights and enjoyments as American citizens throughout the land,"

the Assembly went on to pass pioneering civil rights legislation aimed at guaranteeing the "equal and impartial" access to common carriers, public accommodations, and "public places of resort" that had been evoked in the 1868 constitution.
A week later they passed an act "to enable mechanics, laborers and others to recover their wages" if withheld by nonresident proprietors of plantations. In April
the General Assembly took a further step and appropriated $100,000 "to arm,
equip and maintain the Militia of this State," now to be named the National Guard
of the State of Louisiana and to consist of the present militia "and such volunteers
as shall enroll themselves or enlist therein."[64]

In the outlying parishes, confrontations were multiplying between local Republicans and hostile Democrats, some of whom were already appropriating the term
"militia" to describe their own armed bands and White Leagues. In St. Martin
Parish, Alcibiade DeBlanc, a vigorous white supremacist, had organized a White
League and styled himself a "Col. Com'd'g. State Militia." A deputy U.S. marshal
came after him on the steamer *Iberia,* and eventually arrested DeBlanc and the
DeClouet brothers. But federal forces were few and far between, and others who
shared the sympathies of DeBlanc and DeClouet were determined to challenge
Republican rule and crush the political mobilization of the freedpeople on which
it rested.[65]

As political conflict within the state intensified, Louisiana's bloody battles re-
captured the nation's attention. A massacre of more than one hundred black Republicans at the Colfax courthouse in Grant Parish in April of 1873—"the bloodi-
est single act of carnage in all of Reconstruction"—provided vivid evidence of the
fury of white supremacists incensed by the exercise of political power by black
voters.[66] Legal proceedings emerging from the killings tested the willingness of
local courts to convict white vigilantes, and eventually reached the U.S. Supreme
Court. At the same time Louisiana was about to be pummeled by a series of economic blows originating outside its boundaries. If social relations had been tense
in a period of hesitant economic recovery, they would be further embittered by a
staggering financial reversal.

Beginning with the collapse of the investment house of Jay Cooke in September of 1873, a financial panic rattled the economies of the Atlantic world, ruining
investors, driving down commodity prices, and threatening sugar planters in both

Louisiana and Cuba. The extended period of deflation that followed was traumatic for agricultural commodity producers, and the accompanying unemployment and falling wages jolted wage workers and small farmers alike. Economic crisis, as it often does, undermined recent political gains and cast fragile economic arrangements into doubt.[67]

In Louisiana's nearby competitor, Cuba, slaveholding sugar producers had years of intensive technological innovation behind them and a labor force to which 100,000 captives from Africa had been added in the decade between 1856 and 1866.[68] In the years after the 1873 crisis, the island's planters shuddered, complained, and went into debt, but most survived. They wondered what the future would hold if prices did not recover, but they continued to plant new cane and supervise large harvests. Cuban sugar exports in 1874 and 1875 totaled around 750,000 metric tons each year, although by 1876–1878 they faltered somewhat. In the United States market, Cuban exports lost some ground to beet sugar, but eclipsed Louisiana's production of cane.[69]

Louisiana planters, by contrast, were still trying to adjust to the regime of free labor and possessed neither the financial resilience nor the mastery of their workforce necessary to mount a convincing economic defense against deflation. The protective tariff that had long sheltered U.S. cane growers was no longer sufficient protection against Cuba, which was feeding semi-processed sugars to refineries in Boston and New York. Meanwhile, producers of beet sugar were crowding cane producers politically and economically. By 1875 Louisiana's sugar output of 74,130 metric tons was one-tenth the size of Cuba's in the same year, and accounted for only a small fraction of total U.S. consumption.[70] The straitened economic circumstances of Louisiana planters reinforced their unwillingness to concede benefits to those who labored for them, just at the moment when those workers had achieved postwar gains and a heightened organizational sophistication.

Pleading penury, planters in St. Mary, St. James, and Terrebonne parishes sought in late 1873 to cap or lower the monthly wages they would pay in the future. Sugar workers in Terrebonne Parish, already frustrated by the withholding of a portion of their pay until the crop was sold at the end of the season, responded immediately. In January of 1874 several hundred laborers met in a mass

meeting at the Zion Church on the outskirts of the town of Houma and constituted themselves as an association, in preparation for collective action. Local
workers under Republican leadership also vowed not to work for less than $20 a
month, and proposed forming "sub-associations" to rent land and work it col-
laboratively. This latter demand echoed the earlier experience of freedmen and
women with "labor companies" during the war, suggesting that the desire for autonomous access to land had not abated, even in the face of most planters' stead-
fast refusal to rent them any. The circumstances of a nationwide depression, like
those of wartime, may have stimulated a renewed search for the resources outside
the wage nexus, alongside the use of the labor strike as a means of bargaining over
rates of pay.[71]

The economic crisis and strikes came as voters in the bayou parishes were repeatedly electing men categorized as black or colored to the Louisiana House of
Representatives and the Senate. William Murrell, the minister from Lafourche,
and Milton Morris, from Ascension, had been returned to the House in 1872,
while William H. Keyes of Houma and the former slave and aspiring law student
Louis A. Martinet had been elected for the first time. Frederick Marie, the vigorous defender of laborers' rights in the 1868 Constitutional Convention, was back
in office, and Isaac Sutton was on hand from St. Mary. Thomas A. Cage was serving now in the state Senate, elected from Terrebonne.[72] The ingredients for lively
cross-class and cross-racial coalitions—or for endless factional fractures—were in
place.

Mass action by wage laborers, if it came to be seen as involving a question of
respect for property rights, was precisely the kind of mobilization likely to divide
black workers from their more cautious political allies. The conservative press
quickly denounced Representative W. H. Keyes as an inciter and supporter of the
strike in Terrebonne Parish. In late January 1874, the *Daily Picayune* accused him
of having called upon workers to seize the land and prevent strikebreakers from
working. Alf Kennedy, who served on the Police Jury of the parish, was similarly
said to have headed an armed group of fifty who came down the bayou to stop
work on Southdown Plantation, owned by Henry Minor.[73]

Henry Minor was apparently able to persuade the black sheriff to assemble a
local posse, which was then joined by the Metropolitan Police. The issue was

framed as a question of trespass rather than of politics, and the Republican governor sent units of the state militia to further reinforce the posse and the Metropolitans. Although the Democratic press used the familiar incendiary headlines ("War in Terrebonne!"), the conflict remained nonviolent and its results inconclusive. Strikers returned to work without a wage increase, though wages did creep up over the coming months. Representative Murrell filed a calming report on the events with his colleagues in the legislature, in which he concluded that hotheads from Lafourche Parish (whom others described as white "bulldozers") had overreacted to a peaceable but "boisterous" meeting of laborers in Terrebonne.[74]

In early 1874 some men in the bayou parishes—most, if not all, categorized as black or mulatto—decided to come together officially to propose themselves as companies of state militia. They would, of course, be under the orders of General Longstreet in New Orleans for their formal duties. But they would also be a local, legal, and armed force under the immediate command of their own captains. In March 1874 Benjamin Lewis, the schoolteacher from Thibodaux, proffered his services and those of more than fifty companions from Lafourche and Terrebonne parishes. His unit was mustered in as Company C of the Sixth Regiment Infantry, Louisiana National Guard, and issued Enfield rifles. Lewis was named captain, to be assisted by First Lieutenant Anatole Panalle and Second Lieutenant William Robinson.[75]

For these volunteers, signing up for the militia was a highly consequential choice. On a practical level, they joined the numbers of those who benefited from state patronage, drawing substantial new salaries. Although Benjamin Lewis earned somewhere between $40 and $75 a month as a schoolteacher, the school in Terrebonne was only funded for four months a year. The salary paid to a captain in the militia would thus significantly increase his income.[76] In return for their salaries, however, the militia faced an increasingly mobilized and violent white counterrevolution, in a climate of ceaseless contest over nearly every act of black assertion. In an echo of black military service during the Civil War, Benjamin Lewis and others were proving black citizenship by donning a uniform and taking risks. Admiration for such a stance was waning among white northern voters as the ideal of sectional reconciliation gained strength. But armed defense of voting rights and public voice still held an evident appeal among the black men in Lafourche and Terrebonne parishes who had signed on as privates.[77]

Adjutant General Longstreet was apparently reluctant to give this new militia high visibility. The record notes laconically that owing to the "revolutionary condition of the country," they "suspended their drill in the manual arms" for a time. But in July a second company came together in Terrebonne Parish. Its captain was Benjamin Peney from Houma, assisted by First Lieutenant James Madison and Second Lieutenant Scott Brown. There was now a militarized pro-Republican presence on both sides of the bayou.[78]

The sight of armed men of color drilling in public infuriated local Democrats. That the militia members were at times accompanied by their wives and sisters, who presumably provided moral support and a climate of solidarity, only made it worse. The chairman of the Democratic Party in Lafourche Parish, H. H. Michelet, reported angrily that this company of "negro Militia armed with state arms" had been marching every Saturday evening on the commons in the town of Thibodaux. He characterized the militia as "warriors" accompanied by "colored Amazons."[79]

Confronted by relentless hostility from Michelet and his allies, Company C and Company D depended for their coherence not only on the legitimacy of their commissioning by the state but also on local ties, local courage, and continuing support from their own social networks. A look back at Benjamin Lewis's listing in the 1870 census hints at some of the people who may have helped sustain the unit in the face of Democratic mockery. Lewis's composite household in Lafourche Parish's Third Ward was located near the sugar town of Raceland, a short distance along the bayou from Thibodaux. The daily activities of its five members wove together the world of rural labor with that of small-town activism. As a teacher, Lewis met the families of his pupils as well as the members of the local school boards—who included the Reverend William Murrell, now a state representative. Tench Goodly, age twenty-two, the black boatman, traveled up and down the bayou in the course of his work, and later settled in Lafourche Crossing in the First Ward, closer to town. Taylor Nelson, a black farm laborer, worked on nearby plantations but was also a member of the school board for the parish and later served on the parish Republican committee. His wife, Mary Nelson, presumably kept in touch with neighbors in the Third Ward and traveled to Thibodaux for events of various kinds. William E. Kerr, age thirty-seven, the "retired United States soldier," remains a mysterious figure, a white man living in a predominantly black household. "Retired U.S. soldier" was not a conventional occupational description; perhaps he was injured in the war and no longer worked. Perhaps—but the evidence is silent on this question—he had served in the invading or the occupying Union forces in the mid-1860s.[80]

African American Union veterans were also numerous in the neighborhood, including Nelson Christian, who had served as a private in Company E of the Seventh Louisiana Infantry (Colored), and Lewis Henderson, a captain in Company A of the Seventy-sixth Louisiana Volunteers. These veterans were possessed of military training, worldly experience, and ties to each other.[81] Their account of their prior service may have helped to stimulate the development of the local militia.

White supremacist Democrats responded with an increasingly vituperative insistence on drawing the color line, declaring the issue to be "Shall the white people of Louisiana govern Louisiana?" They moved aggressively to eliminate all possible middle ground, to bring hesitant Democrats to see the wisdom of violent rejection of granting any shred of legitimacy to the Republicans, and to thwart anyone who tried to lower the political thermostat by encouraging cooperation between parties or across the color line. Through the summer of 1874 excited planters and their allies, including the DeClouet family, organized armed White Leagues in many of the rural parishes. In the course of this campaign the most aggressive again appropriated the term "militia" to describe their own extralegal armed mobilizations. They and their allies in New Orleans spoke openly of overthrowing the state, facing down any possible federal troops, and putting an end to black political power.[82]

The federal government and General William H. Emory reacted with distaste, but glacial slowness, to the news of murders, sedition, and planned insurrection in Louisiana. There were only nineteen federal soldiers on hand at Jackson Barracks in New Orleans in the summer of 1874, and Republican governor Kellogg was fearful of an immediate conflagration. Following months of concerted white-supremacist mobilization, the young White Leaguers whom one historian has described as the "silk-stocking vigilantes" of uptown New Orleans were yearning for a fight. General Emory, ensconced in Mississippi, considered sending Lieutenant Colonel John R. Brooke and soldiers of the Third Infantry on an express train from Holly Springs, Mississippi, to New Orleans. But he could not seem to find a train until 9 o'clock at night on September 13, at which point Brooke and four companies finally left for Louisiana. Before federal troops could reach New Orleans, however, the White Leagues moved to take over the city, defying Governor Kellogg and naming their man Frederick N. Ogden "provisional general of the Louisiana State Militia." On September 14 White League forces barricaded the streets. With a huge crowd watching their advance, the young gentlemen and their allies advanced on the Metropolitan Police, who fell back. After brief fighting, the league and their allies found themselves in the hoped-for—but distinctly precarious—situation of having overthrown the legally constituted government of the state.[83]

The *Picayune* exulted that "a dozen gallant lives, worth more than all the sneaking carpet-baggers and ruffian soldiery that ever squatted on a State's carcass, have been sacrificed on the altar of liberty; the blood of gentlemen and patriots has dyed the stones of our thoroughfares, and the shock is over. The Kellogg dynasty has passed into black and bitter memory, and Louisiana throughout its borders today is free." As Colonel Brooke's federal troops made their way toward the city, the Democrat D. B. Penn tried to reassure President Ulysses S. Grant that he and his colleagues felt only "unswerving loyalty and respect for the United States Government and its officers" and that what had transpired was only a war against "usurpers, plunderers, and enemies of the people."[84]

Colonel Brooke, however, knew a coup d'état when he saw one, and prepared to take control of the city with federal troops. Despite all of their boasting about shredding the uniforms of bluecoats, the Democrats in fact deferred to federal forces. General Emory named Colonel Brooke acting military governor of New Orleans, in which capacity he received the formal surrender of Penn and the White Leagues. Brooke held the title of acting military governor for only twenty-four hours, long enough to pass authority back to Governor Kellogg.[85] Twenty-five years later, at the close of the Spanish-Cuban-American War, Brooke would take on the more lasting title of military governor of the island of Cuba—and

again be called upon to interpret the rules of the democratic game in a very fragile polity.

The young Colonel Brooke, in effect, handed authority to a state governor
whose regime the federal government endorsed but would not sustain. For black
men and women in the countryside, the trio of "civil, political and public rights"
asserted in the 1868 state constitution had rested on the maintenance of recognized legal standing, electoral activism, and practical military guarantees. Each of
these in turn required support from Washington, from the statehouse, and from
within the rural parishes themselves. Washington and the state Republican Party,
however, were increasingly unreliable guarantors, and by the mid-1870s rural activists were left nearly on their own. Their last hope was to build locally, bridging
to a generation that came of age after the end of slavery, and fusing labor demands
with political claims.

CHAPTER THREE

Crisis and Voice

Southern Louisiana, 1874–1896

We were much surprised to hear lately a rumor to the effect that a considerable number of the working class of white men expressed themselves dissatisfied with the Democratic Party, and threaten to vote with our opponents next fall. We are unwilling to admit the idea that white men, feeling the obligation of race, should thus prove recreant to duty.

Weekly Thibodaux Sentinel, January 8, 1876

IN OCTOBER OF 1874, CAPTAIN BENJAMIN LEWIS, THE BLACK SCHOOL-teacher who led the state militia in Lafourche, stepped in as a substitute county commissioner ("police juror") in adjacent Terrebonne Parish, just in time to help designate the polling places for the November election. Serving with Lewis on this council were W. H. Keyes and Alfred Kennedy, both of whom had been involved in the sugar strikes earlier that year. The council named Lewis himself one of the commissioners of election at Poll no. 2, at the Lejeune Store on what was called the "old Beattie Place" in upper Terrebonne. As commissioner, Lewis would be charged with supervising the depositing of ballots and their subsequent tallying.[1]

Federal intervention in New Orleans in September of 1874 had prevented the White League from overthrowing the Republicans by force, but it did little to resolve the pervasive crisis of legitimacy. The elections of 1874 and 1876 would each reenact the same struggle for the soul of Reconstruction Louisiana. The bayou parishes, with a history of mobilization on both sides, were a key battleground. Voters, and their kin and neighbors who could not vote, left an extensive

61

paper trail in the newspapers of the time and in their testimony to the myriad in-
vestigators who tried to untangle the results of their actions. This testimony,
which is as vivid as it is unreliable, offers a glimpse of what it meant to vote, and
for one's vote to be counted, during the years when the expansive citizenship envisioned in the Fourteenth and Fifteenth amendments was so sharply challenged.

The numbers of registered Republican and Democratic voters were quite
closely balanced in several of the bayou parishes, and each contest was a hard-
fought one. Despite threats of bulldozing and electoral chicanery, many freedpeople were still voting as they chose to. A planter who ran for state Senate on
the Democratic ticket in 1874 reported that he watched "every man in my employ, without exception, vote against me, one after another." Thus despite the in-
timidating presence of the White League in adjacent parishes, the 1874 elections
sent the Republicans W. H. Keyes and Frederick Marie back to the state House of
Representatives from Terrebonne, along with Isaac Sutton from St. Mary and Victor Rochon and the former slave Louis Martinet from St. Martin. The bayou parishes showed themselves to be capable of sustaining a cadre of activists of color,
backed up by intrepid voters.[2]

The counting of ballots and filing of returns were nonetheless perpetually contested. The refusal of ferociously hostile Democratic politicians to view the Republicans as respectable opponents tended to drive a wedge between radical
Republicans, who wanted to ground the party among black voters, and recon-
ciliationist Republicans, who sought to build a base among whites by pulling away
from an expansive vision of black rights. The more conservative option would
also find increasing support in the North.[3] When the Louisiana House of Representatives refused to seat some of the Republican winners of the 1874 elections,
and a state committee of inquiry confirmed this decision, a congressional committee intervened with a compromise that awarded a majority of the seats in the
Louisiana House of Representatives to Democrats. In the process most of the recently elected black representatives from the bayou parishes—including Marie,
Wright, Rochon, and Martinet—were unseated in April of 1875.[4]

Voting was less and less a right to be defended by the force of law and more
and more a privilege to be exercised at one's own risk. The government in Washington was not inclined to station troops in Louisiana over the long run, whatever

the demonstrated necessity of federal protection. Through 1875, as Benjamin Lewis's militia drilled and marched on the commons in Thibodaux, federal troops were withdrawn from the state, making it unlikely that Republican voters would have any external assistance in the event that they found themselves under armed attack.[5]

In March of 1875 the U.S. Supreme Court decided the appeal of three white men convicted of attacking black Republicans in the 1873 Colfax massacre in Grant Parish.[6] The majority opinion in *United States v. Cruikshank* threw out the convictions, though it left open the question of whether private rather than state action to repress voting could be punished by the federal courts. Ruling somewhat narrowly, the Court argued that "private" intimidation of voting based explicitly on race had not in fact been specified as a charge in the case. Murder was not a federal crime; direct involvement of state officials in vote suppression had not been demonstrated; and the private individuals had not been proved to be acting from motives of racial hostility. The Court reminded one and all that "the Constitution of the United States has not conferred the right of suffrage upon any one." The Fifteenth Amendment specified a particular form of abridgment that states could not institute, but did not confer a federally protected "right." To the extent that voting was a right, it was interpreted as one to be created by the individual states. A black right to vote guaranteed by the fragile, fractious, and divided civil authorities of Louisiana, of course, might look increasingly like no right at all. Moreover, black voters muscled away from the ballot box or punished for voting Republican now had no clear federal judicial recourse so long as the perpetrators were not state actors and did not avow their purpose to be racist.[7]

The symbolic effect of turning back the only convictions that had been obtained in the Colfax massacre was immense. True, the indictment against the accused men had been badly drawn up, and the judicial implications of reiterating the limits of federal constitutional language on suffrage may have been modest. The claim by the attorneys defending Cruikshank and his confrères that the courts could only punish "state action," not private action, had not been echoed in the Court's own decision. Democrats nonetheless viewed the decision as a great vindication. In practice, legal impunity for white vigilantes seemed confirmed. To Louisiana Republicans, bringing criminal charges against members of the White

Leagues or their allies now appeared a waste of time. From the vantage point of black Republicans in Terrebonne and Lafourche parishes, the local militia were, for all practical purposes, the only remaining line of defense at the ballot box.[8]

As the elections of 1876 approached, Louisiana Republicans were demoralized and physically vulnerable. Louisiana Democrats presented candidates whose goal would be to dismantle Reconstruction, dislodge black officeholders, and achieve the departure of the last federal troops, even while claiming not to violate the postwar amendments. Destroying the "Negro militia" in Terrebonne and Lafourche would be a high priority of local Democrats if they won. The newspaper in Thibodaux was explicit in its call to close ranks along lines of color: "We were much surprised to hear lately a rumor to the effect that a considerable number of the working class of white men expressed themselves dissatisfied with the Democratic Party, and threaten to vote with our opponents next fall. We are unwilling to admit the idea that white men, feeling the obligation of race, should thus prove recreant to duty."[9]

High stakes did not bring out the best behavior in either party. Democrats, who could smell the possibility of a victory that they might turn into a purge, made resources available to buy out Republican voters, and in the northern parishes employers exercised the classic weapon of threatening black voters with firing and eviction. Republican leaders in the bayou parishes, uncertain of what was coming next, floundered. Anatole Panalle, who had served with Benjamin Lewis but was now viewed by the Democrats as an "honest colored Republican"—and the meaning of this phrase would soon become clear—held the post of supervisor of elections in Lafourche and was in charge of drawing up the lists of registered voters. The composing of such a list, in a close election expected to divide along the color line, became a source of intense conflict. The wily H. H. Michelet, head of the Democratic committee, persuaded Panalle to leave the registration books overnight at Michelet's coffee house. Although Panalle was still sufficiently respected by his Republican colleagues that most refrained from accusing him publicly, his actions certainly looked bad. Panalle was soon removed from office, presumably on Republican orders from above, and replaced by Marcelin Ledet.[10]

Marcelin Ledet was an intriguing character. He apparently grew up in one of the predominantly white settlements in the southern part of the parish often characterized as "Creole," where voting Republican was unusual but not unknown. The Democrats certainly hated him, holding him to be an "unscrupulous white man." H. H. Michelet warmed to the task of description, reporting Ledet to have "lived in open concubinage with a colored wench whom he abandoned to steal the lawful colored wife of a white republican." It was Ledet's job to ensure fair elections in November of 1876, and most people seem also to have assumed that it was his job to defend Republican interests as well. The boundary between the two tasks was unclear.[11]

Most of what we know about this crucial election at the local level comes from utterly partisan sources, and is further skewed by being embedded in the massive national political wrangle triggered by the same polling. The published back-and-forth concerning the events of November 1876 is nearly endless, since the Hayes-Tilden presidential results were up in the air, with enormous implications for the future of Reconstruction and of national politics. As part of their offensive, Democrats challenged many of the Republican local victories in the bayou parishes. The testimony in these contested elections cases is a perilous goldmine of descriptive material—colorful, rhetorical, self-serving, and suffused with charges of opportunism and offstage intimidation. There are multiple sets of testimony, including one developed by a congressional committee in New Orleans while the national dispute raged in December 1876, and another compiled after the outcome was clear, in March and April of 1877. People said quite different things under the different circumstances.[12]

The charges and countercharges provide a picture of the way in which entire communities, voters and nonvoters, male and female, had been drawn into the contest. The conservative *Thibodaux Sentinel* published the following note under the headline "Heard From":

> The box that was to have been opened at Poll No. 1 on election day, and which so mysteriously disappeared, has been heard from. It was located in the Stoddard School house in the rear of Thibodaux, and it is said that the Radical women and children of the Town voted there. This, very likely, will account for the 250 majority obtained by the Radicals according to the statement of the *Union*.[13]

A witness further charged that Republicans had brought a "female organization" into the parish to discourage men of color from voting for the Democrats, and recounted the following episode: "I witnessed in the second ward here, on the day of the election, a colored woman go to the polls where her husband was coming to vote, and she grabbed his registration papers and the ticket that he had. I do not know whether she put the ballot in the box herself, but I believe she did."[14]

In their accusations, Democrats blended charges of formal irregularity with claims of intimidation and implications of an inappropriate division of decision-making responsibilities within families. White Democrats hoped that the image of black women "bullyragging" their husbands could replace the picture of white vigilantes in Colfax shooting at black Republicans. But Seymour Snaer of Terrebonne, candidate for district attorney in Lafourche, took a different perspective: "black women say, or they would express themselves in such a way, that they had children and that they knew by the prejudice the democrats had against the colored people that if the democratic party came into power they would not have probably the occasion to give the proper education to their children and would not live so happily as under the republican administration." Snaer was affirming, in effect, that within black communities during Reconstruction, political decisions were often viewed as a collective responsibility with cross-generational consequences, not a simple expression of individual preference.[15]

In an era before the secret ballot, control of the physical space of the polling was also openly sought by both sides. In Lafourche Parish, Marcelin Ledet had initially announced that many of the polling booths for the 1876 elections were to be located within plantation quarters. White Democrats were furious at this assumption of the power "to go into men's plantations and to establish polls in or about sugar houses, most of which were at work." Under pressure from both Democrats and from the Republican judge and planter Taylor Beattie (one poll had been located in the quarters of Dixie plantation, owned by his wife), Ledet seems to have acceded to moving several of the polling places, including the one for Poll no. 17, which would now be held at a warehouse on the public road that fronted the R. H. Allen plantation. The Republican commissioners of Poll no. 17, however, seem to have been operating on the assumption that the earlier designation still held. In the early morning they opened the poll halfway between the road and the sugar mill, inside the quarters, in a room of a house formerly occupied by a work-man named Buck Payne.[16]

When the poll was opened in the quarters, eighty-six voters—eighty-five of them black and one of them white—cast Republican tickets. Michelet later complained bitterly that the locating of the poll inside the quarters prevented Democrats from voting. Not only were white farmers unwilling to brave it, he said, but some of the black men on the plantation who wanted to vote Democratic could not do so under the pressure of publicity. Throughout the bayou parishes, small numbers of black voters were indeed moving toward the Democrats—out of fear, clientelism, prudence, or exhaustion. The planter R. H. Allen's carriage driver, for example, was said to have inclined in this direction.[17] At stake here was the question of whose gaze would intimidate which voters. From the point of view of the Democrats, a warehouse owned by a planter was an appropriate place to vote; a worker's rented house was not.

Poll no. 10, by contrast, was located in a "negro chapel" in the deep bayou country of the far south of Lafourche Parish, in a neighborhood occupied by families described at the time as poor and Creole, though some of their descendants would today probably be designated Acadian. There seems to have been a Democratic majority in the area. The circumstances of balloting and the counting of the votes at Poll no. 10, as best one can disentangle them, were certainly irregular, whether one believes the testimony of the Democrats or the Republicans. C. A. Fenstel, a German-speaking Republican who served as one of the three commissioners at the poll, reported that Manuel Acton Sullivan, the Democratic federal commissioner, had comported himself with confidence and exuberance: "Mr. Sullivan, he comes down and he seems to be the boss of the whole thing, and just about 6 o'clock we opens the polls; well, we went on until about 2 o'clock, and then some wine come down for Mr. Sullivan from Mr. Herrin, and Mr. Sullivan he drunk the wine, and, by God, he didn't offer me none. They were two pretty good bottles of wine, and about 5 o'clock there comes down some whisky." To defend his honor, the Democrat Sullivan later explained to a visiting congressional committee that he had drunk wine at breakfast and dinner only because he was reluctant to drink bayou water, and that the bottles of whiskey were most welcome to men who had been in a cold chapel all day.[18]

According to Fenstel, Sullivan the lawyer was thus able to stay warm enough to write out tally sheets, while the poor sober Republicans, slower of hand, could not. According to Sullivan, the Republicans were incompetent, and Fenstel himself not "acquainted with the English language." When the time came for the Republican commissioners to review the tally sheets, Mr. Sullivan found that the gun in his pocket "inconvenienced" him because it kept falling on the floor, so he laid it on the table next to the ballot box. Mr. Fenstel apparently got the message:

> Q: Did you sign these tally-sheets from the returns of that poll?
>
> A: Well, of course I signed them; there was a man with a revolver, and I was out in the woods, and I was twelve miles from home, and he was a bigger man than I was, and of course I signed the returns; I wasn't a fool.

Mr. Sullivan kept the ballot box company for the evening, then took it in his buggy to Thibodaux very early the next morning.[19]

There was already a crowd at the courthouse, including folks from out of town who must have risen early to be sure to catch the performance. ("Was there anybody else present? Why, sir, there was nearly everybody present. Why, sir, there must have been between fifty and seventy-five persons present.") Sullivan (intoxicated according to some, always a sober man according to others) proffered the box, which was no longer sealed, saying "Here is your box," or, perhaps, "Here is your goddamned box." Marcelin Ledet asked, "Where is the commissioners of election?" and Sullivan apparently replied, "There is no commissioners of election; I brought the box myself." The seals, Sullivan later opined, had perhaps fallen off due to the bouncing of his buggy. Ledet, presumably as everyone expected him to, refused to accept ballots brought in under these circumstances.[20]

That was the signal. A man named Mr. Winder jumped onto a chair and said, "I demand that that box be accepted; the time is now come when the rights of the people must be enforced." This caused considerable "excitement." Word quickly spread of the showdown, in which Democrats hoped to force Ledet to take the box. It is hard to know whether the Poll no. 10 box was chosen as the exemplary object of discord simply because the opportunity presented itself, or because it could credibly be argued to contain a Democratic majority (enabling Democrats to contest the final results on the grounds of its refusal), or because Mr. Sullivan was especially adept at asserting control over ballot boxes, and Mr. Fenstel exceptionally disinclined to dispute it. But there it was: an embodiment of Democratic misbehavior for Mr. Ledet, an object containing the will of the people for the Democrats.

Soon Benjamin Lewis and the "Negro militia" arrived on the scene, though there is no record of their having been ordered to do so by any higher authority. Some apparently came in from out in the country, and then obtained arms in town. This caused more excitement, and a great deal of shouting. The Democratic leader H. H. Michelet later claimed that a group of Democratic supporters, most of them Confederate veterans, had been armed and eager to sweep away the militia, whom they characterized as "vandals." The "gray heads" among the Democrats, Michelet said, had with difficulty restrained the young, in the interests of adding the parish's vote for the Democratic gubernatorial candidate, Francis T. Nicholls, to the statewide total rather than risking the annulment of the vote.[21]

H. H. Michelet, however, was a master of bombast—both when he testified in French and when he testified in English. His emphasis on what his allies *could* have done may conceal an uncomfortable awareness of what they in fact did not do. Like his white-supremacist colleagues in New Orleans in September of 1874, who portrayed their scripted advance against the Metropolitan Police as a magnificent military engagement, Michelet was drawn to the image of "sweeping away" those whom he had long refused to credit with any legitimate political voice. But in Lafourche and Terrebonne parishes the forces on each side were still much too closely matched for any such sweeping to take place. Michelet and his friends could not in fact force Ledet to accept an unsealed ballot box of indeterminate contents, presented within a mise-en-scène intended to oblige a Republican to submit to a brazen show of Democratic disregard for electoral procedure.[22]

At the end of the day Ledet prevailed, and the votes from Poll no. 10 were not entered in the consolidated returns submitted in November. Republicans won by a narrow margin, helping to put the former slave T. A. Cage into the state Senate and Dr. C. B. Darrell, a white Republican, into the federal House of Representatives. Democrats would fight for over a year to reverse these election results, working in the shadow of their struggle over the presidency.

At the end of January, the famous Compromise of 1877 was struck. Ruther-
ford B. Hayes and the Republican Party were judged winners of the vote in the
electoral college and gained the presidency. The Democrats, in turn, would get
state power in Louisiana. It was understood that President Hayes would promptly
order the definitive withdrawal of federal troops from Louisiana. Marcelin Ledet
was brought back to testify a second time about the parish election of 1876. Pro-
claiming himself contrite, he took the Democratic line, saying that he had thrown
the election for his Republican friends and was now sorry that he had done so. His
former allies wondered what exactly had happened to him. Louis A. Wiltz, acting
governor of Louisiana, reversed the victory of C. B. Darrall in the Third Congressional District and certified a "corrected statement" giving the office to Democrat
J. H. Acklen.[23]

With the national settlement of 1877, Republican power in Louisiana was
mortally wounded, although the party continued to hold some influence through
patronage at the federal Customs House in New Orleans, and through alliance
with planters in some of the sugar parishes who favored a high protective tariff.
The last federal troops—so few as to be essentially symbolic—were formally "relocated" away from the statehouse, though they were not physically withdrawn
from Louisiana.[24]

The White Leaguers were eager to take over the entire state militia, and had
begun drafting new rules and regulations even before President Hayes issued the
formal order reassigning federal troops.[25] Once in power, the Democrats moved
quickly against the members of Benjamin Lewis's militia, declaring their terms
expired. Oscar Crozier, the Republican tax collector, tried to mediate between
the old militia and the new state government. Crozier, who had served in the
state Senate in 1874–75, owned a small sugar plantation worked with black labor
in Terrebonne Parish as well as several small lots in Lafourche, and was usually described as a mulatto. Governor Francis Nicholls, who wanted to tread warily in
these first months of what Democrats would soon call Redemption, agreed to
postpone action temporarily, but the militia had no choice but to disband.[26] With
a mixture of irritation and gloating, H. H. Michelet charged that the black militia
members, with their guns, eventually "scattered over the state."[27]

The actual fate of the members of "Benjamin's militia" varied. Former first lieutenant Anatole Panalle had made his peace with the Democrats during the 1876 election and continued to serve on the school board. Captain Benjamin Lewis lived on in the memory of his enemy H. H. Michelet as a near-legendary and incendiary bandit. In reality, Lewis had simply moved across the bayou to the First Ward of Terrebonne Parish. In 1880, now married to a woman born in Louisiana and the father of two children, Lewis still gave his occupation as schoolteacher. The neighborhood was similar to the one near Raceland where he had lived as a single man a decade earlier: large numbers of laborers categorized as black and mulatto lived alongside a smaller number of farmers and laborers listed as white, as well as black railway workers from Virginia, Mississippi, Tennessee, Alabama, and Maryland.[28]

Years earlier, John J. Moore, the former slave and later Republican Party activist from St. Mary Parish, had predicted that if the violence against black people became bad enough, they would be forced to leave politics alone. But Moore himself had in practice been hard to intimidate, returning to the town of Franklin to organize in the immediate aftermath of the assassination of the two most prominent Republicans in town. Now, a decade later, the choice of candidates had been forcibly narrowed, the possibility of electing black officeholders nearly eliminated, and the physical safety of Republican voters left hostage to local gangs. Nonetheless, the Republican Party of Terrebonne Parish, by focusing on matters of national concern, managed to ally with a few pro-tariff sugar planters and hold on to a pocket of local power. Black men in Lafourche, Terrebonne, and St. Mary kept on voting, though the resumption of Democratic power made it more and more difficult to ensure that their ballots would be counted.[29]

As the curtain came down on Reconstruction, white-line Democratic dominance was reasserted in the legislature, in the town halls, and in the militia. A new state constitution in 1879 expunged the guarantee of equal "civil, political and public rights" that had figured in the 1868 constitution, though it stopped short of openly mandating racial separation. Much of the power of the state could now be exercised directly against the interests of former slaves and their descendants. They, in turn, were obliged to look elsewhere for support: either upward, to the federal government, or laterally, to their immediate places of work, neighbors, and coworkers.[30] In this pursuit, communication up and down the river and the bayous was of great importance, and families in towns like Donaldsonville and Thibodaux who had easy access to New Orleans could use strategies not open to those living on scattered cotton farms in isolated parishes to the north. In their increasingly embattled situation, activists in New Orleans and in the bayou parishes relied on one another to maintain momentum and morale. No longer able to serve in the militia and often thwarted at the ballot box, they continued to work in the spheres of education, political debate, and labor organizing. The evolving structures of labor in the sugar country did provide some of the conditions for mobilization, and the lively discussion of rights and strategy nurtured by Reconstruction made it possible to give it another try.

The struggle to give meaning to freedom was, of necessity, subject to transformation in the face both of repression and of new opportunities. Those who managed to resist despair were obliged to redirect and reinvent their struggles within tighter and tighter constraints. These constraints reduced the number of their potential allies and raised the costs and risks of the exercise of voice, but they did not altogether destroy the "social energy" that had been activated.[31]

Some men of color who had previously held public office tried to secure economic independence through farming, and they were able to keep a certain freedom of action. Former slave Thomas A. Cage lost his seat in the state House of Representatives to one of the many Democratic challenges to the results of the 1876 elections, but he became one of the rare black residents of Terrebonne Parish to rent and operate a cane farm, and he remained active in the Republican Party. With six cows, 60 acres planted in corn, and 190 acres planted in cane, Cage was no longer dependent on selling his own labor, though he may have owed some allegiance to the man from whom he rented.[32] In Lafourche Parish, Henry Franklin, listed as a mulatto, who had served as clerk of the District Court in 1870, began to accumulate skills and resources that would later earn him the reputation of being "one of the wealthiest and most prosperous colored men in Louisiana."[33]

Most ordinary farm laborers in the bayou parishes, however, lived in the countryside itself and owned little property. Their home communities included large sugar plantations with mechanized mills and small backland settlements in which houses clung precariously to the land between the bayous. During the decades that followed the elections of 1876, Louisiana's sugar industry achieved a certain renewal, pushing forward and increasing its output by about 75 percent between 1875 and 1885. Plantations like Upper Ten, Laurel Valley, and Leighton installed modern equipment and brought in harvests of between 490 and 725 thousand-pound hogsheads of sugar a year, while giants like Rienzi, Raceland, and Arcadia produced over a thousand.[34] In the process, life in the quarters changed, as chattel slavery receded from view and new forms of modernized production emerged. At the same time, social life on the larger plantations also evolved as Acadian farmers, Sicilian laborers, and Irish immigrants moved more fully into the world of cane and its subsidiary activities.

On the large mechanized plantations a rigid racial segmentation of labor was nonetheless still in force. The resident labor force on the rapidly modernizing enterprises like the Leighton plantation remained overwhelmingly black. On Upper Ten plantation, in Lafourche Parish, only one white man between the ages of eighteen and forty-five was listed as living on the plantation in 1878: William Bodien, age thirty-eight. There was a single colored artisan, Wesley Hollins, a cooper, and then twenty-three colored laborers. These names were followed by those of another five colored laborers listed as residing on Sabatier Upper Ten, which may have been a tenancy of the larger plantation: Celestín Tardiffe, age eighteen; Lewis Goodin, age twenty-eight; Clay Williams, age twenty-eight; Israel Lucas, age twenty-nine; and Mark Harris, age twenty-five. Given their ages, it is reasonable to assume that nearly all of these black laborers had been born of slave mothers, and most had probably lived through the occupation of Lafourche Parish by Union forces. Some may have made it to the freedmen's schools, where they could have encountered Benjamin Lewis.[35]

Upper Ten plantation was close to Thibodaux, and laborers who had gone to town in previous years could have seen Benjamin Lewis's militia drilling in front of the courthouse and one or another fracas around the ballot box. The reversal of Reconstruction in 1877 was aimed, among other things, at demobilizing these young men, and young women along with them. But as the events of the decade that followed indicated, some, including Clay Williams and Israel Lucas, refused to heed the warning. They would soon take part in labor strikes and find themselves in court to answer for their actions.

Although a sharp racial segmentation of the labor force characterized most of the sugar fields and mills, in the deep back country instances of open intimate interaction could still be found, vestiges of the more Caribbean pattern of social relations that had characterized French and Spanish Louisiana. One such idiosyncratic community was Laforest plantation, occupied by twenty-five farmers, eighteen of them listed as white, seven as colored. None of the resident males between eighteen and forty-five was listed as a laborer. It is perhaps not surprising that it was on this plantation that the educational inspector had in 1875 found a racially integrated school, taught by Colonel Laforest himself, "a highly educated gentleman" and an "old planter" of the neighborhood.[36]

A few small plantations also combined black and white labor: the Signorelli plantation had a white overseer, eight white laborers with Creole or Acadian names (including Theodule Boudreaux and Desiré Melançon), and five colored laborers with a mixture of Anglo and French surnames, including Moses Todd and Valerie Antoine. The population of the surrounding Twenty-second Precinct was largely composed of small farmers. Many of the men designated as "white" were listed as living on their own "place"; many of the men designated as "colored" were living on land that belonged to someone else.

In some of the mixed-farming areas, cross-racial interaction went up to and included that great southern taboo—interracial marriage. In Lafourche Parish's Tenth Ward, the 1880 manuscript census lists Sheldon Guthrie, age thirty-eight, white, born in New York, "farms on shares"; his wife, Roselia Guthrie, age twenty-three, mulatto female, born in Louisiana; and their daughter, Sarah Guthrie, mulatto, born in New York, age two. Louisiana governor Samuel D. McEnery might later thunder that "God Almighty has Himself drawn the color line," but apparently Sheldon and Roselia Guthrie had not attended either to Him or to McEnery when they established their household in Lafourche Parish.[37]

Residents of these naturally isolated backlands settlements, as well as workers on the intentionally isolated large-scale plantations, often sought out the public life available in the small- and medium-sized towns of the sugar country. The former slave Junius Bailey, for example, born in Assumption Parish, had been a teenager at the time that the Lewis and Peney militias were active in Lafourche and Terrebonne. By the 1880s, Bailey apparently taught school on the Laurel Valley plantation, where the resident population included a white shopkeeper, a white carpenter, a white overseer and clerk, a colored blacksmith, three white laborers, and twenty-four colored laborers. A member of the black Masonic lodge in Thibodaux, he entered politics in the unpropitious year of 1878 and began to make his presence felt. On September 25, 1883, he delivered what was characterized as a "noted address" at an emancipation celebration in Thibodaux, and in 1884 he presented his candidacy for sheriff in the parish.[38]

In Donaldsonville, at the intersection of Bayou Lafourche and the Mississippi River, Pierre Lacroix Carmouche moved into public life as an artisan rather than as an orator. The son of free parents from Ascension Parish, and the grandson of a manumitted slave, Carmouche grew up speaking French, shifting to English when he went to school. Forced to leave school when his father died, he worked for a while as a barber and with a dentist. In the 1880s his ambition drew him to New Orleans, where he trained as a blacksmith and apparently got to know an older generation of activists. This was in some ways a return journey: His grandfather, Juan Bautista Pedro, had married in New Orleans in the year of the 1803 Treaty of Cession.[39]

By the 1880s in New Orleans, men of color had been muscled out of most public offices, but a strong current of egalitarian aspiration and organization continued to manifest itself in the dockworkers' union and among Afro-Creole activists who worked out of Masonic lodges and their own small shops. Louis Martinet, who had begun his legal training while serving in the state House of Representatives, would soon build up a practice as a notary public, certifying property transactions and facilitating small-scale legal initiatives by his neighbors in New Orleans. Rodolphe Lucien Desdunes, whose father was a wheelwright from Haiti and whose mother had been born in Cuba, carried on the family tobacco shop. Desdunes was an active Mason who took a broad view of the struggle, which he saw as encompassing the principles of the French and Haitian revolutions, the Louisiana Constitution of 1868, and the history of the fight for equal rights across the Caribbean. As Reconstruction was rolled back, he labored to sustain a radical interpretation of the Republican Party's commitments in the face of Democratic dominance and a new and much-narrowed state constitution of 1879. With a thoroughly cosmopolitan worldview, Desdunes combined a deep commitment both to Christianity and to the principles of the French Declaration of the Rights of Man, all interpreted within an Atlantic/Caribbean context that highlighted the leadership of black fighters like Toussaint Louverture.[40]

In August of 1884, one of the living embodiments of the Cuban version of that Atlantic struggle was making his way to New Orleans on a steamer from Honduras. Antonio Maceo, rebel hero of Cuba's Ten Years' War against Spanish rule, settled with his family and that of Máximo Gómez into a rented house on St. Phillip in the integrated neighborhood of Faubourg Tremé. He and Gómez had come to energize the Cuban exile community in New Orleans, New York, and Key West and to raise money for the independence struggle they wished to reinitiate on the island. Their shared house was located just a few blocks from the Perseverance Masonic Hall and Economy Hall, both key places of sociability for the population of color in New Orleans, and was near the homes of various French- and Spanish-speaking members of Desdunes's own Masonic lodge, Friendship No. 27.[41]

New Orleans activists like Desdunes and Martinet were well aware of the Cuban War of Independence, and they would later celebrate Maceo's military accomplishments in the pages of the newspaper they founded in the 1890s. It is difficult to know whether they met with Maceo during the months that he lived among them. Maceo spoke more French than English, and the Afro-Creole milieu may have been linguistically more welcoming than that of anglophone men of color. The Cuban Masonic lodge in New Orleans met in the same building on Basin Street as the lodge that Rodolphe Desdunes attended, though on a different day. Antonio Maceo was on his way to becoming an icon of black masculinity and bravery throughout the Atlantic world, and a decade later idealists of color in New Orleans would cite his name alongside that of Toussaint Louverture in the hagiography of black struggle. But perhaps the living Maceo, weighted down with financial worries and political discouragements, kept to himself in Faubourg Tremé. Spanish consular officials in New Orleans were presumably watching their most charismatic military enemy carefully, and there was no reason for him to draw attention to himself beyond the boundaries of the Cuban exile community.[42] But members of that exile community, particularly tobacco workers, may have served as bridges to Louisiana activists. Ramón Pagés, for example, identified as a leader of the "Spanish" cigar makers in New Orleans, was a featured speaker at an equal rights meeting organized some years later by Desdunes and Martinet. Two years after that Ramón Pagés was on a ship full of exiles heading to join the fight for independence in eastern Cuba, suggesting that he himself was a Cuban separatist all along.[43]

Like their counterparts in Cuba, the activists of New Orleans combined traditional mutual-aid organizing with a broader set of commitments to political goals. In January of 1887, for example, a local Republican paper in New Orleans announced the formation of a new educational society titled the "New Amis Sincères," aimed at "the protection of the colored Creole population against wrong and injustice, the promotion of public education, the establishment of a library and the erection of a hall." Its vice-president was a local shoemaker, Homer Plessy, later to become famous as the plaintiff in the landmark antisegregation case *Plessy v. Ferguson*.[44] The same paper provided news of the labor strikes that were spreading across the country and detailed coverage of the activities of the Knights of Labor. Rodolphe Desdunes, in his writings, blended his republicanism with support for labor activism in the countryside; he viewed repression of rural workers as of a piece with white supremacist assaults on the civil, political, and public rights of men and women of color.[45]

In their Louisiana organizing, the Knights of Labor built on significant discontent among sugar workers, who by now had a long tradition of asserting their interests. A planter from St. Mary's had complained in 1886 that employees "are becoming more and more unmanageable. By degrees they are bringing the planter to their way of thinking in regard to how they should work and no telling at what moment there will be a serious move to compel the planter to comply with any request."[46] He was right to be uneasy. Fresh from successes in the North, the Knights of Labor had begun to organize among town dwellers and railway workers and they now turned to the sugar workers. Beginning with the railway town of Morgan City, then moving out into the countryside, the Knights eventually reached even isolated bayou communities like Little Caillou.[47]

The Knights were a cross-class and cross-racial organization, though they were known to tread carefully in matters of racial etiquette. Most of their local assemblies in the South were segregated, but some combined men and women, black and white, from the trades and from the fields. However hesitant they were on the question of racial integration, the Knights' ideology of producer solidarity was a far cry from the racialized rhetoric of the Democrats. The Knights, in their emphasis on unity among working people, proposed a new system of "marking" allies and enemies—one that was not, on the face of it, reducible to racial categories.[48] Moreover, their actions necessarily brought black workers directly into the public spaces of assembly and political action from which white supremacy was trying to bar them.

By 1887 there were said to be twelve local assemblies of the Knights in New Orleans, and thirty outside the city. District Assembly 194, in the Bayou Teche area, claimed 5,000 black members. Donaldsonville, at the fork of the Mississippi River and Bayou Lafourche, held three local assemblies, at least one of them composed of black field laborers. Pierre Carmouche, the blacksmith in Donaldsonville, was one of those who seized upon the Knights as an organizing tool, recruiting men to the organization from across his home parish of Ascension. Carmouche was a longtime activist with a reputation for physical strength; years later one of his neighbors recalled that he could hold a sledgehammer at arm's length.[49] Junius Bailey, the schoolteacher in Thibodaux, also joined the Knights and, when the time came to present formal demands, drew on his skills in formal oratory and the conventions of written communication. Figures like Carmouche and Bailey bridged the gap between town and country, uniting artisans and professionals with laborers and giving the organization exceptional breadth.[50]

In neighboring Lafourche Parish, the first signs of immediate labor agitation were noted in early 1887 by the French-language pages of the *Thibodaux Sentinel*. The paper reported on January 22 that some fifteen black workers, belonging to three of the most important plantations around Raceland, had just gone on strike.[51] A search of the court records housed in the old jail in Thibodaux turns up further details: on January 19 a group of men apparently tried to halt work on the Mary plantation, a large estate covering 1,800 acres and valued at $20,000. Jordan Brannon, Briscoe Wheeler, Johnny Phillips, William Pearson, Peter Young, and James Lagarde were charged with unlawful disturbance and riotous assembly.[52]

Clay Williams, Adam Elles, and Israel Lucust were at the same time charged with trespassing on the Upper Ten plantation—a somewhat surprising charge, given that Williams and Lucust (sometimes spelled Lucas) had in 1878 been listed as residents of Sabatier Upper Ten. Perhaps living in the quarters was one thing; coming into the fields to exhort workers to lay down tools was quite another. Adam Elles was specifically charged with having prevented Nelson Christian from working. This may have been an interesting encounter, since Nelson Christian seems to have been a black Union veteran. Christian would by 1887 have been well into middle age; he may have thought these wildcat strikes highly imprudent.[53]

The testimony of the owner of Mary plantation, Richard Foret, conveys something of the drama of these events. Foret recalled that he had come to Raceland on his way to Thibodaux, and "on my way I met a crowd of colored men going down the bayou on the levee . . . When I got to the depot Mr. Sevin told me the crowd were going down to stop my hands from working . . . as a matter of fact my hands stopped working at 12 M that day." Foret sent a clerk from Raceland to warn the overseer of what was happening. The witness Wiley Jackson later said that he himself had remained at Raceland, "on the levee at the store, sometimes at the depot and down at the little boat." The levee along Bayou Lafourche had evidently become the scene of a tense political promenade, as people went back and forth with news, exhortations, and alarms.[54]

Versions of who exhorted what to whom differed, as is generally the case in judicial records of this kind. The clerk implied that Foret's hands had been intimidated: "I told the boys on Mary plantation to keep on working but they said no the men who had been there had said if they didn't stop they would come back and run them out of the field." But the witness Lewis Anderson, who referred to the workers not as boys but as hands, believed that they were acting voluntarily in response to the strikers' call not to work for 60 cents a day: "the Foret hands agreed at once to stop. They didn't make any threats they didn't have time to make any threats because the others were willing to stop."[55]

The issues under discussion included the classic one: how much could a man or a woman expect to be paid for devoting strength and stamina to working in another man's cane field? The prevailing rate of 60 or 65 cents a day until the harvest began, paid in "pasteboard tickets" redeemable only at the company store, looked pretty paltry. The process of mobilization also reopened the familiar questions of property rights: Who could set foot on a plantation during work time? Could a worker, perhaps even a resident of the quarters, be charged with trespassing on his home plantation? By its nature, the confrontation touched on the even larger issue of whether black men and women had the right to a voice on questions of public concern.

The January strike—modeled to a degree on the informal negotiations common at the beginning of the calendar year—showed no immediate signs of success. But the strength of the Knights of Labor was continuing to grow in the region, and it seems to have tapped into energies that had previously gone into the candidacies of male Republicans and their supporters in the earlier "female organizations." By February, Morgan City in St. Mary Parish had what was described as a "female lodge of colored Knights of Labor."[56] Women had long been an integral part of the field labor force, and their support and solidarity would be critical for the success of any large-scale strike. By March of 1887 a member of the Knights of Labor, Local Assembly 8408 in Schriever, was optimistic. He wrote that although pay was currently 65 cents per day for first-class and 50 cents for second-class men, there was the prospect of a good crop and abundant work: "We expect an increase in wages by April 1."[57]

As summer ended and the late fall grinding season approached, there was a real prospect that mass action would attempt to force the hand of planters. The local Democratic paper began to remind its readers of the open confrontations of the late Reconstruction period, which it now recalled under the title "Benjamin's Militia: A Negro Company that Outraged Lafourche."[58] In a lengthy article filled with transcriptions of correspondence and testimony, the *Thibodaux Sentinel* of October 15, 1887, evoked the old demons of violence and arson by "black banditti." The timing was not accidental: four days later, District Assembly 194 of the Knights of Labor met in Morgan City to try to set a rate of wages for sugar workers for members in St. Mary, Terrebonne, Lafourche, Iberia, and St. Martin parishes. The terms included a call for better wages, no payment in scrip, and extra pay for night watches. Junius Bailey, the schoolteacher who was now president of the joint local executive board, Knights of Labor, headed the signatories of the letter sent to planters in Lafourche: "should this demand be considered exorbitant by the sugar planters . . . we ask them to submit such information with reason therewith to this board not later than Saturday, Oct. 29 inst. or appoint a special committee to confer with this board on said date."[59]

Planters had no intention of doing so. They were prepared to call the Knights' bluff, confident that workers dependent upon the plantation owners for lodging as well as employment would have to back down. But on the morning of November 1, workers throughout the region downed tools. White observers were stunned by the extent of the work stoppage. Across Lafourche, Terrebonne, and St. Mary parishes, to the west as far as Berwick's Bay, labor halted. It was the eve of the grinding season, and there was a risk of killing frost with every passing day; but the fields were empty.

As is the case with any such mass movement, journalistic accounts of the laborers' action must be treated with caution—particularly in their estimate of the number of participants in the first days of the strike. The figure of "10,000 strikers," usually accompanied by the note that 90 percent of them were black, has made its way from contemporary newspaper accounts into almost all subsequent narratives, even though there is no way that journalists at the time could have had a precise idea of the number of participants. The Democratic press had long used imagery evoking mobs and masses when describing black workers, and the number 10,000 may have carried shock value at just the moment when planters were calling on the governor for assistance from the militia. Sympathetic newspapers like the *Weekly Pelican* were quick to echo the figure in order to emphasize the Knights' capacity to mobilize. Nonetheless, even leaving aside the grand totals pulled more or less out of thin air, the sugar strike of 1887 was a major event. Like the great strikes elsewhere in the country in the 1880s, it marked those who participated in it, those who declined to participate in it, and those who repressed it.[60]

The sugar strike rested on a cross-class alliance between field laborers, most of whom were themselves former slaves or the descendants of slaves, and men and women based in town, who had moved away from the world of fieldwork to become artisans, teachers, urban laborers, and organizers. In the southern bayou parishes, ministers and schoolteachers had repeatedly been involved in the mobilization of forms of protest that pushed beyond the boundaries of the permissible. In the mid-1870s this pattern had been embodied in Benjamin Lewis, militia

Quarters of the Evan Hall sugar plantation, Ascension Parish, Louisiana, 1888. Frequently living in facing rows of plantation-owned cabins, black sugar workers could organize among themselves, but were vulnerable to eviction in the event of strikes.

leader with a band of "valiant warriors," on the one hand, and conscientious and successful teacher in the local schools, on the other. In the 1880s, Junius Bailey occupied a similar role, teaching school in the countryside, running for office on the Republican ticket, and at the same time drafting demands for the Knights of Labor that would unleash an enormous work stoppage.

Both by design and as a result of overlapping leadership, large-scale rural mobilization had become intertwined with associational and electoral politics in town. Each new initiative thus threatened elements of white supremacy on two fronts:

the workplace and the public sphere. Although the black and interracial militias of the 1870s had been destroyed, there were still black fire companies and mutual-aid associations that drew members from town and country and displayed their numbers publicly. After the Vigilance Fire Company and Pride of Iberia Hook and Ladder Company, for example, visited Thibodaux in the company of "over five hundred excursionists," it was reported that the firemen "proceeded in a body to serenade the mayor, but the gentleman was either absent or did not want to receive *negro serenaders*."[61]

In the workplace itself, the continuity of gang wage labor gave sugar workers a leverage and a mechanism for self-defense that sharecroppers in the cotton districts could rarely aspire to. The same labor segmentation that fenced black workers into specific jobs and not others created spaces in which solidarity could be constructed and enforced by the workers themselves.[62] Living in the planter-owned quarters, though otherwise a source of vulnerability, had an organizational advantage, for it made communication quick and group action feasible. When General William Pierce and the now lily-white militia under his command were sent into the bayou parishes to restore the "peace" that was said to be threatened by the "beligerent attitude of strikers," they encountered precisely this solidarity. Pierce reported that when his troops arrived on one plantation, "the negroes hooted and used violent language, the women waving their skirts on poles, and jeering." The militant and the playful were being combined in an exuberant show of refusal, reminiscent of the very early days of Reconstruction. Such displays required courage, and a certain confidence that deadly force would not be used in retaliation.[63] In this, the strikers of 1887 were mistaken. Pierce's militia might exercise restraint while on formal duty under his command. But a great deal of the old "bulldozer" spirit was alive among their members—particularly one unit from Shreveport, who were out of uniform and had to be restrained from directly taking on the strikers.

Backed up by a militia whose expenses they were prepared to defray, planters succeeded through intimidation and the importation of strikebreakers in getting some sugar houses back to work. Equally important, Democrats and Republicans among them had joined forces, developing a Peace and Order Committee under planter leadership to police the town of Thibodaux. In nearby Houma, they arranged for a Gatling gun to be placed on the steps of the courthouse in case of disorder. Orders went out for the arrest of strike leaders.[64]

Striking workers expelled from plantations took refuge among kin and supporters in the town of Thibodaux. With work resuming on some plantations, but strikers still holding out on others and in town, the situation was unstable. General Pierce nonetheless declared the problem of public order essentially solved, called upon planters to act on their own to defend private property, and exited the scene with most of his troops, leaving behind the rowdy unit of the Shreveport militia.[65]

Barred from entering or leaving the town without a written pass from the Peace and Order Committee, black workers and their families were now boxed into Thibodaux itself and cut off from the countryside. As late as November 21 some still comported themselves with confidence, and perhaps bravado, on the sidewalks. Mary Pugh, widow of Richard Pugh, owner of Live Oak plantation in Lafourche Parish, reported meeting "negro men singly or two or three together with guns on their shoulders going down town & negro women on each side telling them to 'fight-yes-fight we'll be there.' " But Mary Pugh's own sons were busy molding bullets in preparation for a coming battle. Judge Taylor Beattie declared martial law in the town. By this point, both Beattie and the Pughs interpreted the conflict not as a labor struggle but as a racial confrontation. They saw violent repression as justified, "or else white people could live in this country no longer." Beattie judged "the question of the supremacy of the whites over the blacks" to be at stake. Armed white vigilantes took the strike as a cue to use direct force against men of color, firing into the saloon owned by Henry Franklin.[66]

On the morning of November 22, the white Peace and Order Committee had blocked the entrances and exits to Thibodaux, apparently leading some "number of Negroes" to believe "they were being cordoned about ready for a moment of slaughter, and they fired upon the guards to gain an outlet to the swamps and to freedom." Two of the white guards were hit, neither fatally. The members of the Peace and Order Committee then turned on the strikers who were still in town, pulling black people from the houses in which they had taken refuge, shooting unarmed men, and raging along Canal Street for hours. Whatever rifles Mary Pugh believed herself to have seen among the strikers were apparently not used. Not a single white man was killed; all the dead were said to be black.[67]

No credible official count of the victims of the Thibodaux massacre was ever made; bodies continued to turn up in shallow graves outside of town for weeks to come. Men who fled to New Orleans brought stories of the terror. More than a decade later, Henry Franklin's son would recall that his father had been driven from Thibodaux by "regulators." The white editor of the *Thibodaux Star,* who had participated in the killings, made no effort to conceal his glee at the sight of "negroes jumping over fences and making for the swamps at a double quick time." He concluded, "We'll bet five cents that our people never before saw so large a black-burying as they have seen this week."[68]

The viciousness of the repression and the manifest incapacity of the Knights of Labor to provide any mechanism of defense for their members have tended to eclipse the achievement of the strike itself. Ten years after the close of Reconstruction and the demobilization of the Republican militias, a new generation of black workers and their allies had mounted the largest collective mobilization seen in the state since the Civil War. They lost their campaign for higher wages, and some lost their lives. But they made it clear that they had not been silenced and could not be ignored.

Even after their wage demands had been defeated, sugar workers still had a fragile line of defense in their continued electoral power. Under Louisiana's 1879 constitution, suffrage was in theory open to men over the age of twenty-one regardless of color or previous condition of servitude.[69] Although violence, corruption, and vote suppression were rampant, they carried the risk for the perpetrators that a congressional inquiry might thereby reject the results of the election. The 1884 U.S. Supreme Court decision in *Ex parte Yarbrough* had seemed, at least on paper, to offer some prospect of federal protection of black voting as a constitutionally guaranteed right rather than as a state-conferred privilege.[70] Even in the Louisiana legislature itself there were still some faint echoes of Reconstruction politics: William Posey, born into slavery, had run for the Louisiana legislature on the Republican ticket in 1884, and "cleaned up" in St. Mary Parish, winning a "clear-cut Republican victory." In the state as a whole, registration lists in 1888 still counted 128,150 "colored" voters, and 125,407 whites.[71]

In practice, many black voters on the electoral lists had great difficulty in casting a free ballot, particularly in the northern parishes of the Louisiana Delta where powerful Democratic landowners "counted in" the votes of their employees at their leisure. But the bayou parishes were still contested ground. As late as 1889 the Third District Republican Convention was chaired by Thomas A. Cage, the former slave from Terrebonne Parish. For the election to fill a vacant congressional seat, however, the District Republican Party chose H. C. Minor, the wealthy owner of Southdown plantation who had called in a posse against his employees and now campaigned through the sugar parishes with promises of high tariffs. Such were the awkward coalitions of this effort to renew Republican power.[72]

The white leadership of the Republican Party hoped that white voters whose major concern was the health of the sugar industry could perhaps be drawn into an electoral alliance through the issue of the tariff, driven by their apprehension that lower-priced Cuban sugar would undercut the market for Louisiana sugars. Black voters, for whom a Republican Congress was the only remaining hope for the defense of their voting rights, thus found themselves urged to elect a high-tariff sugar planter. Workers who had faced the Gatling gun on the steps of the courthouse in Houma in 1887 cannot have been much heartened by the fact that this Republican ticket was also supported by Judge Taylor Beattie, the man who had helped bring in the militia. The *Weekly Pelican* in New Orleans urged black voters to resist intimidation and bribery, noting that this might be "the last chance the colored people of the Third District will ever have. If they do not now show themselves worthy of the care of the Republican Party, they may at last be left to the tender mercies of their natural enemies."[73]

These Democratic "natural enemies" saw the rebuilding of a black/white Republican coalition as utterly anathema. The White Leagues from St. Martin Parish—called "Regulators" by their opponents—apparently broke up the 1889 election in Lafayette Parish, and shortly afterward a gang assassinated a black farmer named Cormier, his wife, and their fifteen-year-old daughter. The *Pelican* identified General DeClouet, a St. Martin Parish planter, as "Commander-in-Chief" of the vigilantes, and despaired of any effective prosecution of the crime.[74]

When the votes were counted, H. C. Minor had carried Terrebonne Parish, still a Republican stronghold, and Iberville. But he was swamped in Assumption, Ascension, Lafourche, and Lafayette parishes, and lost the district by 7,000 out of 30,000 votes.[75] Nationally, the Republicans retained control of the Congress. In 1890 they had an opportunity to pass the Lodge Elections Bill, which would have given the federal government new enforcement power in cases of vote suppression, but they let it drop. This turned out to be the last legislative chance to defend black voting rights. The next round of elections was deadly, locally and nationally. In Terrebonne Parish, the opponents of the ever-controversial Louisiana State Lottery were said to have "placed armed men at the polls, turning away all Negroes."[76] Nationally, the new Democratic majority elected in 1892 repealed almost all of the federal Enforcement Acts, which dated back to the 1870s. There was now virtually nowhere to turn for protection against informal vote suppression, and white supremacists would soon initiate legislated vote suppression as well.

In the grim aftermath of the massacre in Thibodaux, Mary Pugh, whose sons had joined local vigilantes in shooting at unarmed strikers, drew up her own balance sheet: "I think this will settle the question of who is to rule[,] the nigger or the white man? For the next 50 years but it has been well done & I hope all trouble is ended." Her chilling resolve reflected the racial dichotomies and the vicious *realpolitik* that had long characterized white supremacist propaganda in Louisiana, as well as the Democratic fantasy that a sufficiently brutal blow would render their neighbors of African descent "as humble as pie," to quote Mary Pugh again.[77] But even the terrifying killings of November 1887 did not achieve the desired result, and Pugh was premature in predicting a final resolution of her version of "the question of who is to rule." According to the iconoclastic white labor organizer Covington Hall, whose uncle was a planter in Terrebonne Parish at the time of the strike, "Neither Judge Beattie (or his son) ever again held elective office, though both tried more than once." Hall added that "Negroes still voted—else, ruthless as had been the suppression of the strike, matters would have been worse."[78]

The Democrats of Louisiana knew the role they wished the descendants of formerly enslaved workers to play. Black men and women were to remain *labor*. They were to offer their strength and stamina where it was needed, making no claims on a civic identity. As laborers, they would be segregated from white hired hands, who would in turn occupy somewhat different places in the production process: working inside the mill rather than in the fields, running machinery rather than cutting cane, planting on shares rather than laboring in a gang. The conduct and comportment of each group could then in theory be held to a specific etiquette, and their interconnection minimized. Potential alliances would be thwarted, and civic silence enforced selectively upon black workers. But it was easier said than done.

To ensure public as well as private separation, and to make clear the formal repudiation of the egalitarian guarantees of the 1868 constitution, Louisiana's Democrats moved toward legislating a requirement of forced segregation. Ever since 1879, when the new post-Reconstruction state constitution had eliminated the phrase "public rights" from its preamble and authorized a state-supported university exclusively for black students, Rodolphe Desdunes and other activists of color had dreaded the possibility of legally mandated segregation in public places and in the schools. In 1890 the axe fell, and the Louisiana legislature passed the Separate Car Act, obliging railroad companies to provide separate accommodations for black and white passengers and authorizing conductors to judge the color of a passenger and order him or her to the designated car. A telling exception was made for black nurses attending white children, whose presence in the white car would be authorized. This was openly "caste legislation," intended to etch racial designations into law and to signal that people of any apparent or known African ancestry were unfit for the company of white people unless their role was explicitly servile.[79]

The community of Creole activists in New Orleans quickly joined forces to challenge the law in the courts. Desdunes and his colleague Louis A. Martinet had legal training and years of experience with the power of the written word— Desdunes as an essayist, Martinet as a notary public. Moreover, Martinet could build on his own constituency, the hundreds of people who had passed through his notarial office over the years to put their rights in writing. One after another lodge, church, and mutual-aid association had recorded their founding and their property transactions at Martinet's office on Exchange Alley. No sooner had a Committee of Citizens been formed to oppose the Separate Car law, and a newspaper, the *Crusader,* been founded to advance the cause, than the vigorous associational life of New Orleans spilled onto its pages. The Grand Lodge, Knights of Reciprocity, for example, announced its activities in support of the Republican Party and its intent to "meet fraternally and discuss and have explained laws or measures looking to the relief of all classes of citizens." The members included men from longstanding Creole families of color, such as the Duparts, as well as those with anglophone surnames like Watts and Mitchell.[80]

For those organizing against the Separate Car Act, the issue was not their own access to comfortable travel, but the far-reaching implications of caste legislation of this kind, and the likelihood that each segregationist initiative would trigger another. Soon the New Orleans school board passed a resolution calling for expulsion from the schools of children they deemed "colored." Desdunes responded bluntly: "We know our rights and feel our wrongs. In spite of that resolution, in spite of militia laws, in spite of frauds, persecutions and murders, we will continue to believe ourselves the equals of other men by virtue of an authority higher than any human injustice."[81]

In May of 1892 it seemed, momentarily, as if the committee's challenge to what they named "white supremacy" had succeeded. An article optimistically titled "Jim Crow is Dead" reported the committee's victory in the case of Daniel Desdunes. Ordered to the white car after he had bought an interstate ticket, Rodolphe Desdunes's musician son had refused to move, and subsequently was brought before Judge John H. Ferguson's court in Orleans Parish. Following a recent Louisiana Supreme Court ruling in a separate case brought by the railway companies, Judge Ferguson had no choice but to dismiss the charges against Desdunes. Insofar as it imposed restrictions on interstate journeys, the Louisiana Separate Car Act was in transparent violation of the U.S. Constitution.[82]

To fully challenge the project of legally sanctioned segregation, however, the committee had to test the law on an intrastate journey. And so it was that their colleague and neighbor, the shoemaker Homer Plessy, bought a first-class ticket from New Orleans to Covington, Louisiana, and refused to leave the car when ordered to do so by the conductor. He was brought before the same Judge Ferguson, and his attorneys filed to stop the prosecution on the grounds that the law was unconstitutional. This time the case would be appealed all the way to the U.S. Supreme Court. It was a long, uphill political and judicial struggle, reinforced by the support of a brilliant white northern Republican lawyer and novelist with extensive southern experience, Albion Tourgée, but weakened by the increasing indifference of the northern Republican Party itself. Within Louisiana, the Committee of Citizens drew on a base of support that it characterized—optimistically—as extending "from the doctor down to the laborer without whom the fields of Louisiana would probably become a howling wilderness."[83] As the Plessy challenge to the Separate Car Act made its way through the courts, Louisiana's Democrats moved to attack universal manhood suffrage as well, empaneling a constitutional commission in 1892 to develop mechanisms for imposing new qualifications on the suffrage. The activists of the *Crusader,* unlike some of the "reform" Republicans of Louisiana, categorically opposed what was called the "qualified suffrage." They were scathing on the claims of the formally educated to be possessed of superior political wisdom: "the refined and cultured classes who would adopt it have been the author of all the evils put down to the credit of Louisiana."[84] For these Afro-Creole activists, imbued with the ideals of the 1848 French Republic, the Louisiana Constitution of 1868, and a pragmatic awareness of the balance of electoral power in the state, defending the broadest possible male suffrage was a matter of political life or death.

In the early 1890s in Louisiana, the three main prongs of the white supremacist project—the subordination of black laborers, forced segregation in public spaces, and the suppression of black voters—were pushed forward together by the Democrats, and opposed together by the men and women who rallied around the *Crusader.* Only occasionally could they count on what was left of the state Republican Party, caught up in its own factional struggles and compromising expedients. The platform of the state's emergent People's Party called for "equal justice and fairness," and its convention included some black delegates. But the Populists' fragile social and electoral base was among small-scale farmers, most of them white, in the northern parishes. The party was weak in New Orleans and the sugar parishes. The legal challenge embodied in the Plessy case was thus far more than an attack on a specific piece of legislation concerning the railroads. In the absence of any effective electoral recourse, it was an emblem of the collective refusal of caste by those whom the law had targeted. As such, the challenge drew support from out in the sugar country as well as in the city. Pierre Lacroix Carmouche, the blacksmith and former Knights of Labor organizer in Donaldsonville, sent in his contribution, as did his fellow members of the local True Friends society. A schoolteacher in Donaldsonville similarly took up a collection and conveyed her heartfelt support for the initiative in a letter.[85]

Like any political campaign, the effort had its detractors, not only among white journalists who characterized Plessy's supporters as "silly negroes" but also among members of the New Orleans community of color who feared that a judicial challenge was doomed. To doubters, Desdunes had already addressed a reply in August of 1891. Under the arresting title "Forlorn Hope and Noble Despair," he spelled out a credo for continued struggle in the face of nearly insurmountable obstacles. Noting that "we have always kept in view the derelictians of the dispensers of justice," he enumerated the ominous decisions of the federal courts that boded ill for a judicial challenge to Louisiana's imposition of a caste distinction in public transportation. But he urged his readers on: "there is no proof sufficient, extant, going to show that the people as a whole have thrown up the sponge in the struggle against injustice." He used the story of a Roman father to develop his concept of an empowering version of "noble despair." The "old Roman" had become angry "upon learning that his son had fled before the presence of three adversaries." When asked what the son could possibly have done, the father replied: "He should have died . . . or trust to a noble despair to save him." Forlorn hope, for Desdunes, was a synonym for a just cause that might yet triumph; and noble despair conferred the resolution necessary to resist against seemingly impossible odds.[86]

Four years later, with the judicial effort still under way, Desdunes looked to the fragile remaining electoral power of African American voters and made the point as plainly as he could: "The Negro is assailed in his manhood and in his dignity as a citizen by men who are claiming the sweat of his brow as their own, and yet would make it appear that he is unworthy of citizenship and justice." The appropriate response seemed clear: "Let him register as he never did before, and walk up to the polls and cast that ballot for liberty at the peril of his life if need be."[87]

Within a few months, the U.S. Supreme Court would turn back the Plessy challenge and allow the white supremacist project its legal "thin disguise" of declaring separate to be equal. Louisiana's Democrats could now claim that obliga-

Rodolphe Lucien Desdunes, author and equal-rights activist in late-nineteenth-century New Orleans. Desdunes, a cigar seller whose parents were from the Caribbean, helped organize the test case *Plessy v. Ferguson*.

tory and invidious racial distinctions were merely consensual social arrangements, and that forced segregation had no relationship to the rights guaranteed in the Fourteenth Amendment. Crushed, the New Orleans Committee of Citizens disbanded, and the *Crusader* ceased publication. The struggle to maintain voice and equal public rights had now been defeated both in the cane fields and in the courts. There remained only the fragile thread of formal electoral rights, and these were under frontal attack. The constitutional commission empaneled by the Louisiana legislature in 1892 had proposed a suffrage limitation amendment containing a poll tax and a literacy/property requirement. The first time around, proponents of legalized vote suppression overplayed their hand. When the amendment was submitted for ratification in 1896, the state's voters, unsure of its target and fearful of its effects, turned it down overwhelmingly.[88] For the moment, the broad suffrage introduced in the 1868 Louisiana Constitution and maintained in the 1879 one remained law. For men of color, registration and balloting entailed incalculable and sometimes fatal risks, but they now constituted virtually the last terrain on which cross-racial and cross-class efforts could be mounted. With each passing day, however, such efforts required more and more of what Desdunes characterized as "forlorn hope and noble despair."

CHAPTER FOUR

Finding the Spaces of Freedom

Central Cuba, 1868–1895

> *Resolved that we, the colored people of the State of Louisiana, as*
> *the especial objects of the abolition of slavery in our land, with*
> *hearts overflowing with gratitude, loving liberty for our neighbors*
> *as we love it for ourselves, desire to share with our enthralled*
> *brethren in the island of Cuba these great and glorious benefits*
> *that have at last come to us.*
>
> Resolution of a meeting at Central Church, New Orleans, 1873

IN THE SOUTHERN UNITED STATES, THE ABOLITION OF SLAVERY EMERGED from a war to maintain the Union against the secessionist initiative. The Civil War settled the question of sovereignty, but did not resolve the question of the locus of legitimate political power in the South. In Cuba, too, the dual dramas of slave emancipation and the struggle for sovereignty unfolded simultaneously and on the same stage. But in Cuba the ideas of home rule and antislavery were combined very differently. Those organizing for Cuban independence against Spanish colonialism in the late 1860s built upon antislavery sentiment, and slaves themselves joined and strengthened the separatist forces as a means toward individual and family emancipation. Put somewhat differently, the war for southern independence was waged to preserve slavery; the wars for Cuban independence aimed to end it. Cuban nationality was, in the minds of many patriots, conceived in abolitionism and nurtured on cross-racial alliance.[1]

On the ground, the Cuban picture was somewhat less clear. Within the daily world of work and family the search for legal freedom and the effort to achieve national freedom could overlap, but they could also conflict. The lengthy wars for independence provided opportunities and risks as both Cuban separatists and Spanish loyalists sought to win the allegiance of Cubans of color. For rural slaves, the challenge was to find ways to break through the isolation and compulsion of the plantation regime and press for concessions, without bringing down the full force of military repression. Their immediate interests could draw them toward the Cuban separatists or, occasionally, toward the colonial regime itself. For slaveholders near the areas of fighting, the dominant fear was the risk of loss of control. The woods seemed alive with bandits and rebels who might ally with runaways, and the threat from the *monte,* the backlands, preoccupied Spanish officers and Cuban planters alike.[2]

It had become clear by the late 1860s that slavery and prosperity in Cuba rested on an unstable base. As the planter José Quesada tried to maintain an effective workforce on the Santa Rosalía plantation in Cienfuegos, for example, he faced high prices for new slaves and had difficulty maintaining authority over those already in residence. Among the descendants of slaves from Santa Rosalía, a woman known as Rita Lucumí, brought from Africa as a child, is recalled to this day as the one who attacked the overseer with a *guataca* (heavy hoe) and cut off his eyebrows.[3] Moreover, planters seeking to replace aging or recalcitrant laborers with newly purchased slaves faced a growing crisis of supply. The Civil War in the United States had finally brought sanctions to bear on contraband slave voyages under the U.S. flag, and the transatlantic slave trade came to an end in the mid-1860s. Cuban planters were hardly inclined to relinquish slavery as a result, but they did have to face the reality that in the long run some other form of organization of labor would need to be developed. They had long relied on the importation of forced laborers of working age, and the harsh conditions of the plantation tended to yield a low birth rate and a high death rate.[4]

As British, Spanish, and U.S. actions halted the transatlantic slave trade, domestic tensions in Cuba threatened the internal political order. Spanish rule on the island had become increasingly militarized and intrusive, constraining the freedom of action of Cubans at nearly every level. Some Cubans found the colonial system a source of security, but many others were inclined to assert an independent identity and question the legitimacy of Spanish rule. And each time the sugar industry faced a crisis, tensions between merchants (often Spanish) and plantation owners (many of them Cuban) worsened. However often supporters of Spanish rule repeated their conviction that Cuba was the "ever-faithful isle," rebellion was in fact an ever-present possibility.[5]

The first major anticolonial conflict broke out in October 1868 in the eastern end of the island, a region of relatively modest sugar plantations and many small farms. It began as a conspiracy organized primarily by men of European or mixed ancestry, born on the island, and it reflected regional as well as general Cuban grievances. The rebel leadership declared a formal commitment to the abolition of slavery, and some slaves of rebel owners were freed to join the uprising. In early 1869 the revolt spread to the area of Santa Clara. In the city of Cienfuegos, the insurgents were led by Adolfo Fernández Cavada, a veteran of the Union Army in the U.S. Civil War. They recruited support from among the young men of the town, including some sons of Spanish officers, and took to the field. Residents in the rural areas responded as well, and the insurgents were soon able to occupy the town of Lajas, take over several sugar mills, and burn cane fields. Reestablishing control, the Spanish authorities began systematic repression of those suspected of disloyalty, executing some and deporting others.[6]

The dynamics of recruitment, repression, and warfare gradually worked to transform the goals and social composition of the rebellion. To the east, in the districts of Puerto Príncipe (later Camagüey) and Santiago de Cuba (later Oriente), the insurgent forces incorporated significant numbers of people of color, including slaves. Slaves who joined the rebels became—in theory—free citizens of the "republic in arms," although they were initially subject to special regulations. The war brought with it an extension of citizenship within rebel ranks, but it was an uneven process, pushed forward by the rapid emergence of black and *mulato* leadership, yet constrained and questioned by those participants who still viewed Cuban nationality as largely excluding those categorized as black. Women as well as men joined the independence movement, and lists of prisoners taken by the Spanish included white women given the honorific "Doña," such as Doña Concepción Machado, and women of color described with phrases such as *morena libre* (free black woman), as was María Andrea Jiménez.[7]

The Spanish colonial government sent troops to try to suffocate the rebellion while it also began to prepare selective concessions on the question of slavery. The Moret Law, passed by the Spanish parliament in 1870, presented itself as an abolitionist document, but as a practical matter freed only children and the elderly. The net effect was a reformist gesture that put the colonial government on record against slavery, but disturbed the supply of labor as little as possible. Its provisions for registration of slaves, arbitration of disputes, and gradual emancipation nonetheless accelerated the breakdown of the social relations of slavery triggered by the outbreak of war.[8]

After young children and the elderly were subtracted by the 1870 law, the slave population of the districts that would later make up the central province of Santa Clara was 56,500, down from 72,100 a decade before. The presence of another 15,900 indentured Chinese workers in the region helped to sustain the size of the labor force under the direct control of planters. On the south-central coast, the sugar district of Cienfuegos held 13,600 slaves, of whom 11,200 were field slaves, alongside 1,700 Chinese workers. Well aware of the centrality of slave labor to their prosperity, landowners and merchants in Cienfuegos were a bastion of opposition to the abolition of slavery. Beginning in 1869, the city's Casino Español, a social and political club for those who championed a Spanish identity, served as a forum for both rural and urban conservatives. A British consular official in Havana was blunt in his estimate of the overall importance of the Casino's various branches: "the authority of the Spanish Govt. is entirely superseded by the Casino Español which is, as you are no doubt aware, composed of all the Pro-Slavery and intolerant members of Spanish society here, from the wealthy Planter down to the meanest pedler." In Cienfuegos, one of these intransigents was Manuel Blanco, heir to José Quesada's Santa Rosalía plantation, where in 1877 he claimed mastership over Rita Lucumí and more than a hundred of her fellow workers.[9]

Despite the war, large-scale planters in the central districts were often able to fortify their mills and carry on with the planting, cutting, and processing of cane. During much of the conflict, this area constituted the far western edge of the main zone of action of the rebels, whose forces were concentrated to the east. Still, the threat and reality of insurgent attacks, of recruitment among slaves, and of a general agitation on the question of slavery opened up new possibilities for slaves themselves.

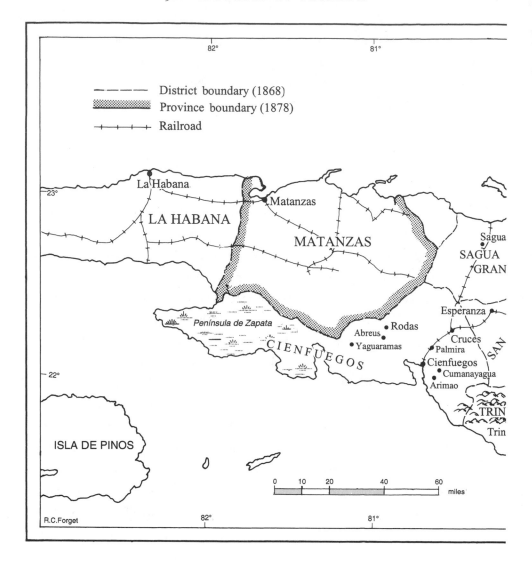

In some cases, the openings were modest and individual. In an effort to combat sentiment in favor of independence, the Spanish authorities confiscated ("embargoed") the goods of some citizens suspected of disloyalty. For Liberato Leiva y Arnau, from the district of Yaguaramas, these goods included a slave named Domitila. When Leiva's goods were embargoed, Domitila began working on her own account in the town of Cienfuegos, moving from the personalized control of a master to the more impersonal pursuit of a daily wage. Some years later, in the

80°   79°   78°

CENTRAL CUBA
ca. 1868
With the districts that later
formed the Province of Santa Clara

23°

la Grande
LA
DE
CLARA
Remedios   Yaguajay
Santa Clara
TA
REMEDIOS

SANTA CLARA

22°

IDAD
idad
SANCTI SPÍRITUS
Sancti Spíritus
PUERTO PRÍNCIPE

Puerto Príncipe

80°   79°   78°

process of dis-embargo, Leiva appealed to the colonial government to try to retrieve Domitila. For this suspected proponent of Cuban independence, the maintenance of authority over an individual slave was quite compatible with whatever
notion he had of Cuban rights. But for Domitila, the rupture between insurgent
slaveholders and the colonial state had brought a provisional freedom.[10]

In the context of instability created by the war, even routine financial operations could become disruptive. When a judge arrived at the Ingenio Angelita in

northern Cienfuegos in November of 1869 to prepare for an auction of twenty slaves of that plantation, the slaves fled to the cane fields and the nearby *monte*. When the slave workforce was counted that night, twenty-four men and twelve women were missing. When a representative of the justice of the peace returned the next day accompanied by several officials and six *voluntarios* (militiamen), the entire workforce rebelled. Dreadful as labor on the plantation was, the prospect of removal from family, provision plots, and huts may have been worse.[11]

Central Cuba was drawn more fully into the vortex of war as insurgent troops under Máximo Gómez moved out of the east, crossed the defensive trench constructed by the Spanish, and invaded the sugar regions in early 1875. This bold stroke, not authorized by the civilian rebel leadership, was aimed at widening the war and broadening its base. But the presence of a major insurgent force did not sufficiently strengthen the local rebellion, and the region's insurgent leaders were reluctant to submit to the high command of the invasion force newly arrived from the east of the island.[12]

As a measure of social control and a means of military defense, the Spanish military helped planters to garrison the sugar estates and recruited contingents of local loyalists into units known as *guerrillas.* But the presence of soldiers could not in practice prevent contact between plantation residents and insurgents. The dispersed rural population was exceptionally difficult to police, and the line between insurgent and civilian, or between runaway and rebel, was by no means clear. The massive Santa Susana plantation, in Santa Isabel de las Lajas, enumerated some 285 slaves in 1875. But at the end of the list there appeared another 38 names of slaves—all listed as *prófugos,* runaways. The runaways thus constituted 12 percent of the plantation slave population, and an even larger percentage of the workforce. More dramatically, the proprietor of the Dos Hermanos plantation pled in 1876 for a tax reduction on the grounds that the majority of the slaves on his estate had been "carried off" by the insurgents.[13]

The Spanish colonial state was caught between two contradictory strategies for sustaining control over slave laborers in a context of war. It could try to counteract insurgent propaganda by instituting some reforms and promising liberal measures in the future, including a proximate end to slavery if peace were achieved. The Moret Law of 1870 was a step in this direction, as were local efforts to encourage surrenders of black insurgents through the hint that they might not be forced back into slavery. Yet in the long run the forces unleashed by the rebellion could only be contained if the rebellion itself was defeated, and the logic of counterinsurgency favored direct repressive action.

In late November of 1876, Spanish general Arsenio Martínez Campos moved to reassert full control over the central region. Establishing his headquarters in Cienfuegos, he deployed new contingents of Spanish forces as Máximo Gómez and the main body of the insurgent army retreated eastward. In addition to direct military actions, Spanish forces collaborated with planters in irregular actions. A mysterious order in December of 1876, from Spanish lieutenant colonel Manuel María de Vivanco, stationed in Arimao, to the captain of the Guerrilla de León, captures the flavor. Upon presentation of the letter, the captain was to form a group of twelve foot soldiers, provide them with three days' rations and a cooking pot, and send them with Manuel Blanco, the slaveholding proprietor of the Santa Rosalía plantation, on a mission whose purpose Blanco would explain. The men were to leave town secretly, if possible without the knowledge even of the other members of the force. It seems likely that the goal was some combination of irregular warfare and discipline of slaves suspected of contacts with the enemy. Similar actions continued over the months that followed. By June of 1877, Vivanco reported to Manuel Blanco that the last black rebel holdout near the Santa Rosalía estate had run out of ammunition. To achieve the death of two black men and the surrender of six women had required the combined effort of ninety Spanish soldiers and seventy pro-Spanish Cuban militiamen.[14]

In an attempt to encourage desertions from the insurgent forces, Martínez Campos offered rewards to rebels who surrendered and promised leniency to prisoners. In their effort to suppress all forms of insurrection, local commanders were nevertheless inclined to shoot on sight those thought to be rebellious slaves, and they frequently treated black insurgents as "runaways" rather than as military enemies. In 1877 the local authorities of Sancti Spíritus, the easternmost district in Santa Clara, suggested to the commanding Spanish general that teams of slave hunters be constituted from among local folk and that a reward of an ounce of gold per slave or Chinese worker captured be offered. If no one subsequently claimed ownership of the slave or Chinese worker, he was to remain the property of the person who had captured him. The surviving military records do not reveal the extent to which this strategy was put into effect. There seems to have been some concern that it might go against the spirit of other decrees on the question of slavery, although the officers consulted were inclined in favor.[15] The divisive and racializing intent and effect of the measure could hardly be clearer.

Although the actions of the rebels had placed full abolition on the agenda for the future, most planters and administrators in Santa Clara did not waver in their public commitment to slave labor. The Casinos Españoles reiterated their support for the government and for slavery. Despite the disruptions of war, the ending of the transatlantic slave trade, and the legal freedom granted by the Moret Law to children and the elderly, the 1877 agricultural census showed that the vast majority of workers on Cienfuegos sugar estates, as in the region as a whole, were still enslaved. Salaried workers, rented slaves, and Chinese contract laborers remained a small minority.[16]

The continued presence of enemies in the nearby hills nonetheless undermined slaveowners' control of their workforce. On November 7, 1877, the administrator of the Santa Rosalía estate reported that two armed men, one white and one black, had suddenly appeared where the work gang of the neighboring Soledad estate was laboring, asked some questions, and told the gang that they were not obliged to work there anymore. The two men then moved off, firing a shot as they departed. Witnesses could not identify the white man, but the black man was said to be named Luis, a resident of Santa Rosalía, where he worked as a *montero,* keeping track of cattle. The administrator thought he remembered that Luis had been arrested earlier for having gone to buy goods for the enemy and for having helped them to steal cattle. He urged the estate's owner to take steps to prevent Luis from "going around on his own account," and warned that he could cause real trouble someday. The administrator suspected that the white man was from the nearby settlement of San Antón, and recommended taking steps against him as well.[17]

The boundary between slave plantations and neighboring farms remained porous, and some members of the workforce moved easily across it. During the late 1870s the administrator of Santa Rosalía complained of slaves who fled the estate, but had the audacity to come home to their huts to sleep. Moreover, he suspected that runaways were providing cattle from the estate to the enemy. There was a blurring of familiar slave grievances—over food and punishment, for example—and the new possibility of active collaboration with insurgents.[18]

The combination of Spanish strategies nonetheless took their toll on the Cuban separatists, and the rebel forces were worn down by exhaustion, division, and direct repression. The rebels had not succeeded in halting work on the major plantations, many of which were heavily garrisoned, and they had not managed to sustain a rhythm of recruitment to the cause that could match the Spanish counteroffensive. Meanwhile, conflicts over questions of race and leadership undermined cohesion among the insurgents as Spanish authorities continued to proclaim that this was a "race war" and that a rebel victory would mean a black Cuba.[19]

Many Cuban separatist leaders stumbled in the face of this maneuver by asserting their own respectability as civilized white citizens, while downplaying and downgrading the actual role of black insurgents. For a rebel army that relied among other things on the dynamic leadership of Antonio and José Maceo as well as Guillermo Moncada, all of them free men of color from the east, such a response by white rebels was profoundly divisive. In central Cuba, where the black rebel general José González Planas was widely admired and where local black officers like Benigno Najarro of Las Moscas sustained the fight in the hills, the effects were equally dire.[20]

As the collective struggle faltered, individual rebels tried to find some way to reincorporate themselves into the productive life of the island. The Spanish government held out the hope that vacant lands in the east might be distributed among those who "presented themselves" for surrender and among others ruined by the war. During the last full year of the war, the Spanish colonial authorities set up carefully supervised new rural settlements, often surrounded by palisades, and tried to keep track of the movements of their inhabitants. In 1877 former residents of the abandoned country towns of Congojas and San Agustín in Cienfuegos asked the Spanish authorities for permission to return, hoping to find some food in the old plantings. Permission was granted, but the reclaimed settlements were to be garrisoned with eighteen soldiers, comparable to the detachments sent to the neighboring plantations. The vigilant eye of colonial authority would watch over this attempt to rebuild subsistence and community.[21]

In early 1878 the main rebel leadership capitulated and signed the controversial Pact of Zanjón, a document that left nearly all of the major issues unresolved but brought an end to what was known thereafter as the Ten Years' War. Cuba remained a colony, subject to stringent control, though it was conceded some of the political privileges, including representation in the Spanish parliament, already granted to Puerto Rico. An end to slavery was promised, but the terms were not specified. As part of the demobilization of the rebel forces, slaves under arms were declared legally free, but the broader goals of abolition and social transformation were unachieved. Antonio Maceo and several of his allies denounced the pact in the dramatic "Protest of Baraguá," but there were few resources with which to continue fighting. Their forces were crushed within months by a renewed Spanish offensive. After delicate negotiations, Maceo himself departed the island with honor intact and began to regroup in Jamaica and Central America, hoping to rekindle the struggle.[22]

The most immediate effect of the Pact of Zanjón was to open up a wider space for political and social action, providing a stimulus to the Autonomist Party (Partido Liberal Autonomista), whose members sought concessions from Spain rather than independence. At the same time it became easier for Cubans to organize voluntary associations of various kinds. At the outbreak of the war in 1868, some cultural organizations perceived as too Creole and hence prone to separatist sentiment had given way to the pro-government Casinos Españoles. In Cienfuegos, for example, the Philharmonic Society had been seen as particularly suspect: its members were interrogated and the society itself abolished.[23] With the end of the war and the reforms conceded in the Pact of Zanjón, it became possible for Cubans to resume and expand their associational life.

A Cienfuegos branch of the Autonomist Party was founded in 1878, a sign that reformism aimed at electoral power was taking hold in the aftermath of war. These years also saw the birth of new mutual-aid and educational societies among those who defined themselves as people of color. Two free black women, Ramona

Lombillo and Flora Borrell de Águila, founded a society titled La Caridad (Charity) in Cienfuegos in 1879. That same year a group of artisans of color in Sagua la Grande formed La Fraternidad, taking on the name that would be associated throughout the next decade with the struggle for full civil rights by Cubans of African descent.[24] The town of Sancti Spíritus had three organizations for people of color and Trinidad two. These organizations were officially recognized and did not offer open opposition to the government. But their very existence indicated the possibility of new forms of collective action and signaled a broadening access by people of color to the public sphere. Once the civil standing of such groups was secure, they could shelter activities well beyond mutual aid and education.[25]

The partial opening for associational activity could not, however, accommodate the goals of those who favored immediate separation from Spain. Anticolonial conspiracies continued to form, and on August 24, 1879, two hundred men under the leadership of Belisario Grave de Peralta rose up in arms in the eastern province of Santiago de Cuba. In the days that followed several insurgent chiefs followed suit, including José Maceo and Quintín Bandera, also a man of color. There was significant dispute among Cubans about the wisdom of renewing armed struggle, but once the die was cast many veterans of the earlier conflict joined in.[26] By early September the Spanish captain general telegraphed the commander of the eastern region (Santiago de Cuba) to report that news of slaves fleeing the estates and joining the insurrection had produced "una desconfianza inmensa" (immense anxiety) in the entire island. A few days later the Spanish commander, Camilo Polavieja, reported that he would need to undertake exemplary punishments, including shooting plantation rebels in front of their fellow slaves.[27]

This new separatist uprising, later labeled the "Guerra Chiquita" or "Little War," found some echoes in the sugar zones of central Cuba. Serafín Sánchez, a veteran of the Ten Years' War, attempted to carry the rebellion into the districts that had now been organized as the province of Santa Clara. Some local activists did the same. Domingo Estepanopoli y Coloma, for example, was arrested by the Guardia Civil in Sancti Spíritus in 1879. He was apparently a former participant in the earlier insurgency who had declined to endorse the Pact of Zanjón. Found in possession of a letter from the Cuban Revolutionary Committee naming him a *comandante,* and a piece of blue, white, and red cloth (presumably for the making of flags or cockades), he was accused of inciting rebellion.[28]

The possibility of new alliances among slaves, free people of color, and rural whites frightened slaveholders. Again the boundary between large estates and small farms came to seem dangerously porous. An informant from San Antón in the Cienfuegos district wrote confidentially to the neighboring Santa Rosalía estate in midsummer to warn the owner of trouble. He reported that the word was spreading that "tonight or tomorrow the *vecinos* (residents) of this district are going to rise up along with the slaves of the plantations." There is no further evidence that the people of San Antón, a tiny community of small farmers situated down the hill from Santa Rosalía, actually succeeded in mounting an insurrection in the summer of 1879 to echo the one to the east in Santiago de Cuba. But the informant's assumption that the free residents of the neighborhood would unite with slaves when the time came may well have alarmed Manuel Blanco, whose estate held some 150 slaves and was spread over 500 acres, with its eastern boundary stretching toward the foothills of the Trinidad Mountains. The plantation administrator took the precaution of canceling night work and increasing his vigilance over the slave barracks.[29]

No one could confidently predict the lines of alliance or division that would develop between the free rural population and the enslaved estate workforce if open warfare broke out against Spanish rule. The Spanish military had earlier sought to employ local free residents to pursue black and Chinese insurgents who could be construed as "runaways," dividing different sectors of the colonial population and making racialized repression individually profitable to selected rural dwellers. But the military also treated the entire free rural population as perpetually unreliable, needing to be garrisoned, supervised, and spied upon, for fear that they would rise up in alliance with slaves on the estates. Constructing the multiracial free population as the categorical political *opposite* of slave, ironically, took hard work, and required driving a wedge of fear between the two groups in order to undermine the links of kinship and sociability that might join them.

Free people of color in the countryside often had close ties to those held as slaves. Gradual emancipation had multiplied the points of contact across the divide between slave and free, and families might well have grandparents and grandchildren freed by self-purchase or the Moret Law, while the parents continued to be held as slaves. When Anacleta, a free black woman, had her son Severiano baptized in August of 1877, she chose as godparents Marcelino and María de la Cruz, both Creole slaves of the Ingenio Angelita. In the province of Santa Clara as a whole, the 1877 census had counted some 55,000 people of color as free and around 42,000 as enslaved. Although the greatest immediate risk of rebellion might lie with the plantation slaves, the center of gravity of the population of color was among the free, and no slaveowner or Spanish administrator could take their loyalty for granted.[30]

As in earlier conflicts, Spanish officials tried to lure noncombatant free people of color away from the new separatist uprising, while at the same time attempting to paint that insurgency as "black" in order to deter white recruits. These efforts disconcerted Carolina Rodríguez, the sister of a white insurgent, who wrote to her brother that conservatives in Santa Clara were maneuvering to gain the support of black and *mulato* residents. Her framing of the issue—that the Spaniards were "urging the blacks against the Cubans"—revealed both her distress and the continued presumption by some white insurgents that *they* were the real Cubans, with whom those labeled "blacks" should logically ally. In effect, she still placed the category "black" outside that of Cuban.[31]

The colonial authorities ordered 10,000 additional soldiers to the central region, but in November of 1879 uprisings were nonetheless reported in Remedios and Sancti Spíritus, and the insurgents were incorporating additional slaves into their forces through attacks on plantations. By repudiating the Zanjón pact and its half-measures on abolition, the rebels of 1879 could appeal more directly to slaves than had their predecessors. As in the last years of the earlier war, insurgents aimed to undercut estate production and enlarge their ranks by incorporating and liberating slaves, and slaves could use the threat of flight to the hills to back up their own challenges to plantation owners. These convergences of interest did not necessarily imply a meeting of the minds on the aims of the war itself. But this insurgency had also taken on a more radical character than the previous one, both through the increasing predominance of black and *mulato* leaders and through a more thorough break with white Autonomists and other reformers on the island.[32]

The Autonomist Party in Santa Clara, as elsewhere, hastened to disassociate itself from this new insurrection. The partial political openings created by the Pact of Zanjón had given the Autonomists space in which to oppose the conservative and "integralist" Constitutional Unionists, and they did not want to lose those freedoms through a further militarization of the island. Moreover, the slaveowners among them had little desire to see an armed conflict that would incorporate their slaves and their smallholding neighbors into attacks on property and the established order.[33]

The Spanish authorities were eventually able to capitalize on the increasing schism between rebels and reformists. In December of 1879 General Polavieja obtained the surrender of Belisario Grave de Peralta in the east, and extracted a statement from him that condemned the actions of his black insurgent colleague Guillermo Moncada as leading to race war. In Santa Clara the faltering rebel effort ended with the capitulation of Emilio Núñez and Serafín Sánchez in October of 1880. Soon the official state of war was lifted in the province of Santiago de Cuba as well. In theory Spanish authority was now reestablished, and gradual slave emancipation under colonial auspices could proceed as scheduled.[34]

In February of 1880, as the "Little War" was drawing to a close, the Spanish government promulgated a law of abolition that attempted to remove the issue of slavery from the political arsenal of its opponents while accommodating the needs of slaveholders through an intermediate period of *patronato* (tutelage or apprenticeship) during which former slaves were required to work for their former masters for token wages. Under this law, the name of slavery was abolished, but full juridical freedom would come in small doses, with a lottery to free the bonded laborers in descending order of age across the period 1885 to 1888.[35] But after twelve years of war and innumerable challenges from slaves, the power relations of a smoothly functioning slave society were a thing of the past. Many of those still in bondage, now denominated *patrocinados,* continued to push at the limits of their masters' control through self-purchase, legal challenge, flight, or negotiation. Some also escaped bondage because of the carelessness of their owners: eleven

slaves belonging to Manuel Blanco of Santa Rosalía, for example, were freed because they had not been properly registered.[36] Meanwhile the atmosphere of im-
minent freedom shifted the balance of power enough to heighten open conflict.

A new administrator on Santa Rosalía reported in June of 1881 that the bound
laborers were refusing to work on the festival of San Juan, and had only resent-
fully gone to the fields when promised an alternate holiday. In October of 1881 he
clapped the black man named Ciriaco in irons for reporting late to work. But a
few days later Ciriaco had gotten the irons off on his own and had fled the plantation. Ciriaco had eventually been returned to the plantation, but more and more
force was required to keep bound laborers at work—and abolitionists working
through the Spanish parliament would soon succeed in outlawing the use of stocks
and irons.[37]

In 1885 the overseer at Santa Rosalía, Pedro García, wrote in fury to Manuel
Blanco to protest a "scandal" that had just occurred. A black woman named
Andrea had been owned as a slave by the previous proprietor of Santa Rosalía,
José Quesada, and was now claimed as a *patrocinada* by Manuel Blanco as his heir.
Pedro García, who seems to have been a fairly rough character, accused Andrea of
trying to captivate everyone who came to the estate, and he insisted that "a mí no
me magnetiza ella ni nadie" ("nobody—not her or anybody else—magnetizes
me"). Her behavior, he said, was provoking him to give her a crack on the head.
Instead, he quit, fuming that he had not taken on this job in order to be kicked
around by black women, particularly not of her kind. It is hard to know which aspect of the incident is more notable: her boldness or his apparent incapacity as a
manager to do anything about it. Subsequent events would show Andrea Quesada
to be a woman with a long memory, willing to challenge just about anyone.[38]

The next administrator at Santa Rosalía tried to keep careful track of the now-
inevitable shift toward legal freedom for those still enslaved on the estate. He titled a ledger "Book No. 1 of the blacks, Santa Rosalía" and began a page for each
man and woman held under the *patronato*. The ledger, however, often candidly
listed them as "slaves" until they purchased or won their final legal freedom. The
small stipends called for by law were noted, alongside the individual purchases on
credit from the plantation store that often canceled them out. First names were
often followed by an African ethnonym such as Congo, Gangá, or Lucumí. When

two slaves shared the same first name, the older one often carried an African ethnonym, the younger the marker Criollo (Creole, meaning Cuban-born). Thus there was Alejandro Lucumí and Alejandro Criollo. By the second or third generation, the surname of the former master, José Quesada, often appeared: Alejandro Criollo's son was named Cayetano Quesada. Several surnames of proprietors in the district were also used, including Apezteguía, Capote, and Zulueta, perhaps reflecting earlier purchases of slaves from elsewhere. A few men carried terms such as Emancipado (Freedman) or Maquinista (Machinist), or simply Grande (Big) in lieu of a surname. Very few of the *patrocinados* took the last name Blanco, after the current proprietor.[39]

The majority of the *patrocinados* on Santa Rosalía achieved their legal freedom one at a time, at dates scattered through 1885 and 1886. Some may have "indemnified" the master for their remaining months and obtained a certificate attesting to their freedom; others were freed under the provision of the 1880 law that called for a fraction of each owner's *patrocinados* to be liberated by lottery each year after 1884. Antonio Apezteguía, for example, a thirty-five-year-old man born in Africa, was still under the *patronato* at Santa Rosalía in 1885. He earned 3 pesos a month, with a dime deducted for each of his many sick days. Out of the balance, he paid for three pairs of shoes: one for "old Francisca," one for Liborio, and one for himself. He became free on September 8, 1886, just a month before final abolition.[40]

The purchases made by *patrocinados* on Santa Rosalía reflect both their initial consumption priorities—fabric, shoes, tobacco, oil for lamps—and their family ties. In the autumn of 1886, the two *patrocinados* named Ciriaco and Paulino each deposited 1 peso per month with the estate owner, apparently to support their aging mother Francisca. So too did Inocente, who may have been a third brother. Francisca Quesada, *la vieja,* was an important figure in the lives of many of Santa Rosalía's black residents. Donato Lucumí's stipend of 3 pesos for April 1885 was collected by Francisca in the form of a length of *rusia* fabric. Donato Lucumí's wage was often 6 pesos a month rather than the 10 common among younger men. In December 1885, he did buy a jacket for 3.60 pesos, ordered from town. But a year later he seems to have been hungry or short of funds; he was apparently caught stealing *boniatos* (sweet potatoes).[41]

Ciriaco Criollo, almost certainly the same young man who had been put in irons a few years earlier, bought thread in February, and then four kinds of coarse fabric (*crehuela, silesia, dril,* and *rusia*) in the following months. He gave charity to the victims of cholera, purchased a pair of undershorts in December, and then, in January of 1886, achieved his freedom and spent several days in town. It is not difficult to envision the careful process of accumulation and the contribution of his mother Francisca as a seamstress that underlay this first trip to town as a free man. But it is only in retrospect—for we know that he would later join the rebel forces—that we can also surmise that Ciriaco Criollo perhaps discussed more than a little politics along the way.[42]

As the laborers of Santa Rosalía moved toward formal freedom, they marked their new status with a change in their dress and in their work rhythm, expanding their autonomy and their effective range of action. The month before Rita Quesada was listed as having achieved her freedom, the administrator recorded several deductions from her pay for "6 days in town and 2 without working." In the year after she achieved formal freedom, her wage rose from 3 pesos a month to 8, but she did not work at all on the estate from June through December of 1886, in contrast to the year before.[43]

On the neighboring Soledad plantation, the situation was doubly awkward, with apprentices suspended between slavery and freedom, and the new Yankee owner, Edwin Atkins, suspended between the abolitionist principles of his Boston Unitarian upbringing and the accounting principles of an eager investor. When E. Atkins and Company took ownership of the Soledad estate in 1884, following a foreclosure on the mortgage, it became not only owner of the land but proprietor of *patrocinados*. Within a few weeks the new administrator, J. S. Murray, was reporting back to Atkins in Boston on the apprentices' efforts to obtain their full freedom: "Many of the 'patrocinados' are buying their liberty and I can't refuse them as the law permits them to do so." He appended a list of the amounts he had received for such self-purchases, and unself-consciously noted that of the six *patrocinados* who had paid him for their freedom, three—Victor Gangá, Benicia Criolla, and Eduvijes—"are in reality over 60 years of age, therefore free according to law." This had not deterred the assiduous Mr. Murray from collecting 68, 85, and 119 pesos, respectively, from them.[44]

Through the last full year of the apprenticeship system, 1885, the Soledad administration tried to build the labor force beyond the *patrocinados* and Chinese workers long resident on the estate. J. S. Murray reported almost daily on his struggle to obtain willing workers at the lowest possible wages, in competition with other estates in the district and with recruiters eagerly seeking laborers to work in Panama on the French project to build an interoceanic canal. Murray used the services of a Chinese labor contractor, Damián Machado, and he hired local workmen. In 1884 he had welcomed back *libertos* (freedpeople) whom a previous overseer (perhaps the same irascible Pedro García who later tangled with Andrea Quesada) had driven off. But within a year Murray was locked in conflict with the *libertos,* as he insisted upon "a contract oblidging them to work at regular hours and at established prices." They refused and he "ordered them all away from the estate." Within two days Murray reported that they had "come to terms and all beged to stay." He seemed pleased: "I sent off only the two head men. They now know how they stand with the estate and I don't intend to loose controll of them in the future."[45]

He spoke too soon. In June an old wall on the estate was taken down, leaving the "negros pig styes without protection so they will have to sell them or have them stolen it is imeterial to us which." Unsurprisingly, within a few weeks Murray was reporting "a good deal of trouble with the negros who want me to pay them at the rate of $3½ per month for having taken from them the raising of pigs for sale." He reported having put three of their "ringleaders" in the stocks—a procedure outlawed some years before. Murray thought the time had perhaps come to "give all the negros their liberty at the price established by the goverment, fixing a salary of from $8 to $10 deducting 50% each month."[46]

In instructions written back from Boston to Cuba, Edwin Atkins sought a solution to the conflict as he saw it: "Regarding the negroes I shall be glad when they are all free, but we do not want to lose the bal of Patrocinado a/c as it stands in your ledger; can you arrange to retain their cedulars until you get their value crediting them $8–$10 per month until they work it out?" In effect, the capital represented by the "property" held in these thirty-seven men and eighteen women was part of the book value of the estate. Until relinquishing that property could be shown to produce an equivalent credit, the *patrocinados* were not to be given the identity papers *(cédulas)* that would enable them to move about freely. Under the circumstances, Atkins's assurance that he would be "glad when they are all free" sounded somewhat hollow.[47]

By the middle of the summer of 1886, J. S. Murray was finally coming to the conclusion about to be reached by masters throughout the island: continued legal bondage, carrying a special, invidious, and deeply resented role for *patrocinados,* was no longer worth the modest financial savings and illusory capital account that it represented. Murray decided to offer the remaining *patrocinados* the option of purchasing their freedom for twenty dollars each, or in installments at five dollars a month. He anticipated that he would be able to "organize them better when all of one class." Besides, he concluded, "we will have to give them their liberty in a short time." Indeed. Those who accepted his offer of freedom on the installment plan in late May of 1886 would find themselves making the last monthly payment in September, just a few weeks before the Spanish crown declared the extinction of the *patronato.* A capitalist logic in favor of ending slavery, so often posited by re-formists and so rarely acted upon by Cuban planters, thus arrived at Soledad six-teen years after the beginning of formal slave emancipation and moments before the question became moot.[48]

Although they were now "all of one class," the former slaves at Soledad were subjected to special constraints. At the end of the 1886 grinding season, Murray described a campaign he had undertaken against "negros who have horses." He had sent them off, he explained, intending to take them back as workers only when they got rid of their horses. "Of course some will let them loose in the potreros [cattle pastures] others will hide them in the woods for a few days." It is not clear whether Murray's greatest concern was the mobility that having a horse gave to a workman, or the attention and grass the horses would consume. But he resolved that "I will get rid of them all in the end and do not intend they shall have them back."[49]

On nearby Santa Rosalía, the former slave Felipe Criollo succeeded in 1886 in earning enough to purchase a saddle, having presumably gotten access to a horse to go under it. He thus joined the category of "negros who have horses," achieving the mobility and distinction Murray was trying to block among former slaves at the more prosperous Soledad. With a horse, one could go overland to Cienfuegos, about ten miles away, or ride a few hours in the opposite direction to cross the ford on the Arimao River. Beyond the town of Arimao lay the mountains. Former slaves could now move out into an expanded neighborhood, only loosely bounded by a polygon of roads and trails. Port city, foothills town, and mountain hamlets all came within reach, as did innumerable villages in the sugar region itself.[50]

The process of "gradual emancipation," with its promise of a transition tightly controlled by masters, had gone into free fall: the province's 1877 slave population of 42,000 dropped to 23,300 patrocinados by 1883, and then to 13,000 as the liberations by lottery began in 1885. On October 7, 1886, the Spanish government, two years ahead of schedule, decreed the definitive end to the patronato, freeing the 25,400 patrocinados still held in bondage on the island. Soon the administrator at Soledad was voicing a complaint that would have been familiar to his counterparts in Louisiana a decade or two earlier: "As usual just before grinding begins the laborers commence moving around from one estate to another asking for an increase of wages." To the dismay of employers, free labor had arrived.[51]

Former slaves in Santa Clara, however, unlike freedpeople in the major sugar parishes of Louisiana, moved into their new legal status in a setting in which they were neither the majority of the population nor even a majority of the people of color. Flight, manumission, war, and gradual emancipation had incorporated people of African descent as free residents of the cities and the countryside over many decades. Now, with the destruction of slavery, the status of free people of color was no longer defined by contrast to those who were legally bound. For centuries, notarial and judicial records had entered free people of color with the notation moreno or morena (black) or pardo or parda (brown), and the term libre (free). But once all were free the term libre added nothing. Did that mean that the color terms should stand alone, or were they also now moot? Everything about the precise status of free and freed people would need to be negotiated through trial and error, individual initiative, and general policy. Equally important, this delicate negotiation would take place in the shadow of political competition between Constitutional Unionists, Autonomists, and Cuban separatists. Those seeking to achieve a full citizenship not constrained by color might well have some political room for maneuver.

The vitality of the Cuban sugar industry in the late 1880s and early 1890s provided a further avenue for negotiation. In contrast to workers in the bayou country of Louisiana, former slaves and other rural free people in Santa Clara found themselves facing an expansive market for labor. Although the Cuban sugar economy as a whole had some notable weaknesses, the central districts of Cienfuegos and Sagua la Grande were still flourishing. Cuban planters produced sugar for the U.S. market without the annual threats of flood and frost that so handicapped Louisiana growers. Capital was also flowing to central Cuba, both as direct investment like that of E. Atkins and Company and as loans to plantations still controlled by Cuban or Spanish landowners. The magnificent Constancia estate, in northern Cienfuegos, produced by 1890 the largest crop of any single sugar plantation in the world. It was owned by the family of the Marqués de Apezteguía, who combined Spanish, Cuban, and U.S. capital into the newly formed Constancia Sugar Company. Soon the huge neighboring estate named Caracas, owned by the Terry family, grew to overtake even Constancia in production.[52] It was no wonder that J. S. Murray of Soledad felt a bit beleaguered by the bargaining of his employees.

Immigrants from Spain and former slaves from the region together formed the core of the postemancipation field labor force, supplemented by Chinese workers and some other local rural people. New arrivals from the Iberian peninsula or the Canary Islands were put to work on the ditches, roads, and rails as well as loading cane, and were sought as carpenters and mill workers. Former slaves, who knew the art of cutting cane cleanly to encourage healthy regrowth, were generally employed as cutters, lifters, and cartmen and tended to be concentrated in the agricultural sector. The names of many of those who had been *patrocinados,* particularly the men, thus reappear in the payrolls of estates in the late 1880s and the 1890s, alongside increasing numbers of Spaniards.[53]

The records of the Santa Rosalía estate provide a glimpse of the evolution of labor on a medium-sized plantation. An enumeration of what was called the *dotación* at the time of the establishment of apprenticeship in 1880 had listed eighty-one men, forty-nine women, and sixty-one children. All of the bound adults were of working age; the children included many who had been freed by the Moret Law, and most were ten years old or younger. On the eighth of each month over the next years, these *patrocinados* were, in theory, paid the stipend required by the law of apprenticeship. After the final end of the *patronato* in 1886, the administrator of Santa Rosalía again drew up a list titled "individuals of color who work in the fields" who would on January 8, 1887, receive their pay for the previous three months. Monthly salaries had evidently been withheld—a procedure that had been illegal during the period of formal apprenticeship—and were now being provided in a lump sum. The male/female imbalance had increased: from 1.7 to 1 in 1880 to 2.2 to 1 in 1887. Seventy-four men now appeared on the pay list, and thirty-three women. Twenty-four children collected a few pesos each for three months' work. No woman earned the 29 or 30 pesos characteristic of the highest-paid men, but Juliana Zulueta, probably about forty years old, and Fernanda Quesada, probably a sixteen-year-old, brought in 19 and 20 pesos, respectively.[54]

By 1887 most of the adult workers were listed with the word *libre* (free) after each name, a carryover from the old mode of listing manumitted slaves. The majority carried a surname, generally that of the previous owner of Santa Rosalía, José Quesada. Others had taken or retained the surnames of slaveholding families of the region. In several cases African ethnonyms continued to serve as surnames, as they had earlier: Donato and Diego Lucumí, Alejandro Congo, and Manuel Gangá, as well as Alejandro Criollo, appeared on the list.[55]

In the Cienfuegos district as a whole, the 1887 census counted a population of 57,000 individuals categorized as white and about 28,900 "of color," a figure that apparently included the Chinese. In the municipality that held the district capital, and in several others, the population counted as white outnumbered that counted as of color by two to one, while in Cruces and Palmira, sugar districts located to the north of Soledad and Santa Rosalía, the population of color was nearly equal in size to that defined as white. Perhaps most striking was the sheer variety of rural establishments. When the tax collectors in 1880–81 enumerated the farms in Cienfuegos growing neither tobacco or sugar, but large enough to be taxable, the list ran to nearly five hundred.[56]

The proliferation of small farms and the availability of vacant land created alternatives to plantation labor. The growth of central mills drawing cane from multiple suppliers likewise brought new opportunities for small renters and landowners. After signing a contract with a nearby *central,* farmers could plant their land in cane and plan for the mill to grind it. Smallholders thus gained a foothold in an industry that had previously been restricted to those prosperous enough to fund their own milling. Small- and medium-scale cultivators, termed *colonos,* now supplied cane to those plantations capable of functioning as central mills, and owners of impoverished estates no longer able to mill their own cane did the same.

The negotiating of *colono* contracts involved considerable tugging and hauling. In 1884 J. S. Murray at Soledad complained that the "colonos are giving us much more trouble than we anticipated, San Pelayo, Roque and Cantignon all refuse to sign new contracts unless we make them large advances, for more than their property is worth."[57] The contracts were often draconian, providing for a share of the benefits to go to the individual grower but pegging remuneration to the price of sugar in order to minimize the financial risk for mill owners. The mill would make advances, supervise certain aspects of the growing, and receive the cane, settling the account once a season. Cane farmers without ownership of their own land, though also denominated *colonos,* had even less independence. Farmers who took charge of planting specific cane fields belonging to the Soledad plantation were charged rent, "so that nobody occupying our land will ever acquire a title," as Edwin Atkins bluntly explained it.[58]

The central mill also had a strong interest in controlling the work rhythm of its supplier *colonias,* an intrusion that *colonos* themselves might well resent. A routine communication to Edwin Atkins from an administrator on Soledad conveys something of the tension: "Some of the Colonos have been weeding lately, but I am not prepared to state to what extent. I will take the mayoral [overseer] with me and go through the whole thing thoroughly, and your instructions regarding delinquents shall be carried out."[59] The moment of the harvest carried a potential for bitterness on both sides if weights were falsified, cane arrived too late or was too dirty, or if the mill stopped grinding and a *colono*'s cane was left to spoil. Some *colonos* tried to resist the terms laid down by the estates, and their obstreperousness placed limits on the expansion of large plantations. In 1891 *colonos* in Santa Clara organized to try to raise the level of compensation beyond the standard rate, and they seem to have met with some success. But for those who hoped that renting a *colonia* was a step up the agricultural ladder, it could be frustrating to find that the next rung had been carefully removed.[60]

For former slaves, a move into the ranks of *colonos* remained difficult. The names of some individuals of color do occasionally occur in lists of the operators of cane farms, though it is impossible to discern whether they were former slaves. The *parda* Clara Quintero and the *morena* Doña Rufina Blanco, for example, were listed as the primary occupants of the *colonias* Jatillo and Cañadita in Santa Isabel de las Lajas in the 1890s.[61] But a more common pattern seems to have been for former slaves to look for space in which to establish mixed farms on which they might plant a modest amount of cane alongside subsistence and market crops. The land area of the province of Santa Clara was by no means fully occupied: some 11,000 *caballerías* (about 363,000 acres) of territory were under cultivation in 1895, but a larger area was listed as in large and small timber. Settling on previously uncultivated lands might offer only a bare livelihood, but it did create some distance from the world of the plantation.[62]

Former slaves sought out and in some cases found plots of land that could be settled without occasioning too much opposition. Some of these smallholdings, known as *ranchos, finquitas,* or *conucos* and generically referred to as *sitios,* evaded the gaze of official record keepers, only to appear suddenly in the record when a titleholder sought to sell a piece of property and found that it had been "improperly" settled by squatters. Other such *sitios* were bought and paid for or were occupied under customary arrangements. To the administrators who ran the nearby estates these small farms were competitors for the time of rural people, who should properly be devoting themselves to estate labor. When J. S. Murray tried in 1885 to describe the exasperating unreliability of former slaves, for example, he wrote to Atkins that the *libertos* (freedpeople) "are now only working when they feel like it, and keeping up a constant loafing during the day in the ranchos," by which he meant the huts, gardens, and provision plots. By rights, those not employed on the estate should also keep their distance. Three years later, after final emancipation, Murray consigned "the old negroes" to a patch of land known as the *sitio,* and planned to "fence them off along the public road so that they will have no entrance to the estate."[63]

The neighborhood around the Soledad estate, now called Pepito Tey, still contains settlements like San Antón, the hamlet where a neighbor had in 1879 predicted to Manuel Blanco that rebellion might erupt among free residents in alliance with plantation slaves. The ruins of the Santa Rosalía plantation sit a short distance up the hill to the west, and cane fields abut the plantings of smallholders. Gerardo, Francisco, and Humberto Quesada, who now occupy the farm inherited from their father, Cayetano Quesada, believe that it was probably their grandfather who planted the avocado tree adjacent to their house. Records in the Cienfuegos archive verify that this was Alejandro Criollo, freed from bondage on Santa Rosalía in the 1880s. The payroll books suggest that after emancipation he and his son Cayetano Quesada shifted from year-round to seasonal work on the plantation, probably combining wage labor with planting on land that they had discreetly occupied. A few miles away lies El Palmar, another jib of land that lay outside the Atkins properties. At some point in the 1880s or 1890s it too became a hamlet, and former slaves were among the first to settle in the neighborhood. The residents included people with the surnames Quesada, Galdós, and Sarría, former slaves of the nearby Santa Rosalía, Santa Teresa, and Soledad plantations. The land itself was owned by a Spanish shopkeeper who allowed them to build and plant there.[64]

In the rich flatlands around the large plantations of Lajas and Cruces, a bit to the north, such niches were harder to find. Most of the owners of nonplantation property who appear on the tax lists around Lajas in the 1880s were individuals who could claim the honorific Don, and were probably categorized socially as white. But one can follow a slowly growing group of smallholders listed as *morenos* (blacks). The *morena* Mercedes Alonso, for example, occupied a *sitio* called La Palmita, and was in 1880–81 taxed about 16 pesos a year. Her neighbor the *moreno* Tomás Mora occupied the even poorer *sitio* Santo Tomás, and paid just 4 pesos per year in taxes.[65]

Establishing a foothold on the land had consequences for both subsistence and citizenship. Even a modest holding could, in theory, provide a basis for lodging a claim to vote. In 1881 the son of Mercedes Alonso, Salvador Díaz, boldly presented himself to the electoral board in Lajas as the renter of his mother's property, on which she paid, according to him, 15.20 pesos annually in taxes. The electoral board seems to have been caught off guard by this request, and referred it down to the municipal council, which under law had no formal authority in the matter. The council granted Díaz the right to vote, though it is not clear whether he actually voted.[66]

The smallest and most isolated rural properties often remained out of the sight of list makers. If the families that farmed them were, like those in El Palmar, informal tenants, their occupancy left little trace. Such tenants-at-will paid no tax, had no legal security, and could make no claim to the vote. But mere possession, even without title, was still worth a good deal, and a legal vulnerability to desahucio (eviction) did not necessarily translate into actual expulsion. Victor Clark, a researcher who visited Cuba at the beginning of the twentieth century, was breezy about such squatters: "The cost of dispossessing a squatter where land was cheap and a suit might reveal a questionable title on the part of the plaintiff prevented proceedings in many instances where there was just cause, and the litigation among large proprietors prevented their giving attention to petty offenders."[67]

In the memory of elderly present residents, by contrast, desahucio and the risks of eviction loom somewhat larger. Fermín Tellería, for example, recalls that his father, Trino Tellería, made payments toward purchase of a house, but later found that the owner had recorded them as rent to prevent Tellería's acquisition of legal title. Nonetheless, there is no doubting the long-term importance of settlements on the land sanctioned by custom only. Access to some land on which to plant provided an important margin of maneuver for those who labored seasonally for wages in the cane. As small farmers, sitieros, they might set their own limits on how much of the year they would work for wages, rather than simply awaiting the planter's declaration that it was now tiempo muerto, dead time. J. S. Murray wrote in May of 1888 that labor was scarce, "as there are 20 estates and colonias planting in this district and all the sitieros have returned to attend to their own plantings."[68]

On the higher ground and marginal lands people of various origins thus occupied adjacent plots of land, perhaps with a measure of conflict between old-timers and newcomers, often with ties of kinship to hold them together. Between the bay of Cienfuegos and the hill town of Arimao, communities like San Antón and El Palmar reflected the fragile coexistence of wage labor and subsistence and market farming. Beyond Arimao and up into the mountains, the land became rugged and the cane fields vanished. By the time one reached La Sierra, Las Moscas, or San Blas, this was clearly coffee and small-farming country. From the point of view of former slaves and other rural workers, land on and beyond the periphery of sugar estates could provide a kind of refuge. From the point of view of planters, these communities at the edges provided wood and a trade in foodstuffs, but were suspected of harboring cattle thieves, bandits, and others who escaped the direct supervision of local authorities.

Despite competition for labor and the existence of some alternatives for former slaves, the Cuban sugar industry continued to grow, and estates did not undergo a period of turmoil comparable in intensity to that of wartime Louisiana. The abrupt abandonment of properties by Confederate owners in Louisiana during the Union occupation, and the reorganization of plantations under lessees or Treasury Department officials, had provided temporary openings for cooperative agriculture among the workers left behind, leading to a short-term shift to the cultivation of foodstuffs. But in Cuba's expanding sugar regions, estates that ceased to grind were likely to be quickly converted to *colonias* supplying a central mill. The cultivation of foodstuffs would coexist with, but rarely displace, the growing of cane.

The world of the sugar plantation in central Cuba was porous and multiracial, though it also showed some lines of ethnic and racial division. When asked about the private guards on his estate, for example, Edwin Atkins replied that "they were mostly composed of men recruited from Spanish laborers who had nearly all of them served their time in the Spanish army."[69] Although their ostensible purpose was to protect the estates from external threats, it is not difficult to see in these guards certain echoes of the post-Reconstruction white militias of Louisiana. As Spaniards on horseback on the lookout for Cuban bandits, or as white men on the lookout for trouble from black men, their authority compounded their distinctiveness.

The ethnic diversity of the labor force nonetheless made for frequent interactions across these lines. A complex plantation population of overseers, machinists, artisans, and younger freedpeople lived in the midst of a vast population from all racial groups who worked as day laborers, cane farmers, and small-scale cultivators. Moreover, town and country were intimately linked—by stevedores who loaded the sugar onto boats, by families who moved back and forth in search of work, and by members of the elite who alternated life in the port city of Cienfuegos with residence on an inland estate. On plantations and on cane farms, people categorized as Spanish and Cuban, white and black, Chinese and *mulato,* came and went, bought and sold, talked and drank coffee, collected wages and argued about the pay scale. The squalid barracks built during slavery remained, with the same atrocious consequences for public health and personal comfort; but the prisonlike control to which their inhabitants had been subjected was now largely gone. There was even some incentive for an improvement of conditions. In the summer of 1887 labor seemed short and wages high, and the administrator on Soledad tried to convince the owner: "the large Baracons for the men are in a very bad condition in wet weather, why not gut one of the large negro Baracons, floor it and give them a desent place to live in?" After all, he observed, "good quarters will be an inducement to good men."[70] And since the new workmen were often single males, their presence also increased the frequency of long-term cross-racial intimate unions. Today families in the neighborhood still have photographs tucked away of a white grandfather in his Spanish army uniform, alongside pictures of a black grandmother born into slavery.[71]

For modernizing planters these were exciting years, and the heterogeneity of the workforce was a natural concomitant of expansion. Landowners and merchants invested in local infrastructure to facilitate the transport of raw cane and the export of finished sugar. In an appeal for permission to build new rail lines for private use, Fermín de Solá wrote exuberantly in 1890 that Cienfuegos was providing a brilliant example of work and of "faith in the future."[72] Edwin Atkins's Soledad estate now comprised 12,000 acres, and Atkins boasted that he carried 1,200 to 1,500 men on the payroll at crop time. Despite the shocks of war and abolition, the island's overall production of sugar was climbing.[73]

At the same time, this seemingly smooth shift from slave to wage labor, and the accompanying expansion and diversification of the labor force, carried with it an implicit set of boundaries on the meaning of freedom for former slaves. For employers, these changes in wages and lodging marked the limit of advancement for those who had finally become juridically free. But for former slaves themselves it could seem hard to work as a laborer in the cane six and a half days a week, live in a barracks, sleep in one's clothes in a hammock, subsist on jerked beef, rice, and lard, receive fifteen to twenty dollars a month, and be laid off when the harvest was over. The alternative was to scramble to be able to rent or settle on a piece of land at the edge of the cane zone, try to build a hut, get one's goods to market, and make enough to satisfy the tax collector and feed a family. Even those families who managed a successful division of labor by dividing their time between town and country struggled with the precariousness of wages and employment.[74]

The abolition of slavery, moreover, had not in itself brought respect or equal rights, and the defeat of open political revolt had not diminished ordinary Cubans' resentment of Spanish privilege and elite opportunism. Although a few bold individuals of color in the countryside sought to be included on the electoral lists, the heterogeneous and mobile working population was still largely excluded from the vote by property requirements. There were nonetheless increasing signs that some former slaves and other people of color would seek greater participation in public culture, particularly through mutual-aid organizations of various kinds. Even the city of Cienfuegos, known for its conservatism, soon had several newspapers defining themselves as "autonomist republican" or "democratic autonomist," as well as an upsurge of journalistic efforts directed toward the population of color. Spain, moreover, adopted universal manhood suffrage at home in 1890, and might be pressed to extend it to the colonies as well.[75]

The conservative Constitutional Union Party had little electoral use for assertive nonelite Cubans. But the Autonomists, supporters of electoral reform and limited self-government, potentially stood to gain from wider mobilization. They had, however, come to a position of opposition to slavery relatively late in the day, and they were reviled by Cuban separatists, who sought complete independence for the island and saw reforms as delusions for the gullible. At the national level, the Autonomists were socially distant from the agriculturalists and urban laborers who constituted the majority of the population, but at the local level they developed cross-class webs of clientage and reciprocity. Sugar towns like Santa Isabel de las Lajas, in the Cienfuegos district, and mixed-farming areas like Yaguajay on the north coast of Santa Clara province, served as fertile ground for such organizing.[76]

The Autonomists' ambitions and their handicaps are both revealed in the fracas surrounding an ill-fated political meeting in Cienfuegos in October of 1886. The Autonomist deputies J. Fernández de Castro and Miguel Figueroa were scheduled to speak in the Teatro Zorilla, the only meeting place their party had been able to secure, located in a section of town largely populated by people of color. The deputies arrived in Cienfuegos in the company of delegations of Autonomists from the region, including the sugar towns of Lajas, Cruces, and Palmira. They were met by a crowd of supporters, including people of color, who greeted them with music. It was later charged that as the speakers made their way to the theater, several people of color accompanying them hurled corn kernels at the houses of suspected Constitutional Unionists.[77]

According to the colonial authorities, the theater was packed, many of those in attendance being "people of little education, people of color in the majority." When Fernández de Castro first criticized the Spanish government, the audience divided into those who applauded and those who hissed. When he claimed that the Autonomists could take credit for the abolition of the *patronato* and thus the definitive end of slavery, he was met with shouts of "mentira!" ("a lie!"). The hall broke out in disorder as some cheered for Spain, others for autonomy, and chairs began to crash.

Accounts sympathetic to the Autonomists claimed that a crowd had already gathered outside the theater, prepared to disrupt the events. These descriptions did not mention any phrase by Fernández that might have triggered the protest, emphasizing instead that people outside threw bottles and rocks at the theater and even fired weapons. Having disrupted the meeting, the crowd apparently tried to move on to the house in which the Autonomists were lodged, whereupon groups who supported the Autonomists began to oppose them. These latter groups were said to be composed "especially of persons of color." The mayor called out the army and Civil Guard to prevent further clashes.[78]

At the Teatro Zorilla a large number of people who generally did not have access to the vote, but who did claim the right to political voice, had burst into the field of public debate.[79] Fernández de Castro and Figueroa lodged with local nota-ble Rafael Cabrera, and seem to have been able to attract a broad base of support. From the point of view of the forces of order, such mobilization was by its nature problematic. The police chief opined that Fernández de Castro could have avoided these troubles if he had taken into account "la clase de público a quien se dirigía" ("the kind of public whom he was addressing"). But Fernández de Castro, once a conservative and now an Autonomist, needed to find support in several quarters. The Autonomists were fighting a genteel but uphill battle, and they had to try the weapons of debate, parliamentary boycott, and, in extremis, popular mobili-zation.[80]

Gabriel Quesada, for example, a young man of color living in Cienfuegos, saw great hope in a campaign of public demonstrations in pursuit of equal rights, in-cluding a peaceful but controversial initiative to integrate the city's main theater. Local Spanish authorities proved relatively accommodating, and in 1893 Quesada reported enthusiastically on his group's success to Juan Gualberto Gómez, the distinguished journalist of color who led the national association of societies of color.[81]

Collective action in support of political initiatives was increasingly visible, but so too was antigovernmental action of a different kind. In the countryside ban-ditry and kidnapping provided a continual spectacle of individual daring and state repression. The island's press followed these dramas in which bold men on horse-back—black, white, and *mulato,* African, Creole, and Canary Islander—demon-strated their ability to operate against and outside established authority. By 1888 small groups of outlaws had taken to the hills in Santa Clara, though it was unclear what combination of hunger and fear of persecution was responsible for their de-cision. The governor declared a "state of war" in the province. In the district of Cienfuegos as elsewhere the bandit Manuel García took on nearly mythical pro-portions, and men operating in his name succeeded in exacting tribute from many of the sugar estates.[82]

In response to the spread of serious banditry, the government extended its presence further into the countryside, using brute force to try to find and capture bandits, vagrants, and other suspicious characters. Six to seven thousand soldiers were mobilized to chase Manuel García through Havana and Matanzas in 1890, with predictable consequences for rural dwellers. Although many Cubans may have hoped for law and order of a kind, they hardly wanted Spanish soldiers breaking down their doors and arresting members of their families in the process. Some of the bandits, moreover, claimed more or less credible ties to Cuban nationalists who were conspiring to renew the anti-Spanish insurgency. Such assertions only increased the Spanish desire to eliminate those who made them, but these statements provided the bandits with a public identity somewhat more appealing than that of cutthroats and highwaymen.[83]

Planters could often insulate themselves from direct bandit attacks by paying the "taxes" imposed by the outlaws. Yet no payoff could fend off a larger crisis brewing in the sugar industry. The 1891 Foster-Cánovas Treaty between the United States and Spain had facilitated access by Cuban sugars to the U.S. market, providing a stimulus to production that enabled Atkins, Terry, Apetzeguía, and others to build their fortunes. But in 1893 a jarring financial crash rocked investors from Boston to Cuba and far beyond. By 1894 the island's commercial relations with the United States, and Spain's inability to negotiate an effective new treaty, had become the central preoccupation of those connected to the sugar industry. With the Wilson-Gorman Tariff Act in 1894 the U.S. Congress imposed new tariffs on raw sugar and undermined the entire structure of Cuban trade with the United States. Spain imposed its own new tariffs in response. As Edwin Atkins phrased it, "the cost of living in Cuba advanced and the price of sugar dropped, credit became impaired." By January 1895 wages had fallen, and Atkins reported that the administration at Soledad plantation had to contend not only with rains and "customs house complications" but also with "strikes owing to low wages." On Soledad itself, the "poor laborers with their thin clothes were suffering from cold and an epidemic very like intestinal influenza."[84]

With their commercial relations with the United States at risk, Cuban planters let out a collective howl of indignation at the economic catastrophe that threatened to engulf them. Workers discharged at the end of the crop season faced an uncertain future. In Cienfuegos, the effects were somewhat muffled by the relative prosperity of estates like Soledad, which employed thousands of workers even after the crash and the trade crisis. The signs were nonetheless ominous, not

Cuban exiles, including Antonio Maceo and Agustín Cebreco (back row, third and fourth from the left), at a planning meeting in Costa Rica, 1892.

only for planters and sugar workers but for everyone entwined with the sugar economy and anyone who bought supplies in the market.[85]

The Cuban separatist movement in exile believed that the moment was fast approaching when it would be time to fight what José Martí, founder of the cross-racial and cross-class Cuban Revolutionary Party, described as a brief but necessary war of liberation from Spain. Organizers like Gabriel Quesada in Cienfuegos had won concessions from the Spanish colonial government that might draw them and their followers into the legal culture and away from armed insurgency, but their mentor, Juan Gualberto Gómez, saw such campaigns as preparatory to a broad anticolonial effort. Gómez was in clandestine contact with Martí and the other exiles who were laying the groundwork for a renewed Cuban separatist rebellion. Antonio Maceo, in San José, Costa Rica, was ready to go, and his fellow exile Agustín Cebreco had a farm near the Caribbean port of Limón, an ideal point of departure for embarking toward Cuba. Máximo Gómez, the admired veteran from the Dominican Republic, was now working closely with Martí. The pieces were falling into place.[86]

A nationalist ideology that called for armed struggle, social justice, and political separation from Spain could, in theory, bring together multiple groups with multiple grievances across the island. But such a convergence was not automatic. True, deepening economic crisis and consequent unemployment provided a field for recruitment to a possible rebellion. But colonial authorities' strategy of selective concessions could also draw energies into initiatives framed within the colonial system, particularly as Spain had moved toward a broader franchise at home and might begin to extend it to the colonies. A full-scale insurrection would also require insurgent Cubans to leave their jobs and families, regroup in the *monte,* and then return to attack garrisons, cane fields, and mills. For men and women in the countryside around Soledad and Santa Rosalía it remained an open question whether the plantations, which had so recently been engines of employment as well as sites of subordination, should be treated as friend or enemy. In February of 1895, the most insistent of the Cuban nationalists rose up in rebellion again, and called the question.

CHAPTER FIVE

A Wartime Cross-Racial Alliance

Cuba, 1895–1898

The ship has entered onto the high seas.

Rebel general Antonio Maceo, after his forces advanced from the
mountains into the open valleys of central Cuba, December 1895

BY EARLY 1895 CUBANS WERE WELL ACCUSTOMED TO RUMORS OF CON-
spiracy—and to the Spanish claim that behind each manifestation of Cuban separatism lay the possibility of "race war." Again and again Cuban separatists denied
the charge and invoked instead a transracial concept of patriotism. But when rebels in eastern Cuba declared themselves in revolt on February 24, 1895, they had
to convince people both that the goal was worth fighting for and that the fight
would not lay bare dangerous divisions among Cubans. Rural residents of central
Cuba who had been in contact with the emissaries of separatist leaders Antonio
Maceo and José Martí would have heard the formal goals of the rebellion, and
might well endorse them. But for now the fighting was some distance away, and
the Spanish response was still unknown. Most people chose to wait, watch, listen,
and consult in order to come to a judgment about the nature of the revolt and its
probable risks and prospects.[1]

Spanish colonial authorities initially responded to news of uprisings in the districts of Santiago de Cuba, Guantánamo, and Matanzas by going on the alert, arresting the usual suspects, and minimizing the importance of the revolt. The gov-

ernor of the western province of Pinar del Río nervously communicated to the governor general that all was tranquil there—for the moment. With a flurry of activity and the discovery of a cache of arms, he believed that he had thwarted the formation of a rebellious *partida* (band). He arrested those he thought responsible for bringing in arms, including the secretary of the municipal court of the town of Viñales, the owner of an "insignificant shop selling food and drink," and two *campesinos* (country people). In mid-March a group of "bandits" had attacked the local volunteer loyalist force, but the governor assured his superiors that the act was not political. In Havana the authorities quickly moved to detain Juan Gualberto Gómez, the veteran organizer of the Sociedades de Color, and held him incommunicado in the Morro Castle. The civil governor of the central province of Puerto Príncipe (later Camagüey) was uneasy about the meetings that were reported to be taking place on sugar plantations in his region. On February 28 he had received word that "malcontents" were assembling at a farm called Unión to endorse the uprising; he issued orders to arrest them. In mid-March he reported that a man named Mirabales was stealing horses and fooling country people into joining a separatist band.[2]

The expeditionary force of General Antonio Maceo made landfall on the first of April near Baracoa, on the northeastern coast of Oriente, survived an enemy ambush, and began gathering recruits. One coffee farmer later testified, "As he was the soul of the revolution, as soon as we heard that he was there, all of us that had 15 or 10 or 20 men went to join him."[3] Maceo and his longtime colleague Agustín Cebreco were on home territory here, and the movement quickly picked up strength. Even elderly veterans of the Ten Years' War joined the fight: Gaspar Caballero, an African-born field worker from the sugar-growing district of San Luis, enlisted as a soldier in the first days and was later transferred to work growing provisions for the troops.[4] Within a month after arriving on the island, Maceo wrote to his wife that he had 6,000 men under his command and much territory under rebel control. He added an exultant postscript: "No day goes by without people coming to join me, all the youth of Santiago de Cuba have gone to the countryside; we have doctors and lawyers with us." Elsewhere in the province José Martí had also landed, and the rebel generals Máximo Gómez, Flor

Crombet, José Maceo, Calixto García, and others rapidly recruited men and matériel.[5]

From the beginning, this rebellion had a markedly cross-racial, cross-class, and even cross-national character. With the Protest of Baraguá in 1878 Maceo, Cebreco, and others had confirmed their uncompromising adherence to independence, abolition, and racial equality. José Martí, the son of Spanish parents, was a strong proponent of full independence and of the patriotic repudiation of racial divisions. Máximo Gómez, born in Santo Domingo, had co-signed the March 24, 1895, Manifesto of Montecristi, which denounced discrimination and called for a forthright alliance between black and white Cubans. Even more decisively, the rebel fighting force assembled in Oriente encompassed soldiers of every socio-racial group. Most units included black, white, and *mulato* soldiers, although some regiments, recruited through the networks of locally respected black commanders like Quintín Bandera, were largely composed of men of color.[6]

Spanish rulers and Cuban conservatives had long invoked the "threat of another Haiti," using a specter of that eighteenth-century revolution leading to a black republic to try to fend off alliances of this kind. But in the years since the "Little War" in 1879–80 this demagogic claim had lost much of its force. The end of slavery and the expansion of a thoroughly multiracial rural workforce had undercut the stereotype of black Cubans as a subjugated mass, liable to volcanic eruption. José Martí and other nationalists had also created an idealized history of long-standing cross-racial alliance in pursuit of abolition and freedom, thus constructing the black insurgent as a grateful partner rather than as a continuing threat. Hoping to counteract racially divisive arguments by the defenders of Spanish rule, Martí and Antonio Maceo led the way in equating racism and slavery with colonialism, and freedom and unity with Cuban nationalism.[7]

Prejudice of various kinds might still flourish in the countryside, but workers of all color groups interacted every day in a multitude of transactions. Although multiple forms of racial etiquette constrained these interactions, face-to-face relations rarely displayed the bitter white-supremacist edge that so often characterized encounters in the countryside of Louisiana. The testimony of witnesses in a later civil suit conveys something of the atmosphere in the first days of the Cuban uprising in the east. A mechanical engineer from the United States who had worked for many years in Cuba described his apprehension at the arrival on the Santa Teresa plantation of a body of sixty to one hundred armed men who then took what they needed from the plantation store. "Some of them had cockades and other marks that would identify them. To tell the truth I wasn't anxious to get any nearer to them than was absolutely necessary." But a Cuban weighman and accountant, nephew of a local cane farmer, described the same events in a matter-of-fact tone: "the insurgents was a thing which did not preoccupy me much. I attended to my business first. I do know that I saw them there and we were even drinking beer with some of them, and as I knew that nothing could happen to me as I was like them, I did not care for anything at all."[8]

The improvised character of initial recruitment to the rebellion meant that friends and co-workers often "rose up" together, whether they were the young, white denizens of a Havana café or a team of cartmen on a Cienfuegos plantation. Any tendency toward racial homogeneity in these small groups would thus be mirrored in the rebel companies they formed, but the heterogeneity of the population in the countryside and the diversity of the rebel leadership worked to blur sharp lines of division by color. The picture of the social composition of the rebellion thus varies, depending on where and when one catches a glimpse of these clusters of men, and occasional women.

Conspirators had been in and out of the province of Santa Clara in the early 1890s, collecting funds and passing on news, but power in towns like Cienfuegos remained in the hands of an intransigent pro-Spanish elite. Manuel Blanco, for example, lived in town as a member of the merchant community of the city, while sending instructions to his administrators on the Santa Rosalía plantation. His neighbor the Marqués de Apezteguía shared his commitment to sugar and to trade, as well as his close relationship to Spanish authorities and, in emergencies, to Spanish troops. Although some landowners had supported the Autonomist Party, Blanco and most of his fellow planters and merchants dreaded a cross-racial Cuban nationalist movement with strong undertones of social egalitarianism. In 1895 they closed ranks, declared their firm loyalty to Spain, and began to raise companies of loyalist *voluntarios*.[9]

Some of the younger members of the planter class, however, were drawn to the idea of a renewed fight for Cuban independence. As word of rebellion in the east reached Cienfuegos, the son of the owner of the Ingenio Manuelita tried to take a boat to Santiago de Cuba to enlist under the black insurgent general Jesús Rabí. He was betrayed and captured by Spanish forces. The insurgency nonetheless picked up steam more quickly this time than it had in 1868. By mid-February 1895 a group of insurgents was reported to be meeting at Los Guaos, near Soledad, and telephone lines were cut, presumably to disrupt the Spanish military response, though the anticipated local uprising did not follow. The black shop-keeper and veteran of the 1868 war Benigno Najarro provided refuge to the white nationalist Alfredo Rego in his shop in the hill town of Las Moscas, east of Cienfuegos, as the two plotted and planned.[10]

While some residents of Santa Clara province took to the hills, others waited and watched through the early spring. A few of the rebels had prior reputations as bandits, and did not inspire confidence. Moreover, many residents of sugar towns like Lajas and Cartagena had provided support to the Autonomist Party and were hesitant to make the shift to armed struggle in pursuit of full independence. Recruitment to this rebellion would not be automatic, even among those who chafed at the bonds of the colonial order.[11]

At first Edwin Atkins, in residence at his Soledad plantation, was relatively confident: "The political trouble is causing much annoyance, and it is hard to keep men at work in the fields as they are scared but I do not expect any serious trouble here or in Trinidad." But by late June rebellion began to be reported near the city of Santa Clara, and a party of a dozen or so rebels was reported to be under pursuit to the east, in the area of Cumanayagua. Atkins reported that there was little work to be had in the area and that "many, particularly negroes, joined the insurgents or took to the woods to live by pillage." In July an expeditionary force led by the Cuban exile Serafín Sánchez landed on the coast of Santa Clara province, and the movement began to gather strength in the region. Benigno Najarro gathered seventy men, rose up, and assumed the rank of lieutenant. José González Planas, the veteran and longtime activist in the Sociedad de Color in the town of Lajas, followed suit on July 8. In the hills and valleys of Santa Clara province, something recognizable as a local rebel force had begun to coalesce. By August and September recruitment to the rebel Cienfuegos Brigade reached a peak, with about four hundred new soldiers incorporated.[12]

What was seen by planters and the Spanish military as an increase in "trouble" reflected a complicated process by which friends, neighbors, and strangers in the countryside came to constitute themselves as insurgents or, as they would say, revolutionaries. The conversations, grievances, and solidarities that preceded these decisions are nearly impossible to reconstruct. But the results were there to see. The manager of the Soledad plantation wrote in July that small parties were "seen in various places, one in this vicinity, but they are all hurrying up country. Yesterday our carpenter met a party of four back of Vaqueria, like most of them armed with revolvers and machetes."[13] At almost the same moment a forty-one-year-old *mulato* corporal from the local pro-Spanish volunteer force, Francisco Álvarez Oliva, decided to change sides. Local officials put out a warrant for his arrest, charging him with "desertion to the insurrectionist camp, with his weapon and ammunition."[14]

In mid-July 1895 the Spanish civil and military governor of the province of Santa Clara, citing recent acts of "savagery" carried out by insurgents, issued a set of decrees that indicated the uneasy state of the countryside. *Campesinos* who needed to go back and forth between town and country were to carry appropriate identification at all times, and could not be abroad between dusk and dawn. Machetes could be kept at home for agricultural labor but could not be carried outside one's own farm. As in earlier conflicts, the necessary mobility that accompanied agricultural work and the sharp implements used in the fields became hard to separate from the activities of conspiracy and the weapons of war.[15]

Country people who had not chosen to join the insurgency were caught up in these conflicts, and struggles over familiar issues took on a new edge. On the Central Narcisa in Yaguajay, a cash-poor administrator proposed in July to pay the workers for the month of May, but not yet for June. A group of twenty-five to thirty workers charged that he had refused to pay some of them anything at all, and went to complain to the mayor of Yaguajay. The mayor visited the plantation and apparently persuaded some of the workers to wait for payment. The next day the mayor, in response to a telegram from the provincial governor, summoned the estate administrator for an explanation, and a hundred workers massed in front of the municipal offices. The administrator apparently promised to produce the money within four days.[16]

Six days passed. On July 27 Manuel Lombano Blanco, born in Santander, Spain, and Guillermo Ruiz, born in Santa Clara, addressed a written petition in the name of the workers to the Spanish lieutenant colonel in charge of the zone. Lombano signed; Ruiz had someone sign for him. A group of one hundred workers, constituting themselves as a "commission," went to military headquarters to deliver their petition. They reiterated their pleas for food and lodging, and apparently added that they feared for their lives because of the insurgent bands that had come near the estate at night. Lieutenant Colonel Millán Ferrez forwarded the petition to higher authorities, reporting also that the workers' attitude was *tumultuaria* (rebellious). He told the workers to return to the estate and guaranteed their security. At 7 P.M. he sent a company of soldiers to the estate, where the workers had reported themselves "threatened." The soldiers ended up trying to "contain" the workers who sought access to the company store. The following day the workers refused to remain on the estate, saying "they have nothing to eat and nowhere to sleep." The governor reiterated his order to provide lodging and a day's rations to the "commissions" of workers. By August 5 two hundred workers from Central Narcisa were reported to be out on strike.[17]

At just this moment the Spanish military records fall silent, and we do not know what became of the hungry and increasingly desperate workers of Central Narcisa. But such conflicts over work and pay were adding to the climate of insecurity in the countryside. As during the earlier anticolonial rebellions, the presence of insurgents in the countryside now heightened tensions within sugar estates. Bracing for potential insurgent attacks, the Spanish colonial authorities did not need upheaval on the plantations. Those in charge of keeping peace on the island could not do their job properly if an estate administrator or local mayor exacerbated conflicts over pay. But no amount of military intimidation or negotiation could erase the consequences of the failure of an estate to pay its workers. Displaced and hungry cane workers could turn from petitions to strikes, and perhaps from strikes to insurgency.

On Edwin Atkins's Soledad estate, it gradually became evident that a cluster of kin and neighbors who carried the surname Sarría, adopted from the previous owners of the plantation, were moving toward open rebellion. These recruits were drawn from among the men and women whom the manager J. S. Murray had found so difficult to control in the late 1880s, including the "negros with horses" whom he had vigorously sought to dismount. Virtually all of the men and women now named Sarría would have witnessed Murray's high-handedness, his use of the stocks, and his general dismissal of their property and aspirations. "Some of the negros give as an excuse that they have no body to cook for them" Murray had written in 1886, "as I have sent off a number of negro women that would not work nor pay rent for their rooms. They want all the privileges of both freedmen and patrocinados, but none of the responsibilities and it will take some time before they can understand their possition."[18]

On August 10, 1895, Claudio Sarría, who had been a cartman on Soledad, officially joined the insurrection, as did Anastasio Sarría. Their neighbor Ciriaco Quesada—the single, thirty-four-year-old former slave from Santa Rosalía— joined on the same day. Ambrosio Sarría followed them a month later.[19] These early recruits seem to have been exceptionally strong characters, often with reputations as resistant workers. Ciriaco Quesada carried a long history of contentiousness and refusal to submit dating back at least to conflicts with the administrator of Santa Rosalía, who had put him in irons in 1881. It is unlikely that anyone was surprised when Ciriaco Quesada chose to accompany Claudio Sarría into the rebellion in the summer of 1895.[20]

In October 1895 the insurgent high command, aiming to defeat Spain by destroying the export economy, ordered sugar estates not to grind any more cane. Soon any estate that continued to prepare for the harvest was vulnerable to armed attack and to the torching of cane fields. On November 20, a rebel party of "eight negroes" appeared at Soledad with the order to burn cane, and had some discussion with the management. Fires began in and around Soledad in earnest in late November, and the manager again reported that "a small party of negroes" had set them, under the supervision of a larger group of rebels. Atkins promptly lobbied the Spanish authorities to obtain protection, and soon a detachment of Spanish soldiers was stationed on the estate.[21]

Faced with the order to burn cane fields, the rebel Claudio Sarría may have been drawn in two directions at once: Soledad was the home of most of his kin, and therefore a place to which he would return again and again. But it was also the symbol of a very recent slavery and of humiliations at the hands of the administrator. Letters from Soledad initially portrayed Claudio Sarría simply as a vengeful individual with a gang of bandits. But by late December J. N. S. Williams, a manager at Soledad, linked him to a larger network of "sitio negroes" who had been living at Soledad. The *sitio* at Soledad seems to have been an area of land planted in food crops, home to quite a few former slaves. In late 1895 Williams expelled most of these "sitio negroes," but initially allowed an older man named Aniceto to remain. He soon repented, writing to Atkins that "I have made up my mind that the next time Claudio comes around that house to pull it down and send the negro and his family off the place. They are spies, I am pretty sure, and it is only consideration for your personal wishes respecting the old man that he has been kept on."[22]

It was by now clear that attacks on the estate were coordinated actions by rebel units. Atkins's employee Peter Beal reported from the Guabairo *colonia* on December 9, 1895: "Yesterday at five o'clock P.M. the Cabecilla [chieftain], known as el Mexicano, appeared in this colonia with some fifty or sixty men and immediately commenced setting fire to the cane from Naranjito down to the railroad and beyond." Beal later testified that the burnings in those weeks had been carried out by "The Mexican, Alejo Torres and Claudio Sarría, Juan Salas, Tata Monte, and Sixto Roque." J. N. S. Williams reported that "Claudio Sarría, Rafael Monte, Torres, and Najarro have united their forces with the Mejicano for their own safety," and he estimated that the group comprised some three hundred men. Most of these names are recognizable and reflect the heterogeneity of the local leadership: Captain Claudio Sarría and Rafael Monte were former slaves; Lieutenant Benigno Najarro was a black shopkeeper and early conspirator from the mountain town of Las Moscas; Lieutenant Colonel Sixto Roque was a white local cane farmer; and a Mexican-born farmer, Lieutenant Juan Ramírez, was known as *el mejicano.*[23]

Soon full-scale war swept in from the east and reached the province of Santa Clara. Under the leadership of Máximo Gómez and Antonio Maceo, the main body of the rebel army had broken out of Oriente and begun an audacious invasion westward. Local insurgent units joined them along the way, and the combined force crossed the Trinidad Mountains and the Arimao River to reach the rich sugar country in early December of 1895. Skirting the heavily fortified town of Cumanayagua, the invading rebel army pushed through the countryside northeast of Cienfuegos, inland and north of Soledad and Santa Rosalía plantations. On December 15, 1895, at Mal Tiempo, just east of Cruces, the rebel forces defeated the Spaniards in a ferocious battle and continued their march westward. To guard their southern flank, Quintín Bandera, a black rebel general famed for his bravery and independence of mind, remained in the area of Trinidad with a group of soldiers from Oriente.[24]

On January 17, 1896, Atkins received news that "all the rebel forces from the eastern departments seem to be en route for here" as 150 cavalry and infantry from Quintín Bandera's command paid a formal visit to Soledad. For the moment, relations were courteous: "They were here under trying circumstances, hungry, barefooted and half naked, yet not one of them appropriated the smallest thing to himself without permission . . . With exception of the officers, they were all colored." The next day local insurgents visited, seeking sweet potatoes, and were reported to have "behaved very well indeed."[25]

In early February of 1896 the rebel high command ordered Higinio Esquerra to gather the scattered local bands formally included in the Fourth Corps and bring them together as an infantry under Quintín Bandera. On February 21 Claudio Sarría and Rafael Monte, another former slave from the area, apparently burned buildings at San Esteban. P. M. Beal reported to Atkins from Cienfuegos that "we are now passing the most critical time since the beginning," and that flying squadrons of *guerrillas*—the pro-Spanish Cuban irregulars who had been recruited under the command of Spanish officers—were forming to "operate against the smaller roving bands."[26]

The question was now starkly posed to the residents of the central sugar zones: would able-bodied men and women join with the rebellion, or would they seek security elsewhere? Spanish fortifications girding the estates posed practical obstacles to joining, as did the presence of armed guards on many plantations. But the deeper question was one of risks, rewards, and meanings: What did this insurrection seem to promise and what did it mean for a man or woman to join it? And how long was it going to last? José Martí had anticipated a short war. But Martí was now dead, killed in battle soon after his arrival on the island.

Key to the decision to join up would be the image of the insurgent army itself, combined with the multiple imaginings of what a free Cuba might bring. Most of the rank and file of the rebel forces from Oriente who swept through Santa Clara were men defined as black or *mulato* and strongly identified with the dynamic figure of Antonio Maceo. Alongside them fought many Cubans who counted themselves as white, and even a few renegade Spaniards. The presence in the rebel leadership of admired veterans of color from the Ten Years' War, including Quintín Bandera, José Maceo, and Agustín Cebreco, under the command of the Dominican Máximo Gómez and the Cuban Antonio Maceo, made credible the picture of the insurgency as a transracial revindication of Cuban freedoms, as described by José Martí. The official ideology of the rebels portrayed racism as a legacy of slavery and colonialism, destined to be eliminated in a democratic Cuban republic. But families who had only recently escaped slavery might still reasonably wonder whether it made good sense to risk their lives and imperil their modest material gains in pursuit of these ideals. And among white doubters, the shadow of years of talk of black savagery and "another Haiti" still lingered.[27] In late 1895 nationalist hopes nonetheless ran high and rebel advances were impressive; those inclined to join up often found a horse and took off toward wherever the action was.

In the core plantation areas around Cienfuegos, those who chose not to join could seek security within what the Spanish military described as the "fortified zone." On some of the wealthiest estates, fortifications permitted continued grinding and inhibited recruitment to the rebellion, particularly of permanent workers who were former slaves or their descendants. A search of enlistment registers, for example, turns up very few recruits with the surnames Terry, Zulueta, or Acea, suggesting that relatively few former slaves of these major landholders made their way to the rebel lines.[28] Estates outside or on the fringes of the fortified zone, particularly those located near the foothills, were far more porous. Thus the surnames Sarría, suggesting residence during slavery on Soledad plantation or nearby Rosario, and Quesada, suggesting residence on the Santa Rosalía estate, do recur in the companies recruited in the neighborhood of Cumanayagua.

In addition to Claudio Sarría, for example, who had joined up early, Felipe Sarría, son of Dolores Sarría, joined in December, and Rufino and Lorenzo followed him in January and February of 1896.[29]

For many of the local residents of Cienfuegos, recruitment was a personal, face-to-face affair, as friends and neighbors who had joined the insurgent army confronted those who had not. On Hormiguero plantation, for example, workers watched as virtually the entire invading force rode or tramped across estate lands in their march to the west. Even those who resisted appeals to enlist found it hard to resist requests for information. One Canary Islander who managed cane farms on Hormiguero ended up giving information to a friend who was an insurgent; the Spanish soldiers, by contrast, were strangers to him, and he did not speak with them.[30]

The moment of recruitment itself could be ephemeral. Rural workers were, after all, committed to their homes and to their families and might have second thoughts about abandoning them, particularly if this meant marching out of their home district. Miguel Angel Abad had a small farm of his own but also worked on a *colonia* supplying the Hormiguero central mill. He watched the passage of Gómez and Maceo through the estate as they torched cane and moved westward. Local insurgents came out of the woods to join them, though most of the workers on the estate did not. Abad had a friend in the invading force "who wanted me to go with them," and he joined up. But after a few hours, "I slowly fell to the rear, and as soon as I found I could separate myself, I started running for my house."[31]

Overall, the rebel Cienfuegos Brigade added 1,057 recruits in 1895 and 557 in 1896.[32] These newcomers immediately confronted the realities of military authority and decision making, as scattered bands came under more centralized authority. In the adjacent province of Matanzas, individual black recruits were frequently relegated to the role of unarmed "assistant," and entire units composed largely of black and *mulato* rebels serving under officers of color suffered discrimination from units under white leadership.[33] The picture for the province of Santa Clara is less clear. Much of the rebel high command in the province was composed of individuals described as white. General José de Jesús Monteagudo, commander of the Villa Clara Brigade, appears to have presented himself as white, and was surrounded by white officers. Under his authority, the patterns characteristic of Matanzas might well be repeated.[34] By contrast, the Cienfuegos Brigade was commanded in 1896 by José Rogelio Castillo, who had served under the orders of the black lieutenant colonel Jesús Rabí in the Ten Years' War. In the Cienfuegos Brigade, of twenty-five officers of the rank of *comandante* and above (including lieutenant colonel and general) for whom racial identifiers are available, five were black or *mulato*. In northeastern Santa Clara province, General José González Planas, the founder of the society of people of color in Lajas, took command of the Remedios Brigade and exercised authority over troops of all colors.[35]

Cuban grievances against the Spanish state, and popular imaginings of a "free Cuba," provided points of convergence among what may in fact have been quite different visions of a postwar future. The rallying of Cubans from different classes and racial groups also reflected the increasing precariousness of the role of non-combatants *(pacíficos)* and the rapid closing off of alternatives for survival in a ravaged countryside. To the extent that workers were brought into the insurgency by immediate hardships, a change in conditions could alter patterns of support. The manager of Soledad estate had been inclined in September of 1895 to disparage the importance of the insurrection, and reported that his conversations with workers suggested that "should wages advance, the lines of insurgents would be rapidly depleted, many of the white men being there through inability to obtain work."[36]

Spanish authorities were quick to try to activate this division, invoking the sup posed danger of black supremacy in the insurrection. The head of the Spanish forces, General Arsenio Martínez Campos, had reported back to Spain in June of 1895 that one group of Cuban soldiers who had surrendered declared themselves autonomists, some with hopes of future independence, but fearful that "the triumph today of the insurrection, with the impoverishment of the homeland, would be to conquer not freedom but anarchy: it would be to descend and convert [Cuba] into a Republic of Haiti, with black people predominant." Each party to this conversation, of course, had by this moment a powerful interest in affirming such an interpretation. The captured Cubans may have wanted to escape further punishment; the Spanish general wanted to reassure his superiors that the insurgency did not reflect the true desires of most Cubans. To the extent that the sentiments cited by Martínez Campos actually reflected the views of some white rebels, black soldiers' fears that they would always be viewed with suspicion and be denied their fair share of respect and promotions would have been confirmed. The contrary narrative of cross-racial nationalist unity nevertheless continued to be voiced by rebel leaders and reiterated by some of the rank and file. As the military fortunes of the rebels rose and fell, celebratory and suspicious interpretations are likely to have risen and fallen as well. Neither one, no matter how confidently voiced, should be taken to reveal a timeless "truth" about the role of race in the rebellion.[37]

The propaganda campaign of the Spanish state found echoes in the reports of the angry administrator of Soledad plantation, J. N. S. Williams, who characterized the conflict in increasingly racialized terms. He judged 80 percent of the insurgent force to be composed of people of color, and raged that "among these negroes are to be found the most degraded wretches in this country, men who do not recognize any leader and who are willing to seize upon any excuse for rapine and pillage."[38] Another Soledad administrator, P. M. Beal, later said that Claudio Sarría had "all the negroes bearing the name of Sarria at his service."[39]

Whatever the substrate of prejudice or egalitarianism alive in the countryside, the day-to-day reality was grim, both in the rebel ranks and near the front lines. One fifty-eight-year-old black laborer on the Hormiguero estate described the drama of insurgent attacks on cane fields and the rebels' attempts to halt work on the estates. He recalled that the rebels had threatened workers that "anybody that remained would have his neck torn off—would have his head cut off." Some fifteen or twenty days later the insurgents returned and found laborers again in the field: "They came again and found us working, and told us, 'didn't we tell you not to work' and we replied 'we are working because it is necessary for us to work,' and then they said 'Stop working at once: take your tools away or we will cut you down, all of you, with machetes.' "[40] By early 1896 the only estate in Cienfuegos to grind normally was Constancia, owned by the Marqués de Apezteguía and garrisoned with 1,700 Spanish troops.[41]

February 1896 saw the arrival of General Valeriano Weyler to replace Arsenio Martínez Campos at the head of the Spanish forces, and the beginning of a more aggressive military strategy aimed at isolating and starving out the insurrection. By the fall of 1896 the Spanish were systematically destroying unauthorized cultivation in the countryside.[42] At the same time, Spanish forces tried to establish official zones in which crops could be grown to feed those who remained loyal. They taxed local landowners and recruited local men, both Spanish- and Cuban-born, to create an armed force to protect the plantings. Several such zones were established in Palmira and Cienfuegos, though they were always vulnerable to surprise attacks. The colonel of a Spanish brigade in Cienfuegos felt it necessary to remind those protecting the zone that official orders required that one "sacrifice one's life before one's military honor."[43]

Direct Spanish engagements with the insurgents in the area around Cienfuegos often involved not the regular Spanish soldiers, but loyalist *guerrilla* forces on patrol. In mid-June of 1896, for example, a *guerrilla* commander in Santa Isabel de las Lajas reported on operations carried out the day before. Leaving the Central Caracas, they had passed through the Central Andreita, several smaller farms, and the Central Hormiguero, finally spending the night at the Portugalete plantation. At 6 A.M. they apparently came across the encampment of an insurgent leader, the black man named Rufino Cuellar. They reported him killed while trying to escape.[44]

In the fall of 1896 General Weyler formalized the Spanish policy of establishing camps to which noncombatants were to be consigned. The aim was to dry up the sources of insurgent support by "concentrating" rural folk into or near the towns. For the men and women in the camps, who were referred to as *reconcentrados,* the cost of "protection" was economic paralysis and devastating epidemic disease. One such camp was established on the Hormiguero estate in Cienfuegos; others were established in the foothills town of Arimao and along the rail lines.[45]

Something of the tone of the assault against Cuban civilians can be inferred from a private letter written by the civil governor of the province of Santa Clara to General Pedro Pin, commander of the Spanish forces in the region. Written in a meticulous hand on his private letterhead, the note asked General Pin to recommend that his officers take steps to prevent the abuses being committed by Spanish soldiers who sacked the brothels of the towns they entered. They "use" the women without paying them, break up the furniture, steal their belongings, and "mistreat them without pity," the governor wrote. This was quite literally rape and pillage, though the governor phrased his criticism of the soldiers somewhat differently: "If they take their pleasure and do not pay them, so be it; but the rest of their actions are odious."[46]

The operations reports of the Spanish forces in Santa Clara province for 1897 make equally depressing reading. In the month of February, for example, Colonel Juan Manrique de Lara's unit operated out of an encampment near the town of Trinidad. Beginning on the 8th he brought together a column composed of 950 infantrymen, 95 members of the *guerrilla* (the pro-Spanish irregular force), 96 civil guards, 10 local *guerrilleros* (pro-Spanish fighters) and one artillery piece. They began a march through the countryside. As he received reports of insurgent presence in one place or another, the colonel would send groups off in pursuit. Periodically the Spanish forces were fired upon by insurgents holding particular hills; they fell into ambushes; they succeeded in routing one or another small insurgent force and found a body or two left behind. But their most notable activity was simply destruction. They located the areas where insurgents grew crops *(prefecturas)* and burned them. They found country people without appropriate papers and detained them. They came upon huts in the countryside and burned them. In their first two days of march they reported destroying 150 huts and *prefecturas,* and every few days the process was repeated.[47]

The story was similar in the Cienfuegos region. The First Battalion of the Infantry Regiment of Bailén spent much of June of 1897 moving back and forth from an encampment in Cumanayagua, near the Rio Caunao. Their reconnaissance activities rarely yielded more than a cow or two, the occasional prisoner (including one seven-year-old), and some abandoned weapons, but they burned houses and farms along the way. They managed to be absent for an insurgent attack on Cumanayagua itself, but claimed to have hastened in pursuit of its attackers.[48]

While the Spanish forces burned huts and gardens, insurgents continued to set fire to cane fields. In September of 1897 the mayor of the municipality of Cruces sent a terse two-page report to the Spanish military, detailing the destruction of his region by fires, which he attributed to the insurgents. He listed the seven major sugar mills that had been destroyed, enumerating the workforces thus displaced. The mayor's rough estimates would place the lost jobs at harvest in Cruces alone at close to 7,000. Moreover, he reported that all of the smaller farms of the region had "disappeared," leaving no house standing except some of those on the sugar plantations.[49]

For rural residents to survive in this climate of violent contest over terrain, repeated attacks, and continual arrests of civilians was a challenge. A high degree of resourcefulness and improvisation was required, and small bands of civilians sometimes formed in the countryside to escape Spanish authority and forage for themselves. The insurgent forces were also passing through a grim time, having suffered the devastating news of the death in battle of Antonio Maceo in December of 1896. Some rebels deserted the ranks, and it was increasingly difficult to recruit new soldiers to replace those who had fallen or departed.[50]

The Spanish, in forcing rural Cubans into camps, made it clear that they viewed even *pacíficos* as potential enemies. But at the same time, the colonial authorities tried to promote a new version of the old notion of autonomism and to create structures of rule that might make it possible to gain the loyalty of Cubans weary of war. Throughout the long and desperate conflict between Spanish forces and Cuban rebels, the Spanish colonial government had sought to deny the very possibility of Cuban citizenship. Now they tried to persuade residents of Cuba that if they remained loyal, they would have wide access to a substantial Spanish citizenship, regardless of color. The 1890 expansion of the electoral franchise within Spain itself could provide the basis for offering broader rights of participation to Cubans, in the context of a looser imperial structure.

In 1897 the Spanish parliament thus belatedly conceded several basic demands of the political reformists and constituted a new "autonomist" government for Cuba. In principle, a wider suffrage and a more expansive politics were now possible. A November 1897 decree extended Spain's electoral law of 1890 to the island, and local authorities began to compile lists of eligible voters. The Hormiguero worker and insurgent recruit Miguel Ángel Abad, he of the hasty retreat home, soon appeared on the electoral list of the nearby municipality of San Fernando.[51]

In response to pressure from the urban-based movement for equal rights for Cubans of color, led by Juan Gualberto Gómez, the Spanish government had already in the early 1890s conceded that the honorific title of "Don" (a formal "Mister") could be claimed by men of color, and had accorded formal equal rights of public accommodation and education regardless of color.[52] Juan Gualberto Gómez himself had opted for rebellion, but the Spanish government hoped to rekindle the peaceful political engagement of some of those who had benefited from the colonial regime's concessions.

The changing of courtesy titles signaled a new formal equality of legal standing, and surviving electoral lists from Santa Clara confirm the presence of Cubans of color among those recognized as electors. But the official habit of marking differences and distinctions was not easily relinquished. The electoral census of March 1898 for Sagua la Grande listed hundreds of electors in each district of the municipality, but carefully accorded the title "Don" to some and omitted it from others, generally following the names of the latter with the color terms *pardo* (brown) or *moreno* (black). The lists from the cities of Santa Clara and Cienfuegos were more discreet, eschewing the distinctions and labeling every voter as "Don." Some rural districts dispensed with titles altogether.[53]

The electoral lists are equally interesting as snapshots of rural society. The district of Arimao, at the eastern edge of the zone of Cienfuegos, included the Soledad estate, the small-farming area around the town of Arimao itself, and the hill town of La Sierra, toward the mountains. On the district's 1898 voting list appeared Manuel Lago y Tacón, the Spanish immigrant second carpenter at the Soledad mill, who later began a family with Bárbara Pérez, the former slave from the Pérez Galdós family estate of Santa Teresa. Francisco Achón, almost certainly a Chinese workman from Soledad, and eight men with the surname Quesada, very likely former slaves from Santa Rosalía, appeared as electors as well. Twenty-three of the registered voters in Arimao carried the surname Sarría, and most of them were former slaves or their descendants from the Soledad and Rosario plantations. Indeed, the number of registered voters with the name Sarría exceeds the number of insurgent recruits of the same name.[54]

Actual practice at the ballot box, of course, cannot be retrieved from registration lists, and there is no telling how many of those who registered under the new Spanish rules were also providing aid and comfort to the insurgents. Moreover, the disruptions of war rendered these late electoral rights proffered by Spain largely moot—Spanish forces were not in effective control of much of the countryside. But the drawing up of integrated electoral lists could in itself establish a precedent. If the Spanish colonial authorities now endorsed an expanded color-blind suffrage, echoing Cuban nationalist notions of a citizenship that transcended race, then it might seem that peace was bound to consolidate electoral rights, no matter who emerged victorious.

In late 1897 and in the early months of 1898, however, peace seemed a long way off. José Martí and Antonio Maceo were dead, and recruitment to the insurgency had stalled. Spain was no closer to defeating the insurrection, but still controlled the major cities—including Havana, Matanzas, Santiago, Cienfuegos, and Santa Clara—though it seemed to some observers that the Spanish officers much preferred simply to garrison the towns rather than to expose their troops to the debilitating effects of irregular warfare in the tropics. Rebel general Máximo Gómez, aware that colonial rule without authority in the countryside was inherently unstable, optimistically predicted a rebel victory through a renewed offensive in the summer of 1898. With insurgent forces strong in the east, the city of Santiago de Cuba braced for attack.[55]

Yet in the rank and file of the rebel army, many soldiers were sick and demoralized. Dr. Carlos Trujillo, chief health officer for the insurgent Cienfuegos Brigade, estimated that two-thirds of the men in the brigade were suffering from malaria.[56] Quietly, some left the fight to find care for their illness or work with which to support their families. Rafael Iznaga, for example, was a soldier in the rebel Cienfuegos Brigade. But his name also appears on the payroll of the Soledad plantation for January of 1898. He seems to have taken something of a leave of absence from the war, and earned 7 pesos hauling wood.[57]

These temporary departures from the ranks of the insurgency reflected the complex choices made during wartime. Alongside and within the formal armed struggle for national independence were thousands of individual struggles for survival, for resources, and for respect. Thus Rafael Iznaga had chosen to become a *mambí*, a rebel soldier; his brother Victoriano had not. Victoriano, however, served as a messenger to the rebels.[58] Ciriaco Quesada, the former slave from Santa Rosalía, had enlisted in the rebel Cienfuegos Brigade and survived the war, but neither his name nor that of Captain Claudio Sarría appears on the list of discharged soldiers compiled in the late summer of 1898. His neighbor Cayetano Quesada, who was suffering from serious respiratory problems, also seems to have left the rebel ranks before the final mustering-out, probably to settle in San Antón, the hamlet tucked between the Soledad and the Santa Rosalía sugar plantations.[59]

Other country people, of whatever ancestry, had chosen from the beginning to keep their distance from the rebellion itself. Santa Rosalía's cane fields were torched early in the war, and most of the residents retreated to town or to neighboring Soledad. Then, in 1897, many were sent to a nearby Spanish "reconcentration" camp. But Ramón Ramos Quesada, apparently born free of a slave mother, remained behind to guard the cattle and to help keep the owner Manuel Blanco apprised of the state of things in the war-torn hills southeast of Soledad. The year earlier, he had drafted and signed careful updates on the food provided to the Spanish forces, as well as on the overall condition of the estate. Depending on how the war turned out, Ramos Quesada might expect to keep a foothold on the land when it was all over.[60]

Atkins's Soledad plantation continued to operate throughout the war, and its pay lists are full of workers with the surnames Sarría, Quesada, Iznaga, and Galdós, most of them former slaves or their descendants from the Soledad, Rosario, Santa Rosalía, La Vega, and Santa Teresa estates. They worked alongside Spanish immigrants and long-free Cuban country people, a multiracial work force parallel to the multiracial rebel army and the multiracial electoral lists.[61]

The locally recruited, pro-Spanish *guerrilla* also drew members from the heterogeneous rural population. In the neighborhood of Soledad an irascible Spanish cane farmer, Juan Piñol, led such a group from a headquarters on the nearly ruined Santa Rosalía plantation. Santa Rosalía was strategically located on the Caunao River between Cienfuegos and the town of Arimao and still had enough livestock to keep the *guerrilla* in meat and mules. Foragers and enforcers under cover of war, these men were widely detested as renegades. But this did not prevent some local people from casting their lot with them.[62]

Over the long years of war, women faced choices somewhat different from those of men. A few took up arms: Caridad Quesada, now in her eighties, recalls that one older woman from Santa Rosalía had been a *mambisa,* a rebel fighter. In Yaguajay, to the north, Faustina Heredia, born free in 1877, accompanied Mateo de Jesús Hernández to the insurrection, and they married behind rebel lines.

CARTERA DE IDENTIFICACION
DE PENSIONADOS DEL
EJERCITO LIBERTADOR

FIRMA DEL INTERESADO

The identity card of Faustina Heredia, who fought alongside her husband in the the ranks of the Liberation Army during the 1895–1898
war for independence.

Many more women passed on information or supplies. Bárbara Pérez lived and
worked as a laundress in the foothills town of Arimao, which was garrisoned with
Spanish soldiers. According to her son, Tomás Pérez y Pérez, she washed the uniforms of Spanish soldiers and sometimes found loose ammunition in the pockets.
She would set it aside and then, telling the guards that she needed to collect wood
for a fire to boil the wash water, head to the *monte* and pass the bullets along to the

rebels.[63]

These patriotic and combative examples remain vivid in modern memories. In the written record, however, one is equally likely to come across strategies aimed at individual and family survival and at securing a postwar future. Gregoria Quesada, a slave and later a *patrocinada* on the Santa Rosalía plantation, was perhaps kin to Cayetano and Ciriaco Quesada, both of whom had joined the rebellion. Shortly after emancipation Gregoria Quesada moved to the town of Cienfuegos, settling near the public fountain on the side of town nearest to her former home at Santa Rosalía. She lived among men and women with the familiar surname Sarría, themselves almost certainly migrants from the Soledad or Rosario plantations.[64]

In 1888 and 1894 Gregoria Quesada had paid a total of 118 pesos to an older woman of color, Eleuteria Almoguea, for two pieces of property in the mountain community of La Sierra, on the far side of the Arimao River, toward the Trinidad Mountains. Three years later, in the discouraging year of 1897, when the countryside was ravaged and the political struggle stalemated, Gregoria Quesada paid Lutgarda Díaz y Nodal 200 pesos for an eight-acre *sitio,* also in La Sierra. It seems unlikely that in 1897 Gregoria Quesada could even travel there, given the Spanish policy of *reconcentración* and the risks of raids of one kind or another. She seems instead to have been envisioning a postwar future, when she and her children might rejoin a rural community and settle in. The plot she purchased bordered on lands owned by the Almoguea family; perhaps she and her neighbor Eleuteria Almoguea had thought this through together.[65]

The long Cuban fight for independence took an abrupt turn in April of 1898 when the United States declared war on Spain. At the international level, the decision was momentous, effectively trumping the Cuban struggle with an enormous infusion of naval power and inaugurating a new phase of overseas expansion by the United States. For people on the ground, particularly those near the port of Cienfuegos on the south coast, it was dramatic news followed by dramatic action. Isidro Vera, Sr., recalls that his father, who lived near the mouth of the bay, never forgot the shock of the American artillery as it attacked the lighthouse on May 14, sending projectiles overhead and inland.[66]

The U.S. declaration of war also made it possible for additional Cuban exile activists to join the fray. Expeditionary forces of Cuban exiles had previously set off from the U.S. coast in secret. Now they could head to the island openly. On May 25, 1898, for example, the steamer *Florida,* escorted by the U.S. warship *Osceala,* landed on the north coast of Oriente with 500 Springfield rifles, a million bullets, and 300 recruits for the Cuban rebel army. The Cuban force was under the command of the veteran rebel general José Lacret Morlot, and included doctors, dentists, pharmacists, and foot soldiers. Lieutenant Martín Morúa Delgado, a man of color from Santa Clara who worked as a clerk, was among them. So was Ramón Pagés, the cigar maker who had spoken up in favor of universal "public rights" at an equal rights meeting in New Orleans convened by Louis Martinet and Rodolphe Desdunes two years earlier. The Louisiana activists who had organized the Plessy challenge had followed the progress of the war in Cuba in the pages of their newspaper, *The Crusader.* Now at least one participant in the debates in New Orleans would join the Cuban struggle on the ground.[67]

In June of 1898, Cuban rebel troops commanded by Generals Calixto García, Agustín Cebreco, Jesús Rabí, and others participated in the final siege of Santiago while U.S. forces attacked on land and from the water. The city fell in July. Within a few weeks the war was over, but in a disconcerting and unresolved way. Spain and the United States debated the terms of peace in Paris, without Cuban representation, while the occupying U.S. forces hurried to isolate the Cuban rebel army. The Cuban rebels, in turn, convened an Assembly at Santa Cruz in the east to sketch out a postwar future. Throughout the countryside people were apprehensive and puzzled. What now? Would the Cuban soldiers be paid? Would farmers find credit to rebuild and plant? Would Cubans exercise sovereignty over their island?

In newspapers and in public debate within Cuba, the focus was on politics and on the prospects for national independence, but for many families the immediate question was food and land. The rebellion itself had been fought by country people, but only rarely had its leadership declared formal claims to land. Questions of property had been little discussed, except for a fleeting early rebel decree calling for the distribution to soldiers of land "acquired by the Cuban Republic either by conquest or confiscation."[68] Instead, an ideology of independence, justice, and transracial patriotism had framed the struggle. But now it was neither the Cuban generals nor the ideologists of the separatist cause who were in power. A U.S. military occupation force under General Leonard Wood was in control of Santiago, and would have to formulate a policy on whether former soldiers could claim land in the eastern countryside.[69]

In Cienfuegos, Gregoria Quesada now held title to the piece of land in La Sierra, but likely had no animals or tools with which to begin to work it. Rafael Iznaga, the rebel veteran who had cut wood on Soledad, might reasonably expect to be employed again by the Iznagas of Newport, Rhode Island, owners of La Vega plantation, where his parents had been slaves. Bárbara Pérez moved with Manuel Lago, the Spanish immigrant carpenter, to El Palmar, at the edge of the Soledad plantation. (Years later, their son Tomás Pérez y Pérez recalled the garden plot, the ducks the family raised, and the tendency of the cows to invade his mother's kitchen.) One by one, Cubans of color and their white neighbors tried to find niches to occupy in the countryside or in town.

Former rebel officers, like General Higinio Esquerra, who had been a farmer before the war, were somewhat better situated when it came to building a post-war livelihood. As men of local influence, they could negotiate rental contracts as *colonos* (cane farmers) when estates resumed grinding, thus capturing a fraction of the benefits of economic recovery. Veterans, black and white, who had served under them might continue to look to them for favors and credit, in exchange for political loyalty. And employers could benefit from former officers' ability to recruit their followers to work on the estates.

These rank-based clienteles could quickly reproduce the asymmetries that had developed during the war. Educated Cubans, who were disproportionately white, had enjoyed easier access to officer status in the rebel Liberation Army, a privilege that had become more noticeable as the war went on. Already in late 1897 there had been signs that some black rebel officers were being sidelined, and the last months of 1898, with their promise of victory, saw the commissioning of large numbers of white middle-class and professional latecomers to the struggle.[70] There was every risk that these privileges, etched into rank and renown, would pattern access to resources after the war. The U.S. occupiers, moreover, showed a marked preference for elite interlocutors and allies and a persistent scorn for the cross-racial rank and file of the rebel forces.

But the links between structures and outcomes are rarely simple. Cubans, particularly Cubans of color, entered the peace with multiple and sometimes contradictory experiences. Many had achieved respect as soldiers, even if they risked disrespect again as residents—not yet citizens—of an island occupied by a country known for its racial hierarchy and segregation. The much-vaunted, often romanticized, solidarity across the color line during wartime was not entirely a myth: it was an ideal that had to a certain extent replaced prior assumptions of deference. A great deal remained to be decided and defined, from electoral rights to property laws to racial etiquette, and thousands of black veterans were living proof of the possibility of cross-racial collaboration. This would be, in effect, a second beginning for the process of defining a postslavery order in Cuba.

CHAPTER SIX

Democracy and Antidemocracy

The Claims of Citizens, 1898–1900

*What care I whether the test which we have put be a new one or
an old one? What care I whether it be more or less ridiculous or
not? Doesn't it meet the case? Doesn't it let the white man vote,
and doesn't it stop the negro from voting, and isn't that what we
came here for?*

Ernest B. Kruttschnitt, president, 1898 Louisiana

Constitutional Convention

WITH THE INTERVENTION OF THE UNITED STATES IN CUBA'S WAR FOR
independence, the threads of investment, markets, and exile that had bound the
two societies snapped taut. But if the ties were clear, their meaning was not.
When the McKinley administration invoked the Spanish government's abuses as a
rationale for war, African American newspapers noted bitterly that the administration seemed far more concerned with affronts to individual rights committed
by Spaniards against Cubans than those committed by white citizens against black
citizens in Georgia or Louisiana. For their part, many Cuban patriots worried that
the invading army would carry with it a claim to U.S. sovereignty over the island,
and perhaps elements of the U.S. racial order as well.[1]

Even as the United States headed toward war with Spain, politicians and the
courts were reexamining the relationship between citizenship and suffrage within
the United States. In early 1898 a convention was convened to write a new state
constitution for Louisiana. Along with their confrères in other southern states,
the Louisiana delegates set in motion a profound challenge to what was left of the

guarantees of the Fifteenth Amendment to the U.S. Constitution. Efforts to limit voting by African Americans had been a theme of southern Democrats' political existence since the passage by the U.S. Congress of the Reconstruction Acts had opened the vote to black men in 1867. What was new in the 1890s was white leaders' willingness to hazard a frontal assault on black suffrage itself, first by statute and then in a set of new state constitutions designed expressly for this purpose.[2]

In both Louisiana and Cuba, the rights of former slaves and their descendants were vulnerable to abridgment on several fronts. Laborers in the cane fields of each society tried to maintain their claims of citizenship, sometimes as soldiers, sometimes as voters, sometimes as workers. Moreover, these two stories of postemancipation adaptations become by 1898 a single story, a pair of trajectories crossing and colliding at every turn.

The intersection of these two dramas carried with it an intertwining of people as well. Among the U.S. soldiers who shipped out to Cuba in 1898 were African American volunteers from New Orleans, Donaldsonville, and points in between who brought with them aspirations for respect and citizenship as well as their own interpretations of the Cuban independence struggle and its fallen leader Antonio Maceo.[3] The man President William McKinley chose as the first U.S. military governor of Cuba in 1899 was General John R. Brooke, the Pennsylvania-born officer who had been posted to various Louisiana towns in the 1870s to try to protect black voters from white vigilantes. In 1874 Colonel Brooke had served for twenty-four hours as acting military governor of the city of New Orleans, called upon to intervene between the White Leaguers who had seized the Louisiana state house and the shaky Republican governor William Kellogg to whom the reins of government were to be handed back. In Louisiana in 1874 and in Cuba in 1899, John R. Brooke embodied the power of the federal government of the United States in situations where structures of sovereignty and rights of representation were unresolved, and he exercised formal authority over polities that would soon be beyond his control.[4]

Throughout the 1890s the political situation for black citizens in Louisiana had been precarious. In 1888 the state had counted 128,150 voters classified as "colored" and 125,407 classified as "white."[5] This equilibrium was the background fact that had kept Republican, populist, and fusionist politics alive, while fueling white-supremacist efforts at fraud and vote suppression. Although in the sugar parishes the Knights of Labor had been crushed, cross-racial organizing continued in various parts of the state. On the New Orleans waterfront black and white longshoremen and stevedores struggled to work out a modus vivendi that would protect their interests, and in the northern parishes lumber workers and members of the People's Party joined forces across the color line.[6] These alliances were fragile, riven with danger, and threatened by explicit and implicit racism, even within their own ranks. They placed black working people in positions of great vulnerability, as the black physician Dr. Sterling Price Brown quickly learned when he came to the aid of black waterfront workers during strikes in the mid-1890s. Together they were attacked by a "mob of white hoodlums," workers whose previously cross-racial union had expelled black cotton screwmen and then tried to block them from seeking work separately.[7]

Louisiana Democrats were on top, but insecurely so. They had seen urban politicians make some concessions to waterfront workers, black and white, and rural Populists win white and black votes in the northern parishes. Despite vote suppression and intimidation, African Americans still represented a potential swing vote between competing white-led parties or factions. Louisiana Populists had since their founding meeting encompassed both black and white members of the Knights of Labor and the Farmers' Alliance, and were gaining enough strength to alarm Democrats. "Fusionist politics," embodying elements of the cross-racial electoral coalitions shattered by successful white-supremacist mobilization in the 1870s, reemerged in 1894 and 1896 as a potential threat to Democrats' continued dominance. Populist coalition-building was most pronounced in the northern parishes, but electoral maneuvering in pursuit of black voters also took place in New Orleans and in the sugar regions, with their history of Knights of Labor activism and a planter class divided between White League Democrats and pro-tariff Republicans.[8]

The issue reactivating elite Republicanism in Louisiana was the perennial one of tariffs, for sugar producers were in perpetual need of protection from lower-cost Cuban imports. The national Democratic Party and the administration of Grover Cleveland had become increasingly hostile to such measures, and in response some south Louisiana planters moved toward a strategic alliance with congressional Republicans. The result was the formation of a statewide National Republican Party, built around pro-tariff planters and looking for new coalitions in pursuit of state power. In 1896 the bayou sugar parishes provided a key base for an alliance of the People's Party and this National Republican Party.[9]

For the planter Republicans, such an alliance was purely strategic. But like any coalition, it could potentially empower its junior partner. Republican planter Henry McCall, to reassure his peers that there was no threat of a resurgence of significant black political power, argued that "the old war and reconstruction issues are dead; the force bill and election laws are buried never to be resurrected; the issues of the future are to be industrial, economical, and social."[10] John N. Pharr, owner of a large plantation in St. Mary Parish, presented himself as a National Republican gubernatorial candidate who could make a new kind of cross-racial alliance work. In his speeches, the man who had expelled strikers from his plantation in 1887 took a more inclusive tone: "I was reared with the Negro and worked side by side with him for twenty odd years. I may say for all my life, I never have found him other than a good laborer and as honest as most other men."[11]

Underneath Pharr's seemingly respectful call for an electoral alliance lay a fatal weakness, implicit in his use of the phrase "side by side." True, working "side by side" could generate mutual respect. But Pharr, the owner of vast acreage and an employer of day laborers, meant the phrase metaphorically, in the manner of industrialists who extolled the "harmony of interests" between labor and capital. The white man and "the Negro," in his construction, were "side by side," but asymmetrically so, for the one was to remain a "good laborer" seeking only a wage, the other a citizen eligible to accumulate property and run for office. Black voters might choose to cast their ballots for Pharr, and he might choose to seek and then acknowledge their votes. Once out of the meeting hall, however, neither was likely to be under much illusion about the character of the bargain. Fusion politics did not carry with it a local fusion of interests.

Pharr's paternalism and hypocrisy were evident, but the problem went deeper. The evolution of labor patterns in the cane fields of postemancipation Louisiana had nearly precluded the possibility that black and white workers would actually work side by side in *shared* tasks, a situation far more likely to produce effective alliances and solidarity than sheer physical proximity.[12] In their everyday lives black and white sugar workers were largely separated, and their tasks and places of work and residence were different, even within the boundaries of the same plantation. Wage work in the fields was overwhelmingly black except for a modest number of Italians, most of them seasonal migrants. Wage work in the sugar factory was overwhelmingly white. The "quarters" housed workers who were black; the overseer's house and outlying buildings housed employees and tenants who were white. This pattern was not simply a mechanical "legacy" of slavery. It was the result of sharply segmented employment practices as well as the crushing of the labor movement.[13]

There were, moreover, many ways of being poor in the countryside, and they did not necessarily imply the same immediate political and economic interests. White sugar workers were likely to be renters or smallholders who took wage employment only seasonally or town dwellers with a salaried job at the mill, both of which engendered interests quite different from those of black wage-paid field laborers who lived and worked on the plantation year-round. Land rental and ownership were largely off-limits to black agriculturalists in the sugar areas of the bayou parishes, and the few families of color who succeeded in getting a foothold there usually did so as sharecroppers, not owners or cash tenants. Everyone in the cane-growing parishes might be thought to have an interest in maintaining high sugar prices, but owners, renters, and day laborers could be expected to differ on the share that should go to wages. And although laborers' wages depended on a buoyant sugar market, wage earners would not necessarily share small farmers' desire to keep up the prices of other commodities.[14]

Populists tried through various means to link the interests of small farmers with those of wage laborers, but theirs was an uphill fight. The strategic alliance with National Republican planters, moreover, threatened to undercut the Populists' class appeal even further. One local paper tried in a single breathless sentence to meld the concerns that held the coalition together: "The Terrebonne Times is Devoted to the Advocacy of Republican Principles in National and State Affairs Especially to the Protective Policy of the National Government to all American Industries and the Interests and Welfare of the Laboring Classes." Veterans of the 1887 Knights of Labor organizing drive in the sugar fields were likely to be skeptical of the depth of this fusion.[15]

The way in which divergent political and economic interests were framed could be as important as the interests themselves.[16] Democratic politicians and the Democratic press insistently portrayed black workers and black voters in a language that was designed to undermine mutual respect. The racist epithets and stereotypes that filled the daily papers reinforced an insidious construction of the "black vote" as something that Democrats could steal and Republicans could court when it suited them. One of the most frequently reiterated claims of those who sought to limit the franchise was that men whose votes were stolen were themselves "not worthy of the rights of citizenship."[17] The element of bad faith in this charge was breathtaking, of course, for it was the thieves who mocked those they had robbed. But the rhetorical purpose of the claim was to associate black voters with corruption, so that disfranchisement could be presented as "reform."

Both Populists and National Republicans benefited from a relatively inclusive franchise, and both also relied on the votes of white farmers and laborers who might be excluded if literacy or property requirements were introduced as a means of disfranchising black citizens. For the moment they opposed disfranchising initiatives. But a "lily-white" variant of their electoral alliance was also possible. Reducing the size of the electorate might even seem to some Republican candidates to be preferable to having corrupt Democratic polling officials "count in" votes attributed to black citizens whose names were on the registration lists, but who had cast no such ballots. No black voter would have been well advised to rely on the National Republicans as allies in the long run.[18]

In the elections of the spring of 1896, Democrats brought out the usual invective and racial slurs. One paper referred to the opposing slate as "John N(igger) Pharr," and the "Populist-negro social equality ticket." Invective alone, however, could not suppress votes. In St. Landry Parish, black women were beaten with barbed wire to intimidate families inclined to support the Populist–National Republican fusion ticket, and a Populist candidate in East Baton Rouge Parish was shot. Nonetheless, the bayou sugar parishes all went for the National Republican John Pharr, as did the northern hill parishes. Officials in the majority-black river parishes, alerted by their leadership that it was the "duty of Democrats to rob

Populists and Republicans of their votes whenever and wherever the opportunity presents itself," fraudulently "counted in" black votes they could not gain by other means. Democrats thus claimed 56 percent of the total recorded vote, to howls of protest from the Populists and Republicans. The narrowness of the margin was bound to tempt competing factions to build alliances for the next round. Later in 1896, an equally awkward legislative coalition of Populists, National Republicans, and urban Citizens' Leaguers almost succeeded in sending a reformer to the U.S. Senate. But the old race-baiter Samuel D. McEnery—who viewed the color line as a law endorsed by God Almighty—squeaked in.[19]

With the state house and the Senate delegation secure, Louisiana Democrats returned to the key task: destroying the electoral base for future challenges of this kind. The first step was urgent, with a presidential election looming in November of that year. The rolls still held around 130,000 black voters, 44 percent of the total registered electorate. Some even thought it possible that the Republican McKinley might carry the state if local Republican and Populist voters were able to cast their ballots freely. The Democrats chose an initial stealth weapon designed to appeal to antimachine "good government" types as well as white-line Democrats: requiring the use of the secret ballot. When accompanied by a prohibition on providing assistance to illiterates in the voting booth, an election law mandating the secret ballot could cut a wide swath through a working-class and small-farmer electorate accustomed to going to the polls with a prepared party ballot. By giving election officials discretionary authority to further purge the lists of eligible voters at will, a new registration law would complete the task, cleaning out any undesirables who persisted. The whole package could be presented as a reform, muscled through the legislature, and applied without further ado to the upcoming elections. In building the case for disfranchisement, Democrats tapped into a widespread sense that elections were fraud-ridden and needed "reforming," but their goals were absolutely partisan and resolutely white-supremacist.[20]

The secret ballot alone brought a devastating drop in opposition votes, which fell 75 percent from the April to the November 1896 elections. The registration act then etched the consequences into the electoral lists themselves, requiring voters to re-register annually or biannually, with registrars given complete discretion to refuse to register anyone. In the state as a whole, the number of "colored voters" fell by almost 90 percent, reaching 12,902 by the end of 1897. If the plummeting numbers of voters in the state tell the story in broad outline, the figures are even more stark at the local level: in Lafourche Parish, home of the great mobilizations in the cane fields in 1887, there had been 3,283 black voters registered in 1896. By January of 1898 there were only 51. In the parish of Ascension, black registration had been 2,621 in 1896. In early 1898 it was 281. Of the small group that remained, 75 had written their names and 206 had made their marks. It was easy to see that a literacy test could almost finish the job.[21]

Democrats wanted more than this de facto transformation of the electorate, however. They sought to achieve a classic political "lockup," in which the formal rules of the game would consolidate their advantage. They shifted from statutory to constitutional stratagems and moved to convene a constitutional convention. Elections to the convention reflected the consequences of the prior statutory limitations: only one Populist and one Republican were elected to a gathering composed overwhelmingly of Democrats. The convention began its deliberations in New Orleans in February of 1898.[22]

Black men in Louisiana, some of whom had been voting for thirty years, now faced nearly absolute and permanent expulsion from the political process. This assault would target the surviving activists of the Reconstruction generation as well as the supporters on whom they depended. If the 1896 Supreme Court decision in *Plessy v. Ferguson* had signaled the final repudiation of the 1868 ideal of equal "public rights," the new state Constitutional Convention promised political death. As the convention's deliberations unfolded, Louisiana equal-rights activists were still reeling from their defeat in *Plessy.* The Citizens' Committee had disbanded in despair, and Louis A. Martinet gave up his New Orleans activist newspaper, the *Crusader.* He continued to devote his attention to his notarial practice, recording the incorporation of such voluntary associations as the "Afro-American Mutual Aid Protective Association," the "Ladies of Determination Benevolent Mutual Aid Association," and a mutual-aid group called simply "Dignité."[23]

Few strategies remained for African Americans in Louisiana who sought to defend their access to political voice and resources. But in both New Orleans and the bayou parishes some men, mindful of the importance of black Civil War military service in securing the passage of the Fourteenth and Fifteenth amendments, saw a new opportunity to press a claim to full citizenship by volunteering for service in the war looming in Cuba. It was a gesture that could appeal to educated men of color eager to demonstrate their capacity for leadership, to young working men willing to enlist as privates, and to publicists who could argue that patriotism deserved civil respect.

Pierre L. Carmouche, the former Knights of Labor organizer from Donaldsonville, was one of the first to grasp this possibility. By 1898 he was a successful blacksmith with a cross-racial clientele. A patriotic man, he was also reported to be "one of the most particular in matters pertaining to the race." Having followed the progress of the anticolonial struggle in Cuba, he avowed that "the success of Maceo in Cuba" was "the height of his ambition." It is not difficult to discern how Carmouche might have made the connection: an 1895 issue of the *Crusader* records on its front page a contribution to the Plessy challenge of a dollar from Pierre Carmouche and the "True Friends Association" of Donaldsonville, and in another column the progress of Máximo Gómez and Antonio Maceo's forces in the war in Cuba.[24]

On February 15, a week after the disfranchising convention had convened in New Orleans, the U.S. battleship *Maine* exploded in Havana Harbor. On February 26, Pierre L. Carmouche addressed himself by letter to the Republican secretary of war in Washington and then to Democratic governor Murphy Foster of Louisiana, offering his services and those of 250 men of color of Ascension Parish, "on short notice, in defence of our country, at home or abroad."[25] Louisiana's white Democrats were now in an awkward position, for the offer reintroduced the possibility of black military service in a moment of heightened patriotism.

Pierre Carmouche was well ahead of national policy on the question of war itself and on the issue of black recruitment, but his enthusiasm was shared by other people of color in New Orleans. The forced disbanding of the racially mixed state militia in 1877 had not killed the martial spirit among Louisiana's men of color. An "independent military company" organized in August of 1887 had made bold to fire the salute at memorial services for the Colored Grand Army of the Republic of Mississippi and Louisiana at Chalmette Cemetery in New Orleans in 1890, whereupon the state legislature had outlawed all military organizations operating without permission from the governor. These "Faith Cadets," as they called them-

selves, had effectively gone underground, and were now ready to jump at the opportunity to mobilize for the war, if only the president would make the call.[26]

The national African American press quickly weighed in on the issue of war. As
the weeks went by many papers moved away from their earlier skepticism regarding President McKinley's interventionist policy and adopted a full-throated call
for black patriotism, black recruits, and black officers. Some continued to raise
questions about the wisdom of offering to fight for a nation that would not guarantee basic rights to its black population—either the vote itself or protection
against lynching. Increasingly, however, this contrast became a mechanism for trying to press claims of equal treatment rather than an argument against enlisting.[27]

During these same weeks, in Louisiana itself the process of disfranchisement
rolled onward. The Constitutional Convention was a sorry spectacle, a Demo-
cratic-dominated conclave drafting the clumsy coda to widespread de facto vote
suppression in the state. Its chair, the White League veteran E. B. Kruttschnitt,
announced that "this convention has been called together by the people of the
State to eliminate from the electorate the mass of corrupt and illiterate voters
who have during the last quarter of a century degraded our politics." Others were
even more blunt, calling for the adoption of an "understanding" clause that would
enable registrars to enfranchise all white applicants and disfranchise all black
ones. The debates and machinations were fractious nonetheless, in part because
white Democrats from majority-black parishes stood to lose power as the official
registration in their parishes evaporated, leaving less room for the stuffing of ballot boxes to produce fictive totals that would uphold their relative importance
within the state party.[28]

The core provision was an educational test designed to exclude 90 percent of
black men of voting age. Further proposals put on the table for discussion were
riddled with mean-spirited exclusions, and tortured exceptions from the exclusions. An alternate property qualification would, it was hoped, "preserve the franchise to 5000 or 6000 illiterate whites," while admitting only 1,000 blacks.[29]
Booker T. Washington himself, accompanied by one of the few remaining black
state legislators, appealed directly to the Louisiana delegates to content themselves with class limitations on the franchise, rather than blatant proxies for race.
But he failed. Section 5 of Article 197 of the final document allowed all qualified

men who could testify that they had voted prior to January 1867—that is, prior to the congressional extension of the vote to black men—and their legitimate male heirs to register during the first nine months of 1898 and acquire a permanent right to vote, without meeting the literacy and property requirements otherwise introduced by the new constitution. Naturalized immigrants could also register during this period without meeting the new requirements.[30]

Up to the last minute, even the white-supremacist Senator McEnery thought Section 5 ill-advised, because it seemed so clearly in violation of the Fifteenth Amendment. Its design, the arguments made in its favor, and its likely consequences were unequivocally racial. But instead of dropping the clause, the convention tried to ensure that the rest of the disfranchising mechanisms—which were formally race-neutral—would remain in place even if the grandfather clause were to be ruled unconstitutional. Beneficiaries of the grandfather clause were required to claim it before September of 1898, after which it would no longer be available. Hence the courts would be "powerless to interfere with the successful inauguration of the plan."[31] They also secured the consequences of their actions by making individual disfranchisement unappealable: when Charles Soniat from New Orleans proposed that those denied registration should have the right of appeal to the courts, his motion failed.[32]

Governor Murphy Foster prided himself on the final text: "The white supremacy for which we have so long struggled at the cost of so much precious blood and treasure, is now crystallized into the Constitution as a fundamental part and parcel of that organic instrument."[33] An attorney who had participated in the convention reported to the Louisiana Bar Association without any apparent embarrassment that it had been the delicate task of the convention to "falsify the accepted teaching of history and roll back the wheels of political revolution without bloodshed; to take away the ballot from almost, if not quite, a majority of the voters in the state."[34] Kruttschnitt, the convention's chair, was equally candid, but more cynical. He explained that the convention would have preferred to have inscribed "universal white manhood suffrage, and the exclusion from the suffrage of every man with a trace of African blood in his veins. We could not do that, on account of the fifteenth amendment to the Constitution of the United States." They had, therefore, turned to what he believed the U.S. Supreme Court had recently

judged to be "permissible expedients." The result might be inelegant, he acknowledged, but "Doesn't it let the white man vote, and doesn't it stop the negro from
voting, and isn't that what we came here for?" The official journal of the proceedings of the convention noted that this declaration was met with applause.[35]

The *Washington Bee,* an African American weekly closely allied with Republicans of color in New Orleans, drew attention to the contrast between the language of freedom used to justify U.S. intervention in Cuba and the reality of vote
suppression in Louisiana. "While . . . the greatest of our commonwealths are voting in their State legislatures millions of money, with which to arm, equip and
mobilize State troops, in the event of a war, and while a great wave of sympathy is
sweeping across the entire geographical confines of the Republic for 'Cuba Libre',
in a great southern State, also swept by this same wave for free Cuba, political
chains are being forged for black men, the like of which have caused even South
Carolina and Mississippi to blush with envy."[36] Equal-rights activists in Washington, D.C., and their allies in New Orleans began to plan, discreetly, a judicial
challenge to the Louisiana Constitution as contrary to the Fourteenth and Fifteenth amendments. But time was against them. The registration offices in Louisiana were open every day during early 1898 to accommodate those men who
stepped forward under Article 197 to claim a permanent right to vote by invoking the grandfather and naturalization clauses. By September of 1898 qualifications would revert to the ostensibly color-blind literacy and property provisions,
which would be harder to challenge in court. Adding to this difficulty was the
timing of the next national election under the new rules, two years away, so no
plaintiff could be argued to have been excluded from a specific round of balloting
for federal office until then.[37]

The effects of constitutional disfranchisement were at once practical, symbolic,
and punitive, and they were designed to undercut alliances along and across class
lines—permanently. Gone was the time when sugar workers and farmers in St.
Mary Parish could elect a man like John J. Moore, who hoed in the cane for a living, so that he in turn could vote in the state legislature on civil rights and laborers' lien legislation, as had happened in the 1870s. Sugar workers lost even the
cold comfort of withholding support from white Republicans like Judge Taylor
Beattie, as voters in Lafourche Parish had done after Beattie's apparent complicity

in the 1887 Thibodaux massacre. Shortly after the imposition of the new rules, the total number of "colored" voters registered in Lafourche Parish fell to zero. The number in Terrebonne was 45. Not only would the Republican Party in Louisiana collapse completely, but the faint final hope of using the ballot to extract concessions from Democrats would fast disappear as well.[38]

On April 25, 1898, while the special Section 5 "permanent" registration books were still open in Louisiana, the United States Congress declared war on Spain. As the magnitude of the necessary mobilization became clear, the question of black military service arose with new intensity. African American Republican figures from Louisiana like Henry Demas and P. B. S. Pinchback, as well as grassroots organizers like Pierre Carmouche, reiterated their ability to recruit volunteers. Four regiments of black regulars in the U.S. Army, previously stationed on the western frontier, were sent to Tampa, Florida, and shipped out in mid-June to participate in the invasion of eastern Cuba. They would soon acquit themselves well in the battles of Las Guásimas and San Juan Hill, gaining a place in military lore—but no right to promotion to commissioned officer status in the regular army.[39]

In Kansas and Illinois the governors (a Populist and a Republican, respectively) opened recruitment of companies of state volunteers who would serve under black captains, and North Carolina did the same.[40] At a mass meeting in favor of black enlistment convened in New Orleans in early May, Henry Demas addressed an enthusiastic crowd generously estimated at 5,000, some of whom were Union veterans of the Civil War. But two major problems loomed. First, the existing mechanism for the enlistment of volunteers was the state militia, precisely the institution from which black men in Louisiana had been entirely excluded in the aftermath of 1877. There was little prospect that Governor Murphy Foster would reverse this ban. Second, even if federal mechanisms for recruitment were introduced, President McKinley had not yet committed himself to the commissioning of black officers from among any such volunteers. For many of the African American proponents of enlistment, the idea of black officers was an integral part of the campaign. But whatever the risks of trying to prove political manhood or leadership ability through warfare, it looked as though black volunteers in Louisiana might have nowhere to go to try the gamble.[41]

A solution was found in the medical science of the era, with the argument that black soldiers were particularly suitable for war in the tropics. There were two variants to the argument: a racialized version, in which black people were imagined (falsely) to be inherently resistant to yellow fever, and an environmental one (endorsed in the African American press), in which residents of the Gulf States were viewed as more likely to have been exposed to the illness and to have acquired immunities. The concept of "immune troops" emerged as one around which Republicans and Democrats could both rally, and in mid-May Congress authorized the president to raise as many as ten "immune regiments." In an opportunistic flicker of the old Republican ideal of black warriors, President McKinley now called on Louisiana to allow the formation in the state of black as well as white units, assuring Governor Foster that they would not be the state's responsibility. Colonels C. J. Crane and Duncan N. Hood, both white, arrived in New Orleans to sign up waiting volunteers.[42]

The response was immediate. The "Faith Cadets" assembled at their old headquarters in New Orleans, elected officers, and then offered their services in a body to Colonel Crane. They were mustered in on June 20, 1898, as Company A of the Ninth U.S. Volunteer Infantry. Other men of color from New Orleans followed suit. Henry O. Franklin, whose father had been driven out of Thibodaux following the massacre in 1887, became second lieutenant of Company C. Dr. Sterling Price Brown, the physician who had worked with black dockworkers, became first lieutenant in Company D. Lafayette Tharp, a labor leader who had struggled to prevent the racial split among the New Orleans longshoremen in 1894, worked with Colonel Crane to recruit soldiers to the Ninth Volunteers, and was appointed second lieutenant in Company E, where he acted briefly as chaplain of the regiment.[43]

Upriver in the sugar parish of Ascension and the town of Donaldsonville, the blacksmith Pierre Carmouche had already "neglected his business in order to enthuse his people and to instruct them as to their duties as defenders of the country." Dozens of men were persuaded. In early July Carmouche traveled downriver with his companions to New Orleans, where they were mustered in as Company L. In all, nine companies of black soldiers from Louisiana and three from Texas formed the three battalions of the Ninth Volunteers, while Colonel Hood recruited white men to the Second and Tenth Volunteers. The press reported on the encampments of "immunes" being set up on the banks of the Tchefuncta River north of Lake Ponchartrain, and noted that under the immune bill these soldiers were "not connected in any way with the state, and just as soon as the men arrive at the camping grounds the government will begin taking care of them."[44]

An acquaintance of Lieutenant Henry Franklin, Miss Stella A. E. Brazley, wrote him a poem that expressed her hopes for the regiment, and her interpretation of its mandate. Antonio Maceo, the martyred Cuban rebel general, was central to her vision: "Go! seek the spot where Maceo fell / And strike his slayers; spare them not." But Stella Brazley had an even larger view, one that embraced an idealized martial ancestry and the leaders of the Haitian Revolution:

> Ye scions of a warlike race,
>> Renew the prestige of your sires,
> And by your valor win the place
>> Where glory flames with radiant fires,
> With those great heroes, brave and pure,
> Men like Maceo, Toussaint L'Ouverture.[45]

This evocation of heroic assertion by black generals echoed a long romantic republican tradition among people of color in Louisiana, and could not have been further from Governor Foster's picture of what he had agreed to in permitting federal recruitment of "immunes" in the state.[46] Variants of these two visions would clash from the beginning to the end of the history of the black Louisiana regiment.

In the nineteenth century, volunteer companies of the U.S. Army generally served under captains of their own choosing. But if these black soldiers imagined that the men whom they elected, or those who had recruited them, would become their captains, they were mistaken. Under a federal ruling, a white man would be named as captain of each black company. The refusal to commission black captains in the immune regiments was a serious blow to the long-standing African American campaign of "no officers, no fight," and the men of the regiment struggled against its implications. At a mass public meeting, the recruits called for the elected captains to be commissioned, and letters written to the press drew attention to the humiliations and disrespect that the federal ruling entailed. Given the exigencies of military discipline, the predicament of the elected captains demoted to lieutenants is largely hidden from the official military record. But it is visible in telling silences in the regimental history and in the tense exchanges between captains, lieutenants, sergeants, and privates recorded in court-martial testimony.[47]

Serious strains were thus built right into the structure of command of the Ninth Volunteer Infantry. At the moment of mustering-in, Pierre Carmouche and his fellow volunteers—among them artisans and laborers from New Orleans and men from the sugar plantations around Donaldsonville—had to choose between giving up their hope of service or bending to the humiliating rule. The manuscript muster roll of Company L hints at the drama in an awkwardly worded paragraph marked by insertions and erasures: "The company was recruited at Donaldsonville, La. July 4, Lieut. Carmouche being largely instrumental, and traveled by rail from thence to New Orleans, July 8, 1898. Where it was filled up and organized by Cap. Coleman and Mustered into the service of the U.S. July 13." These inked lines substituted for the usual formula that attributed recruitment to the captain, and they made a fine distinction between "recruited at" and "organized by." Credit for the first went grudgingly to Carmouche, a man of color. But responsibility for "organization" was attributed to Willis Prague Coleman, a white man as punctilious in his insistence on racial deference as Carmouche was on the question of equal rights. (Later, in Cuba, Captain Coleman punched a black private from an Illinois unit who was, in his view, standing too close to him in the commissary and talking too loudly to the grocer. "Remember you are not holloring behind your G. dm'd nigger officers now, I'm a white man," Coleman allegedly said, before grabbing the man by the throat.)[48]

Even before the Ninth Infantry left for Cuba, tensions were visible both within the ranks and with the surrounding society. These black men with rifles stationed at Camp Corbin in the summer of 1898 were a walking challenge to Louisiana

Lieutenant Pierre Lacroix Carmouche, of Donaldsonville, Louisiana, in 1899. Carmouche, a blacksmith, initiated the recruitment of Company L of the Ninth U.S. Volunteer Infantry among African American men in Ascension Parish. The regiment was sent to garrison the town of San Luis in eastern Cuba during the first U.S. military occupation of the island.

Democrats' repudiation of black political power, and their presence reversed the disarming of prior black militia. Although in principle Louisiana's Democratic congressmen had supported the recruiting of immune regiments, it did not take long for the soldiers to crash against local white claims to deference—particularly deference to the police. In mid-August a soldier from the regiment was shot in downtown New Orleans by a policeman. Private Thomas Bazile, the black cook in Company H, evidently now thought the time for armed self-defense had arrived. If the victim had been white and the aggressor a black soldier, Bazile insisted, the assailant would have been made to answer for his actions. Perhaps unfamiliar with the gravity of the charge of mutiny in the ranks, Bazile apparently incited his fellow soldiers "to join the crowd that was gathering and go to the city and get the man that had killed their comrade and to bring him to camp." Over a hundred men gathered with their weapons to hear Bazile's words. But Second Lieutenant Lafayette Tharp, the black longshoreman who stood well over six feet tall, told Bazile to "hush" and ordered the men to stay put—which they did. According to Tharp, Bazile continued to insist "that he was a man and was willing to die that night." Luckily for Bazile, the unit was about to ship out, and no court martial was then sitting. By the time Bazile's case was heard two months later in Cuba, wide allowance would be made for his naiveté (Tharp had apparently told him he was "as green as grass"), and some clemency was granted because of his subsequent good conduct. He eventually got off with six months' imprisonment at hard labor and a fine.[49]

Lieutenant Tharp, for his part, was caught between his own aspirations for discipline and respect, on the one hand, and the restless new recruits he was supposed to train and control, on the other. A longtime activist on the New Orleans waterfront, Tharp was bitterly aware of what he described as the "spirit" of the "entire population of the city of New Orleans for the past twenty odd years," and seems to have feared the worst. As the unit was preparing to leave Camp Corbin, Tharp gave custody of his two children by his first marriage—Naomie Annie, age twelve, "now in the convent of the Sisters of the Holy Family," and Edwin Lafayette, age ten, "now in the Thomy Lafon's Boys' home"—to a local pastor, Reverend Isaac Hall. These children, educated in institutions created over the years by Creole activists, would remain there during Tharp's absence, though Reverend

Hall was authorized to place Edwin Lafayette "in Straight University or any other institution of learning as in his judgment he may deem to the best interest of the boy." Meanwhile their father, as a second lieutenant in Company H of the Ninth Infantry, would try to demonstrate leadership and good judgment in a deeply contradictory situation. Tharp was not alone in his struggle between optimism and pessimism: the notary who traveled out to the camp on August 2, 1898, to record the custody document was Louis A. Martinet, the attorney who had assisted in bringing *Plessy v. Ferguson* to the U.S. Supreme Court and then closed his newspaper in despair after its defeat.[50]

Ten days later, just as the Ninth Volunteers were about to ship out for Cuba, the Spanish government accepted the peace protocols offered by the United States. As of August 12, there was no longer any clear enemy to fight except yellow fever. The Louisiana volunteers would be sent to join the occupation of the eastern provinces, which were now ravaged by disease and starvation. The volunteers' formal march down Esplanade in New Orleans to the troop transports was nonetheless an occasion for celebration, and black citizens lined the streets to wish them well. For Lieutenant Carmouche, the journey across the Gulf of Mexico was also an inspiration. The grandson of a woman born in slavery, and long an admirer of Caribbean freedom struggles, he could now report home to his family that he had seen with his own eyes what his wife described as "the Island of Hayti the land of Toussaint Louverture."[51]

The local population of Santiago de Cuba had been astonished as forty-two merchant ships loaded with supplies for U.S. soldiers steamed into Santiago harbor in the days following the Spanish surrender there. But what were they to make of the fresh arrivals of soldiers, now that the war was over? The comportment of the U.S. troops in the city of Santiago had already caused considerable alarm, and now more were on the way. The English-language press in Santiago, moreover, predicted the worst about the incoming "Immunes."[52]

The first duty of the Ninth Volunteers was to join the camp at San Juan Hill, and soon they were attending to the sick and wounded there. By late August the fantasy of black immunity had been shattered, and the regiment was felled by fever. Initially too weakened to proceed to their next posting, by September 19 the volunteers had recovered sufficiently to take the train to San Luis, twenty-five miles inland. With troop mortality in Santiago at horrendous levels, the high command thought it safest to garrison the new arrivals in upland communities. San Luis was the eastern province's second-largest town, located across the Boniato ridge, in a rich sugar-growing valley. It was also near the family home of General Antonio Maceo, a hero to thousands of Cubans and a model for African American activists, including Lieutenant Pierre L. Carmouche.[53]

The majority of San Luis's 11,000 residents were categorized by the census as black or mixed. One soldier from the Kansas regiment stationed there wrote, "I am convinced that these people are of our Negro race, although they cannot speak the English language, but they have the complexion of our race." A delegation of officers from the black U.S. regiments visited the Maceo family to pay their respects, and spoke with his sisters, who were apparently now eking out a living by doing laundry for the occupation forces. Captain William Coston, chaplain of the Louisiana unit, also wrote feelingly of the Maceo family and their sacrifices. Coston pronounced himself much impressed by the Cuban population of the towns of San Luis and neighboring Songo, finding them to be extraordinarily hospitable. A Kansas infantryman reported, "These people treat us as best they can and they do everything to make friends with us."[54]

The soldiers' role had certain rewards. Several of the black volunteers in Santiago wrote home with pride at being "master" of the situation, for they had refused attempts by white American civilians, including a local hotel keeper, to draw the color line in Cuba. This sentiment was shared by some of the black regulars who had served at San Juan Hill. John E. Lewis of the Tenth Cavalry later wrote, "Give me Cuba rather than any section of the South that I have ever been in, and I hardly know of one Southern state that I have not been in. Here . . . a man is a man for what he is worth. The great Cuban, Gen. Rabbi (a Negro), stopped over on his way from Bayamo to Havana, Cuba, and it was surprising how the Cubans turned out to do homage to that black Cuban general. It was the best of people who turned out. There was no color line drawn there."[55]

Daily life in camp, however, was noticeably less stirring. In a letter home, three privates from the Eighth Illinois Infantry gave a description of their routine that captured something of the oddness of the situation: "When the men leave the barracks, they walk down to the brook and wash, and go around the Cuban houses. You sit by the door and the family sits around in a circle, and there you are. You can't understand them, nor they you."[56] For Chaplain Coston, however, a spiritual connection did not necessarily require a shared language. He reported optimistically that local residents had joined the troops for open-air church services. He was also pleased to officiate at several weddings of U.S. soldiers with Cuban brides.[57]

The region of San Luis was itself in the midst of upheaval. General Henry W. Lawton and General Leonard Wood, successive U.S. commanders of the Department of Santiago, issued orders down in the city, while Cuban soldiers remained armed in the hills. In principle, foraging was to halt now that hostilities had ended, but the U.S. authorities decreed that no rations were to be issued to the Cuban soldiers. Cuban general Agustín Cebreco, a man of color from the nearby town of Cobre, wrote urgently to General Máximo Gómez that this put the men under his command in an impossible situation, and he doubted that a strict regard for private property rights was called for under the circumstances.[58] Shortly thereafter, an Assembly of Cuban delegates was convened by the rebel forces in Santa Cruz del Sur (Camagüey) to try to shape the island's political future. The formal Assembly received little respect from the U.S. command, but activists across the island continued to press for Cuban autonomy in local affairs. On November 1, 1898, a group of Cuban proprietors and artisans in San Luis addressed a bold letter to the man they addressed as "Citizen General Leonard Wood." They explained that the local municipal judge—presumably a holdover from the colonial era—was unsuited to his job. These residents had thus constituted themselves as a steering committee, choosing a Cuban rebel officer, José Alayo y Torres, to replace the unsatisfactory judge. Their letter was to inform Wood of the committee's actions and to secure his approval. They signed their missive "Patria y Libertad" (Homeland and Liberty), and proceeded on the assumption (correct, as it turned out) that despite the U.S. assertion of the right to make such appointments, Wood had better things to do than try to reverse their choice.[59]

General Wood, meanwhile, was putting together an urban police force and a provincial Rural Guard, aiming to kill two birds with one stone: provide employment to selected rebel soldiers while establishing a local armed force under his direct orders to patrol the countryside. It was not quite clear who the targets of the Rural Guard would be—criminals, bandits, unruly rebel soldiers, or any presumed lawbreakers of their choosing. To head the force in Santiago, Wood chose an unlikely veteran: a Spaniard named Rafael Ferrer who had asserted the rank of lieutenant in the rebel forces in 1897, but had never been formally commissioned. (It seems possible, given his birthplace, late recruitment date, and lack of a formal rebel commission, that Ferrer had been a deserter from the Spanish Army, but the record is silent on this.) Ferrer and his men set up camp on November 4 on the Santa Ursula plantation east of the city of Santiago. Almost immediately the owner expressed outrage at what he saw as their taking of his property and Ferrer's abuse of his employees.[60]

On November 11, 1898, this newly formed Rural Guard set off to patrol the northern districts of the Santiago region, including the area occupied by the Ninth U.S. Volunteers.[61] On November 14, Ferrer and his men turned up at the sugar house of the Norma plantation, which was being used as a dining area for the black Louisiana soldiers. Something happened that afternoon in the mess hall that would reverberate from San Luis to Santiago to New Orleans and back. Louisiana newspapers later said that a drunken black U.S. soldier had stolen a pig, and resisted arrest by a Cuban policeman. But this version is not corroborated by the regimental records, which make no reference to any pig, or by early reports from the officers in command, who reported that Private Willie Clark of the Ninth Volunteers had been attacked unprovoked and killed by Lieutenant Ferrer of the Rural Guard. Whatever the story of the initial conflict, the aftermath echoed Thomas Bazile's earlier call to arms, back in the camp at New Orleans. "Enraged and unknown persons"—presumably soldiers from Clark's regiment—came to the sugar house and confronted the Rural Guard. Lieutenant Ferrer and two other guardsmen were killed, along with the owner of the plantation store and his son.[62] A Cuban child was caught in the crossfire and several of the U.S. soldiers were wounded as well. General Leonard Wood, apprehensive of the consequences of the confrontation, hastened to San Luis.

There were as many contradictory versions of the incident as there were reputations to protect and axes to grind. The chaplain of the Ninth Volunteers—who was not with the unit at the time—later portrayed it all as a tragedy arising from a misunderstanding. Colonel John R. Marshall of the Illinois regiment in San Luis reported, following an inquiry, that Lieutenant Ferrer had shot Private Willie Clark without provocation. General Wood, in contrast, concluded that the incident was entirely the fault of the black U.S. soldiers—but also entirely unforeseeable, hence not *his* fault. An account published in Havana framed it as black U.S. soldiers, whom the reporter characterized as "a horde of ferocious savages," versus Cubans, omitting the fact that Lieutenant Ferrer was a Spaniard. Accounts published in the New Orleans press treated it as a drunken brawl—and believed Democrats' denunciations of black recruitment thus justified. Two members of the Ninth Volunteers were confined in prison in Santiago and several months later were tried by a military court. Major Duncan B. Harrison, who commanded a battalion of the unit, acted as defense counsel, and they were acquitted.[63]

There is no longer any means by which to disentangle these stories in order to figure out to what extent the shootout was an echo of the earlier confrontations between black soldiers and white policemen in New Orleans, to what extent it was inflected with tensions between Cubans and the occupiers, and to what extent it was an alcohol-induced argument. It does seem that in camp in San Luis that November, things were seriously awry. The strategy of imposing on each volunteer company a white captain who was at the very least unfamiliar with, and at worst utterly contemptuous of, the men under his command, contributed to indiscipline—not exactly by provoking mutiny, but by undermining the respect and reciprocity on which a volunteer unit relies. Tension had been building for months between overbearing white captains and restless, assertive black lieutenants.[64]

In the days that followed, along with a flurry of summary courts martial of privates, Captain W. A. Dayton of Company D, one of the white Louisiana company commanders, was ordered into confinement. The depth of Dayton's own indiscipline is suggested by the order sent to the Officer of the Day at San Luis on November 29:

> The regimental commander directs that you remove from Capt. Dayton's tent all of his weapons, then every intoxicating drink found there, then place a sentinel there, a reliable man; with instructions to allow no weapon or intoxicating liquor to be

given to Capt. Dayton, to allow no civilian to enter his tent except in your presence, and to report promptly to you, any attempt of Capt. Dayton's to leave his
tent, except to go to the water closet. You will read these instructions to Capt.
Dayton as soon as he can understand you.

Captain Dayton, availing himself of the privileges granted to commissioned officers in the volunteer units, resigned shortly thereafter. Command of the company was taken over by Lieutenant Sterling Price Brown, the black physician who
had worked for years with New Orleans dockworkers.[65]

Colonel Crane tried to keep the soldiers in line and out of further contact with
Cuban civilians. He prohibited the sale of rum and sugar cane to the soldiers and
ordered Cuban vendors away from the camp. General Wood, who held that
Ferrer had fired in self-defense, appointed a new head of the Rural Guard and ordered the U.S. troops to break camp and reestablish themselves several miles outside of town. Within a few weeks steps were being taken to shift units out of San
Luis altogether. Wood clearly wanted the incident forgotten, and it has indeed
proved nearly impossible to excavate details from the military records. For soldiers of the Ninth Volunteers, however, it was a watershed event, still recalled
years later. In a pension request filed in 1901, Lieutenant Lafayette Tharp identified the place and time of his illness during his military service as "Camp Acheva,
three and a half miles north of St. Louis, Cuba in the third camp in the mountain
after the riot at the sugar house."[66]

The Democratic press in the United States gave incidents of this kind a racial
reading, linking black disorder to black assertion. The *Times-Democrat* of New Orleans explained to its readers that "these regiments have been enjoying social
equality in the island, where a large proportion of the population is of negro or of
mixed blood, and where that race line which the Anglo-Saxon insists on does not
exist. Every one of these men will come back filled with the idea that he can play
this social equality racket here, as well as at Santiago." This reference to "social
equality" as a "racket" reflected a long-standing campaign by white-supremacist
publicists to describe the civil and political equality sought by black activists as
something called "social equality," which could in turn evoke specters of forced
association and race mixing. This discursive maneuver had served them well in the

recently decided *Plessy v. Ferguson,* transforming what the 1868 Louisiana Constitution had described as a "public right" of equal access to public conveyances into an ominous assertion of "social equality." The court's rejection of Plessy's claim could thus seem justified to those who thought "social equality" utterly undesirable, those who thought it regrettably unattainable, and those who thought it constitutionally unreachable. And once "social equality" edged out "civil equality" or "public rights" as a descriptor of what was at stake, its negative aura could be expanded further to swallow up rights that even a few years earlier would have been thought constitutionally guaranteed.[67]

Newspapers like the *Washington Bee* refused this characterization of events; they insisted that it was Cuba that was menaced by the extension of racism and an explicit color line from the United States.[68] African American journalists thus increasingly framed the question of Cuba in didactic terms, linking the question of political rights at home and abroad. Would the service of black soldiers secure them against disfranchisement in the United States? And what system of government, with what basis in social and racial distinctions, would the United States try to create in the island of Cuba, using the authority that would soon be confirmed by the Treaty of Paris? U.S. intentions concerning the long-term status of the island were unclear, and even short-term strategies were not yet thought through. The boundaries of citizenship—indeed, even the existence of Cuban citizenship—remained to be defined.

On January 1, 1899, de facto intervention gave way to formal U.S. rule as President McKinley named General John R. Brooke as military governor of Cuba. Having justified the occupation as an apprenticeship in democratic practice, the Republican administration in Washington would now have to decide what principles of suffrage to apply to Cuba, where no constraints of federalism stood in the way of promulgating egalitarian electoral rules if the U.S. government chose to do so. There was also a large gap between the project of U.S.-supervised pacification and the reality of postwar life in the countryside. The occupying U.S. Army was stretched thin, and its appointed proxy, the Rural Guard, was only loosely under U.S. control. Many civilians had come out of the Spanish "reconcentration" camps physically weak and dependent on relief supplies. Former rebels, still armed, searched for the means to survive and reintegrate themselves into productive life.[69] In smaller towns outside the reach of U.S. forces, Cuban rebels had often stepped in to take up authority quite directly. From Cienfuegos in central Cuba the Boston-born planter Edwin Atkins reported with unease that insurgents "under negro officers" were in power in the nearby town of Arimao. Everything remained uncertain. The U.S. government would soon offer Cuban soldiers $75 each to turn in their weapons, but many found this an undignified proceeding. Others bristled at the way U.S. officers berated Cubans and disparaged their sense of civic duty.[70]

Cubans of African descent, in particular, had good reason to expect that the postcolonial order should be different from its predecessor. They sought both symbolic and substantive evidence that the expulsion of Spain would bring an end to invidious racial distinctions. Their acts and gestures, however, disconcerted those U.S. observers for whom a color line was a given. When the Cuban general Máximo Gómez made a visit to Cienfuegos in February of 1899, he was welcomed by North American and Cuban officials, lodged in the home of a millionaire planter, and fêted in an exuberant procession. "One dignified officer was seen marching with a negress on his arm (so the boys said) and everything was mixed," wrote Edwin Atkins. Along the railway lines, insurgent forces of the region assembled to greet Gómez, and people of color were in the majority. Atkins was scornful of this display and suspected that Gómez was trying to stir up sentiment in favor of independence. Be that as it may, those who lined the tracks were showing their sense that they too were legitimate participants in public culture.[71]

Added to these assertions of civic equality came urgent claims to resources. Already in 1898, Cuban rebel soldiers had sought to take possession of unused farmland in eastern Cuba—and even General Wood thought their claims might well be morally justifiable. By May 1899 families in the central province of Santa Clara were reported to be returning to the countryside and beginning to plant gardens. Those who were able to grow tobacco themselves, or work on shares on tobacco farms, could hope to obtain some ready money. Farming, however, required tools and animals, both of which were scarce. General James Wilson, governor of Matanzas and Santa Clara provinces, proposed to distribute agricultural implements and seeds to rural Cubans; he also intimated that an expanded suffrage for the upcoming municipal elections might be more appropriate than a restrictive one. But Governor Brooke, who thought the provision of tools and credit a step toward "pauperism," rejected these proposals.[72]

The interests of "pacification" nonetheless required that Governor Brooke attend to at least some of the claims of veterans of the Cuban rebel army. Back pay had been promised to them for their time of service, and this question would absorb months of debate and millions of dollars. Meanwhile, a host of smaller but vital questions pressed in on the military government. Who, for example, could rightfully assert ownership of the horses that rebel soldiers had commandeered during the war? Horses had long been both a symbol and a tool of mobility and autonomy, and many veterans were in possession of horses captured in raids or contributed by sympathizers for the purpose of the fight against Spain. Defending established property rights sounded like an appropriate goal to the occupiers, but how were such rights to be defined in the aftermath of a war in which soldiers had foraged for mounts and supplies?

Brooke seems quickly to have realized that it would be unwise to try to dismount men who viewed themselves as liberators of their nation. In June of 1899 he issued an order that authorized soldiers, on credible oral testimony by two witnesses that a horse had been in the soldier's possession prior to the armistice, to inscribe the animal in the local livestock registry. This was, in fact, quite a departure from the standard requirement of continuity of title, and a few months later Brooke backtracked, ruling that such registration would establish ownership only against other oral claims, not if someone else held written title to the animal. But the procedure had been established, and local municipalities appeared to be sympathetic: the city council in Cienfuegos had already made a similar ruling, encompassing not just horses but "animals" more generally.[73]

Although Brooke's intent seems to have been purely pragmatic, others grasped the possible implications of this new mode of defining ownership. A conservative Cuban politician, Rafael Martínez Ortiz, recalled Brooke's order bitterly. "It was a bad decree, which set a terrible precedent," the cause of general unpleasantness and lack of confidence. Even more important, he believed, it had tended to lead the mass of people "without culture" astray, encouraging a mistaken understanding of morality and justice.[74] In his angry denunciation, Martínez Ortiz touched on a crucial link between politics and property. Rural people, including former slaves and their descendants, were well aware that their autonomy depended in large measure on their access to resources, from the horse they rode to the mule that could carry produce to market. Rural people might also believe that across years of customary use some pigs, houses, or garden plots had become the property of themselves and their kin—though prewar legal title to those resources might be held by planters or urban investors. In the eastern regions, where there had long been abundant public land (tierra realenga), similar claims could be made for the right to settle on such land. But to titleholders, any step that placed a moral claim based on merit or labor above a written claim based on past title could seem a threat to the social order, even if its intent was merely to formalize a fait accompli.

Rural Cubans pressed their claims to such resources in part because the prospects for those who had nothing to sell but their labor were generally grim. During the halting postwar reconstruction, laborers on the sugar plantations earned only 60 to 80 cents a day, without food. Frederick Folz, an officer of the U.S. occupation forces, concluded that "the wages . . . are not sufficient to enable a man to support a family and save enough to buy the yoke of oxen, cart, plow and pony, necessary to his independence." He reported that "the laborers are not even allowed to cultivate gardens as they would then spend less of their wages at the Owner's Store; on other estates they are given land and encouraged to an independence which however stops just short of selling them the land." A laborer might occupy land rent free "in consideration of his being available for employment on an Ingenio," or farm on shares, or occasionally pay a small rent. "The owners naturally wish to keep the reins in their own hands, and to be able to send off people whom they do not find desirable tenants or useful hands." Even under these constraints, workers made their preferences felt. Plantations with a reputation for good treatment were reportedly able to hire good laborers, "while those Ingenios where the slave idea has governed are finding the supply short."[75]

Those who refused to submit to the "slave idea" of management included both white and black workers. Fifteen years after emancipation, and following decades of immigration of Spanish laborers and the incorporation of white Cubans, the rural wage labor force was a thoroughly cross-racial body. Various racial biases could be seen in hiring, with white men often favored for mill work and given preferential access to better housing, but the small farming sector, the field work crews, and the waterfronts were multiracial. Thousands of white men worked as cane cutters alongside black and *mulato* men, as well as a smaller number of black women. An image of white and black standing shoulder to shoulder, or working side by side, was often literal rather than merely metaphorical, and nowhere more so than in the ranks of the veterans of the Cuban Liberation Army and in the cane fields.

The moment when groups of Cuban veterans came home provided an opportunity to secure a foothold that might resist later efforts at expulsion. The process is perhaps best understood through a close-up lens: at the edge of Soledad plantation, there lay a large expanse of burned-over land in the old *corral* (municipal grazing grant) of San Antón. An urban contractor and businessman named Antonio Ravella held title to at least fifty of the acres. Ravella and his wife died in Cienfuegos during the war, and the heirs, including their daughter María, did not immediately settle the estate. Shortly after the war the black veteran Cayetano Quesada, his father Alejandro Quesada, and his white comrade-in-arms Zacarías González apparently moved onto the land and began planting. Their initiative combined what may have been a customary right to a garden plot enjoyed by the former slave Alejandro Quesada with a patriotic claim to unused land made by the veterans. These claims, however, were not at this point channeled through the legal system, which was in considerable disarray, and would in any event have been unlikely to acknowledge them. But the veterans' de facto possession of the land did generate an indirect written record: when, in 1901, the Soledad plantation sought to expand in this direction by purchasing 150 acres from María Ravella, she had to hold back two of the component lots because they were "held improperly by other persons." She promised to expel the squatters, who presumably included Cayetano Quesada and others, but either she did not try or she did not succeed.[76]

Cuban veterans who moved onto land in this way generally did so quietly, counting on local support and legal inertia to work to their benefit. Their claims, however, were in some sense sheltered by the more open and public campaigns for universal manhood suffrage and for back pay for veterans, both of which rested on an implicit theory of citizenship and the debt owed to patriots. Claims made by women might seem at first glance to fit uneasily within this construct. But again, a close-up view shows the strategy of assertion and alliance at work. The former slave Gregoria Quesada lived in a working-class neighborhood near the public fountain in the city of Cienfuegos, and had acquired several small pieces of land in the foothills town of La Sierra. Meanwhile, one of her family's assets, a mule marked with a brand "like three tubes," remained back at the Santa Rosalía plantation, where Gregoria Quesada had been held as a *patrocinada* in the 1880s. After the war ended, Gregoria Quesada approached the administrator and then the overseer of Santa Rosalía to try to retrieve the mule. The overseer, Constantino Pérez, told her that no one could remove an animal from the plantation without written permission.[77]

Meanwhile, another former slave from Santa Rosalía, Ciriaco Quesada, had made his way back home following his service in the rebel army. The surviving records do not indicate whether he and Gregoria Quesada were kin, but they seem to have become allies. As a veteran, Ciriaco Quesada had certain resources that Gregoria Quesada did not. He may well have taken advantage of Governor Brooke's decree in the same month of June 1899 to inscribe a horse in the property register in nearby Arimao. As the struggle over Gregoria's mule unfolded, this same decree suggested a new tactic that the two former slaves could use to counter the power of the overseer and the administrator. On August 17, 1899, Ciriaco Quesada and his brother Paulino went to Santa Rosalía to inquire about Gregoria's mule. The overseer stood on ceremony: he would not yield the mule without a written order from Manuel García Blanco, the administrator, who lived in town in Cienfuegos. Indeed, the overseer seems to have been rather proud of himself; he subsequently reported the confrontation, and his own firmness, in a letter to the administrator.[78]

The general understanding concerning veterans' horses, however, could yield a written text about the mule, which in turn could be deployed against the overseer. Ciriaco Quesada apparently proceeded to the town of Arimao and obtained a written order from the mayor, certifying that the mule was inscribed in the property register under Ciriaco Quesada's name and was therefore to be turned over to him. The veteran Francisco Álvarez Oliva was now serving in Arimao as a sergeant in the Rural Guard, and was willing to lend a hand to his former comrade-in-arms. The two of them showed up at the plantation first thing the next morning and asked to see Constantino Pérez, the overseer. Pérez seems to have become a bit disconcerted, and blustered that the inscription in the property register was of no consequence—Ciriaco Quesada could have registered all the cattle on the estate in his name in Arimao, and that would not change anything. The sergeant then made it clear that he would, if necessary, go get the mule himself. Pérez no longer had much choice, and sent for an employee to bring the animal. Sergeant Álvarez Oliva proffered a carefully written receipt, signed with a flourish, and he and Ciriaco Quesada departed with the mule. The overseer was reduced to fuming in a letter to the administrator that they should try to collect from Ciriaco Quesada for the three years' worth of grass that the mule had eaten on the estate—if only to make the point that Ciriaco Quesada should never have brought the mayor of Arimao into the dispute.[79]

The problem for local elites and for the U.S. occupation government was potentially acute. If some local mayors, municipal councils, and rural guardsmen provided aid and comfort to veterans seeking to transform de facto possession of a horse into written title, or a customary claim to a mule into ownership, how was one to draw a secure line around existing rights of property? Relatively modest one-time concessions could expand into a disruptive redistribution unless municipal authority, in towns large and small, was vested in the hands of those who shared a more restrictive notion of entitlement to property and a greater deference to U.S. guidelines. Only then could one be sure that the authorities would promulgate and enforce an appropriate and property-based concept of what the politician Rafael Martínez Ortiz had called "the moral and the just."

This implicit link between questions of property and questions of governance, however, seems to have remained largely unspoken on both sides. Even conservative figures like Martínez Ortiz refrained from openly repudiating the moral claim of veterans to some kind of material gratitude from the nation, and in turn no veterans' leader raised the possibility of a full-scale land reform. To the extent that property rights were discussed publicly, attention focused on the demarcation

In August of 1899, Sergeant Francisco Álvarez Oliva, who had joined the Cuban Rural Guard after serving in the Liberation Army, assisted the former slave Ciriaco Quesada in a dispute over a mule. Together the two veterans retrieved the mule, leaving this receipt for the plantation administrator.

of *haciendas comuneras,* undivided lands held by multiple owners as tenants-in-common. Although facilitating subdivision and sale of these *haciendas* was a major concern of investors, few participants in the debate openly favored allowing settlement by *non*-titleholders. The conviction that veterans were entitled to plant burned-over or abandoned land and make it their own seems primarily to have found expression in local actions and implicit understandings among neighbors and veterans themselves, rather than on the surface of public debate.[80]

The claims of citizens, however, had expanded to encompass a multitude of assertions, written and oral, formal and informal, material and political. In sugar towns like Lajas and Cruces, women and men born into slavery and freed in the 1880s often managed to put together 50 pesos or more to buy a house lot in town. A few, like Gregoria Quesada, had purchased small farms in the foothills. Other changes in landholding patterns and practices, like Cayetano Quesada's settlement of a substantial burned-over tract, crept in largely unrecorded, but reflected a pattern of measured challenge and negotiation. Each achievement of a foothold on the land increased by a perceptible margin the ability of a rural worker to have some say in the terms of his or her wage employment. And each successful local assertion could potentially be accompanied by a claim of voice in public affairs as well.[81]

In December of 1899, General Leonard Wood took over from General Brooke as U.S. military governor of Cuba. In the view of Secretary of War Elihu Root, the time had come to move away from military improvisation and to put more robust structures of indirect rule into place. Both Secretary Root and Governor Wood were Republicans, notionally bound by their own party's endorsement of black suffrage and by its criticism of the new disfranchising constitutions in the southern states. But like the southern disfranchisers, they portrayed voting as a privilege, not a right. And that construction could open the door to multiple ethnic, class, or racial limitations. General Wood was unapologetic about his enthusiasm for restrictions: "The individual who on reaching twenty-one has not shown enough energy to accumulate $250, nor to have learned to read and write, nor to have defended his country in a state of war, is a social element unworthy to be counted on for collective purposes. Let him not vote!"[82]

Lest anyone miss the racial implications of such a policy in a society only fifteen years removed from chattel slavery, Secretary of War Root framed the choice clearly: "When the history of the new Cuba comes to be written the establishment of popular self-government, based on a limited suffrage, excluding so great a proportion of the elements which have brought ruin to Haiti and San Domingo, will be regarded as an event of the first importance." The coded reference to race was unmistakable: the words "Santo Domingo" had long conveyed to many white ears the overtones of "black peril," dating back to the eighteenth century. And at this turn of the nineteenth to the twentieth century both Haiti and the Dominican Republic were governed by presidents of African descent.[83]

The U.S. occupation government outlined qualifications for voters at the upcoming municipal elections in Cuba that restricted the vote to males over the age of twenty-one who were either literate, property-holding, or veterans of the Cuban Liberation Army. Each component was exigently defined: literacy meant the ability to read *and* write; property had to be of the value of two hundred and fifty dollars, American gold; service in the Cuban Liberation Army had to be documented with evidence of honorable discharge. The decree explicitly extended voting rights to residents of Cuba who had been born in Spain, as long as they had not made a formal declaration of allegiance to the Spanish crown. The inclusion of those born in Spain expanded the white electorate substantially, while the silence concerning those born in Africa or China quietly reduced the ranks of voters who had been slaves or indentured workers.[84]

In the postwar census taken under U.S. supervision, some 26,000 male citizens of color over the age of twenty-one were counted as able to read and write. These men would be eligible to vote, as long as the registrars' criteria were no more exacting than those of the census-takers. But three times as many men of color over twenty-one could *not* read and write (78,000), and another 2,000 could read but not write. Of these 80,000 men, only those who owned substantial property or could prove honorable discharge from the army would have the right to vote. Under these rules, the Cuban municipal elections would see more voters of color than any recent Louisiana election, but a disproportionate number of people of color would still be excluded.[85]

Claims to public voice and standing, once successfully asserted, are nonetheless difficult to roll back. Ciriaco Quesada had stood his ground in the face of the overseer at Santa Rosalía and helped reclaim the contested mule. Cayetano Quesada had lost his horse, appropriated by a superior officer, but had cleared and planted new land to cultivate for his family. Both men saw themselves as veterans, as did their neighbors.[86] Would they step back from claiming the right to vote, simply because their names did not figure on the rolls of those formally mustered out of the army in 1898? In Cuba as in Louisiana, the question of the boundaries and content of citizenship now hung in the air as both a practical and a constitutional question, one whose resolution would shape the contours of public life in the early twentieth century.

CHAPTER SEVEN

The Right to Have Rights

1901–1905

The Constitution, if we are honorable, will protect universal suffrage.

> José B. Alemán, debate in the Cuban Constitutional Convention,
>
> January 30, 1901

AS THE TWENTIETH CENTURY OPENED, THE ABILITY OF FORMER SLAVES and their descendants to participate in political life was gravely at risk on both sides of the Gulf of Mexico. The Louisiana Constitutional Convention of 1898 had brushed all challenges aside, hammered home the last measures, and handed its disfranchising text to a legislature accountable only to an already drastically reduced electorate. Seeing no need to submit the new constitution to a popular vote on ratification, legislators simply promulgated it as law. In Cuba, the U.S. occupation government, though led by northern Republicans rather than by southern Democrats, showed a parallel disregard for the concerns of participation and process. Imagining themselves able to design a polity from scratch, the occupying authorities tried to exclude those from whom they might expect trouble, and drafted a highly restrictive set of rules for the June 1900 municipal elections in Cuba. The disfranchising schemes for Cuba, however, lasted little more than a year, while those of Louisiana would remain largely intact for more than half a century.

Permanent disfranchisement, however, was not quite a fait accompli in Louisiana in 1900. As a result of the statutory restrictions of 1896, registration figures had shown 74,133 white voters and 12,902 colored voters in the state in January 1898. With the 1898 constitution, the number of white voters was pumped back up, and that of colored voters crushed. As of March 1900, the state's registration books held 125,437 white voters and just 5,320 colored voters. The formal equilibrium of the 1880s and the statutorily imposed disequilibrium of the 1890s had given way to avalanche.[1] But the state still held a substantial number of African American activists and stubborn white Republicans, and the courts had yet to rule on the convention's brazen challenge to the Fifteenth Amendment. A coalition of men and women of what might be termed "neo-abolitionist" convictions was organizing in Washington, D.C., to try to stop the disfranchising process across the South. The egregious Louisiana Constitution, whose voter eligibility rules were unequivocally racial in intent and in effect, seemed a likely target.

The first potential judicial challenge came to hand early in 1900. A. L. Gusman, a white attorney in New Orleans, had taken on the case of a man named Samuel Wright who had been sentenced to death for assault with intent to commit rape. Gusman decided to challenge Wright's indictment by denying the legitimacy of the unratified Louisiana Constitution of 1898, and thus of the Jefferson Parish grand jury that had issued the indictment, because the convening of a twelve-member grand jury violated the prior Louisiana Constitution of 1879, which called for a sixteen-member grand jury. Gusman argued that the "so-called Constitution of 1898" was illegitimate. He recalled that the state's voters had rebuffed the legislature's earlier efforts to achieve disfranchisement through amendments to the 1879 constitution. The imposition of new qualifications through statute, rather than through constitutional amendment and ratification, therefore constituted a violation both of Louisiana's 1879 constitution and of the federal guarantee of due process, while undermining the principle of popular sovereignty itself and the U.S. Constitution's Article 4 guarantee to each state of a republican form of government. Gusman quoted the U.S. Supreme Court as having ruled that "suffrage once granted will be protected. He who has it can *only* be deprived of it by due process of law." Faced with this onslaught of constitutional argumentation, Sheriff Lucien Marrero of Jefferson Parish—a Confederate veteran and former Democratic state senator—asked that the case be dismissed on the grounds that the federal court had no jurisdiction and the plaintiff no cause of action. Accepting the sheriff's plea, and apparently characterizing portions of Gusman's argument as a "political question" over which Congress alone had jurisdiction, the Circuit Court ruled in favor of Marrero on February 3, 1900, clearing the way for Wright to be executed.[2]

On February 19, 1900, Gusman initiated an appeal to the U.S. Supreme Court, and Sheriff Marrero consigned Wright to the state penitentiary to be put to hard labor. By this point, familiar figures in the world of African American activism were beginning to rally to this campaign, despite their uneasiness at using a defendant in a criminal assault case to advance their argument for equal access to suffrage. James Lewis, a black Union veteran, stood bond for Gusman's appeal in February. Jesse Lawson, a black attorney in Washington, D.C., helped to coordinate the New Orleans and Washington ends of the campaign, lining up a white lawyer from a distinguished abolitionist family, Arthur Alexis Birney, to assist in preparing the case and arguing it before the U.S. Supreme Court. Behind Lawson was the discreet support of Booker T. Washington, whose carefully worded and accommodating public statements were accompanied by private maneuvering to promote legal challenges to disfranchisement.[3]

The case reached the U.S. Supreme Court in December of 1900. Birney and Gusman argued that the restricted electorate under which the Louisiana Constitutional Convention was convened, compounded by the failure of the state to submit the constitution for ratification, violated the principles of popular sovereignty and constituted a breach of "the pledge given in the act of reconstruction" by which Louisiana had been readmitted to the Union. In the process "a large majority of the legal voters of the State have been, through the anomaly of conventional sovereignty, eliminated from the electorate of the State, and over 190,000 native-born Americans placed in the thralls of political bondage, and made aliens in the land of their nativity and exiles in their own homes." Samuel Wright could have no redress in Louisiana state courts operating under an invalid constitution, whose proceedings the attorneys characterized as "insurrectionary, revolutionary, usurpative and unconstitutional."[4]

The U.S. Supreme Court disposed of the matter in short order in January of 1901. Professing to be unaware of what kind of case this could be said to be, since the appellants had not used the recognized legal procedure of habeas corpus, they ruled that Gusman, as a "private person," whatever his "friendship or sympathy" for the prisoner, or his "concern . . . as to the enforcement of unconstitutional laws" had no standing to bring such a case. The Court dismissed the appeal, and both Samuel Wright and the Louisiana Constitution of 1898 were left to their fates. Five years after *Plessy v. Ferguson,* the Court ignored the argument about the legitimacy of Louisiana's constitution and spoke not a word about race.[5]

Seeking a better case and a more direct target, activists in Washington and New Orleans announced in May of 1901 that the National Afro-American Council was taking steps to test directly the validity of the "grandfather clause" of the Louisiana Constitution. On July 10, 1901, David J. Ryanes, a former slave born in Tennessee and long a registered voter in New Orleans, presented himself to the supervisor of registration for the parish of Orleans, Jeremiah Gleason. Gleason blocked Ryanes from registering, invoking Article 197 of the 1898 constitution, which permitted registration only by those who could meet property or educational requirements and those who had entered their names during 1898 on the "permanent" registration list open to men entitled to vote on January 1, 1867, their adult sons and grandsons, and most naturalized immigrants.[6]

Ryanes, represented by a local white attorney, Armand Romain, filed suit against Supervisor Gleason in the Civil District Court of the parish of Orleans, alleging that Gleason's refusal to register him violated his "rights and privileges as a citizen of this State and of the United States." Attorney Romain was a Republican and a 30th degree Mason in the Scottish Rite Lodge who had commanded a battalion of the Ninth U.S. Volunteers during the military occupation of Cuba, earning warm praise in letters written home by Lieutenant Pierre Carmouche. Defeated as a Republican candidate in 1896, Romain may also have relished a fight with the state's leading white-supremacist Democrats.[7]

District Judge Somerville dismissed the case on August 19, 1901, on the grounds of no cause of action, and also provided an eleven-page disquisition on suffrage as a privilege, not a right. Ryanes tried to register again, was refused again, and brought suit against Gleason again. Armand Romain filed a more carefully worded brief arguing that Article 197 of the 1898 constitution was plainly an "unlawful plan of suffrage qualifications based upon discrimination on account of race, color or previous condition of servitude, which is, therefore, in violation of the Fifteenth Amendment of the Federal Constitution." Taken together, the literacy/property restrictions and the grandfather clause of Article 197 were designed "to disfranchise only poor and illiterate colored persons of the African race," and hence denied them equal protection. Romain sought a writ ordering the supervisor of registration to "inscribe the name of the relator herein upon the books of his office as a duly qualified elector and voter."[8]

Romain's brief for David Ryanes, in its final revised version, was a carefully framed appeal to the Fourteenth and Fifteenth amendments. Louisiana's new rules did not, on their face, speak of color, although throughout the deliberations of the constitutional convention the legislators had made no effort to hide the intent of the new restrictions, and the "permanent register" of 1898 was a transparent mechanism to favor white voters.[9] The grandfather clause and naturalized immigrant provisions alone had brought 37,877 white voters onto this register, seven times the total number of men ranked "colored" who had squeezed onto the rolls on the basis of all modes of qualification combined.[10]

The Democratic Party fielded an impressive defense team for Supervisor Jeremiah Gleason: the state attorney general, Walter Guion; the Democratic strategist Ernest Benjamin Kruttschnitt, former chair of the 1898 constitutional convention; and the attorney Walter L. Gleason. They would present their arguments to Judge St. Paul of Division C of the District Court—himself a former delegate to the disfranchising convention and a member of the commission that had designed the rules in the first place.[11] Proceedings in the case began in July of 1902 with testimony from the plaintiff. David Jordan Ryanes, of 2618 South Rampart Street, in the Ninth Precinct of the Eleventh Ward of the parish of Orleans, was sixty-one years old and had been living in Louisiana since 1860. As best he could recall, he had first voted in 1867, when the Reconstruction Acts expanded the franchise to include black men. He had voted ever since, "Up to this Constitution which stopped me." He identified himself as being of "the African race." He had never been indicted or convicted of a crime, and could write "a little bit," though not enough to prove literacy at the registration office.[12]

Romain sought to enter various voter registration tabulations, divided by color, into the record. The attorney general objected, and the judge upheld the objection. The figures were nonetheless appended in case of appeal, and were stark: in Ward 11 of Orleans Parish, where Ryanes lived, the number of registered voters who were classified as "colored" had plummeted from 1,100 in 1896 (following 1880 registration rules), to 239 in 1897 (following the restrictive statutes), to 65 in late 1898, before creeping back up to around 180 in 1899–1900. In the same period the ward's white registrants had declined only from 3,776 to 3,084.[13]

Romain's case against the new constitution rested on seeing its different elements as together expressive of its intent and effect: the literacy and property requirements excluded both black and white citizens, and the grandfather clause then readmitted only whites. In trying to register a plaintiff who failed to meet the purportedly race-blind literacy and property criteria, however, the Louisiana activists could point to no single clause on which to base their claim of a Fifteenth Amendment violation, that is to say, an explicit abridgment by the state "on account of race, color, or previous condition of servitude." They needed to persuade the court to read all of Article 197 and discern its logic. This the court refused to do, treating each clause separately. Judge St. Paul of the District Court argued that if the plaintiff could not meet the property and literacy qualifications, then he had no grounds to complain that he also could not meet the grandfather criterion, whether it proved to be constitutional or not. St. Paul ruled in favor of Supervisor Gleason, judging the matter to have been settled already by the prior suit in Division E. Attorney Romain objected strenuously that the earlier case had been dismissed without a hearing, and was in any event about a separate set of facts. But he got nowhere.[14]

Along with their fellow delegates to the 1898 convention, Kruttschnitt and St. Paul had designed the disfranchising rules to be marginally judicially credible. The work of exclusion was done by the race-neutral literacy and property provisions, and the transparently racial grandfather clause did not itself exactly abridge Ryanes's right to vote—it was simply unavailable to him as an alternative. The actual intent and the practical effect were quite clear, but the wording was designed to make it possible to claim otherwise. Judge St. Paul had no difficulty in giving to the text the formal reading designed for external consumption, rather than the practical one that the delegates had acknowledged during the convention itself— and that he as a delegate had heard with his own ears.[15]

As Armand Romain prepared to appeal Ryanes's case to the Louisiana Supreme Court, a crucial Alabama voting rights case, *Giles v. Harris,* was making its way toward a hearing in the U.S. Supreme Court. Jackson Giles, a black man who worked in the federal courthouse in Montgomery, Alabama, had sought through the federal courts to be reinstated on the electoral rolls after being excluded under the new 1901 Alabama Constitution. On April 27, 1903, the U.S. Supreme Court turned Giles back, judging his case to be an inappropriate appeal to "enforce political rights," as opposed to constitutionally protected civil rights.[16]

In New Orleans, a clerk dropped by in July of 1903 and picked up the *Ryanes v. Gleason* case file so that the state attorney general, Walter Guion, who was defending Supervisor Gleason, could ponder it. Guion would ponder it—or at least hold on to it—for the next eight months, as a second Alabama appeal by Jackson Giles made its way through the courts. Unable to win his initial "action in equity" (an action that seeks equitable relief, in this case, specific behavior by the registrar) Giles was now trying to win a case for damages against the registrar. The new case was *Giles v. Teasley,* and was argued in January of 1904.[17]

On February 23, 1904, the justices of the U.S. Supreme Court turned Giles's second appeal aside as well, judging themselves unable to review the action of the state court. In practice, both the registrar and Alabama's registration system were vindicated. Down in New Orleans, the attorney general apparently heard the news, concluded his own brief, and returned the *Ryanes v. Gleason* case file to the Louisiana Supreme Court within the week. Armand Romain, attorney for Ryanes, picked up the papers on March 17 and had two days to read them before the case went to court on March 19.[18]

In contrast to the terse and dismissive documents often filed by the state in previous cases, Louisiana's leading Democratic minds this time delivered themselves of a bulldozer of a brief. Instead of admitting or denying the white-supremacist intent of the 1898 convention he had chaired, Kruttschnitt and the other attorneys for Gleason simply piled up the evidence that the U.S. Supreme Court itself had now walked away from the Fifteenth Amendment. Drawing on the older decisions in *Cruikshank,* the *Slaughter-House* cases, and *Minor v. Happersett,* they hammered home the difference between citizenship and suffrage, and the narrowing of federal authority to intervene in the states in questions of voting.

But the real windfall was the pair of brand-new rulings in *Giles v. Harris* and *Giles v. Teasley*. The southern Democrat Kruttschnitt could now quote with approval the Union veteran Oliver Wendell Holmes. Holmes had argued that if Giles was correct in claiming the Alabama scheme to be unlawful, "how can we make the Court a party to the unlawful scheme by accepting it and adding another voter to its fraudulent lists?" The Louisiana authorities were delighted to follow through on this circular logic: "if the articles of our Constitution be unconstitutional . . . no such relief as is prayed for by [Ryanes] can be afforded by our courts, since there will be no lawful power or authority in [Gleason] to act as supervisor of registration."[19]

In arguing against Ryanes's claim in the Louisiana Supreme Court, Kruttschnitt and his colleagues skirted the question of racially biased intent—on which the 1898 constitutional convention debates were very clear—by noting the lower court's ruling that such evidence was irrelevant and immaterial. The Louisiana authorities then blandly assured the court that each of the qualifications for voters could, in principle, exclude not only black but also white men. Very recently naturalized foreigners and white men whose grandfathers were not eligible to vote in 1867, for example, could not invoke the grandfather clause. Chief Justice Frank A. Monroe, like Judge St. Paul a former member of the constitutional convention, professed to be thus convinced of the race-neutrality of the rules. Monroe also noted that the framers of the Louisiana Constitution had "not thought proper" to include cases of refusal of permission to register among the enumerated civil or political rights for which there was a right of appeal to the Supreme Court. The actions of local supervisors of registration were final. Ryanes's appeal was rejected.[20]

The strategy of judicial challenge had, in effect, reached a dead end. With the U.S. Supreme Court categorically on record in the *Giles* cases, there was no point in appealing the Ryanes case further.[21] At the end of the day, it had become clear that the courts would not defend Jackson Giles, David Ryanes, or any other black voter who had been disfranchised. Holmes had been explicit and emphatic: "Relief from a great political wrong, if done, as alleged, by the people of a state and the State itself, must be given by them or by the legislative and political department of the Government of the United States." Why this wrong should be deemed political rather than constitutional was unclear, given that the Fifteenth Amendment was right there in the Constitution, and that in Alabama as in Louisiana the Democrats had openly sought to render it a dead letter. But the Court proposed to defer to Congress. And the majority in Congress, moved by varying degrees of apathy, racism, and strict federalism, had rebuffed all new efforts at legislation aimed at enforcement of black citizens' voting rights. Neither legislation, nor executive action, nor even congressional inquiry into allegations of abuse could be expected. Disfranchisement by state constitution, begun as a clear challenge to federal authority, encompassing provisions that even some of its strongest proponents expected to see turned back by the courts, was in 1903–1904 accorded the respect of an inevitable expression of the will of "the people of the state."[22]

In his dissent in *Giles v. Harris,* Justice John Marshall Harlan insisted that "upon the facts alleged in the bill (if the record showed a sufficient value of the matter in dispute) the plaintiff is entitled to relief in respect of his right to be registered as a voter." But it was the language of the Alabama authorities in *Giles,* who acknowledged the exclusion of the "mass of the negro population" from what they referred to as "the privilege of voting," that would stand. The key displacement of the vote, from an implicit right of manhood citizenship to a privilege for the select few, had been made. Equally ominous, the term "the people of the state" could be uttered as if its boundaries were rightfully controlled by the leadership of the Democratic Party and the now-reduced state electorate. Jackson Giles and David Ryanes were back where they started, their names struck from the electoral rolls on which they had each figured for decades, their political voice deemed no longer part of "the people."[23]

By 1904 David Ryanes and other working-class African Americans in Louisiana were in some respects even more isolated than they had been at the moments of formal disfranchisement in 1896 and 1898. The cross-class alliance embodied in the collaboration between Ryanes and the activist attorneys was itself undercut by the logic of the constitutional challenge. Jesse Lawson and other members of the Afro-American Council increasingly focused on the precise racial dimension to disfranchisement, the only aspect that the Fifteenth Amendment could invalidate. Lawson assured readers of the *Washington Post* that "we are willing to accept any test for voting that applies alike to white and colored citizens."[24] Armand Romain's briefs recognized that it was the conjunction of the racially specific grandfather clause with the race-blind class restrictions that did the dirty work of biased disfranchisement. Eliminating the grandfather clause alone would not have moved David Ryanes a single step closer to registration—although it would move his illiterate and propertyless white neighbors in the Eleventh Ward a step away. Such grandfather clauses would eventually be ruled unconstitutional by the U.S. Supreme Court in 1915.[25] But by then the Louisiana Democratic Party had achieved its lock on political power, and the loss of a portion of the white electorate would not be much mourned.

Meanwhile the remaining political parties in Louisiana adjusted to the reality of a truncated electorate. The Democrats did not need to be as concerned for their white working-class flank as the property and literacy qualifications edged off the rolls those poor white voters who had not availed themselves of the grandfather clause during 1898. Among Republicans, the "lily-whites" supplanted the earlier coalition-building "black and tans" and moved toward openly racist electioneering.[26] Pierre L. Carmouche, still active in Donaldsonville, tried to find space within the now reduced Republican Party and appealed directly to the federal government in hopes of achieving through patronage a post as naval officer in New Orleans, but to no avail. In despair, he sold his remaining property in Donaldsonville and moved to Detroit, Michigan.[27]

The Populists' own last-ditch efforts to defend universal manhood suffrage had failed, and their potential base of farmers and laborers was both divided and demoralized. Some Populist leaders railed in despair, others drifted toward a white-supremacist variant of the old fusionist coalition-building, supporting the planter Donelson Caffery in a failed campaign for governor. Caffery picked up 9,277 votes on the Republican-Fusionist ticket (1,121 of them in the sugar parish of Lafourche alone), and 4,938 on the People's Party ticket. But he was swamped by the 60,206 votes conferred on the Democrat W. W. Heard. As a practical matter, neither Republicans nor Populists could any longer seriously challenge Democratic supremacy in the state.[28]

An impoverished electoral sphere also handicapped those who sought to organize outside it. Any cross-racial movement that might need a modicum of legal protection and electoral leverage to survive, like the Knights of Labor or the waterfront unions, was left utterly vulnerable. Many activists were forced to retreat to the sphere of mutual-benefit associations and cautious self-improvement. There cross-class alliances could be built on a very small scale, and some cross-racial collaboration could persist at the level of face-to-face relations. But the mode was necessarily defensive, and the scope of such efforts was narrowly constrained.

As the electoral system closed down, apartheid in the sugar fields continued to harden. A researcher writing for the bulletin of the federal Department of Labor noted in 1902 that at the Cinclare sugar plantation and factory, roughly "80 per cent of the population . . . are Negroes, the manager, overseers, engineers, and skilled workmen and their families being the only white persons on the place." At Calumet in St. Mary Parish, the figure was 90 percent. At Cinclare there was "practically no Negro skilled labor," except for "one blacksmith, and two or three carpenters' assistants, who can scarcely be called skilled laborers." Workers lived in the "quarters" and were paid in scrip accepted at the company store, with the unused balance redeemable in cash at the end of the month. The researcher, who seems to have been a white man from the area, wrote with exasperation that the laborers had "an unfortunate notion of freedom, which leads them to desire most those things which they could not possess as slaves—guns, ponies, and the privilege of moving about—none of which things brings them profit of any sort." He passed over without comment the contemporaneous process of exclusion of black men from electoral politics. As of 1900, the electoral register of St. Mary Parish counted exactly one registered voter listed as "colored."[29]

The desolate situation of African Americans in the world of cane should not obscure just how much repressive energy it took to keep it that way. Pierre Carmouche and the soldiers of the Ninth Volunteers, Rodolphe Desdunes and the Citizens' Committee, the churchgoers who raised the money to hire Armand Romain to take the supervisor of registration to court—all of them had shown an eagerness to ally, albeit cautiously, across class and racial lines in pursuit of what the Louisiana Constitution of 1868 had characterized as the enjoyment by all citizens of the same "civil, political and public rights and privileges."[30] They also showed a capacity to mobilize from the top to the bottom of the economic scale within African American communities, linking the former slave David Ryanes to

the distinguished Union veteran James Lewis and the urbane Republican businessman and politician Walter L. Cohen. When the members of the various mutual-
aid associations filed their founding documents with the notary Louis A. Martinet,
some signed with elegant script, others with hesitant letters, and still others with
just a cross.[31] Thirty-eight years after the end of slavery, twenty-five years after
the withdrawal of federal troops, six years after *Plessy v. Ferguson,* and four years after the disfranchising Louisiana Constitution of 1898, Louisiana activists in 1902
were still raising funds and bringing suit. But once the federal Supreme Court decisions in *Giles* arrived in the hands of the Louisiana Supreme Court in 1903–
1904, the door to this phase of judicial and political action was definitively closed.
When Rodolphe Desdunes looked back from the vantage point of 1911, he recalled the *Plessy* case with words that could have applied to the other cases as well:
"The courts have, it is true, refused our aspirations, but . . . our people have had
the satisfaction of forcing the hand of the U.S. government, by acting through the
offices of one of its own constitutive branches."[32] It clearly broke his heart, however, to have to concede that the Constitution's post–Civil War promise had been
betrayed.

Across the Gulf of Mexico in Cuba, from which the Louisiana soldiers of the
Ninth Volunteer Infantry had recently returned, a different political order was
emerging. During the thirty-year period of Cuba's wars for independence, Cuban
theorists of the nation had sought to associate the sin of slavery, and the caste
structure that accompanied it, with Spain and with Spanish colonialism. The most
conservative claimed that white Cuban nationalists had sacrificed blood and treasure to free black Cubans from slavery, thereby cleansing themselves of guilt and
imposing a debt of gratitude on freedpeople and their descendants. The most radical portrayed slaves and free people of color themselves as key architects of Cuban freedom. For them, solidarity across racial lines in the rebel army was the
model of a reciprocal and respectful democratic polity. Alongside this theorizing
of the nation had also been a great deal of practical living in the "republic in arms."
Veterans of the rebel army had served within a cross-class, cross-racial force led
by black, white, and *mulato* officers, and their ground-level alliances could now
serve as the building blocks for a new round of claims.[33]

The U.S. military government in Cuba, however, answered to the same Republican administrations in Washington that had failed to act to protect black voters in the southern United States. The Republican platform in the 1900 election had endorsed black suffrage, as Pierre L. Carmouche and a greeting committee of men of color from Donaldsonville reminded President McKinley when they welcomed him to New Orleans in 1901. But the leadership of the Republican Party was increasingly making its peace with voting restrictions of various kinds, their long-standing class and racial prejudices reinforced by an electoral strategy in which the votes of southern Republicans had become less and less important. The war in Cuba, moreover, had provided an opportunity to accelerate the repair of what were viewed as "sectional" conflicts within the United States, bringing white southerners back into an expansive patriotic coalition. Most Republicans still found explicit racial limitations to be constitutionally inappropriate, but implicit ones were increasingly tolerable when proposed for the southern states. Such thinking, combined with a heavy dose of realpolitik, encouraged the U.S. occupiers of Cuba to introduce limits on the suffrage there as well.[34]

Governor Leonard Wood had restricted voting in the June 1900 municipal elections in Cuba to those who could demonstrate either literacy, possession of substantial taxable property, or honorable discharge from the Cuban army. The strategy of excluding the illiterate and unpropertied, but admitting those who could prove their service in the army, nonetheless misjudged the mood of veterans, the degree of mobilization in the countryside, and the political ambitions of the leadership of the Liberation Army. From the beginning, General Wood discovered that by making the list of veterans a kind of permanent electoral register he gave the officers drawing up the list—themselves often future candidates for office—abundant incentive to add the names of those who had served the war effort in any capacity. The official mustering-out rolls thus tended to grow, as some officers tried to help the men who looked to them for assistance.[35]

To the extent that rural Cubans saw elections as an expression of collective voice, they were likely to push at the boundaries of the formal qualifications for voters. Rumors spread, for example, that a given bundle of $250 in ready cash sometimes served to meet—sequentially—the property requirements of more than one resident. Gregoria Quesada of Cienfuegos, for example, owned at least

$250 worth of property in the hill town of La Sierra. She was female, however, and therefore not eligible to vote. Perhaps Gregoria's property could serve as guarantee for a kinsman, such as her son.[36]

At the end of the day, the local electoral lists for 1900 were noticeably thinner than those compiled in the last year of Spanish rule, when Spain had sought desperately to recruit loyalties by extending universal manhood suffrage. In the sugar regions, however, particularly those with relatively few Spanish immigrants, the electorate was nonetheless robustly Cuban and cross-racial. Local veterans whom Wood might have preferred to keep out of the sphere of politics appear in the May 1900 electoral lists for Cienfuegos: Claudio Sarría, a former slave and veteran from Soledad with a controversial disciplinary record was there, as was Fermín Quesada, later characterized by U.S. military intelligence as a dangerous and illiterate horse thief. There were also numerous black men with close ties to the world of slavery, men whose color and class alone would have troubled Wood: Gabriel Quesada, a *mulato* civil rights activist from Santa Rosalía who later became a policeman; Ventura and Tomás Sarría, brothers of African descent who went on to acquire a farm of their own near Caonao; Trinidad Tellería Santana, a veteran and tobacco worker; Ceferino Quesada, a black former slave from Santa Rosalía.[37]

Elections carried out under Wood's rules, excluding two-thirds of the adult male population, did not yield the results sought by the U.S. occupiers. Although the proportion of white to black voters might resemble that of Louisiana during the interval of statutory (as opposed to constitutional) disfranchisement, the political issues at hand were those of postwar reconstruction, patriotic assertion, and determining who would be part of a new leadership class. Cross-racial alliances were one way to achieve those goals. Many of the municipal councils filled up with what the U.S. occupiers saw as "unworthy" men, who promptly began petitioning the government for universal manhood suffrage. And the inclusion of the soldier clause, though strategically astute, reinforced the pro-independence electorate and undercut the philosophical arguments in favor of literacy and property restrictions. Including some men who were illiterate and unpropertied on the voting rolls left the argument against universal manhood suffrage clothed only in the thin robes of obvious antidemocratic hostility to the majority of the population. This argument was not likely to fare well in a mobilized populace in the throes of nationalist self-definition.

Governor Wood's goal of a local government of what the occupiers often called the "better class of people" was thwarted, but he saw no alternative to the course he had set for establishing formal Cuban independence. Political support in the United States for immediate annexation was already meager, and continued to shrink by the day as the news of war in the Philippines made clear just how costly colonialism could be. The Teller Resolution, voted at the beginning of the U.S. intervention in Cuba, had committed the United States to handing authority over to an independent Cuban government. Anti-expansionist Democrats in the U.S. Congress were, for their own reasons, hounding the Republicans to do so more quickly. The formula of some kind of "organic" relationship between the United States and the island, to be built into a Cuban constitution, seemed to promise the possibility of continued control and a right of reintervention. General Wood, for his part, was in a great hurry to finish up his work in Cuba, because he hoped to proceed to China and distinguish himself in the effort to put down the Boxer Rebellion.[38]

In July of 1900 the military government called new elections to choose delegates to the Cuban Constitutional Convention, in anticipation of an orderly withdrawal of the remaining occupying forces and an end to formal rule by the United States. Wood redoubled his efforts to put power securely into the hands of "responsible" Cubans, but was again disappointed. Instead of men of appropriately conservative views, voters elected thirty-one delegates and an equal number of alternates encompassing an assortment of veteran rebel officers, separatist politicians, and some former Autonomists. Two well-known activist men of color, Juan Gualberto Gómez and Martín Morúa Delgado, served as representatives from Santiago de Cuba and Santa Clara, respectively. Antonio and José Maceo's close colleague General Agustín Cebreco, who had held the countryside around San Luis in the early months of the U.S. occupation, was elected as an alternate.[39]

By the time the Cuban Constitutional Convention was seated in November of 1900, the issue of suffrage had fully escaped the control of both the U.S. military governor and his conservative allies on the island. There was abundant discussion on the floor of the convention of the sacrifices made during the war by the most

humble members of Cuban society. Town councils, mass meetings, and the veterans' associations lined up in favor of writing a positive right to vote directly into
the Constitution—something that the U.S. Constitutional Convention of 1787
had not done, that the Fifteenth Amendment to the U.S. Constitution did not do,
and that Governor Leonard Wood undoubtedly did not want to see the Cuban
convention delegates do.[40] An extended franchise had become an element in a
democratic definition of the nation, consistent with the ideals for which the war
had been fought—as well as being part of future campaigns for office and patronage. But the grassroots support for suffrage seems to have reflected another element as well: an assertion of entitlement to respect and to what has sometimes
been called "the right to have rights." The original rebel document releasing soldiers from service in the Liberation Army conveyed this spirit in its language: the
bearer was formally declared to be deserving of the respect of his fellow citizens.
In this sense universal manhood suffrage was itself expressive, communicating
something about the nature of the new nation.[41]

During the debates in the convention, it became clear that as the nation was
being rebuilt after a harrowing war, certain kinds of exclusions seemed particularly repugnant, an insult not just to individual veterans but to the social groups
that had provided a large proportion of the troops in the Liberation Army. Indeed,
imposing exacting qualifications would seem to reproduce the worst aspects of
the colonial order. A franchise restriction based on the ability to read and write,
for example, implicitly held illiterate Cubans responsible for the deficiencies of
the educational system imposed on them by Spain or, in the case of many descendants of Africans, the bondage in which they had been held throughout their
youth. Although some former slaves like Bárbara Pérez of Arimao had successfully
learned to read through the exercise of stealth and ingenuity, most field workers
had had no such opportunity.

Not everyone agreed with this democratizing enthusiasm, of course, and hostility to illiterates was not confined to the U.S. occupiers. Some white Cuban
officers had moved to exclude black officers from power during the last months
of the war, in keeping with what they saw as the requirements of "civilization"
and national independence.[42] A leading white Cuban intellectual, Enrique José
Varona, later advocated excluding illiterates from the vote. But in 1900–1901 the

overbearing presence of the United States, and the high-handed impositions of Governor Wood, gave this kind of thinking among elite Cubans an unhealthy odor of collaboration and toadying. Some activists used the language of civilization quite differently, arguing for "racial uplift" without expressing hostility to those who had not yet been uplifted. The journalist Rafael Serra, for example, combined an enthusiasm for education with an endorsement of universal suffrage. Growing into the fullest form of citizenship through civic training was, for him, consistent with acquiring its key rights from the beginning.[43]

In the year 1901, a constituent assembly in Cuba simply could not devote itself to debating electoral rules entirely outside the view of the larger population. The founding document that the convention members were drafting was quite literally the precondition for nationhood—the U.S. forces were not going to leave until a constitution had been produced. Suffrage was constitutive of membership in the nation, at least for adult males, and inclusion rather than exclusion was, to many minds, the order of the day.[44]

The convention formally took up the suffrage issue in early 1901. Its members, elected under the restricted franchise, found themselves in an interesting bind. As one member noted uneasily, they were like the Roman god Janus, with one face turned toward the Cuban people and one toward the U.S. occupation government. Among Cubans, the clamor for universal manhood suffrage was unmistakable; among most of the occupiers, the preference for property and literacy qualifications was clear.[45]

The debate on the floor of the convention took an odd tone, because no Cuban delegate—not even the most conservative—would speak out loud against universal manhood suffrage. Options that had been considered behind closed doors were not to be discussed in the open. Instead the delegates wrangled over whether an extended franchise should be written into the founding document, and thus be relatively immune from modification, or left to be spelled out in an electoral law—in case, upon further reflection, legislators wished to back away from the current enthusiasm for a wide franchise. The proponents of universal manhood suffrage, however, had the rhetorical power all on their side: this was, they said, a matter of national honor, of respect for the ordinary Cubans who had sacrificed so much for independence. They further pointed out that both the last

Spanish electoral law and the constitution drafted in the field during the Cuban rebellion had embodied universal manhood suffrage. How was the new Cuban state to offer its citizens anything less?[46]

The final vote was twenty-five in favor, just three against. Doubters hastened to introduce a proposal guaranteeing participation in the drawing up of electoral lists to whatever should turn out to be the minority party or parties, and this measure passed quickly. But on the major symbolic and practical issue, the proponents of an extensive franchise and of the vote as a right, at least for men, had won. And however disappointed Governor Wood might be, he had a still bigger fight ahead. He could not afford to provoke a showdown on the question of suffrage—in part because he was about to provoke one instead on the right of renewed U.S. intervention.

Over the next months the suffrage question would be eclipsed as the occupation government brought all possible pressure to bear on the convention to write into its text the language of the Platt Amendment, recently passed in the U.S. Congress, asserting the right of the United States to return to the island if Cubans should prove unequal to the task of running the country to the satisfaction of Washington. The delegates were given to understand that if they declined to incorporate the key text, the United States would refuse to withdraw its forces. Bowing to the inevitable, a narrow majority of the Cuban delegates reluctantly consented. When the United States stepped off the stage, it would remain quite visible in the wings.[47]

On May 20, 1902, the U.S. flag came down and the Cuban flag went up. The Cuban Republic had begun, and its transracial definition of Cuban citizenship and the rights it entailed now went into effect. The continued U.S. tutelage implied by the Platt Amendment threatened to constrain outcomes, but the popular understanding of politics was now both inclusive and expansive. If former slaves like Claudio Sarría and Ceferino Quesada had made their way onto the electoral lists despite the strictures of Governor Wood's limitations, they were unlikely to be deterred from further participation by the threat of future activation of the Platt Amendment.

The ability of Cubans to organize across racial lines rested on patterns of labor and of workplace sociability that had been developing for some time within the

rapidly growing sugar industry. The halting postwar recovery of Cuban sugar production in 1899 quickly gave way to sustained expansion as Cuba asserted its immense natural advantage in cane growing and its ability to meet the demand of the
U.S. market. The workforce that labored in the fields had been and would continue to be multiracial, drawing in not only the black and white permanent residents of the plantations themselves but men and occasionally women who lived in
nearby towns, thousands of immigrants from Spain, and artisans and laborers who
tilled land of their own during part of the year. Although the Cuban sugar economy did not provide equal opportunity in the modern sense, it provided abundant, if seasonal, employment. War veterans with recent experiences of confrontation and a keen sense of entitlement began the process of building a tenacious
workers' movement, fusing the claims of patriotism with those of social justice.
Cuban social relations were thus neither static nor definitively structured, and the
public sphere remained open for discussion and debate in a way that had become
impossible in Louisiana, where white supremacy as both a formal structure and an
openly avowed goal had achieved a lock on the political system.[48]

Cubans of all classes celebrated the transfer of power on May 20, 1902, with considerable fanfare. The new president, Tomás Estrada Palma, was a respected pro-
independence exile, and the seizing of sovereignty momentarily subdued sectarian
concerns. Workers' organizations in the city of Cienfuegos, for example, built a
majestic arch dedicated to the new Republic. The cross-class and cross-racial alliances that had undergirded the Liberation Army were reinforced by patriotic enthusiasm, seeming to promise a future of unity.[49]

On the eve of the next sugar harvest, however, the patriotic coalition faced an
immediate challenge. A work stoppage by tobacco workers in Havana expanded
by mid-November of 1902 into a citywide general strike, drawing support from
public employees, from nearby towns, and from Cuban workers in Tampa and
Key West. At issue was the admission of young Cubans into skilled jobs in tobacco
processing. Cuban workers believed Spaniards to have a monopoly on the coveted
apprenticeships, and wanted recruitment to these jobs opened up. By November
26, battles between workers and police in the streets had yielded 5 deaths and
114 wounded.[50]

The Veterans' Association, under the respected former general Máximo Gómez, accompanied by the civil rights activist Juan Gualberto Gómez, offered to mediate, and the company against whom the strike had been initiated conceded that it would henceforth admit Cuban apprentices into the workshops "without distinction of race." Within a day or two the other major tobacco producers had followed suit, though their final document referred to the admission of apprentices "without any distinction of nationality." Work resumed by the end of the month.[51]

The focus of action had by this point shifted to the province of Santa Clara, and particularly to the areas around Cruces and Lajas, in the heart of the sugar country. Urban unions in the towns of Cienfuegos and Santa Clara had declared their solidarity with the Havana strikers, and the Rural Guard was dispatched to patrol the wharves of Cienfuegos. Then, on November 27, there came word that numerous groups under red flags were in the streets in Cruces and were seeking to carry the strike to the plantations. The goal was apparently to express solidarity with workers in Havana; no specific demands were presented. The U.S. consul at Cienfuegos reported that work had stopped in the municipalities of Lajas and Cruces, and that administrators at Hormiguero plantation had charged that they "have been threatened by colored men to stop work and laborers have quit work through fear."[52]

The local press provided more detail: "commissions" of workers sent out from the town of Cruces had visited several estates, including Hormiguero, to bring about work stoppages. They succeeded in halting labor on several of Hormiguero's cane farms, but the arrival of police blocked further action. The editors of the newspaper *El Imparcial* expressed apprehension that such activities, if spread to U.S.-owned estates, could have serious diplomatic consequences. U.S. forces were still camped at Pasa Caballos, just across the bay from the city of Cienfuegos, and it seemed that planters might turn to them for help.[53]

The strike organizers benefited from the exceptional mobility and autonomy of workers in central Cuba. While some families continued to live on plantation land, or in the equivalent of Louisiana's plantation "quarters," many others had relocated to nearby towns and hamlets. From small settlements like San Antón, Arimao, and Guaos, they could plan, act, and speak outside the gaze of the plantation administration. In the larger town of Lajas, the Barrio Guinea had emerged as a black neighborhood where former slaves, particularly women, had bought small plots of land along the railroad tracks. Cruces, at the heart of the strike, was a way station on the rail line and home to many families of workers in the cane, as well as to a mutual-aid association called the Centro Luz de Oriente, founded in 1889 and composed largely of Cubans of color. From this had emerged in 1893 a Club de Obreros (Workers' Club). Along with the Centro Africano, a cultural center founded in Lajas in 1889, it served as a point of mobilization in 1902.[54]

At the same time, much of this organizing crossed ethnic lines. Spanish-born anarchist activists who had settled in Lajas and Cruces over the previous years helped to organize a Workers' Guild. Along with Cuban anarchists, they provided elements of the formal ideology of the 1902 movement, and helped spread word of the strikes through their newspapers.[55] During the strike a letter from a correspondent in Santa Clara to the anarchist newspaper *Tierra!* called metaphorically for the "emancipation of all slaves" as well as the "disappearance of all privileges."[56]

Like earlier Knights of Labor organizing in Louisiana, Cuba's sugar workers' unions built on mutual-aid associations and veterans' organizations as well as on work groups in the fields and mills. Prestige gained in the war could also translate into leadership in the unions: Evaristo Landa, a black officer from the independence war, presided over the Gremio General de Braceros (General Workers' Guild). Landa, born around 1857, had been living in the province since the 1880s.[57] By 1902 black leadership of a labor union was unlikely to raise the old specter of a "black rebellion." These organizers were respected veterans representing the cross-racial labor force, and they were voters. Planters might raise alarms, but unlike their counterparts in Louisiana they could not be sure of the support of local elected officials, nor did they have an all-white repressive force at their disposal.

Conflict in the sugar fields thus tended to be defined largely by class, not by race or nationality. Planters themselves quickly pulled together across national lines: Nicolás Castaño, the preeminent local Spanish-born merchant, convened a Cienfuegos branch of the Círculo de Hacendados y Agricultores (Planters' and Farmers' Circle), with the Cubans Emilio Terry and Nicolás Acea as "presidents of honor," Castaño as president, and the participation of Agustín Goytisolo (the Basque owner of San Agustín plantation), Jorge Fowler (the English-born owner of Dos Hermanas in Cruces), and Elías Ponvert (the Cuban founder of Hormiguero). The Cienfuegos Círculo telegraphed the national office to ask it to represent their interests, and specifically called for a reorganization of the Rural Guard and new "laws of repression." The national office, in turn, communicated with President Estrada Palma.[58]

The 1902 strike exposed a fault line that cut across the Cuban nationalist coalition in the province. To sustain his political power, provincial governor José Miguel Gómez, a veteran and founder of the Liberal Party, of intermittently populist leanings, needed both the support of veterans and the consent of the property-owning classes. The coalescence of some veterans around the new workers' organizations imperiled his strategy, put his political machine at risk, and posed the danger of a renewed U.S. intervention. The U.S. minister in Havana was blunt in his evaluation of the Cuban government's weakness: "A strike in the cane fields would mean the greatest possible danger to life and property in this island, a danger with which this Government could not cope with its available forces."[59]

For Governor Gómez, the closest weapon to hand was the Rural Guard, under the direction of José de Jesús ("Chucho") Monteagudo, a veteran and Gómez loyalist. The governor dispatched guardsmen to the Hormiguero plantation and to the town of Cruces, and by the second of December the "instigators" of the strikes had been detained. They were turned over to a judge specially appointed to deal with violations of crimes falling under the provisions of Spanish criminal law, still in force, that prohibited combinations to alter the price of labor.[60] More ominously, on December 7, two workmen, Joaquín Casañas and Amado Montero, disappeared from the San Francisco plantation, apparently in the company of members of the Rural Guard. One was a young activist and former tobacco worker; the other was a veteran who had worked as a security guard on one of the estates. Their bodies were found eight months later.[61]

With the tobacco strike settled by negotiation in Havana, and the rural leadership under arrest, the sympathy strikes based in Cruces came to an end in time for the harvest to begin on schedule. Sugar prices were on the rise, and the editor of a local newspaper hoped that the flow of wages would begin to ease social tensions.[62] In late December, however, another meeting of workers assembled in the Centro Africano de Lajas, drawing members of the multiracial workforce together in public space belonging to a black organization. "We will not ask anyone where they come from, that is to say, where they were born. All we need is the unity of everyone whose shirt is filled with sweat." This time the organizers formulated specific wage demands, and apparently succeeded in calling strikes on estates in Lajas and Palmira. The mayor of Lajas stepped in to arrest the strike leaders, and work was again resumed. When the veteran and union leader Evaristo Landa was released some months later, he felt obliged to pledge his loyalty to a local political figure who had intervened on his behalf.[63]

Despite the force that was used in response to the strikes of late 1902, these efforts made it clear that in the cane fields, mobilization could and would continue to cross the color lines that under other circumstances might divide Cubans and Spaniards. Nor was the repression itself racially coded. Like the Knights of Labor in Louisiana, labor organizers in the Cuban cane fields portrayed the fight as one of workers against plantation owners, not blacks against whites. But in contrast to Louisiana, the forces of order also constructed the conflict as having to do primarily with property and public order, not race. A planter writing to the U.S. consul did call attention to the identity of some of the organizers as "colored men," and another referred to a portion of the Cienfuegos region as the "black continent." But there was no sharp divide comparable to that which in Thibodaux in 1887 had placed the Louisiana state militia—from which men of color had been excluded since 1877—face to face with black strikers, with disastrous results. The Rural Guard of Santa Clara Province was at this point still a close descendant of the wartime Liberation Army, and a significant number of the guardsmen seem to have been veterans of color. The reports concerning the two workmen who were apparently killed by the Guard made no mention of color.[64]

Local networks of clientelism, moreover, were tight enough to permit the strike leader Evaristo Landa to be released unharmed from jail—again in sharp contrast to the fate that befell black Knights of Labor organizers in Louisiana in 1887. Here too the anticolonial Liberation Army was a key precedent, and social networks continued to be built around the links that had developed among men in the same companies and regiments, and between officers and those who served under them. The extensive franchise had after 1901 enabled some officers to transform these clienteles into an electoral base. Thus although the charismatic Liberal José Miguel Gómez moved quickly to suppress social disorder before U.S. forces might feel compelled to intervene, and responded with calculated violence to collective actions that were not under the control of his political machine, he was well aware that his rule rested on a broad cross-class and cross-racial base. Many families of color in the countryside of Santa Clara identified strongly with the Liberals and their base among rural working-class veterans. It would have been self-defeating for Gómez to speak in any variant of the tones of Louisiana's white-supremacist planter-governors.[65]

From the point of view of Cuban planters, the harvest of 1902–1903 now proceeded under an optimistic sign, with order restored in the fields and the anticipation of a new Reciprocity Treaty with the United States to keep up prices. By 1903 total Cuban sugar production again surpassed one million tons—marking an extraordinary recovery from a devastating war. The province of Santa Clara dominated the other five provinces, producing between 30 and 40 percent of the island's total output, a position it would hold until the end of World War I.[66]

Building on this combination of regional prosperity and political strength, José Miguel Gómez and the Liberal Party prepared to extend out from their original power base in Santa Clara. The large population, extensive foreign investment, and expanding production of the province looked like a promising springboard from which Gómez could try to move toward national power. In the spring of 1905 Gómez presented his candidacy for the Liberal Party nomination for the presidency, vying with the eastern veteran Bartolomé Masó for the chance to oppose the sitting president, Tomás Estrada Palma. In addition to mustering the usual powers of patronage and clientele, the Liberal campaign was marked by a keen awareness of the importance of black voters in the electorate and the power of an appeal to equal rights and a transracial concept of the nation. Liberal Party leaders criticized President Estrada Palma for acts of social discrimination on the basis of race (he had omitted the wives of two representatives and a senator of color from the guest list for a state reception) and pilloried his Moderate Party for dropping Juan Felipe Risquet, a man of color, from their congressional ticket in Matanzas. The more conservative Moderate Party soon found itself on the defensive. Throughout the campaign, the Liberals put forward the famous slogan taken from José Martí, calling for a republic "with all and for all."[67]

Estrada Palma, despite his reputation as a man of integrity, panicked at the prospect of losing an election. He undertook blatant manipulation of the electoral process, firing thousands of government employees affiliated with the Liberal Party and corrupting the ballot. A fraudulent election for members of the electoral boards gave rise to fraudulent registration lists, on which 150,000 fictitious voters were said to have been inscribed. On September 22, 1905, a Liberal congressman was assassinated in Cienfuegos, and the Liberal Party withdrew from the general elections in protest at the Moderates' abuse of the electoral process. Estrada Palma declared himself the victor. According to the government's calculations, no Liberal Party candidate had won elective office at any level.[68]

The Liberal Party, whose voters had been cheated and whose operatives could see their prospects of public employment vanishing, moved to take up arms. They fielded what was later described as the "Constitutional Army," although at the time one might have mistaken it simply for an extended, armed transracial clientele based in the key provinces of Santa Clara and Pinar del Río. The old *cuadrillas,* small cross-racial units of fighters, reemerged, now constituting themselves as veterans of the Liberation Army dedicated to defending the revolutionary faith. Once again Cubans of color were conspicuous in the rebel ranks, both as enlisted men and as officers. There was a certain element of mimesis and perhaps even carnival in the exercise, a kind of reenactment of the anticolonial mobilization, but without a Spanish army against which to fight. The entire affair was brief, largely kept under control by José Miguel Gómez, and with little of the ideological sweep of the 1895–1898 independence struggle. But preventing Estrada Palma's antidemocratic appropriation of long-term state power for himself and his allies may have been quite a sufficient motivation for those who took to the field. As Republicans in Louisiana had learned, one-party control could doom political action (as well as patronage) for a lifetime.[69]

Estrada Palma, fearful of immediate defeat, called on the United States to intervene. Unable to think of any other way to avoid either chaos or a Liberal takeover, Theodore Roosevelt's administration deployed troops to Cuba, with the immediate goal of preventing José Miguel Gómez from entering Havana. President

Roosevelt named Charles Edward Magoon head of a "Provisional Government of Cuba," a regime whose very name revealed its self-consciously temporary character. The main function of the U.S. troops was to interpose themselves between the armed Liberals and the city of Havana, and then to protect U.S.-owned property.[70] The next stage would be to pacify and monitor the countryside, carry out a census, publish an electoral list, supervise "clean" elections, and depart.

When U.S. forces arrived in Cuba to undertake this second occupation in 1906, they confronted both a corrupted electoral process and a highly politicized population. Awkwardly, however, it was their closest allies, the supporters of Tomás Estrada Palma, who had perpetrated the blatant electoral abuses that triggered the Liberal revolt of 1906. While Governor Magoon organized an administration in Havana, U.S. troops fanned out into the areas of greatest U.S. investment, particularly the province of Santa Clara. As they settled into their encampments, U.S. forces eyed the armed Cuban veterans with particular suspicion, a suspicion that was undoubtedly reciprocated. In the eyes of most of the occupation authorities, the supporters of the Liberals, among them thousands of men of color, some recently armed and drilled in the ranks of the ephemeral Constitutionalist Army, were a "dangerous" element. But in contrast to the U.S. occupiers in 1899–1902, with their aggressive desire to shape Cuba's political system, this was a half-hearted exercise in neocolonialism. The U.S. soldiers in the Cuban countryside between 1906 and 1909 watched, recorded, and condescended, but they no longer had the capacity to impose long-term boundaries on citizenship and participation. Cuba's commitment to universal manhood suffrage, etched into the 1901 Constitution, was now beyond dispute, however much its operation might appall the occupiers.[71]

The breadth of the potential for political participation was revealed by the new electoral census. Once the 1907 population census was complete, scribes in Havana drew up a list of all the eligible voters—virtually every male citizen over the age of twenty-one. For the area of Cienfuegos, for example, the 1907 electoral lists included even the most modest protagonists in the long-standing struggle to give both social and political content to citizenship. Ciriaco Quesada, he of the 1899 claim to the mule on the Santa Rosalía plantation, was now a registered voter in the barrio of Guaos, adjacent to the Soledad plantation. Alejandro

Quesada, born into slavery, and his son Cayetano Quesada, who settled on land in the hamlet of San Antón, were there as well. Gabriel Quesada, a literate *mulato* activist and baseball player, appeared in the town of Cienfuegos, his occupation listed as policeman. Eduardo Pérez, known as "el Cañón," brother of the literate black laundress Bárbara Pérez, was on the list for Guaos. One after another, black, white, *mulato,* and Chinese sugar workers turned up as registered voters—including those born in Africa and in China, whose claim to Cuban nationality might earlier have been placed in doubt.[72]

This expansive franchise, combined with the explicit guarantee of equal rights mandated by the 1901 Cuban Constitution, obviated the need for broad judicial challenges comparable to those mounted in Louisiana by the Committee of Citizens in *Plessy v. Ferguson* or the Afro-American Council in *Ryanes v. Gleason.* Instead, the attention of many activists focused on the dynamics of electoral competition itself, and in some instances on the question of whether men of color were well represented on the lists of candidates. Moreover, in day-to-day politics, the contest for loyalties provided some protection to those engaged in other forms of collective action, while tending to constrain the use of repression.

The promise of equal citizenship rights did not, of course, directly address the question of claims to resources. Those who could prove their service in the rebel army, and surviving members of the families of those killed, had been able to collect back pay, and these payments often served as an important first step toward the purchase or rental of land. But public discourse in Cuba, as in the United States, rarely addressed the question of what might be thought to be owed, and by whom, to those whose forced labor as slaves had built much of the nation's wealth. As in most other postemancipation societies, this most awkward of questions was generally voiced only obliquely, in the context of compensation for those who had served in the military—that is to say, a small subset of former slaves, virtually all of them men. But by prying open the space for political voice and defending their claim to public rights, rural Cubans had helped to create the political conditions for opening up broader claims to resources, whether as wages, as land or, in one exceptional case, as reparations.

CHAPTER EIGHT

The Search for Property and Standing

Cuba, 1906–1914

It seems unfortunately to be the case here [in Cienfuegos] that men's prejudice, which undermines all sentiment of honorable generosity, is acting not to unite all of the Cuban races, but to head instead down the road of division, and the worst kind of division, division into races.

General Eloy González, handbill distributed in Cienfuegos, April 2, 1907

IN THE SPRING OF 1906, THE FORMER SLAVES OF THE SANTA ROSALÍA plantation made a startling discovery about events that had taken place more than thirty years earlier. It now appeared that a notarized will filed in 1870 by José Quesada, the previous owner of the plantation, had declared his wish to confer *gracias* on his slaves at the time of his death. The term *gracias* was an ambiguous one. It could refer simply to favors, but it also echoed the phrase *libertad graciosa* (liberty without payment) that often appeared in manumission documents. José Quesada had not mentioned by name any of the approximately eighty slaves whom he had registered in the various slave censuses, nor did he specify whether the *gracias* he wished to confer included freedom. Instead, Article 11 of his will stated that upon his death a list of the slaves and the *gracias* to be given them would be found. The balance of his possessions were to go to Manuel Blanco, his manager.[1]

When José Quesada died in 1876, Manuel Blanco inherited the plantation, but the will's reference to *gracias* was apparently ignored. When the Spanish colonial state introduced the *patronato* to replace slavery four years later, Blanco routinely registered the slaves of Santa Rosalía as his *patrocinados*. When the *patronato* was abolished in 1886, most of the former slaves took the surname Quesada and sought to establish themselves on the land or in town, working as wage laborers, small-scale cultivators, dockworkers, or artisans. Some continued to work for the Santa Rosalía plantation itself, alongside Spanish immigrant workers.[2]

When the war for Cuban independence resumed in 1895, former slaves and sons of slaves from Santa Rosalía were among those who joined the rebel army. The young man of color named Ramón Ramos Quesada, however, stayed on the plantation to guard Manuel Blanco's cattle and keep Blanco apprised of the situation in the countryside. The news was not good: pro-Spanish *guerrillas* were commandeering animals and food; insurgents were torching the cane. When the war ended in 1898, the property was in disarray. Former slaves who returned from the war or from refugee camps to seek work in the cane fields found the food inadequate, the new administrator overbearing, and many of the dwellings burned or taken over by new white tenants. Harsh words were exchanged: Asunción Quesada complained to the administrator about the food, and opined that Manuel Blanco's minions wouldn't last long now that the war was over. He was promptly fired.[3]

Manuel Blanco, whose wealth rested on commerce as well as on the plantation, apparently journeyed back to Spain after the war, leaving his nephew Manuel García Blanco behind to manage his affairs. The cranky old uncle never drew up a will of his own, and when he died in 1906 the inheritance was quickly contested. His sister, his nephew, and various kinsfolk living in the Canary Islands vied for shares of his estate. The testament of José Quesada by which Blanco had acquired the plantation now became relevant to the property claims of the Blanco heirs, sending attorneys back to the 1870 notarial volumes.[4]

In the close-knit city of Cienfuegos, word of Article 11 of that will, the provision for *gracias* for Quesada's slaves, now escaped from the sanctum of the notary's office and began to reach an unintended audience. One of the first to get the word seems to have been the sixty-two-year-old Andrea Quesada. A former slave on Santa Rosalía, she quickly inferred that she should have benefited from the *gracias* to which José Quesada had made reference thirty-six years earlier. In her view, José Quesada's last wishes had been violated by Manuel Blanco, and she was entitled to claim damages from the estate.[5]

Andrea Quesada was, by all accounts, a strong personality and a tough customer. She had been in her twenties when gradual abolition began in the 1870s, and in her thirties when the *patronato* was established in 1880. During the last full year that she was held in bondage on Santa Rosalía, as we have seen, the overseer had complained bitterly that she thought she could "magnetize" everyone on the estate, but that he would refuse to let her control *him*. Instead, he submitted his resignation. "I did not take this job to be kicked around by black women, much less of her kind," he had written.[6] It cannot have escaped anyone's notice, however, that he was the one who backed down.

Now, twenty years later, as word of Article 11 of José Quesada's will reached Andrea Quesada, she decided to confront the management of Santa Rosalía again. This time she would use the court system, and she would frame her claim as a formal demand for reparations. In her view, the *gracias* that should have been hers by the 1870 will had been concealed by Manuel Blanco, and the time had come for his estate to repair the damage thus done. She conveyed a notarized power of attorney to a Spanish merchant, Julián Cabrera y Cao, to represent her under the authority of a Santa Clara lawyer, Benito A. Besada, a Liberal Party activist. Cabrera and Besada took legal steps to try to oblige the Blanco heirs to produce the list of slaves and the *gracias* owed them. When that failed, they filed suit to block the Blanco inheritance altogether, in order to impose retroactively what they took to be the original intent of the deceased José Quesada.[7]

Andrea Quesada's representatives implied in their argument before the court that the *gracias* in Article 11 referred to manumission, and that Andrea Quesada should therefore have been freed upon José Quesada's death in 1876, not kept in bondage for another decade. The failure of Manuel Blanco to have made public in 1876 the list of names and gifts mentioned in Article 11, they argued, should invalidate both Blanco's inheritance of Santa Rosalía from José Quesada and the inheritance Blanco's heirs were now preparing to assume. Cabrera fired off notices to the descendants of Blanco who lived in the family townhouse on the Calle San Fernando in Cienfuegos, and to those who were far away in the Canary Islands.[8]

In the tumultuous year of 1906, shaken first by the aftermath of a contested and corrupted election, then by the armed revolt of the Liberal Party, and finally by a U.S. military occupation of the island, there seems to have been a measure of political space within which to press this claim. The heirs of the conspicuously wealthy, conservative Spaniard Manuel Blanco are not likely to have been particularly popular in early republican Cienfuegos. Andrea Quesada's legal representative called the court's particular attention to the *pingües bienes* (juicy fortune) that Blanco had amassed, emphasizing the power that Blanco had exercised across the years he had improperly held Andrea Quesada and others in slavery.[9]

As word spread in 1906 that it might be possible to prove that Manuel Blanco had cheated the former slaves of Santa Rosalía, the field of claimants grew. Andrea Quesada gave her power of attorney to Cabrera on May 22, 1906. On July 26 Silverio Quesada Acevedo followed her lead, as did Torcuato (known as "Cuatro"), Marcial, Alejandro, Germán, Caridad, Clara, Águeda, and Cristóbal Quesada Acevedo. These nine African-born survivors of slavery at Santa Rosalía were accompanied by five Creole men and women: Gregoria (known as "Goya"), Ventura, Eduarda, Luis, and León Quesada Acevedo. A few days later they were joined by eight more men and women. In filing their powers of attorney, all now used a double surname, Quesada Acevedo.[10]

Meanwhile, another group of former slaves from Santa Rosalía went to a second notary. Identified by the courtesy title Don, by their first names (Hilario, Miguel, Ceferino, and Cándido), and by the single surname Quesada, they were labeled "sin otro apellido" (without a second surname), a marker of illegitimate birth that was often applied to men and women of color. These four men from the rural districts of Arimao and Lagunillas conveyed their power of attorney to Ramón Ramos Quesada, thirty-five years old, whom the notary listed with the courtesy title Don. Ramos Quesada, in turn, conveyed the power of attorney to Cabrera, who was representing Andrea Quesada, thus consolidating the various claims.[11]

The leading figures in this twenty-seven-person challenge seem to have been Andrea Quesada, the lawyer Benito Besada, the merchant Julián Cabrera, and the ingenious Ramos Quesada. Ramos Quesada is to this day recalled as a short black man with a primary-school education who was "good at moving papers," and whose nickname was *el abogado*—the lawyer.[12] Among those who came together to participate were thus not only several resisters of long standing, including the charismatic Andrea and the sharp-tongued Asunción, but also the previously more accommodating Ramos Quesada, who had guarded the estate's cattle during the war. They now shared the goal of recovering some portion of Manuel Blanco's property for the former slaves named Quesada from Santa Rosalía.[13]

Like unlettered people in other times and places, those formerly held in slavery on Santa Rosalía had developed a network of access to writing that went beyond their individual levels of literacy. Someone—perhaps Andrea Quesada—had gotten wind of the writing in the notarial records of Cienfuegos that confirmed the existence of Article 11 of José Quesada's will. Then someone—probably Ramos Quesada, who knew how to write—had set about the task of locating and obtaining powers of attorney from those who might be construed as beneficiaries of the newly identified *gracias*. Through the action of a literate intermediary who could link rural former slaves to urban advocates, written texts in the form of legal documents were being created out of oral networks, the better to engage formal rules concerning inheritance in a new set of circumstances.[14]

The strategy of delegating writing and deploying texts in order to prove standing and assert entitlements had a long history. But prior to abolition and the wars for independence, slaves and *patrocinados* who went to court had to plead as second-class claimants for the protection of colonial law. Now Andrea Quesada and the others were taking hold of the legal system as citizens, not supplicants. These former slaves saw a shared interest in this legal action in pursuit of property and standing, and together they had the resources to undertake it. Their initiative, moreover, did not bear the usual marks of individual client-patron relations found elsewhere in the notarial records, particularly those documenting loans by officers to their former subordinates. Ramos Quesada, Andrea Quesada, and their neighbors were aiming higher.[15]

Any such campaign, of course, did require attorneys and allies. While the cooperating lawyer and merchant may have been motivated by principles, or by the promise of a percentage, they may also have seen a political gain in taking up the cause of the Quesadas from Santa Rosalía. Benito Besada, the Santa Clara lawyer who lent his name to the case, had been an activist in José Miguel Gómez's Partido Republicano Federal de las Villas (Federal Republican Party of Las Villas) in the early years of the first U.S. occupation, though he had broken with the party shortly thereafter in a complicated maneuver concerning the Platt Amendment. If he had continuing political aspirations, Besada might have good reason to construct himself as a champion of a local community that had been cheated by a now dead Spaniard.[16]

The core of Andrea Quesada's case rested on the irregularity of Manuel Blanco's suppression of Article 11, and on a broader and more resonant claim to have been improperly held in bondage. The implication of her argument was that the *gracias* intended by her former master included manumission for all of his slaves. This was a bold assertion, and the written record provides little evidence of so sweeping an intention on the part of José Quesada. But such a claim could nonetheless be voiced with confidence in Cienfuegos in 1906. Spanish rule had been ended in a struggle during which Cuban rebel leaders associated slavery and its legacies not with Cubans but with Spanish colonialism. The 1901 Constitution had endorsed transracial citizenship as a pillar of the new Republic. Claims to hold property in men and women were a discredited relic of an earlier epoch, readily denounced in a republican courtroom.

The lawsuit, however, did not prosper. The attorney for Manuel Blanco's recognized heirs invoked the limitations of the passage of time *(prescripción)* and effectively shifted the burden of proof back to the claimant: unless Andrea Quesada could demonstrate that the list of slaves and *gracias* actually existed, and that her name was on the list, the claim should be thrown out. The Blanco family defendants professed to believe that the list perhaps never existed; certainly they could not recall having seen any trace of it among the papers of the deceased. Absent the list, Andrea Quesada was not an heir and thus, the Blanco lawyer argued, had no standing to sue in the first place. The judge in Cienfuegos agreed, and rejected her demands. The appellate court in the provincial capital of Santa Clara overruled the assertion that Andrea Quesada lacked standing, but concurred with the claim of prescription, arguing that too much time had elapsed since José Quesada's death. The appellate court thus upheld the overall decision of the lower court.[17]

At this point, Andrea Quesada and Ramos Quesada were faced with a nearly insurmountable obstacle. To overcome the claim of prescription, their lawyer had tried to argue that the failure to carry out Article 11 of the will made the subsequent ownership of the plantation itself null and void, hence an uncompleted inheritance. The courts had not agreed. Ramos Quesada and the attorneys persisted, however, and appealed the decision to Cuba's Supreme Court. Marcelino Iznaga Suárez Román, who still lives in a settlement adjacent to Santa Rosalía, recalls that years ago his father, Victoriano Iznaga, told him about a conversation he had with Ramos Quesada, who was preparing to travel to Havana to pursue the case. Marcelino Iznaga's father apparently suggested to Ramos Quesada that this was a lost cause, because the former slaves would never have enough money to win against the Blanco family. Ramos Quesada is said to have responded, "Even without money we are going to put up a fight. At least we'll get things clear." ("Nosotros sin dinero vamos a echar la pelea. Por lo menos vamos a aclarar.")[18]

Like the plaintiffs in *Plessy v. Ferguson* in New Orleans in the 1890s, Ramos and Andrea Quesada seem to have taken the view that fighting the case was the next best thing to winning it. At least that way there could be no mistaking the sentiments of those who believed themselves to have been wronged. Pursuing the case all the way to the Supreme Court would also make public Andrea Quesada's status as a rights-bearing citizen, and undercut the claims of those whose power over her had rested on the old relations of slavery. But in 1908 the Cuban Supreme Court upheld the lower court's decision, reiterating the finding of prescription and ruling Andrea Quesada's claim to have come too late. The case was closed.[19]

A group of former slaves had nonetheless succeeded in taking a prosperous local family to court, and lived to tell the tale. Like Gregoria Quesada's 1899 claim to a mule held by the administrator of Santa Rosalía, Andrea Quesada's lawsuit tapped into the wartime construction of Cuba's cross-racial national identity and evoked the idea of solidarity with the victims of Spanish exactions. The surviving evidence, and the larger theory of recompense for illegal enslavement, proved too fragile for the claim to prevail in the face of skeptical judges. But by attributing an act of benevolence to a long-dead master, and deceit to the more proximate one, the lawsuit had asserted a moral and legal warrant for claims by the living. Decades later, various members of the community recalled stories of Blanco's machinations and of irregularities in the Quesada will, even though the lost lawsuit itself had been nearly forgotten. Indeed, the former slaves' thwarted legal claim to a portion of the inheritance occasionally grew in memory beyond the elusive *gracias* to encompass a right to the land of the entire plantation.[20]

Initiatives like those of Andrea Quesada persisted despite the occupation of the island by U.S. forces utterly unsympathetic to assertions of this kind. As part of its military intervention beginning in 1906, the United States sent a U.S. "Army of Cuban Pacification" out into the countryside, particularly to those portions of the island with the densest concentration of U.S. investments. Officers of the Military Information Division were instructed to take the pulse of the public, to identify potential dangers, and to map the terrain. In their role as military occupiers of a country whose population was thought to be generally unreliable, they drew heavily on the services of paid informers and on gossip conveyed by English-speaking residents. They filed field reports composed of a tangle of tendentious judgments and revealing detail, in which ground-level events appeared as if through a narrow and distorting lens.[21]

Both high U.S. officials and low-level officers found the public assertion of rights by black citizens quite distasteful. Republican and Democrat alike, U.S. officers and civilian appointees reflected the trend at home in which claims to political voice by the descendants of slaves were being refused. Equally baffling to these occupiers was the seeming ability of Cubans to form cross-racial alliances. The ideology of the Cuban independence movement, particularly as it was interpreted by white power holders, endorsed black Cuban political participation precisely as part of such alliances, rather than within groups defined by color. Both major Cuban parties vied for black support. But for the occupying U.S. forces, these alliances themselves were unnatural and tainted with overtones of manipulation and criminality. The Military Information officers often found cross-racial political mingling as troubling as the rumors of "Negro conspiracies" that were the favorite alarmist staple of their various informers.[22]

In the same way that General Leonard Wood had in 1901 misjudged the depth of Cuban sentiment in favor of universal manhood suffrage and underestimated the willingness of Cuban politicians to accommodate it, U.S. authorities in 1906–1907 initially clung to the hope that white, English-speaking, unconditional defenders of property and of the U.S. intervention could simply reassert class rule in the Republic. What U.S. officials seem not to have fully understood was that a populist figure like the Liberal leader José Miguel Gómez had a thoroughly Cuban strategy for maintaining a different kind of class dominance, one modeled on the authority of white officers in the multiracial Liberation Army. In a polity in which men of color constituted 30 percent of the electorate, cross-racial politicking, cooptation, and clientelism made a good deal more sense to Gómez than white-supremacist posturing.[23]

Cubans of color were divided on whether to make the best of the major parties' inclusive strategies or try to organize autonomously. What they took for granted, however, was that they were players in the electoral game. When Cubans of color attended political meetings, held public offices, and spoke in public, they were embodying the ideals of racial confraternity of José Martí and Antonio Maceo. But their public presence only heightened U.S. alarm. The majority-black communities of Congojas and Parque Alto, inland from Cienfuegos, for example, seemed particularly ominous to the head of the Secret Service: "The police force of Congojas, a small place just northeast of Rodas, consists of one mulatto. The natives stay at home during the day but at night are off on their horses." And when the Americans oversaw the confiscation of weapons in Cienfuegos, an agent wrote that the "immense advantage of taking even 254 rifles out of the hands of irre-sponsible negroes can hardly be overestimated." Conflating their anxieties about race and class, the U.S. intelligence officers tended to characterize the supporters of José Miguel Gómez and the Liberal Party simply as "dangerous men."[24]

There was a certain irony to the U.S. hostility to the Liberal Party and its sup-porters, whom the occupiers perceived as largely the "lower class of whites" and the "Negro element." To some of the most adamant of Cuban activists of color, this same Liberal Party seemed to be too exclusionary in its leadership to ade-quately represent their interests. Already in 1905 Evaristo Estenoz, a *mulato* vet-eran and labor leader, had argued that men of dignity, if they were to merit the term "free men," should require of society that it treat them with respect. The Liberals, he charged, had required dutiful loyalty of their black supporters, but did not offer such respect in return. Estenoz nonetheless remained with the Liberal Party for the moment, and rose to the rank of general in the 1906 Liberal revolt.[25]

During the early months of the U.S. occupation that followed, Evaristo

Estenoz traveled to Cienfuegos and Santa Clara, where some citizens proved receptive to the claims for fair treatment and a larger share of public offices for veterans of color. Eloy González, son of the respected black Cuban general José González Planas, distributed handbills in Cienfuegos in 1907 denouncing instances of exclusion of Cubans of color from the planning for political events. He argued that "the colored race, which has fought and spilled rivers of its generous blood, deserves the respect due in the public life of its nation to any group that has contributed as Cubans to the building of this mistreated Republic." The U.S. Military Information Division, in turn, filed a report describing him as "a shrewd, poorly educated, aggressive negro residing in this city who has a large following in this part of Santa Clara Province."[26]

Throughout 1907, activists of color continued to frame their political assertions in terms of the ideals of cross-racial fraternity. Veterans of color, including the longtime organizer Evaristo Estenoz, the respected colonel Pedro Ivonet, and the former plantation laborer Ricardo Batrell, spoke out as men who had helped to create the nation itself. They insisted that a claim to respect and reciprocity was not the same thing as a call for racial separatism—much less an incitement to race war. And when Eloy González denounced white politicians for neglecting black citizens, he drew upon the language of transracial patriotism: "men's prejudice, which undermines all sentiment of honorable generosity, is acting not to unite all of the Cuban races, but to head instead down the road of division, and the worst kind of division, division into races."[27] In the face of what they perceived as disrespectful treatment, some activists began to think in terms of a united front of men and women of color, designed to put pressure on the parties by raising consistent demands for black representation.[28]

Most U.S. observers, however, still had great difficulty understanding invocations of equal rights in terms other than "conspiracy." After a meeting in Cienfuegos endorsed by the eminently respectable journalist Juan Gualberto Gómez, Major W. D. Beach of the U.S. Cavalry reported "disquieting rumors about negro gatherings" and mysterious "so-called commissioners"—two cigar makers and a carpenter from Havana who made the rounds of the major towns of the Cienfuegos region. It all added up, a "negro in [his] employ" reported, to a movement to "secure the election of as many negroes as possible to the offices of

Alcalde and other municipal positions at the approaching elections and subsequently to elect their own candidates to the federal offices," as well as a demand for 50 percent representation in the Rural Guard, then scheduled for a large-scale expansion.[29] Politics as usual in a multiracial republic, one might think. But to Cubans who viewed black deference as a prerequisite for participation, these claims hinted at insubordination. And to U.S. officers accustomed to white supremacy, such demands were insolent and tantamount to potential insurrection.

The dynamic of suspicion and misattribution of motive was bound to increase tensions. By treating claims to voice and representation as conspiratorial, the U.S. occupiers portrayed activists of color as inherently dangerous. And by casting doubt on the standing of those who spoke the language of equal rights, both U.S. officials and some Cuban observers affronted the honor of veteran officers like Evaristo Estenoz and Eloy González for whom the wartime sacrifices of Cubans of color were a sacred mark of membership in the nation. The humiliations of military occupation of the island by the United States further complicated the struggle for power among Cubans, who would now for a second time have to earn the right to be a republic and comport themselves properly in elections in order to establish a new regime.

By early 1908 Evaristo Estenoz had become disenchanted with the established parties. Seeking a larger role in the upcoming elections, he and his closest allies formed an Agrupación Independiente de Color (Independent Group of Color), a pressure group of black and *mulato* activists, most of them previously affiliated with the Liberal Party. The formal aims of the Agrupación included not only obtaining a share of government posts but also proving the capacity of the "colored race." A week later the group began publishing a newspaper, *Previsión,* and elaborating a reformist agenda focused on gaining public respect and access to resources controlled by the state. Like their counterparts in Louisiana a few years earlier, the members of the Agrupación denounced a system permitting "privileges and castes" as a "false democracy."[30]

This initiative was, in the words of Estenoz, a symbolic refusal to kneel and beg for respect from the established parties. But it could also be portrayed by its opponents as a symbolic break with the familiar forms of cross-racial unity, even if the ideology of Antonio Maceo was its touchstone. Ultimately only a small

number of the original equal rights activists, and few voters of color, were willing to follow Estenoz down the path of autonomous electoral organizing. The
Agrupación presented a list of candidates for the November 1908 congressional
and presidential elections in Havana and Santa Clara provinces, but they were utterly swamped in the ensuing Liberal victory. In Oriente, they could not put together enough signatures to get on the ballot.[31]

As Estenoz and others were debating the relative merits of organizing through
or outside the two main parties, rural Cubans of all colors struggled to find the
food and wages they needed to survive. However vigorous their sense of deserving respect, their most immediate focus was necessarily land and tools rather than
elective or appointed office. A confidential report filed by an officer in the U.S.
occupation forces described the situation in the area around Soledad and Santa
Rosalía plantations in the summer of 1907: "The people living in the vicinity of
Constancia, Cumanayagua, Soledad, Guaos and, in fact, throughout the country
are practically destitute. The drought has ruined the vegetable crop and they have
no money to carry them over to the next season."[32] Among those living in this
district were the kin and neighbors of Andrea Quesada, who had initiated the lawsuit against Manuel Blanco. In filing powers of attorney that might enable them to
follow her example if she won, these men and women were, in effect, envisioning
multiple strategies aimed at achieving some measure of resources, respect, and
public voice.

Formal claims made through the legal system were matched by informal claims
made in the day-to-day court of community opinion. Even a seemingly precise
notion like "land ownership" had an on-the-ground counterpart quite separate
from the written property register. Alejandro Quesada, a former slave, was one
of those who filed a power of attorney in preparation for legal action against the
heirs of Manuel Blanco. But he and his son Cayetano Quesada, veteran of the
1895–1898 war, had already joined with their white neighbor Zacarías González
to gain a foothold in the tract of pastureland adjacent to the Soledad plantation.
Although the neighbors might consider these *sitios* in San Antón to be legitimate
settlements, the administrators at Soledad plantation were likely to view the veterans as at best tenants-at-will on land of the title holder, María Ravella y Carr. In
1901 Edwin Atkins had sought to buy the land, and tried to commit María Ravella

to evicting the squatters. But for the moment the Soledad sugar mill needed cane to grind more than it needed petty lawsuits. The jib of land in San Antón was of relatively little consequence compared with the large tracts the owners of Soledad hoped to acquire, and the residents were also potential laborers and cane suppliers. Soledad's account books for 1908 list Zacarías González from San Antón as one of the farmers supplying cane to the mill, along with the former slaves Aniceto Sarría and Ceferino Quesada. Cayetano Quesada himself worked for wages on Soledad's Belmonte cane farm.[33]

Those who were earning cash in town could themselves sometimes enter the formal land market. Gregoria Quesada continued with her purchases of land in the foothills town of La Sierra that provided her with a farm on which to establish her sons. By the time she died, around 1913, she would leave twelve different plots of land to her four children, who included a stevedore and a *pailero* (sugar boiler) still living near Cienfuegos, a third son in nearby Abreus, and a daughter who had gone east to Santiago de Cuba.[34]

As in Louisiana during Reconstruction, the search for economic and physical security was intertwined with the defense of the right to a public voice. But in Cuba, unlike Louisiana after 1898, voting and officeholding by men of color were now commonplace. Gabriel Quesada, for example, was a classic intermediary figure, bridging generations, neighborhoods, and skills. He was described in the census as a *mulato,* married, and thirty-nine years old. He had settled in the port neighborhood of Aduana in the city of Cienfuegos in 1900, just after the end of the war, and immediately registered to vote. He knew how to read and write, as did his carpenter neighbor Manuel Quesada, the stevedores Luis José Quesada y Pérez and José Quesada y Pérez, and the young workman Juan Quesada y Beltrán. Their older stevedore neighbor, also named Manuel Quesada, a more recent migrant to the *barrio,* could read but not write.[35]

The resources of the web of kin and neighbors named Quesada had come to spread across an expanded polygon, encompassing the docks and the city of Cienfuegos, the small farms in the foothills and along the Arimao River, the sugar plantations of Soledad and Santa Rosalía, the sugar towns like Abreus, and, in a few instances, the metropolises of Havana and Santiago. Each of the strategies for advancement undertaken by different families held out some promise and some risks. Cayetano Quesada combined wage labor and small-scale farming, even without title to his farm. Gregoria Quesada had careful recourse to the notary for her purchases, and left a will. Gabriel Quesada obtained a salaried job, though he was singled out by the U.S. military as a suspicious character because of his links to other activists of color. In addition, all of the men in the group were by 1907 registered voters, under suffrage rules that made voter registration nearly synonymous with census enumeration.[36]

When in 1908 Evaristo Estenoz reconfigured the Agrupación Independiente de Color into an Independent Party of Color and sought to build support in places like Cienfuegos, he necessarily had to seek support from groups like the Quesadas and from others descended from slave families who carried the surnames Sarría, Apezteguía, Acea, or Terry. But with the workforce on the plantations now thoroughly multiracial, and the same true of the dockworkers' union in town and of most farming communities in the countryside, this was not particularly propitious terrain on which to organize a political party defined along racial lines. Many men of color, particularly the veterans, already had long-standing ties to the Liberal Party and its networks of clientele, often mediated through the multiracial associations of veterans. The complaints of disrespect for black citizens voiced by Eloy González and Evaristo Estenoz probably rang true to those, like Gabriel Quesada, who were directly involved in urban politics. But they and their rural neighbors were likely to be equally convinced of the necessity of avoiding "divisions." They might suffer disrespect from white power-holders, but they also relied on multiple cross-racial relationships and alliances in the workplace and in their public lives. Even the lawsuit claiming rights for many of the Quesadas as former slaves was built on their link to the merchant Julián Cabrera and to the lawyer Benito Besada. Making race the primary axis of political affiliation could undermine this mode of operation.[37]

As the Agrupación made its transition from pressure group to political party, it also found itself at a symbolic disadvantage. Its express goal was inclusion on the basis of mutual respect, not racial separatism. But the Cuban ideology of racial fraternity, while making it difficult to exclude Cubans of color from the polity, also "made it possible to delegitimize any attempt at racially defined mobilization."[38] An activist or voter who began down the path of allegiance to the Partido

Independiente de Color would face this potential accusation, along with all the overtones of danger and ingratitude built up through years of talk of "black conspiracies."

The problem of Estenoz and the *independientes,* however, went beyond the efforts of their enemies to delegitimate them. Estenoz's initiative suffered from a paucity of friends. Respected activists and politicians of color who had achieved recognition through the established parties, including Juan Gualberto Gómez, Martín Morúa Delgado, and Rafael Serra, might be expected to shun the Independent Party of Color out of both principle and self-interest. Each set of leaders, after all, could be seen as seeking to increase their share of a finite pool of patronage. Morúa, for example, was closely entwined in the politics of clientele of the Liberal Party. But quite subtle competing ideologies were also at stake. Rafael Serra, an eloquent journalist and longtime ally of José Martí, had over the years developed a picture of citizenship that emphasized civic participation, education, and mutual aid. Political parties might be an essential element of electoral life, and Serra himself became a senator in 1908. But for Serra parties were not the main vehicle for defining citizenship, and they held a dangerous potential for corruption. His stance implied neither deference nor accommodation to racism. Serra instead envisioned racial democracy as something built up from the base through the exercise of civic virtue. He believed in counteracting the slurs of racists not only with self-help and forbearance but also through exemplary public action.[39]

Serra's ideal of respect earned through virtuous action, fused with an uncompromising claim to full political and civil rights, more closely resembled the ideas of Louis Martinet and Rodolphe Desdunes in Louisiana than those of Booker T. Washington in Tuskegee, though Serra shared in the general admiration for Washington's accomplishments in the field of education. Serra's prescriptions, along with those of the Liberal Party ideologist and power broker Juan Gualberto Gómez, could hold a strong appeal for aspiring men and women of color across the island, particularly the thousands who belonged to one or another society for education and mutual aid. His fellow-journalist Lino D'Ou, whose reputation was enhanced by his record of service alongside General José Maceo, drew on much the same spirit.[40]

Even local militants and autodidacts like the veterans Ricardo Batrell and Eloy González, who might be expected to respond to Estenoz's language of honorable self-defense and assertion, insisted on the value of racial fraternity as a response to the quite visible evidence of white racism. Batrell, so confirmed a resister that he had once taken to the hills in rebellion all by himself, nonetheless kept his distance from the Independent Party of Color.[41] Eloy González, despite the antiblack thinking among urban elites in the final years of the Estrada Palma administration and the racial arrogance of the U.S. occupation authorities, invoked citizenship, earned through sacrifice, rather than the right to retaliation. Even in the face of provocations from those who advocated "whitening" the Cuban population through European immigration, and from journalists quick to evoke stereotypes of black witchcraft and "atavism," the great majority of Cuban activists of color replied in the language of respect, fraternity, and reciprocity. Sensing that this was the moral high ground, they sought not to discredit racial equality as a myth, but rather to propound it as an ideal not yet achieved. To the extent that the new Republic was falling short of the imagined reciprocity and respect that had characterized the struggle for national independence, it needed to be brought back to those ideals, and race-conscious rhetoric was potentially at odds with that goal. It is not surprising that the one document that we have from the local Cienfuegos activist Gabriel Quesada in 1908 is his request to Juan Gualberto Gómez for a copy of the electoral law.[42]

If most voters of color declined to support the Independent Party of Color, they also initially had little reason to anticipate a major backlash against it. In 1908 the Cuban countryside was not particularly propitious terrain for the mobilization of racialized thinking among white people either. There was relatively little evidence of the populist variant of violent racism that mirrored elite racism in Louisiana politics. During the 1902 Cuban sugar strikes, some planters had invoked the danger of masses of black workers, but most observers knew that the strikes were organized along class, not racial, lines. And anyone could see that the Liberal Party's own clientele, built up from units of the Liberation Army, was thoroughly cross-racial and supported by many of the labor unions. White racial domination might still be a discreetly held presumption of most white Cuban political leaders, and racial deference a rule of etiquette during the evening strolls in the public parks. But both those who took this deference for granted and those who hoped to replace it with a greater degree of mutual respect seemed to agree that cross-racial alliances should and would be the fundamental basis of Cuban politics.

In the last months of the U.S. occupation, the possibility of renewing the republican experiment gave new life to the discourse of patriotic unity. Following the presidential election of 1908, Cubans bid U.S. governor Magoon and his troops farewell and welcomed the new, popularly elected Liberal president José Miguel Gómez, along with his old rival-turned-ally, Vice President Alfredo Zayas. In January of 1909, as the United States prepared its departure, Governor Magoon was fêted in Cienfuegos with elegant receptions, paid his respects to the Casino Español, and conveyed his best wishes to the Spanish-born population. In March, the new President Gómez arrived to a crowd of eight thousand people waiting on the wharf, visited the city council and the home of a prominent Cuban planter, and attended the dance held in his honor at the Sociedad Minerva, the city's leading society for people of color.[43]

Once in power, José Miguel Gómez moved quickly to consolidate the Liberal Party, welcoming activists of color who had never left the Liberal fold as well as those who were now ready to return. He did not propose to allow much space for those whose ambitions took them in a more autonomous direction, however. Nor was he eager to cut a deal with a figure like Pedro Ivonet, the former Liberation Army colonel, now member of the Independent Party of Color, who offered to swing votes in exchange for a chance at public office.[44] Frustrated, the leadership of the Independent Party of Color and the newspaper Previsión became yet more hostile to the established parties, and began to prepare for elections in 1910.[45] With formal state power now back in the hands of Cubans, albeit under the shadow of possible future interventions by the United States, the independientes hoped to be able to call the established parties to account on the issue of racial equality.

It is virtually impossible to determine who actually joined the Independent Party of Color during this period. The leaders' own estimates were naturally self-serving, and no one else undertook a count. The newspaper Previsión appears to have circulated fairly widely, promoting demands for reform and a discourse of racial pride. It claimed fifty-three registered municipal committees of the party in the province of Santa Clara alone, and the support of 60,000 members, among them 15,000 veterans, across the island. There is little corroborating evidence for such sweeping assertions, however, and it would be imprudent to estimate Estenoz's support through his own political organ. The party had attracted enough followers to trigger the ire of the Liberals, who charged Estenoz with libel. But many of those who looked to *Previsión* for eloquent denunciations of discrimination may not have looked to Estenoz for a practical political solution to their immediate problems.[46]

Here lay the contradiction within which Estenoz and the Independent Party of Color had to maneuver. They wished to mount, in effect, a great civic campaign against racial discrimination, at a time when the established parties had little interest in defining the struggle for resources in this way. In the process, Estenoz reached for two concepts—"party" and "color"—that seemed to him logically and strategically necessary to this task. But as a result, he opened his group to a formal counterattack that deflected attention from discrimination to focus it on politics and procedure. Moreover, in his effort to assert the manhood of Cubans of color, Estenoz used a language of honor and physical self-defense that could sound quite belligerent: "Any man of color who does not instantly kill the cowardly aggressor who bothers him in a public place is a miserable person unworthy to be a man, and he dishonors his race and his homeland." Estenoz sought to rally Cuban citizens against racial discrimination exercised by foreign shopkeepers—hence the reference to the honor of the homeland. But a casual reader, or a political opponent, could easily see his words as a racialized call to arms.[47]

In an effort to block Estenoz's initiatives, Martín Morúa Delgado, a Liberal senator who identified himself as a man of color, introduced a proposed amendment to the Cuban electoral law that would deny the title of political party to any group containing members of only one race, color, or class, if class was to be defined by birth, wealth, or diploma. With the language changed to refer only to race or color, and with the addition of a qualifying phrase characterizing the groups to be prohibited as those seeking "racist goals," the bill was passed by the Senate in February 1910. Although it would not become law until approved by the House, it immediately placed a cloud over the Independent Party of Color. In this unpropitious climate, Evaristo Estenoz, recently released from imprisonment for his inflammatory editorial in *Previsión,* set out on his electoral campaign.[48]

The best vantage point from which to examine the full potential of the Independent Party of Color during 1910 is not Havana, where José Miguel Gómez and the Liberal Party maneuvered to try to undercut it, or Santa Clara, where its support seems to have been fleeting. Its deepest roots, in terms of both the origins of its leadership and the possibility of anchoring it in a popular political culture, were in the eastern province of Oriente. In the country's second-largest city, Santiago de Cuba, and even more in the sugar-growing and smallholding hinterland of that city, the party found by 1910 a distinctive set of conditions and abundant grievances. The call for a forthright political reply to white racism encountered its most receptive listeners in the east, encouraging Estenoz toward more daring gambles.

Oriente was the birthplace of Cuban revolutions, and the home of a large and long-free population of color as well as thousands of former slaves. It had a tradition of public activism and military action by men of color. Antonio and José Maceo, Guillermo Moncada, Agustín Cebreco, and Quintín Bandera had defied Spanish rule throughout the last decades of the nineteenth century and had risen to the rank of general in the Liberation Army. Captain Hermenegildo Portuondo Río and Colonel Pedro Ivonet, also based in Oriente, had followed Moncada and Maceo into battle and now supported the Partido Independiente de Color.[49] They would try to link their campaign with the memory of Antonio Maceo and mobilize voters against the presumptions of the Liberals. The strongest potential support for the party seems to have been centered in the coastal area around Guantánamo and in a cluster of towns in the southeast, including San Luis, La Maya, Alto Songo, and Palma Soriano.[50] Inland and across the first range of mountains from the city of Santiago, this cluster was in the lush corner of the island where the three regiments of African American soldiers, including Pierre Carmouche and the Ninth Volunteer Infantry from Louisiana, had been stationed in 1898–99. It was also the region in which Cuban troops under General Agustín Cebreco had lingered during those same months, disconcerting U.S. general Leonard Wood.

As soon as war had given way to truce in the summer of 1898, some of these Cuban veterans had sought land and animals, hoping to begin their peacetime existence with access to productive resources.[51] But when the sugar mills resumed grinding and investors arrived on the scene to organize the planting of more cane, access to good land began to be highly contested. The classic Caribbean dilemma became increasingly apparent: rural dwellers needed a combination of food security and wage labor, access to land and access to jobs. But like their counterparts in Louisiana, Oriente's new plantation owners preferred laborers they could control, preferably without alternative sources of income.[52] And, ideally, without political voice.

In the central province of Santa Clara, the expansion of sugar production had been built over decades through the multiplication of cane contracts between central mills and small- and medium-sized farms, an arrangement that left significant room for people to combine wage labor with food cultivation. But Oriente was different. Here, in the traditional refuge of runaways and the homeland of thousands of small-scale farmers, modern sugar mills were now rapidly buying up the land themselves, expelling those without title (as well as some of those with), and organizing production on the basis of gang labor. For rural families of color, particularly the families of veterans, the Independent Party of Color's assertion that they were being treated with disrespect politically could thus resonate with the experience, or the threat, of immediate economic dispossession.[53]

The potential electoral weight of Oriente's population of color was substantial. The province of Oriente as a whole held 87,305 Cuban male citizens of voting age, divided into the categories "whites born in Cuba" (45,710), "whites born in Spain" (2,795), and "colored" (38,481), giving whites a modest overall majority. But in several districts in Oriente, including San Luis, Alto Songo, Cobre, and Guantánamo, the great majority of the population was characterized as *negro* or *mestizo,* the latter term a genteel replacement for some of the older designations for those of apparently mixed African and European ancestry. When the census takers made a formal count of the population of the municipal district of San Luis in 1907, for example, they found 14,212 people. They counted 3,433 of the district's residents as "native white," 993 as "foreign white," and about 3,831 as "Negro." But far and away the largest group was the one they designated "mixed" *(mestizos),* whom they counted at 5,951.[54] Given the electoral rules in force since 1901, such tallies invariably gave these districts an electoral majority of men of color.

Voters in Oriente had shown little interest in the Agrupación Independiente de Color in 1908, dividing their votes between factions of the Liberal Party and the Conservatives, who had replaced the now-dissolved Moderate Party. Nationally, both of the parties had attracted distinguished activists and veterans of color to their electoral lists, including Juan Gualberto Gómez and Martín Morúa Delgado for the Liberals, and the journalist Rafael Serra, Lieutenant Colonel Lino D'Ou, and General Agustín Cebreco for the Conservatives. Indeed, more than a third of the representatives elected to the national Congress in 1908 from Oriente were men of color, including Cebreco and Serra. Although white politicians may have maneuvered to keep the representation of men of color below their proportion in the province's population, seven out of eighteen posts constituted more than a token number.[55]

Now, in 1910, the Liberals held the governorship of the province of Oriente, and the Conservatives dominated the city of Santiago de Cuba. Neither, however, seemed to offer much to the poorer residents of the countryside. Provincial governor Rafael Manduley was a white veteran who had fought alongside Maceo in the 1895 war, but who subsequently cultivated his ties to the elite of Santiago. And though several distinguished men of color figured prominently in the region's congressional delegations, white men tended to monopolize local offices.[56] Evaristo Estenoz, menaced by the pending Morúa Amendment, saw this as the moment to invoke a constitutional right of assembly and try to assert the political identity of the Independent Party of Color. He began a high-profile electoral tour through the province.

Local leaders of the *independientes,* who apparently did not hesitate to sign their names, openly announced their intentions to the provincial authorities. They passed along lists of the party's organizers, communicated the proposed routes for their marches, and specified the dates for their meetings. They comported themselves as regular participants in the electoral process, and reiterated that all would take place in good order. Governor Manduley was nonetheless highly alarmed, and characterized the party's propaganda as criminal, dangerous, and racist. He reported that in the region "blacks" were insolently speaking of the majority they held over "whites." In the stress of political conflict, a dichotomous categorization was winning out over the long-standing social custom of naming multiple gradations of color.[57]

By April of 1910 the governor was writing frantic letters to Havana predicting that Estenoz's followers would march on the city of Santiago, "cut off a few heads," and then retreat to the mountains. A few mayors enhanced his fears: from Alto Songo came a report that meetings of Estenoz sympathizers were "exciting" people against the white race. One of the local men accused of such propaganda, however, assured officials that the meetings were simply "exchanges of opinion." The tone was set by the governor's alarm, however. Local newspapers charged that the *independientes* had sworn before the Virgin of Cobre that they would carry out a war of extermination and vengeance against whites.[58]

It is difficult to extract from these breathless stories a clear picture of what Estenoz actually argued in his stump speeches in 1910, much less how his listeners responded. Newspapers in Havana reported somewhat more calmly that the

Independent Party of Color advocated that municipalities in Oriente with major-ity-black electorates should have black officials—not, on the face of it, a particu-larly incendiary claim. President José Miguel Gómez, however, was prepared to portray all of this oratory as "racist" and inflammatory, and he ordered Estenoz and the leaders of the party arrested on charges of conspiracy in April of 1910. After a trial in which they were defended by an attorney from the Conservative Party, they were absolved of the major charges. But in the interim, the Liberal Party had succeeded in moving the Morúa Amendment through the House of Representatives, and President Gómez immediately signed it.[59]

Amid all this partisan maneuvering, the most interesting question is the hardest to answer: what did rural people think that they might gain from listening to, and perhaps voting for, the Independent Party of Color? A fragmentary court record in the papers of the Audiencia de Santiago de Cuba provides a few clues. In the summer of 1910, local authorities in the town of Holguín had used the routine re-pressive mechanism of charging activists with "illicit association" for gathering at the home of Germán Cruz, a tailor, described as of the "black race" and of "brown color." One of those in attendance testified that the meeting had as its object to discuss whether it would be possible to form a party under the name "Inde-pendiente de Color" (Independent of Color) which could "encompass all ele-ments." One of those present at the meeting, he said, was José María Grave de Peralta, a white man. The Grave de Peralta family had a revolutionary history go-ing back decades. Enclosed in the court record was a sample handbill for the new party, distributed in the town of San Luis, which concluded, "We repeat that there is room for everyone, because we will preach healthy doctrines."[60]

The notion that this was a party fully "independent of color" was something of a stretch—the movement was built, after all, on the shared sense of grievance of activists of color. But the handbill, the testimony, and the composition of the or-ganizing group in Holguín all reinforced the claim that the Partido was a political initiative seeking support across social and racial lines, not a hate group or an ex-clusivist party. On a literal reading of the Morúa Amendment, their meetings could be permissible, as long as they conformed to the prevailing requirement to notify the authorities of such gatherings. The alarm and anxieties expressed by the governor, however, did not leave much room for such a reading.

Despite their careful use of language that repudiated the portrayal of the party as "racist," when the *independientes* persisted in trying to enter candidates in the elections in Oriente, local authorities often refused to accept them, and these rejections were upheld by the courts. The 1910 electoral campaigns thus ended in disarray for the party, which found itself caught between a congressional prohibition of dubious constitutionality, a judicial vendetta later ruled unfounded, and a public relations disaster of significant proportions, centering on the charge that it was the party members who were the "racists." Under the circumstances, it is hardly surprising that few organizations of people of color offered their support, preferring out of a mix of principle and prudence to stay in the good graces of the established political parties and, particularly, of President José Miguel Gómez.[61]

By the time of the 1912 elections, the Independent Party of Color was battered, fractured, and isolated in Havana and faltering elsewhere. Routinely denounced in the press as "racist," it had been crippled organizationally by the passage and signing of the Morúa Amendment to the Electoral Law. Its leadership had split, leaving Evaristo Estenoz and Pedro Ivonet as virtually the only remaining national figures aligned with the party. Estenoz and Ivonet seem to have made two calculations: first, that a demand for the relegalization of the party might be an effective rallying cry; second, that they should base their campaign in Oriente, where the population of color held a potential electoral majority in several districts. A meeting of their remaining followers held in early May 1912 then made a third calculation that would subsequently prove to be fatal: that an armed protest on May 20, 1912, the tenth anniversary of the founding of the Republic, would link them symbolically to the principles of the 1895–1898 war and give them leverage with which to rejoin the political process. Several leaders of the movement met with President Gómez to discuss the Morúa Amendment, and apparently left with the impression that in the midst of his reelection campaign he might support their call for repeal of the amendment.[62]

As the moment for the anticipated anniversary protest approached, Evaristo Estenoz traveled to Santiago with thousands of pamphlets calling for repeal of the Morúa Amendment. At a mass meeting, his supporters distributed invitations to a dance to be held in Belona, where Pedro Ivonet owned a farm. On May 19, Estenoz disappeared momentarily from view. Shortly thereafter, from the town of

San Luis, the mayor cabled the provincial governor to report that in the neighborhood of La Luz and on an adjacent farm about fifty men had gathered, apparently
looking for Lieutenant Colonel Tomás López Zapata, said to be their leader. A
few men were reported to have arrived in town from the city of Santiago, but the
town of San Luis itself was reported calm.[63]

On May 20, the mayor noted that some men known to be *independientes de color*
were suspiciously entering and leaving town on horseback. The next day one resident was said to have been assaulted by a group of men of color. The town remained calm—the sugar mills were grinding, and the nearby villages had celebrated the anniversary of independence with a *tumba francesa,* a dance ceremony
with African roots. But the mayor of the ward of La Luz in San Luis reported that
a gang of *independientes* had entered houses, stolen horses, recruited men, struck
women, threatened whites, and said that they would begin to burn things. On
May 22 a young man, Emilio Gómez, said to be an orator for the Independent
Party of Color, was taken into custody. On that same day, several warships holding
hundreds of government troops left Havana for Oriente.[64]

In the area around San Luis, May 20 had initially added up to a burst of com-
motion, bravado, and theft, with some nonlethal blows struck to accompany
the threats. For the island's newspapers, however, this was part of a broad
"Movimiento Racista," a "Racist Movement," defined by a reported exchange of
gunfire near Guantánamo between the Rural Guard and a band led by Pedro
Ivonet.[65] By May 23 the mayor of San Luis also became convinced that he had a
real insurrection on his hands: there were reports of one hundred men under
the command of Juan Guzmán, and another four hundred under Sixto Sosa y
Zapata—and they had Mausers.[66]

At this crucial moment, however, the mayor blurted out the most awkward
feature of the movement. The rebel bands were "recruiting people of all classes
and colors by explaining to them that it is not a race war but rather in favor of the
reelection of President Gómez and the repeal of the Morúa Law. If steps are not
taken immediately to discredit this version and crush them, they will keep picking
up strength and sympathy among ignorant people who will believe this criminal
uprising to be a political movement."[67] The problem, in other words, was not that

this was a movement founded on race hatred, as the press had insisted in its first dispatches. It was rather that for the men actually in the field and doing the recruiting, their efforts had more to do with mobilizing people to make specific demands upon the state. And with local veterans like Hermenegildo Portuondo Río in the lead, the claim of local *independientes* to the mantle of Maceo was not altogether far-fetched. Moreover, they seemed to be persuading a number of their neighbors to join them. The imputation of "political" goals to the rebels was also reinforced by Estenoz and Ivonet's request, less than 48 hours after the protest began, for negotiations with the national government. The government refused.

By May 26 the reports of armed bands had multiplied, to the point that an employee of the Ingenio Hatillo near San Luis believed there to be five hundred men camped nearby, engaging in what he called *simulacros* (mock battles) in the mountains. Meanwhile, armed repression had begun, combining local army units with the Rural Guard. In San Luis it was the army that was out in force, displaying "vigorous activity in pursuit." Mayors called for further reinforcements, and rumors of landings of U.S. troops began to spread. President Gómez repeatedly declared himself able to handle the protest without assistance, and on May 27 he sent the head of the armed forces, General José de Jesús ("Chucho") Monteagudo, and another shipload of troops to Oriente.[68]

Many of those involved in the activities in support of the May 20 protest may have envisioned, up to the last minute, that their leaders would reincorporate themselves into the Liberal Party as a kind of caucus, having backed Congress down on the question of the Morúa Amendment and given the party leadership a scare by raising the prospect of making off with the votes of citizens of color. Political *gritos,* proclamations made with supporters gathered and rifles raised, were a classic form of public demonstration. It had been only six years since José Miguel Gómez had rallied armed Liberals on horseback to intimidate President Tomás Estrada Palma. A regional revolt, seconded by protests elsewhere in the island, could lead to negotiations and power sharing. Pedro Ivonet's offer to broker votes for José Miguel Gómez, rejected in 1910, could in effect be reiterated with emphasis, backed up with a principled appeal for a public recognition of the special claims of veterans of color. The movement, though led by veterans experienced in guerrilla warfare, had refrained from any serious military engagement. Evaristo Estenoz apparently counted on the established rules of the game to keep his protest within the usual power politics of Cuba.

But the party leadership had drastically miscalculated. President José Miguel Gómez had every reason to court the electoral supporters of the *independientes,* but he would not tolerate an armed challenge from the margins of the fragile new Republic. Nervous about possible renewed U.S. military intervention, the government portrayed the protest as a dangerous act of "racist" antipatriotism. As the press campaign became more and more inflammatory, Cubans were encouraged not to view the movement as a variant on power politics among factions of veterans, each claiming the mantle of 1895 and the War of Independence. Instead, the very idea of the Partido Independiente was portrayed as dangerous blasphemy, in which the symbols of nationality were twisted by ingrates into a thing called "race war." By this logic, such blasphemy could be met only with patriotic counterforce.

Hints of cross-racial support for the protest continued to confound this picture, particularly when reporters stumbled upon white adherents of the movement.[69] And although across the nation the main story line was racial, a conservative newspaper in Santiago de Cuba had reported as early as May 27 on an interview with Estenoz and Ivonet in the town of La Maya, in which they denied that this was a race war, pledging to fight for the repeal of the Morúa Amendment and for equal rights between whites and blacks. Some Conservatives who were eager to use the fact of the protest to discredit the Liberals initially emphasized the constitutional rather than the racial dimensions of the movement for repeal. They soon, however, joined in the general alarm.[70]

By the second week, General José de Jesús Monteagudo had arrived in Oriente to lead the repression of what was left of the movement. By presidential decree, constitutional rights were suspended in the province. The army and Rural Guard units had been supplemented by volunteers from the city of Santiago de Cuba. In contrast to the cross-racial and cross-class army, the volunteer defense force was drawn almost exclusively from white-collar, and predominantly white, occupations: it included 244 merchants (43 of them Spanish) and 152 salaried employees, but only 25 day laborers (the majority of them Spanish) and 10 field workers.[71] Here, in the new Republic, was an ominous echo of earlier pro-Spanish *voluntarios* and *guerrilleros,* reframed as Cuban patriots.

The most sensational reports in the newspapers portrayed the army and the volunteers as protecting defenseless women against racist chieftains *(cabecillas racistas)* and savage hordes. To this visceral argument was added the need to defend both the state and the ideal of the nation. Some former officers in the Liberation Army stepped in to try to save their former colleagues Estenoz and Ivonet from the path of error. Thus Maceo's close comrade General Miró Argenter went on his own to Oriente to attempt to persuade the rebels to change course, and the black general Agustín Cebreco was also proposed as an intermediary.[72] But President José Miguel Gómez and General José de Jesús Monteagudo, who had aspirations of his own to the presidency, were determined to use force to demonstrate that it was they, not Estenoz and Ivonet, who had inherited the legitimacy of the 1895–1898 Army of Liberation. They would counter theatrical displays of force with dead-serious retaliation, and track suspected rebels with tenacity.[73]

Once the protest was framed by its political enemies as the opening battle of a "race war," repression reinforced this framing by defining its targets by race. And once the targets were defined by race, some additional men of color were likely to head to the *monte* in order to stay out of the way of the army, whether or not they had much sympathy with Estenoz. But although the local defense force in Santiago looked a good deal more like the White Leagues of New Orleans in 1874 than like the Cuban Liberation Army of 1895, this was still Cuba, not Louisiana. The language of justification invoked patriotism and equality, not regional resentment and white supremacy. For the immediate victims of state violence, of course, the distinction was moot. For their contemporaries' political interpretation of their deaths, however, it was not.[74]

What the army portrayed as a cleaning out of criminals and antipatriots, the black population in portions of Oriente experienced as a reign of terror. By all accounts, the killings by the army and by the volunteers were widespread, and included noncombatants. Army officers reported killing hundreds of rebels. Chilling stories circulated of women and children machine-gunned by the army, and of men decapitated simply on suspicion of sympathy for the Independent Party of

Color. Whether fully accurate or not, the stories themselves added to the terror. Hundreds of men were summarily arrested. Across the island, newspapers provided sensationalist reporting on the campaign against what was now widely portrayed as a racist uprising.[75]

It seems clear that there had been both a disastrous miscalculation by the Partido itself and a conscious effort by the Gómez administration to exaggerate the threat of insurrection and thus discredit the Partido electorally. By showing himself a resolute defender of property, José Miguel Gómez also hoped to avert U.S. intervention. But in the particular circumstances of Oriente, where the Partido had real local roots even if it did not have widespread support, there was a possibility that initial repression might trigger further violence aimed at redressing social and economic grievances specific to rural dwellers in the east. Rebels' sacking of town halls and the burning of property registers can be seen in this light. Nevertheless, whatever the motives of the rebels, it was President Gómez's decision to give an ambitious general like "Chucho" Monteagudo a free hand to lead the pursuit of rebels, combined with local officials' deployment of a hastily assembled vigilante force, that created the conditions for what Agustín Cebreco later referred to as "episodios tremendos"—terrible episodes.[76]

Events in Oriente shaped reactions to signs of unrest elsewhere, but the drama of protest and repression took a quite different form in the other provinces. The Independent Party of Color had focused considerable organizing effort, for example, on the central province of Santa Clara. The town of Cruces was said to be a stronghold of support, including women's auxiliaries to the party. But initially the only echo there of the May 20 protest came when two suspected rebels were said to have made off with a horse from the Santa Teresa estate. In nearby Lajas, where the party had published a paper called *El Civismo*, the veteran of color Simón Armenteros organized a group of men in the banana fields of the barrio Transvaal, apparently stole horses and saddles, and took to the hills. But veteran officers, including General Eduardo Guzmán in Cienfuegos, volunteered to lead troops against the protesters, and denunciations of the protest multiplied faster than recruitment to it.[77]

In many towns, general anxiety was in much greater evidence than black rebellion. A reporter from the town of Palmira wrote that spirits were much agitated because of what were thought to be "suspicious movements" of the people of color, indicating that they were "meditating" rebellion.[78] Nothing seems to have come of the presumed meditation. And things were said to be perfectly quiet around Cayetano Quesada's neighborhood of Guaos and Caonao. By May 22, reports began to filter in that some of the early accounts of trouble in the countryside around Cienfuegos had been exaggerated.[79]

The Rural Guard encountered the rebel Simón Armenteros and his group several times in the countryside, beginning on May 21 when they captured two members of his band; it soon numbered only fourteen men. By May 24 the group had dispersed, and Armenteros went into hiding in his home neighborhood in Lajas, the *barrio* called Guinea. He had apparently returned to sleep in his house and to try to negotiate his surrender, discouraged by how few had followed him. On May 28 the night guard reported that they had surprised Armenteros and three of his group. A shot was fired and one member of the group was apparently captured, though Armenteros fled. That same week, in the countryside, the Rural Guard apparently surprised the group led by Felipe Acea, killing one of his followers, Rafael Luna Peralta. A white man who was a member of Acea's band went free, and was still around at the site to talk with a journalist some time later. Like their counterparts in Santiago de Cuba, some captured and surrendered members of the party explained that they had fled to the countryside not to participate in an armed rebellion, but out of fear of being arrested. The arrest lists included the editor of the paper *El Civismo,* charged with instigating the rebellion, and Esteban Montejo, later made famous as the "cimarrón" (runaway slave) in a biography by Miguel Barnet.[80]

A last flicker of action in Santa Clara province came in early June 1912, with reports from the town of Aguada de Pasajeros of the capture on the cane farm Orbea of two members of a rebel group led by Antonio Curbelo. But the conflict never developed the sharp lines of demarcation that had come to characterize the events in Oriente. In the city of Cienfuegos, the local Sociedad de Color declared its unconditional support for the government, and the self-defense forces that developed in the smaller towns seemed to cross class and racial lines. In a petition for official recognition (and pay) for the fifty armed men who had formed such a group in Aguada, the residents described the force as primarily composed of workers from that farming region, who needed to be paid since they could not do their usual work.[81] By late June the rebel leader Felipe Acea surrendered voluntarily in a carefully scripted display of dignified deference to the local mayor. The cross-racial alliances that had long undergirded the Liberal Party apparently provided mechanisms for reintegrating dissenters. In the end, Santa Clara's population of color escaped the kind of large-scale repression that had characterized the government offensive in Oriente.[82]

The Machiavellian aspects of government repression of the Independent Party of Color are clear, including the use of racist imagery and the exaggeration of the threat posed by the initial protest. It remains difficult, however, to discern the popular response in the rest of Cuba to the news—both real and exaggerated—of armed protest in Oriente carried out in the name of grievances connected with color. Some listeners were likely to recognize the names of Evaristo Estenoz and Pedro Ivonet as veterans associated with long-standing campaigns for equal rights for Cubans of color; others probably believed the stories of black violence. Some rural residents of Santa Clara indeed fled to nearby towns, but whether this reflected a "white" fear of "black rebels," or peasant apprehension about the effects of confrontation in the countryside, is not known. In the region of Palmira, families reported to have left the countryside for fear of the "seditious movement" were said to be returning home in early July of 1912. A dispatch by the U.S. consul identifies those who fled as "white," but the local press simply described them as rural folk. Similar flights to towns in Oriente included large numbers of people of color, who quite reasonably wanted to stay out of the way of both rebels and the army.[83]

Throughout the summer, the *independientes* were strongly denounced across the island by veterans' groups and by the Sociedades de Color. A combination of military zeal and racial animosity may have motivated some white veterans, and fear may have spurred the Sociedades de Color. But even to many seasoned veterans and activists of color, some of them perhaps readers of *Previsión,* the politicization of racial identities by the party seemed both unwise and dangerous. President José Miguel Gómez was opportunistic, and much of the press openly racist, in invoking the ideal of a color-blind patriotism. But this does not imply that all who opposed the Partido in the name of the ideal were themselves opportunists or dupes. It was—and is—an open question whether the concept of caste is best combated through the invocation of solidarity along a color line or across it.[84]

The concept of cross-racial loyalties had deep social as well as ideological roots. Veterans and sugar workers, moreover, were among the most heterogeneous groups on the island. In a pattern repeated throughout the province of Santa Clara, men and women descended from slaves on Soledad and Santa Rosalía were joined in their daily routines in the cane by neighbors of all color categories. Like the activist Ricardo Batrell from Matanzas, the Quesadas and the Sarrías might claim citizenship with an awareness of color, but the public life they lived was itself transracial, with consequences both in theory and in practice.

The repression in Oriente lent itself to a dichotomous portrait in the press, with the army embodied in a white officer corps and their targets associated with a party "of color." The army's display of the cadavers of Estenoz and Ivonet provided a further occasion for characterizing the conflict in starkly racial terms. But no such picture was plausible in Santa Clara province. The local Rural Guard itself was multiracial in composition, and a showdown between the rebels and the Rural Guard would not be a confrontation of black against white. Again, this was not Louisiana, with its lily-white militia. In late May of 1912, Edwin Atkins had written to General Leonard Wood, now in the War Department in Washington, to report that all was relatively calm in the area around Soledad plantation. But he also noted that "the rural guard in Cuba and also the small army there has been largely filled with negroes." He clarified that he was thinking particularly of parts of Santa Clara, "where I judge that nearly half of the force is composed of negroes. Whether these could be depended upon in an emergency, I do not feel at all sure." By June of 1912 Edwin Atkins was uneasy about whether General José de Jesús Monteagudo could even get his forces to carry out a sufficiently vigorous repression in Oriente, precisely because the army itself was still quite multiracial. His fear of hesitation on the part of Monteagudo was misplaced, but his perception of the heterogeneity of the armed forces was accurate.[85]

Even the agitated reports published in 1912 show cracks in the imagined racial dichotomy. The white member of the Acea rebel group in Cienfuegos, for example, is an intriguing figure. It is not clear quite how he happened to be available when a local journalist went to the site of the encounter between the Rural Guard and Acea's followers. Perhaps his presence among those arrested would have undermined the government's image of a race war, so he was left to roam around on his own after the capture of black members of the gang. Or perhaps some more haphazard set of events left him free. Nonetheless, his membership in the group supports the party's repeated claim that white men had joined it, and echoes the fear of the mayor of San Luis that this might come to be seen as a "political" rather than a "racial" movement. The white man's presence hints that some Cubans could imagine incorporating questions of race into a political movement without its thereby becoming "racial."

Refusing the creation of a dichotomy of color, public figures long associated with the campaign for equal rights rejected the ideology and tactics of the Independent Party of Color, but continued to point out that equal rights had not been achieved. Nicolás Guillén, senator from Camagüey; Generoso Campos Marquetti, representative from Havana; General Agustín Cebreco, representative from Oriente; Lino D'Ou, representative from Oriente; and the indefatigable Juan Gualberto Gómez all signed a petition in early June of 1912 marking their distance from the protest, but trying to contest the characterizations of the conflict as a war of black against white.[86]

Although the dynamic of challenge and response across the island was complex, the sensationalized news of events in Oriente became part of the permanent framing of the events of 1912, even in areas where the local revolt had a different character. In July the press in Cienfuegos echoed the official rationalization for repression and inveighed against the "Infamous ingratitude of part of the race of color against the white who sacrificed so much to give them liberty: first with the abolition of slavery and then for their complete redemption."[87] In order to anathematize the protest in Oriente, the local press thus denied the agency of people of color in the earlier struggle to achieve slave emancipation, and used the powerful image of "ingratitude" to justify repression.

It is difficult to know how the trauma and division of 1912 affected ordinary people outside Oriente who had participated in the war of 1895–1898 and in the early workers' movement. These previous experiences of solidarity might weigh in the balance against the racialized imagery of black barbarism deployed during the repression of 1912, and help maintain the basis for activism and cross-racial

General Agustín Cebreco, from Cobre, in eastern Cuba. Cebreco joined the Cuban rebellion in 1870 at the age of fifteen, survived the 1895–1898 war, and became a national statesman in the first Cuban Republic.

alliances. Indeed, in mid-July of 1912, just as the state of siege was being lifted in Oriente, port workers in Havana threatened to strike to protest the actions of a U.S. company that had fired a group of black workers. Blatant segregation imposed by a foreign-owned company violated both workers' own principles of solidarity and nationalist sensibilities.[88]

But the fears mobilized or generated in 1912 continued to reverberate. White rural dwellers who had fled to nearby towns at reports of "black rebellion" may have regarded their neighbors of color somewhat differently in 1913 than they had in 1911. And country people in Oriente who counted themselves as members of the "clase de color" had new reason to distrust their white neighbors in town, some of whom had been ready to volunteer for repressive action that often degenerated into lynching. Images of danger could lodge themselves deep in individual consciousness, marking potential allies as potential enemies.

The armed protest led by the Independent Party of Color in 1912 reflected a fracture in the nationalist coalition, drawing on the accumulated anger of veterans of color whose ascent had been thwarted as well as on the frustration of other Cubans pushed aside in the postwar world. But the protest was not simply the culmination of prior black struggles. It was one of several expressions of such struggle, representing one position in a long-standing debate. In 1950 Serafín Portuondo Linares, himself the son of a participant in the uprising, argued convincingly that the Independent Party of Color was race-conscious but not racist.[89] In the long run, it was not the protest itself but the repression of that protest that most effectively drove a wedge between Cubans identified as "white" and those identified as being "of color." By the same token, the brutality of that repression neither discredits nor vindicates the Independent Party of Color's claim to speak for Cubans of color. Instead, it shows what the Cuban state was capable of—and what the Liberal Party would subsequently have to live down.

In the end President José Miguel Gómez paid a high political price for his failure to place appropriate limits on the use of troops in Oriente in 1912. He faced hostile editorial cartoons in the press and widespread political criticism for a repression that was routinely characterized as "butchery." General José de Jesús Monteagudo came in for even more scathing caricature. It was not difficult to demonstrate that whatever the government's rationale, its actions were an affront to the memory of Antonio Maceo. Within weeks of the end of hostilities, family members of men detained by the government during the repression renewed a call for amnesty. Groups of women organized a broadly based campaign that gained the support of the main newspaper in Santiago, and within a year they achieved their goal.[90]

José Miguel Gómez, in the end, lost his bid for reelection, and his enemies would in the future find ways to use the events of 1912 to discredit him. Paradoxically, for many families of color in central Cuba it made sense to embrace the Liberal Party again, provisionally overlooking its role in the killings in Oriente in the summer of 1912, and activating instead the cross-racial networks that could maintain a space of electoral action. Those whose houses had been invaded by vigilantes or soldiers in 1912 knew, of course, that black voters were more vulnerable than white, and that the party leadership contained men whose views on race were appalling.[91] But under universal manhood suffrage, the Liberal Party was still in some sense theirs, and continued activism within it helped to guarantee jobs, patronage, and respect for the rights of citizenship gained in the 1895–1898 war and enumerated in the 1901 Constitution. As workers in the cane or claimants in the courts, they had made use of the party's networks and rewards. They were not likely to abandon it easily.

A routine transaction from the notarial records of the city of Cienfuegos in October of 1912 provides a glimpse of everyday politics in the aftermath of upheaval. The notary certified a formal agreement between Canuto Montalvo, the African-born leader of the Centro Africano in the sugar town of Cruces, on the one hand, and Andrés Calleja y Capote, a Liberal Party congressman, and Carlos Suárez y López, a businessman, on the other. On the eve of the November 1912 elections, Montalvo recalled to the other two men their promise to help rebuild the Centro's building, which was in need of substantial repairs. The quid pro quo was made explicit: the repairs were to be done in recognition of the good and selfless services provided to the Liberal Party over the years by members of this organization, referred to in the text as the Casino Africano. There was nothing elegant about this exercise of patronage and politics, and it certainly lacked the principled tone of the calls for mutual respect that animated the 1912 autobiography of Ricardo Batrell or the exhortations to manly resistance of Evaristo

Estenoz. But in its own way it reflected the incorporation into politics not only of individual voters of color but of a group with an explicit adherence to African-derived cultural practices that journalists and reformers often denounced as atavistic. There was little of the supplicant in Canuto Montalvo's tone: just weeks after the worst racially defined violence in the history of the Republic, Montalvo was reminding a local white Liberal that members of the community of African descent were not cowed. If the roof had needed fixing before the events in Oriente, it still needed fixing afterward. Congressman Calleja owed quite a lot to those of his constituents who had opted for cross-racial clientelism rather than third-party organizing. And Canuto Montalvo, of uncertain literacy but long-standing authority within the community, proposed to make sure that Calleja knew it.[92]

The trauma of 1912 did not fully silence those who denounced the problems associated with racial discrimination in the Republic, nor did it quiet the frustrations of many veterans of color. Guarded public discussion continued, particularly in fiction and in journalism.[93] The boundaries of the possible had been forcibly redefined, but the claim to voice and vote within the ideology of shared citizenship remained strong. Even racists, ironically, had staked their claims against Estenoz and the Independent Party of Color on the grounds of transracial patriotism. They thus narrowed the opening for variants of white-supremacist logic that called for the political exclusion of those not deemed white, and they committed themselves to a party politics that built on the participation of all adult males, regardless of color.

CHAPTER NINE

Diverging Paths and Degrees of Freedom

SOUTHERN LOUISIANA IN THE EARLY TWENTIETH CENTURY NEVER SAW A wave of official armed repression comparable to that carried out by the Cuban Army in Oriente in 1912. But the reasons do not lie in any greater tolerance or forbearance in Louisiana's leadership. On the contrary, by 1900 no initiative resembling the Independent Party of Color would have had a prayer of survival in Louisiana in the first place. Mass meetings like those conducted by Evaristo Estenoz in the eastern countryside of Cuba were unthinkable in rural Louisiana—among other things, because there no longer existed any cross-racial right to vote or candidates of color to campaign for.

Sharply contrasting constitutional resolutions of the question of citizenship had solidified the divergence in public culture between Louisiana and Cuba. Public life in postwar Cuba, though hardly egalitarian, was open to men of color. Emerging from military service in the Cuban rebel army in 1898, Major General Agustín Cebreco, Major General Jesús Rabí, Colonel Pedro Ivonet, and Lieutenant Evaristo Estenoz each found a path to political expression. An alternate member of Oriente's delegation to the 1901 Constitutional Convention, General

Cebreco was elected to Congress in 1904 on the Conservative Party ticket. General Rabí refused to hold public office during the first U.S. occupation, but was inspector of mines and forests during the early years of the Republic. Colonel Ivonet worked within the Conservative Party, undertook negotiations with the Liberals, and then joined Evaristo Estenoz in the Agrupación de Color. Lieutenant Estenoz himself was active in the workers' movement before establishing the Agrupación.[1]

The events of 1912 in Cuba demonstrated that in moments of crisis, a color line could be sharply drawn, with devastating consequences. But even in the midst of that trauma, activists of color drew on the national narrative of cross-racial unity and called for the repair of damage done by color-conscious injustice. In Oriente itself, the women's campaign for amnesty, couched in the language of reconciliation, built political alliances to appeal for the release of those swept up in the repression. Once the prisoners formally repented of their involvement with the armed protest and the Independent Party of Color, they were amnestied. Elsewhere in Cuba, mutual-aid and cultural associations maintained their place in public culture and reasserted the full citizenship of Cubans of color.[2]

Nor did the events of 1912 alter the cross-racial organizing strategies of members of the working class. Two years after the killings in Oriente, the first National Workers' Congress convened in Havana. Artisans and laborers from across the island converged to submit reports and listen to speeches. Black, *mulato,* and white activists addressed questions of the length of the working day, the legal protections of workers, and the specific problems facing bakers, tobacco workers, harness-makers, and many others. Each delegation posed for a formal portrait that captured their diversity and displayed their solidarity. The Workers' Congress even crossed lines of gender as well as those of color. Delegates honored Dr. Rosa Anders, an attorney, in their opening ceremony, and the delegation from Oriente included María P. Garbey, a woman of color.[3]

In September of 1915 an event took place that embodied a renewal of the cross-racial ideals of Martí and Maceo. In the same corner of southern Oriente that had seen the protest of 1912 and its repression, Generals Agustín Cebreco and Jesús Rabí, who had served with the Maceos, organized a procession that symbolically affirmed the transracial character of Cuban nationality. Accompanied

Delegates from Yaguajay and Mayajigua, Cuba, to the 1914 National Workers' Congress in Havana. Virtually every delegation to the Workers' Congress was interracial.

by some 2,000 veterans identified as white, black, and *mulato,* they rode on horse-back from the city of Santiago de Cuba to the church of the Virgen de la Caridad in the hill town of Cobre. Often depicted in popular iconography as a young woman of color, this Virgin was said to have appeared centuries earlier to a group of three men in a small boat, one white, one slave, and one Indian. After the veterans arrived at the shrine, one of the officers read a petition to the Holy See signed by Cubans with affiliations to the Conservative Party, the Liberal Party, and the recently established socialists, formally asking that the Virgin of Cobre be recognized as the patroness of the Cuban Republic. On May 10, 1916, Pope Benedict XV granted the veterans' request.[4]

In Cuba as in Louisiana, entangled notions about color, civility, and danger could poison personal interactions and undermine efforts to expand the citizenship of men and women of color. In both places a multitude of racial prejudices continued to be expressed privately and in myriad social situations. But while the federal government had endorsed Louisiana's forcible exclusion of people of color from shared public spaces and from the voting booth, in Cuba the sphere deemed *public* continued to be defined very broadly, and within it equal rights and nationalist unity were widely acknowledged.

A practiced eye could easily detect the element of hypocrisy in the Cuban system. But a practiced eye could also see that these formal guarantees created a space for alliance, negotiation, voting, military service, officeholding, union organizing, and education. In addition, formal equality enabled Cubans of color to assert the dignitary components of citizenship—or, in a crisis, to denounce effectively the violation by the state of the equal respect due to citizens. The armed protest in 1912 marked the outer limits of this claim to public voice in the early Republic. The Cuban state charged the protestors with disloyalty and antipatriotism, providing a rationale for calling out the army. But a competing concept of patriotism provided a language with which to denounce the repression, and formal adherence to the ideal of cross-racial unity enabled repentant survivors to be reincorporated into the polity.

In Louisiana, by contrast, the ruling Democratic Party had put in place an interlocking structure that virtually excluded people of color from the public sphere. The deployment of the militia against the Knights of Labor in 1887 was followed by vigilante violence, and in 1896 the U.S. Supreme Court declared the forced separation of those deemed "colored" from those deemed "white" on the state's common carriers to be both constitutional and natural. State-mandated humiliation as well as private prejudice would now characterize interactions in public spaces. Although a few Civil War veterans of color continued to play limited public roles in the state through the 1890s, and a small group of men of color held federally appointed jobs at the Customs House, Republican Party patronage was fast becoming an uncertain commodity. Men of color returning from service in the U.S. war in Cuba faced open hostility from white employers and pension commissioners. No new black captains or colonels, much less generals, could be found in the veterans' ranks; no mass base of voters existed on which to build even a local political career. The architects of white-supremacist repression had become the leading figures in the state's public life, and by the time of the 1898 disfranchising convention, their successors and allies had achieved a near monopoly on power.

In Cuba, the architects of the 1912 army repression in Oriente paid a significant political price for their association with what came to be seen as a massacre. General José de Jesús Monteagudo had hoped to become a candidate for the presidency; instead both he and President José Miguel Gómez appeared in the press as men with blood on their hands. Memories of the events of May and June 1912 would be used against the Liberals in the elections of 1912 and 1916.[5]

The contrast between Louisiana and Cuba is in these respects sharp, but not total. The divergences in politics and public culture did not prevent many parallels in the individual and family strategies developed by the survivors of slavery. In Lafourche Parish as in the municipality of Cienfuegos, men and women combined wage labor, subsistence cultivation, and market gardening. They sought education for their children, and when possible, they came together to seek higher wages and more regular pay. When the opportunity arose, many men of color in Louisiana sought a fuller citizenship by volunteering for military service, and some of those in rural Cuba joined the rebel Liberation Army in 1895. Tracing these initiatives by former slaves and their descendants has been a major theme of this story. If the shape of postemancipation societies had been wholly determined by the exercise of such initiative and defiance, however, Louisiana might have come to resemble Cuba in the postemancipation world much as it did in the time of slavery. Alternatively, if postemancipation societies had necessarily inherited the most repressive legacies of slavery, these two sugar-producing plantation societies would have followed nearly parallel paths toward exclusion and widely institutionalized racism. But they did neither.

History rarely embodies narratives that are purely heroic or purely tragic, for it does not script itself according to dramatic conventions. The legacy of slavery and emancipation was neither an indomitable spirit of defiant initiative on the part of former slaves nor a relentless commitment to white supremacy on the part of former masters, though elements of both of these are easy enough to discern. The key legacy in both Cuba and Louisiana was a contest over the right to respect and resources, which increasingly encompassed a contest over the boundaries of citizenship. Between the 1860s and the first decade of the twentieth century, these contests absorbed the energies and attention of thousands of individuals, operating with different degrees of freedom within structures that changed in response to their efforts. Louisiana is distinguished from Cuba by the ways in which the scope of this contest came to be successively narrowed. As different structures of formal rights and labor practices took hold in each polity, initial divergences tended to be amplified.

Slavery in the modern world had been a system that relied upon law. To transform a human being into property required the legal construct of a "person with a price." Slavery may have been regionally specific in its geography, but it had to be national in the maintenance of its controlling fiction. Comparison of Cuba and Louisiana after slavery suggests that the same is true of white supremacy as a postemancipation project: not white supremacy as a color prejudice, or even as a kind of psychosocial pathology—these can emerge in many social settings—but white supremacy as an organized structure constraining the public voice and civic standing of those whom it labeled inferior.

If we think of our two cases as complex dynamic systems in motion over time, we can see that in the years after slavery various possibilities were open—ranging from an inclusive citizenship that would transcend color to an exclusionary social order that would constrain public and political rights. As long as the struggle had a strong electoral and labor dimension, as it did in Louisiana during Reconstruction, or involved a cross-racial movement for national independence, as it did in Cuba, it remained a true contest. White supremacy was a political project aimed at ending the contest between contending pictures of citizenship, at locking in a permanent structure of legal, economic, and political privilege. And the project of white supremacy, like slavery before it, required legal backing right up to the top of the system.

In an odd twist of history, the turning points would come at a moment when both Cuba and Louisiana were under the formal authority of Republican administrations in Washington, D.C. Within Louisiana, the collapse of Reconstruction-era political alliances had made it very difficult for workers to sustain any cross-racial collective action, and throughout the 1890s the actions of the Louisiana legislature further pushed men and women of color out of the public sphere. These aggressions against the emancipationist reading of the Fourteenth and Fifteenth amendments to the U.S. Constitution, however, would in the end need authorization from the top. Between 1896 and 1904, from the decision in *Plessy* to the second decision in *Giles,* the U.S. Supreme Court provided that backing, definitively undercutting both public rights and political voice.

From 1898 to 1901, the U.S. occupation government in Cuba attempted to impose a formally democratic but highly constrained electoral system on the island. But within Cuba there was significant momentum behind a broader transracial ideal, reinforced by the character of the fight against slavery, the increasing heterogeneity of the rural workforce, and the experience of the rebel army that had made the nation possible. When the moment of truth came in the Cuban Constitutional Convention in 1901, everyone knew that a recently mobilized national population was awaiting the recognition of a broad range of rights. Even conservative white delegates, even men who were moved by sentiments of prejudice, voted for an inclusive citizenship and universal manhood suffrage. And the U.S. occupiers, more concerned with their long-term economic and geopolitical relationship to the island than with its internal political arrangements, deferred.

In itself, an expansive suffrage was hardly sufficient to address deep problems of economic and social inequality in Cuba. But it served as an important buffer against antidemocratic temptations and provided the framework within which a multitude of labor, mutual-aid, and educational associations, often cross-racial, could proliferate. There was no selective process of voter registration comparable to that found in the individual states of the United States. It was the task of the local census-takers to issue a voter registration card (*cédula electoral*) to each male citizen over the age of twenty-one. Cubans could claim their suffrage rights on the spot, and the census-taker was required to have a book of blank *cédulas* in his briefcase or saddlebag. Those denied a card were apparently quite quick to complain at their omission. Cuba's broad suffrage and transracial citizenship were thereby affirmed in each visit of the census-taker to a household.[6]

The right to vote may or may not actually function as a fundamental political right that is "preservative of all rights," to use the famous phrase from the 1886 U.S. Supreme Court decision in *Yick Wo v. Hopkins*.[7] But it is clear that denying it does undercut all other rights. Louisiana and Cuba in the early twentieth century were both sites of notable electoral corruption, and in neither place would the balloting meet the standards of a modern team of international election observers. But in Cuba the right to vote carried with it both political leverage and an expressive power that its refusal in Louisiana denied. This leverage, in turn, spread out into other realms of action, and particularly to the exercise of collective bargaining and of access to law.[8]

In Louisiana, by contrast, one meaning of formal citizenship without the vote was neatly summarized by a planter from Lafourche Parish. Having read of race riots in Chicago, he wrote to a Chicago newspaper in 1919 to suggest a solution: "Send your negroes back to us, we can work them, we know their ways and they know our ways. We have no prejudice against them as negro laborers and value them as such."[9] Nearly every word in his sentences was revealing. The phrase "your negroes" conveyed the implication of possession and domination that he believed white readers in the North would share. The promise that "we can work them" communicated the relations of employer and employee, not fellow citizens. And the words "negro laborers" relegated them to the day labor that he believed to be their appropriate fate.

These assertions were not simply rhetoric and ideology. They were part of a social organization of production that rested on a sharply segmented labor market. Former slaves and their descendants in southern Louisiana were disproportionately and overwhelmingly confined to the role of laborers. In the 1910 census for Louisiana, the category "farm laborer (working out)" was heavily black. Men of color rarely appeared among those listed as farmers in the bayou sugar country. The census counted only seventy-one "negro and other nonwhite" farmers in the whole of Lafourche Parish.[10] The Cuban census of 1907, by contrast, revealed that in the sugar districts of Santa Clara province the broad occupational label *agricultor* was used for both farmers and laborers, whether categorized as white, black, *mulato,* or Asian. This clustering reflected the continual movement back and forth between subsistence agriculture and wage-paid work, and the presence of workers of every origin in the cane fields. The name-by-name lists, moreover, convey the heterogeneity of the plantation workforce directly.[11]

Nor was it simply a question of those intangibles called "racial attitudes" or "race relations." Individual white employers of Cuban working men and women often displayed the same racialized arrogance that their counterparts in Louisiana expressed so freely, and exercised their prejudices as they hired workers to different jobs. But as Cuba's planters expanded their workforce, the labor supply that they faced was spread out across several different groups (in census terms): "native whites," "Spanish-born whites," "native-born people of color," and, in some cases, "foreign-born people of color," including Haitians and West Indians employed on the new plantations in the east. Thousands of these workers were drawing together in a cross-racial labor movement under cross-racial leadership. Many were soon accustomed to bargaining over matters of rights and wages and to acting as members of electoral coalitions. Employers could not dictate to them in matters of wages or of public rights. When a U.S. company tried to enforce a color line on the Havana docks, workers immediately went on strike.[12]

The Cuban pattern of cross-racial alliances had deep roots both in structures of labor and in a widely shared ideology of nation, and thus survived considerable buffeting from stereotypes, fears, and efforts at division. A sharp difference existed between prejudice as a practice, which characterized both Cuba and Louisiana, and prejudice as a principle of public life, which flourished in Louisiana but not in Cuba. The multiple color terms employed in Cuban social life—*blanco, trigueño, mestizo, mulato, moreno, negro,* and so forth—do not in themselves confer "fluidity" on these categories or on the personal relations of those who inhabit them. Racism need not be based on dichotomous categories imagined to be biological; it can be framed within a continuum whose content is construed as partially cultural, with a social "whiteness" remaining at the top and a multiplicity of categories below. Both of these conceptions contain elements of the same poison. In Cuba, however, private racism of the hierarchical and cultural type coexisted with public declarations of equality; in Louisiana, after forty years of struggle, white-supremacist ideology of the dichotomous and biologizing type had achieved dominance in the political and economic spheres.[13]

In his inaugural address of 1904, Louisiana governor Newton Blanchard made the core of that ideology quite clear. Although his colleagues eight years earlier had claimed to support Louisiana's Separate Car Act on the grounds of custom and convenience, Governor Blanchard could now acknowledge that their real goal had been to deny to Louisiana's citizens of color the very essence of public dignity: "No approach towards social equality or *social recognition* will ever be tolerated in Louisiana. Separate schools, separate churches, separate cars, separate places of entertainment will be enforced. Racial distinction and integrity must be preserved."[14]

There were moments in Louisiana that showed hints of continuing public struggle. But fragile alliances quickly faltered in the face of black disfranchisement, which effectively destroyed the electoral basis for negotiation. White Louisiana Populists who had in the 1890s spoken of interests shared across the color line eventually made their peace with the idea of a lily-white electorate, only to be driven from the political scene. The Louisiana lumber workers who joined the International Workers of the World in 1913 operated within a truncated electorate, a largely segmented workforce, and the quotidian racism that accompanied the political project of white supremacy. They could not and did not sustain the day-to-day links of sociability and political cooperation that would give full meaning to the principles of cross-racial alliance. Men and women designated as "colored," hence outside the political community, would generally have to go it alone. And by the second decade of the twentieth century, this would often mean that they would have to go north.[15]

With each strike and each electoral campaign in Cuba, by contrast, alliances of various kinds were built and rebuilt, reinforcing and being reinforced by day-today linkages on the ground. And as powerful leaders of color rose in different branches of the Cuban labor movement, white-supremacist variants of union organizing further receded from view. It was not a matter of a mythical Iberian color-blindness: people made daily reference to color, and race as a concept continued to be invoked and debated. Eugenicists and criminologists propounded claims of inherent black "atavism," and intellectuals of color worked to develop countervailing ideals of racial transcendence.[16] Although they might still face slights when they went to town, or stigmatizing separation on the doorstep of a plantation social club, former slaves and their descendants had nonetheless succeeded in making themselves not only indispensable to an expanding sugar industry but a force to be reckoned with in a growing labor movement.[17]

All of this cross-racial mobilization could coexist with invidious distinctions and complex hierarchies, particularly concerning relations between men and women. Among town dwellers in central Cuba, there was often a formal etiquette of separation by color in key social situations—the customary evening stroll in the park being the most conspicuous. At the same time, in the political sphere, men of color found it more difficult to advance through the ranks of the established parties than it had been to advance through the ranks of the Liberation Army. No group had greater formal respect in Cuba, however, than the veterans of the 1895–1898 war, independent of color. When Cayetano Quesada— the son of slaves—died in the 1940s, the members of the cross-racial veterans' association of Cienfuegos turned out to bury him with full honors. Two decades later, in 1964, Faustina Heredia, who had accompanied her husband, Clemente Hernández, into battle in the 1895–1898 war, died at the age of eighty-eight. In the official records, she was a soldier's widow, not a soldier. But her neighbors knew otherwise, and the veterans' association of Yaguajay buried this daughter of a free woman of color with military honors, wrapped in the Cuban flag.[18]

The opportunities and dangers that former slaves and their descendants confronted in Louisiana and Cuba thus reflected the large, conditioning structures of the two sugar economies and of the two political systems, as well as the results of their own continuing efforts to affect those structures. If we return for a moment to the metaphorical sense of "degrees of freedom," we can see how it is that neither structures nor struggles could fully determine the outcome. On both sides of the Gulf of Mexico, men and women who had survived slavery sought access to productive resources, to civil recognition, and to public standing. Throughout the 1870s and 1880s in Louisiana, and across the 1880s and 1890s in Cuba, thousands of former slaves and their allies stepped into public view and made their voices heard—as patriots, as citizens, as workers, as veterans, as men and women with a claim to respect. But as each of these struggles was resolved, certain parameters would for a time be set, and the range of possible future states of each society would be reshaped.

It is tempting to try to peel back the "how" of these processes in hopes of finding a unified, clear "why." But if we take our metaphor of multiple degrees of freedom seriously, it is clear that while we can reasonably ask for causal explanations of key moments of inflection in the evolving process, the interactive dynamics of each system make any simple global explanation of the differences in their outcomes unlikely. Suppose, for example, we were to point to their differing environments. Cuba's superb soil and climate allowed for continual expansion of production after the end of slavery; Louisiana's more precarious environment for the growing of cane pushed planters to request endless bounties and subsidies. Cuba's expanding economy drew in immigrants and smallholders from the countryside, ensuring a multiracial workforce; Louisiana employers had less to offer and relied on subordinated black laborers. But it was Cuba's particular history of both immigration *and* mobilization that shaped how its labor force would be composed, and how workers would interact with the political system. With Spanish anarchists, Cuban nationalists, and returning veterans came an insistence on racial equality and a powerful sense of citizenship. At the same time, claims to autonomy, land, and respect as skilled laborers flourished among the many descendants of slaves who planted subsistence and market crops in the interstices of the world of cane. When workers could build solidarity on their shared experiences, while drawing upon the material resources of family smallholdings and the skills of kin and allies who worked in town, a truly cross-racial public life became possible—if the state did not close down that public space. The antiracist ideals of Antonio Maceo and José Martí were hardly binding on Cuba's political class. But in proportion as these precepts were acted upon in daily life, they tended to grow rather than atrophy.

Former slaves in Louisiana had expressed the same desires for autonomy, land, and dignity as their counterparts in Cuba, and had planted subsistence and market crops on land temporarily left vacant by the flight of planters during the Civil War. Between 1864 and 1887 they had organized as workers, entered into the political system, gained some ground in the legal system, and made public claims to voice and respect. But by the 1890s they and their descendants ran up against a planter class that saw little need to make concessions and a federal government unwilling to look behind the fictions by which white supremacists refused the claims of men and women of color to dignified citizenship. Former slaves and their descendants tied to the plantation by residence in planter-owned quarters were joined by modest numbers of black migrants from the upper South, and both groups were subjected to a requirement of constant social deference. Land ownership or even tenancy remained largely out of reach.

By the beginning of the twentieth century, Louisiana and Cuba's sharply contrasting patterns of public life helped to lock inequality into Louisiana's world of cane, while opening up Cuba's. In Cuba, though political corruption was common and women were still denied the vote, virtually all families could have a political identity, and the votes of men of color were avidly sought. Even those born into poor rural families of color in Santa Clara province, for example, could grow up thinking of themselves as valued members of the Liberal Party. In Louisiana, by contrast, politics had been brought within tight bounds, one-party rule reinforced by systematic class and racial disfranchisement.[19] After the Thibodaux massacre of 1887 and the assaults on black voting, activist men and women of color in Louisiana were forcibly cut off from their potential base in the countryside, and their initiatives had to be channeled through the narrowest of openings. No union would organize in the Louisiana cane fields again until the 1950s, and even then the strikes would be defeated.[20]

Despite all of this, men and women who had survived slavery in each of these worlds continued to seek allies, to advance arguments, and to alter their strategies in their daily battles for survival and respect. Bárbara Pérez had emerged from slavery on the Santa Teresa plantation in Cienfuegos and faced expulsion from the house in which she had grown up. While working as a laundress in the town of

Bárbara Pérez, of Cienfuegos. Born into slavery, she learned to read while still enslaved and worked as a laundress after emancipation. She later became a trained midwife on the Soledad plantation.

Arimao she met a Spanish carpenter, moved with him to the hamlet of El Palmar, and gave birth to two boys, Tomás and Luis. When the carpenter abandoned her, she found another partner, and eventually trained as a midwife on the Soledad plantation. Her son Tomás became a cane farmer and a worker on the plantation, eventually directing a multiracial work crew at the lime kiln.

Adèle Colomb, born into slavery in Donaldsonville, Louisiana, had faced a parallel challenge. Left a widow in the 1870s, she had no choice but to let her teenaged son Pierre Lacroix Carmouche leave school and begin work. He trained as a blacksmith and flung himself into virtually every public venue for activism open to a man of color. He obtained appointment as the local tax assessor, sent money to New Orleans to the organizers of the *Plessy* challenge, and persuaded dozens of his black working-class neighbors to enlist for service in the 1898 war with Spain. But upon his return to Ascension Parish and New Orleans after the end of the 1898 war, Pierre Carmouche faced a closed political world, compounded by personal humiliation from the white former clients of his blacksmith shop who scorned his claim to the public standing of an officer and a gentleman. In 1902 Carmouche abandoned Louisiana for uncertain employment in Detroit, Michigan. In 1912 he wrote bitterly to Booker T. Washington: "What I did and encouraged our people to do, in our war with Spain in 98, Is what I would not attempt to do again *Not Unless* it was for the *complete* and *perminent* rights, liberties, oppertunities, and freedoms of the Colored Citizens of America or U.S."[21]

Some of those who had been mobilized in Louisiana in the 1880s and 1890s did stay and continue to make claims, even as their likelihood of success diminished. Mutual-aid associations gathered private resources and forged horizontal ties, with occasional forays into a more public sphere. In 1907 Lieutenant Lafayette Tharp carried out his correspondence with the federal pension office on the stationery of the optimistically named Colored Moral Industrial Progressive Benevolent Union of Young Colored Men, emblazoned with the motto "In Union is Strength." But one by one a generation of veterans of earlier struggles despaired of being heard by the federal government. Lafayette Tharp had returned from service in Cuba weakened by his illnesses there and unable to continue work on the docks. Refused a military pension, he ended up dependent on his church and on a former employer.[22] Others returned from the war to the cane fields, where they resumed wage labor and had to make their peace with continued hardship. Participants in the networks that had sustained the Knights of Labor and the *Plessy* challenge redirected much of their energy inward. Thus toward the end of his career as a notary public in New Orleans, Louis Martinet turned to writing somber wills for an aging clientele and formalizing "family meetings" to appoint guardians for those now incapacitated. The webs of kinship and of mutual aid were respectfully inscribed in his notarial record and served as a bulwark for the ill and the infirm, but broader collective action was now nearly impossible.[23]

Cuba's very different postemancipation order made possible a very different twentieth century. When Bárbara Pérez's son Tomás Pérez of Cienfuegos, born in

Tomás Pérez y Pérez, of Cienfuegos, 1998. Son of the former slave Bárbara Pérez and the Spanish carpenter Manuel Lago, Tomás Pérez worked in the fields and mill of the Soledad plantation. At the age of ninety-six, he recalled details of his family history and of labor relations on the plantation.

1902, reflected back on his life on the Soledad plantation, he recalled cross-racial work teams and shared political struggle. Such memories did not obscure his experiences of hunger or of social slights to his darker-skinned daughters. Indeed, his own story of initiatives along and across the color line was built on a deep personal identification with his mother's journey from slavery to freedom. Again and again, his mother had crossed the potential divide between herself and those rural people who traced their ancestry to Spain or the Canary Islands. The freedom of action of Bárbara and Tomás Pérez had nothing to do with "passing," and did not imply turning one's back on the generations born in slavery. When Tomás Pérez chose as a young adult to claim a second surname that would signal public standing by implying legitimate birth, he did not take on the last name of his Spanish father, Manuel Lago. Instead, he doubled his mother's surname and began referring to himself as Tomás Pérez y Pérez. In the public culture of rural Cuba, he exercised leadership and claimed rights on the basis of his labor, his integrity, and the respect earned by his mother.[24]

Within each of these horizons of possibility, there emerged different degrees of freedom for men and women of African descent. But in both Louisiana and Cuba, there also came to be a vernacular sense of the deeper meaning of freedom, derived from the experience of claiming rights and dignity even in the face of constraint. It is perhaps not surprising that the keenest appreciation of that deep sense of freedom would be expressed by a man who faced the narrower horizon. Rodolphe Desdunes, in 1895, addressed his readers as they prepared for the possible defeat of the *Plessy* challenge at the Supreme Court. "'It is well for a people to know their rights even if denied them,' and we will add that it is proper and wise for people to exercise those rights as intelligently as possible, even if robbed of their benefits."[25]

APPENDIX

ABBREVIATIONS

NOTES

SELECT BIBLIOGRAPHY

ACKNOWLEDGMENTS

INDEX

Appendix: Tables

Table A.1   Sugar, slavery, and population in Louisiana, 1860

Parishes	Sugar produced (metric tons)	Slave population	White population	Population of free people of color
Ascension	7,297	7,376	3,940	168
Assumption	8,031	8,096	7,189	94
Lafourche	6,684	6,395	7,500	149
St. Martin	3,401	7,358	5,005	311
St. Mary	13,939	13,057	3,508	251
Terrebonne	7,721	6,785	5,234	72
Total for the six bayou parishes	47,073	49,067	32,376	1,045
Total for Louisiana's fourteen major sugar parishes	87,344	116,125	68,679	3,397
Total for Louisiana	100,574	331,726	357,629	18,647[a]

Sources: Production figures—United States Census Office, *Agriculture of the United States in 1860; Compiled from the Original Returns of the Eighth Census* (Washington, D.C.: Government Printing Office, 1864), pp. xcix, 68–69. I have converted hogsheads of 1,000 lbs to metric tons of 2,204.6 lbs. *Slave and free population*—United States Census Office, *Population of the United States in 1860; Compiled from the Original Returns of the Eighth Census* (Washington, D.C.: Government Printing Office, 1864), p. 194.

Note: I use the term "bayou parishes" to refer to the five parishes that border Bayou Lafourche, Bayou Terrebonne, or Bayou Teche, as well as to Ascension Parish, which held some plantations facing Bayou Lafourche and a larger number facing the Mississippi itself. Eight additional parishes producing more than 7,000 hogsheads of sugar in 1860 were the river parishes of W. Baton Rouge, Iberville, Jefferson, Plaquemines, Point Coupée, Rapides, St. Charles, and St. James.

a. The free population of color was heavily concentrated in the city of New Orleans, in Orleans Parish.

Table A.2   Sugar, slavery, and population in the province of Santa Clara, Cuba, 1860–1862

Districts *(jurisdicciones)*	Sugar produced (metric tons)	Slave population	White population (including Asians)[a]	Population of free people of color
Cienfuegos	43,151	16,985	28,645	7,720
Remedios	15,373	7,182	26,772	5,443
Sagua la Grande	46,426	19,150	27,240	2,072
Sancti Spíritus	12,605	8,564	27,036	6,933
Trinidad	16,590	10,141	18,193	9,188
Villa Clara (Santa Clara)	11,017	6,921	34,929	10,764
Total for the province of Santa Clara[b]	145,162	68,943	162,815	42,120
Total for the island of Cuba	535,857	370,553	793,484	225,843

Sources: Production—Carlos Rebello, *Estados relativos a la producción azucarera de la isla de Cuba* (Havana, 1860). *Population*—Cuba, Centro de Estadística, *Noticias estadísticas de la isla de Cuba, en 1862* (Havana: Imprenta del Gobierno, 1864). (These figures are from the table "Censo de Población segun el cuadro general de la Comisión Ejecutiva de 1861." They differ slightly from those of other tables in the same volume.)

a. The 1861 census counted the island's 34,828 Asians with the white population.

b. The province was formally constituted in 1879. These are its constituent *jurisdicciones*. The population figures for Ciego de Ávila, later made part of Camagüey, have been subtracted from Sancti Spíritus.

Table A.3 Male laborers and farmers by residence and color, ages 18–45: Lafourche
Parish, 1878

Color and occupation	Resident on plantations	Resident in towns or elsewhere in countryside	Total	Percentage of occupational category
Colored laborer	836	489	1,325	71%
White laborer	232	297	529	29%
Total			1,854	100%
Colored farmer	53	99	152	15%
White farmer	75	796	871	85%
Total			1,023	100%

Source: "Militia List for Lafourche Militia, Lafourche Parish, Louisiana, 1878," uncatalogued document, Court Annex, Office of the Clerk of the Court, Lafourche Parish, Thibodaux, Louisiana. This manuscript list provides data on the adult male population formally eligible to serve in the militia. It appears to be quite comprehensive, although it may exclude some men. Divided by electoral precincts, it could have been drawn from an 1876 voter registration list. By 1878, in practice, men of color would no longer have been called up for militia service.

Note: On plantations with 20 or more resident male laborers, 84 percent of the laborers were designated "colored." On the two largest plantations, the disproportion was stark: Rienzi plantation had 65 colored laborers and 10 white; Raceland plantation had 50 colored laborers and 4 white. Those white men designated laborers and resident on plantations were disproportionately concentrated on the smaller plantations.

Abbreviations

PLCC	Parish of Lafourche, Office of the Clerk of the Court
PN	Protocolos Notariales (Notarial Records)
PTCC	Parish of Terrebonne, Office of the Clerk of the Court
SCC	Supreme Court of Louisiana Collection
Treaty Claims	U.S./Spain Treaty Claims
Ultramar	Sección de Ultramar
UNO	University of New Orleans
USNA	United States National Archives
XU	Xavier University Library

Other Abbreviations

caja	caja (box)
esc.	escritura (notarized document)
exp.	expediente (file)
inv.	inventario (inventory)
leg.	legajo (bundle)
libro	libro (book)
no.	número (file number)
Protocolo	Volume of documents recorded by an individual notary
RG	Record Group
sig.	signatura (call number)

Notes

INTRODUCTION

1. See José L. Franco, *Antonio Maceo: Apuntes para una historia de su vida,* 2 vols. (Havana: Editorial de Ciencias Sociales, 1975), 1:263–283; and Eric Arnesen, *Waterfront Workers of New Orleans: Race, Class, and Politics, 1863–1923* (New York: Oxford University Press, 1991).

2. Franco, *Antonio Maceo,* 1:282–327; Armando Vargas Araya, *Idearium Maceísta: Junto con hazañas del general Antonio Maceo y sus mambises en Costa Rica, 1891–1895* (San José: Editorial Juricentro, 2002).

3. See *Daily Crusader,* 22 June 1895. In DFC, ASC, XU.

4. William Hilary Coston, *The Spanish-American War Volunteer* (1899; reprint, Freeport, N.Y.: Books for Libraries Press, 1971), esp. pp. 133–134, 218; *New Orleans Picayune,* 18 August 1898.

5. See Coston, *Spanish-American War Volunteer,* p. 133; and *La Lucha: Diario Republicano* (Havana), for November 1898.

6. See Frank Tannenbaum, *Slave and Citizen* (1946; reprint, Boston: Beacon Press, 1992); Herbert S. Klein, *Slavery in the Americas* (Chicago: University of Chicago Press, 1967); Carl N. Degler, *Neither Black nor White* (New York: Macmillan, 1971).

7. For a rationale for this approach, see Frederick Cooper, Thomas Holt, and Rebecca Scott, *Beyond Slavery: Explorations of Race, Labor, and Citizenship in Postemancipation Societies* (Chapel Hill: University of North Carolina Press, 2000), intro.

8. See Jacques Revel's notion of the "jeux d'échelles," the play of scales, in Revel, ed., *Jeux d'échelles: la micro-analise à l'expérience* (Paris: Seuil/Gallimard, 1996).

9. The details of these recruiting trips appear in Carmouche's pension file in the U.S. National Archives, file C-24444335.

10. Historians these days are often gun-shy about explicit talk of causation, but a respect for agency and contingency is by no means contrary to a search for causes. Agency itself is a causal notion, and choices have the meaning that they do precisely because they have conditions and consequences.

11. On Desdunes and his allies, see Joseph Logsdon with Lawrence Powell, "Rodolphe Lucien Desdunes: Forgotten Organizer of the *Plessy* Protest," in Sam Hyde, ed., *Sunbelt Revolution: The Historical Progression of the Civil Rights Struggle in the Gulf South, 1866–2000* (Gainesville: University Press of Florida, 2003), pp. 42–70; and Lester Sullivan, "The Unknown Rodolphe Desdunes: Writings in the New Orleans *Crusader,*" *Xavier Review* 10 (1990): 1–17. The quotations are from Rodolphe Lucien Desdunes, *Nos hommes et notre histoire* (Montreal: Arbour & Dupont, 1911), pp.

192–194. The original French of the second quotation uses a figure of speech that is difficult to render in English: "notre peuple a eu la satisfaction de pousser au pied du mur le gouvernement américain agissant par le ministère de l'une de ses branches constitutives."

12. Tomás Pérez y Pérez, interview, 1998. See also Rebecca J. Scott, "The Provincial Archive as a Place of Memory: The Role of Former Slaves in the Cuban War of Independence," *History Workshop Journal* 58 (autumn 2004): 149–166.

1. Two Worlds of Cane

Epigraph: George Lamming, *In the Castle of My Skin* (New York: Schocken Books, 1983), p. 25.

1. See Gwendolyn Midlo Hall, *Africans in Colonial Louisiana: The Development of Afro-Creole Culture in the Eighteenth Century* (Baton Rouge: Louisiana State University Press, 1992); Thomas Ingersoll, *Mammon and Manon in Early New Orleans: The First Slave Society in the Deep South, 1718–1819* (Knoxville: University of Tennessee Press, 1999); Richard Follett, *The Sugar Masters* (Baton Rouge: Louisiana State University Press, 2005); Joseph Karl Menn, *The Large Slaveholders of Louisiana—1860* (New Orleans: Pelican Publishing Company, 1964), pp. 112–114; and Carl A. Brasseaux, "Acadian Life in the Lafourche Basin, 1803–1860," in Stephen S. Michot and John P. Doucet, eds., *The Lafourche Country II: The Heritage and Its Keepers* (Thibodaux, La.: Lafourche Heritage Society, 1996), pp. 21–26.

2. For a more detailed discussion of this and other patterns, see John B. Rehder, *Delta Sugar: Louisiana's Vanishing Plantation Landscape* (Baltimore: Johns Hopkins University Press, 1999). See also Sam B. Hilliard, "Site Characteristics and Spatial Stability of the Louisiana Sugarcane Industry," *Agricultural History* 53 (January 1979): 258; and J. Paul Leslie, "Laurel Valley Plantation, 1831–1926," in Philip D. Uzee, ed., *The Lafourche Country: The People and the Land* (Lafayette, La.: Center for Louisiana Studies, 1985), pp. 206–224.

3. Michael Tadman, "The Demographic Cost of Sugar: Debates on Slave Societies and Natural Increase in the Americas," *American Historical Review* 105 (December 2000): 1534–75; and Follett, *The Sugar Masters.*

4. For data on population and production, see Appendix, Table A.1. See also John C. Rodrigue, *Reconstruction in the Cane Fields: From Slavery to Free Labor in Louisiana's Sugar Parishes, 1862–1880* (Baton Rouge: Louisiana State University Press, 2001), chap. 1; Mark Schmitz, "The Transformation of the Southern Cane Sugar Sector, 1860–1930," *Agricultural History* 53 (1979): 270–285; and Walter Johnson, *Soul by Soul: Life inside the Antebellum Slave Market* (Cambridge, Mass.: Harvard University Press, 1999).

5. Carl Brasseaux, *Acadian to Cajun: Transformation of a People, 1803–1877* (Jackson: University Press of Mississippi, 1992); Gilbert C. Din, *The Canary Islanders of Louisiana* (Baton Rouge: Louisiana State University Press, 1988), esp. p. 135.

6. Testimony of Corporal Octave Johnson before the American Freedmen's Inquiry

Commission [Feb.? 1864], reproduced in Ira Berlin, Barbara J. Fields, Thavolia Glymph, Joseph P. Reidy, and Leslie S. Rowland, eds., *Freedom: A Documentary History of Emancipation,* ser. I, vol. 1, *The Destruction of Slavery* (Cambridge: Cambridge University Press, 1985), p. 217.

7. Roderick A. McDonald, *The Economy and Material Culture of Slaves: Goods and Chattels on the Sugar Plantations of Jamaica and Louisiana* (Baton Rouge: Louisiana State University Press, 1993), chap. 2.

8. Caryn Cossé Bell, *Revolution, Romanticism, and the Afro-Creole Protest Tradition in Louisiana, 1718–1868* (Baton Rouge: Louisiana State University Press, 1997); Ira Berlin, *Slaves without Masters: The Free Negro in the Antebellum South* (New York: Oxford University Press, 1974), pp. 108–132; Kimberly S. Hanger, *Bounded Lives, Bounded Places: Free Black Society in Colonial New Orleans, 1769–1803* (Durham, N.C.: Duke University Press, 1997); Emily Clark and Virginia Gould, "The Feminine Face of Afro-Catholicism in New Orleans, 1727–1852," *William and Mary Quarterly,* 3d ser., 59 (April 2002): 409–448. A superb recent synthesis is Ira Berlin, *Generations of Captivity: A History of African-American Slaves* (Cambridge, Mass.: Harvard University Press, 2003), pp. 88–96, 140–157, 179–189.

9. Lester Sullivan, "The Unknown Rodolphe Desdunes: Writings in the New Orleans *Crusader,*" *Xavier Review* 10 (1990): 1–17; and Rodolphe L. Desdunes, *Nos hommes et notre histoire* (Montreal: Arbour & Dupont, 1911), p. 150. See also Mary Niall Mitchell, " 'A Good and Delicious Country': Free Children of Color and How They Learned to Imagine the Atlantic World in Nineteenth-Century Louisiana," *History of Education Quarterly* 40 (Summer 2000): 123–144. On the ideologies of 1848 in France, see Maurice Agulhon, *1848 ou l'Apprentissage de la République (1848–1852)* (Paris: Le Seuil, 1992), and Agulhon, *Les Quarante-huitards* (Paris: Éditions Gallimard, 1992). The meanings attributed to the term Creole, which in Louisiana generally implies some French ancestry, have long been disputed. The referents and overtones of the word, moreover, have shifted over time. See, for example, Virginia R. Domínguez, *White by Definition: Social Classification in Creole Louisiana* (New Brunswick, N.J.: Rutgers University Press, 1986); and Sybil Kein, ed., *Creole: The History and Legacy of Louisiana's Free People of Color* (Baton Rouge: Louisiana State University Press, 2000). Cuban use of the word *criollo,* by contrast, usually simply connotes New World birth and proximate or remote Old World ancestry, which could be European, African, or both. In neither case, however, is the usage of the term stable or without ambiguity.

10. See Nicolas Theodore Macarty & autres, appelants v. Eulalie Mandeville, F.C.L. intimée [initiated 1847], Docket no. 626, N.O., 1846–1861, SCC, UNO. The five *marchandes* working for Eulalie Mandeville are described in the Testimony of Marie Louis Panis, p. 126.

11. I am grateful to Leroy Soles of Detroit, Michigan, for sharing photocopies of the records that he obtained in the course of his genealogical research on the family of his great-great uncle, Pierre Lacroix Carmouche. See Act. 85, from page 23b, of the volume Marriages (1777–1830), Slaves and Free Persons of Color, located in

the Archdiocese of New Orleans Archives, New Orleans, as well as baptismal records from Ascension Church in Donaldsonville. Pierre L. Carmouche's year of birth is variously given as 1861 or 1862.

12. See Appendix, Table A.1, and H. E. Sterkx, *The Free Negro in Antebellum Louisiana* (Cranberry, N.J.: Associated University Presses, 1972).

13. See Judith Kelleher Schafer, *Becoming Free, Remaining Free: Manumission and Enslavement in New Orleans, 1846–1862* (Baton Rouge: Louisiana State University Press, 2003), prologue. See also James O. Fuqua, ed., *Civil Code of the State of Louisiana* (New Orleans: B. Bloomfield and Co., 1867), chap. 3, Articles 184–188. This process culminated in the Act of 6 March 1857, which held simply that "from and after the passage of this Act, no slave shall be emancipated in this State."

14. Solomon Northup, *Twelve Years a Slave,* ed. Sue Eakin and Joseph Logsdon (reprint; Baton Rouge: Louisiana State University Press, 1968); original edition published in 1853.

15. See Manuel Moreno Fraginals, *El ingenio: Complejo económico social cubano del azúcar,* 3 vols. (Havana: Editorial de Ciencias Sociales, 1978), vol. 1, chap. 4; Laird W. Bergad, *Cuban Rural Society in the Nineteenth Century: The Social and Economic History of Monoculture in Matanzas* (Princeton, N.J.: Princeton University Press, 1990), esp. chaps. 2–3; and Franklin W. Knight, "Origins of Wealth and the Sugar Revolution in Cuba, 1750–1850," *Hispanic American Historical Review* 57 (1977): 231–253; and Reinaldo Funes Monzote, *De bosque a sabana: Azúcar, deforestación y medio ambiente en Cuba (1492–1926)* (Mexico City: Siglo Veintiuno Editores, 2004).

16. See Oscar Zanetti Lecuona and Alejandro García Álvarez, *Caminos para el azúcar* (Havana: Editorial de Ciencias Sociales, 1987), pp. 52–53; and Orlando García Martínez, "Estudio de la economía cienfueguera desde la fundación de la colonia Fernandina de Jagua hasta mediados del siglo xix," *Islas* 55/56 (September 1976– April 1977): 117–169.

17. Carlos Rebello, *Estados relativos a la producción azucarera de la Isla de Cuba* (Havana, 1860), as compiled in Rebecca J. Scott, *Slave Emancipation in Cuba: The Transition to Free Labor, 1860–1899* (Princeton, N.J.: Princeton University Press, 1985), table 4. Slave totals are from tables 5 and 10 in the same volume, where I have grouped the island's 1860 *jurisdicciones* to fit the boundaries of what would in 1879 be designated as Santa Clara province.

18. See Appendix, Table A.2. In nineteenth-century Cuban documents, the Spanish terms *negro* (m.) and *negra* (f.), meaning "black," had multiple usages. On the one hand, each could designate an individual categorized as black because of perceived skin color, African birth, or predominantly African ancestry. Uncapitalized, they often followed a name in a notarial or judicial document. In this usage, they contrasted both with "white" (often unmarked) and with *pardo/parda* or *mulato/mulata,* terms that implied lighter color and/or mixed African and European (or occasionally Chinese) ancestry. On the other hand, the word *negros* (also uncapitalized) was also used at times to refer to all of those held as slaves on a given plantation, or to all of those categorized as having African ancestry, independent of differentiations

of color. This usage frequently had negative connotations. Equal-rights activists, in turn, often adopted instead the phrase *de color* (of color), by which they intended to refer respectfully and inclusively to all people of African descent. In English, the terms *black* and *of color* (or *colored)* have some of the same indeterminacy and inclusiveness, and I have used them to translate the Spanish *negro/negra* and *de color,* generally trying to hew close to the vernacular word choice of a given original text.

The Spanish terms *mulato* and *mulata,* however, do not translate convincingly into English. The English word *mulatto,* with its ugly origins in the word *mule,* sounds archaic, and has strong overtones of nineteenth-century racist tracts. In Cuba, despite the same problematic etymology, the word *mulato* has evolved in contemporary colloquial usage into a relatively neutral, if ultimately ambiguous, descriptor. When using Cuban sources, therefore, I have chosen to leave the term *mulato* in the original Spanish.

19. Appendix, Tables A.1 and A.2, and "Censo de población según el cuadro general de la comisión ejecutiva de 1861," in Cuba, Centro de estadística, *Noticias estadísticas de la Isla de Cuba, en 1862* (Havana: Imprenta del Gobierno, 1864).

20. See Follett, *The Sugar Masters,* chap. 7, on the management skills of planters and the labor regime of enslaved workers.

21. See the correspondence transcribed on pp. 173–195 of *Macarty v. Mandeville,* SCC, UNO. In the late 1830s and 1840s Eugène Macarty was in Santiago de Cuba, Barthélemy Macarty was at the Dolorita plantation and in Hongolosongo, and their sister, Mme Chéry Rigaud, was also in the region.

22. See Thomas A. Becnel, *The Barrow Family and the Barataria and Lafourche Canal: The Transportation Revolution in Louisiana* (Baton Rouge: Louisiana State University Press, 1989), esp. chap. 1, "Early Settlers in Bayou Country"; and Rehder, *Delta Sugar,* pp. 55–60.

23. See Rebello, *Estados relativos;* García, "Estudio"; and Orlando García Martínez and Irán Millán Cuétara, "Testimonio del quehacer constructivo en la industria azucarera cienfueguera" (paper presented to the I Coloquio Internacional: El Patrimonio Cultural de la Ciudad Iberoamericana del Siglo XIX). See also the engravings by Eduardo Laplante in Justo Cantero, *Los ingenios: Colección de vistas de los principales ingenios de azúcar de la isla de Cuba* (Havana: L. Marquier, 1857).

24. "In the Matter of Naturalization of Yarrow Williams," 24 October 1868. In Minute Book, Parish Court of Terrebonne, 17 September 1868, PTCC.

25. Ann Patton Malone, *Sweet Chariot: Slave Family and Household Structure in Nineteenth-Century Louisiana* (Chapel Hill: University of North Carolina Press, 1992), p. 38.

26. See Malone, *Sweet Chariot,* pp. 33–37; and Tadman, "The Demographic Cost," p. 1553. On the effect of slave sales on families, see Northup, *Twelve Years;* and Johnson, *Soul by Soul.*

27. On the ineffectual anti–slave trade treaties of 1817 and 1835 between Spain and Great Britain, and the unevenly enforced penal law of 1845, see David Murray, *Odious Commerce: Britain, Spain, and the Abolition of the Cuban Slave Trade* (Cambridge: Cambridge University Press, 1980). On Caridad de Juraguá, see the history pre-

pared by Orlando García Martínez and Iran Millán Cuetara, available in the Archivo Histórico Provincial de Cienfuegos. The lists of the slaves of Santa Rosalía are in CMJL, CC, BNC, files 173 and 178. The recollections concerning Má Rita are from interviews with Caridad Quesada, Cienfuegos, in 1998, 1999, and 2000. (Note: all interviews are with the author, unless otherwise specified.)

28. On Santa Rosalía, see "Relación jurada . . ." 5 November 1868, in vol. 14, exp. 107, CMJL, CC, BNC. On Soledad, see Rebecca J. Scott, "Reclaiming Gregoria's Mule: The Meanings of Freedom in the Arimao and Caunao Valleys, Cienfuegos, Cuba, 1880–1899," *Past and Present* 170 (February 2001): 181–216. On Santa Teresa, see Rebello, *Estados.*

29. Bárbara Pérez's son Tomás Pérez y Pérez, and her granddaughters Olga Pérez Ponvert and Ela Fundora, shared elements of her life story in interviews in 1998 and 1999. See also Rebecca Scott, "Tres Vidas, Una Guerra: Rafael Iznaga, Bárbara Pérez y Gregoria Quesada entre la Emancipación y la Ciudadanía," in José Amador and Fernando Coronil, eds., *Historia y memoria: Sociedad, cultura y vida cotidiana en Cuba, 1878–1917* (Havana: Centro de Investigación y Desarrollo de la Cultura Cubana Juan Marinello and Latin and Caribbean Studies Program, University of Michigan, 2003), pp. 83–99.

30. See Tadman, "The Demographic Cost."

31. Northup, *Twelve Years,* pp. 159–163.

32. Rebello, *Estados,* pp. 13–17. Following Rebello, I have calculated a Cienfuegos district hogshead *(bocoy)* at 60 *arrobas,* or 690 kg.

33. See Desdunes, *Nos hommes,* pp. 32, 77, 107.

34. David C. Rankin, "The Impact of the Civil War on the Free Colored Community of New Orleans," *Perspectives in American History* 11 (1977–78): 379–416; Sterkx, *The Free Negro;* and Berlin, *Slaves without Masters,* pp. 384–395.

35. See the biographical sketch of Pierre Landry in Eric Foner, *Freedom's Lawmakers: A Directory of Black Officeholders during Reconstruction* (Baton Rouge: Louisiana State University Press, 1996), p. 126; David Rankin, "The Origins of Black Leadership in New Orleans during Reconstruction," *Journal of Southern History* 40 (August 1974): 417–440; and p. 16 of the chapter titled "Soldiers of the Cross," in the manuscript "For a Black History of Louisiana," by Marcus Christian, MCC, UNO.

36. Interviews with Santiago Pelayo and Blas Pelayo, Cienfuegos, 1998. The baptismal record of Blas Sarría, son of Pastor Pelayo and "la morena patrocinada Wenceslaa criolla" is 28 May 1881, no. 698, fol. 242, Libro de Bautismos No. 15, in the Cathedral of Cienfuegos. I thank Kathleen López and Mitzi Espinosa Luis for sharing their transcription of it.

37. See Manuel Lucena Salmoral, "El derecho de coartación del esclavo en la América española," *Revista de Indias* 59 (1999): 357–374; Alejandro de la Fuente, "Slave Law and Claims-Making in Cuba: The Tannenbaum Debate Revisited," *Law and History Review* 22 (Summer 2004): 339–369; and Scott, *Slave Emancipation,* p. 14.

38. Schafer, *Becoming Free,* chap. 5.

39. Murray, *Odious Commerce,* p. 299.

2. Building Citizenship

Epigraph: Text of article titled "Militia," transcription in section "Negro Soldiers (1863–1941)," Box 34, Marcus Christian Collection, Louisiana and Special Collections Department, Earl K. Long Library, University of New Orleans.

1. See C. Peter Ripley, *Slaves and Freedmen in Civil War Louisiana* (Baton Rouge: Louisiana State University Press, 1976).

2. Benjamin F. Butler, Major-General, Commanding, to Hon. E. M. Stanton, Secretary of War, 14 November 1862, in U.S. War Department, *The War of the Rebellion: A Compilation of the Official Records of the Union and Confederate Armies,* ser. I, vol. 15 (Washington, D.C.: Government Printing Office, 1886), p. 592.

3. See Barnes Lathrop, "The Lafourche District in 1862: Confederate Revival," *Louisiana History* 1 (fall 1960): 300–319; and Lathrop, "The Lafourche District in 1862: Invasion," *Louisiana History* 2 (spring 1961): 175–201.

4. *The War of the Rebellion,* ser. I, vol. 15, pp. 619–620.

5. See Peyton McCrary, *Abraham Lincoln and Reconstruction: The Louisiana Experiment* (Princeton, N.J.: Princeton University Press, 1978), pp. 112–114; and *The War of the Rebellion,* ser. I, vol. 15, pp. 619–620.

6. *The Thibodaux Sentinel / La Sentinelle de Thibodaux,* 7 February 1863.

7. Peter M. Yawyer to John P. Yawyer, 10 January 1863, in Yawyer (Peter M.) Letter, LLMVC. On the breakdown of slavery in the Union-occupied parishes, see the volumes of *Freedom: A Documentary History of Emancipation, 1861–1867:* Ira Berlin, Barbara J. Fields, Thavolia Glymph, Joseph P. Reidy, and Leslie S. Rowland, eds., ser. I, vol. 1, *The Destruction of Slavery;* and Ira Berlin, Thavolia Glymph, Steven F. Miller, Joseph P. Reidy, Leslie S. Rowland, and Julie Saville, eds., ser. I, vol. 3, *The Wartime Genesis of Free Labor: The Lower South* (Cambridge: Cambridge University Press, 1985, 1990).

8. See John C. Rodrigue, *Reconstruction in the Cane Fields: From Slavery to Free Labor in Louisiana's Sugar Parishes, 1862–1880* (Baton Rouge: Louisiana State University Press, 2001); Paul Eiss, "A Share in the Land: Freedpeople and the Government of Labour in Southern Louisiana, 1862–65," *Slavery and Abolition* 19 (April 1998): 46–89; William F. Messner, *Freedmen and the Ideology of Free Labor: Louisiana, 1862–1865* (Lafayette, La.: Center for Louisiana Studies, 1978); J. Carlyle Sitterson, "The Transition from Slave to Free Economy on the William J. Minor Plantations," *Agricultural History* 17 (1943): 216–224; and the Berlin et al. volumes cited in note 7.

9. Vol. 8, Memorandum Book, box 3, Alexandre E. DeClouet and Family Papers, LLMVC.

10. See Berlin et al., *Wartime Genesis,* pp. 363–377; Rodrigue, *Reconstruction,* pp. 39–49.

11. See James G. Hollandsworth, Jr., *The Louisiana Native Guards: The Black Military Experience during the Civil War* (Baton Rouge: Louisiana State University Press, 1995). The quotation is from Whitelaw Reid, *After the War: A Southern Tour, May 1, 1865, to May 1, 1866* (Cincinnati: Moore, Wilstach and Baldwin, 1866), p. 244.

12. See Ira Berlin, Joseph P. Reidy, and Leslie S. Rowland, eds., *Freedom: A Documentary*

History of Emancipation, 1861–1867, ser. II, *The Black Military Experience* (Cambridge: Cambridge University Press, 1982).

13. See ibid., table 1, p. 12. Family memory concerning Pierre Carmouche senior was conveyed to me by Leroy Soles of Detroit, 2003.

14. See Eiss, "A Share in the Land," pp. 46–89; and Lawrence Powell, *New Masters: Northern Planters during the Civil War and Reconstruction* (New Haven: Yale University Press, 1980).

15. Eiss, "A Share in the Land"; Rodrigue, *Reconstruction,* p. 49.

16. On politics, see McCrary, *Abraham Lincoln,* p. 304 and chap. 10. Evidence on labor arrangements comes from Records of the Assistant Commissioner, Louisiana, RG 105, Records of the Bureau of Refugees, Freedmen, and Abandoned Lands, USNA, reproduced on microfilm on M1027 (hereafter USNA, M1027). On Orange Grove, see Monthly Report of 1st Lieut. J. S. Wadsworth, Asst. Inspr. Freedmen, for the Parish of Terrebonne, for the month ending April 30, 1866, USNA, M1027, reel 28; and Monthly Report of George A. Ludlow, Asst. Inspr. Freedmen, for the Parish of Terrebonne, La., for the Month ending July 31st, 1866, USNA, M1027, reel 29. On a few plantations in Lafourche Parish freedpeople still worked under rental arrangements and grew corn rather than sugar as late as 1868. See Monthly Report of John H. Van Antwerp, Asst. Inspr. Freedmen, Parish of Lafourche, La., for the month ending September 30, 1868, USNA, M1027, reel 31.

17. On the reluctance to lease, see Monthly Report of Capt. C. E. Wilcox, Asst. Inspr. Freedmen, Parish of Lafourche, La., for the month ending January 31, 1866; and Hqtrs BRFAL, State of Louisiana, Inspection Report for Jan., Feb., March, 1866, both in USNA, M1027, reel 28.

18. From the article titled "Militia," in the *New Orleans Daily Crescent,* 18 November 1865, transcription in "Negro Soldiers (1863–1941)," box 34, MCC, UNO.

19. See Hollandsworth, *Louisiana Native Guards,* chap. 10; and Joseph G. Dawson III, *Army Generals and Reconstruction: Louisiana, 1862–1877* (Baton Rouge: Louisiana State University Press, 1982), app. 3. Quotation is from Wm. Dougherty, Provost Marshal and Asst. Inspr. of Freedmen, Inspection Report of Plantations, freedmen, &c. in the parishes Jefferson and Orleans, Right Bank, January 1866, in USNA, M1027, roll 28.

20. Dougherty, Inspection Report, January 1866.

21. See Henry S. Wadsworth to Col. J. I. Grigg, Inspector General, January 31, 1866, in USNA, M1027, reel 28. See also Rodrigue, *Reconstruction,* chap. 6.

22. See Claude F. Oubre, " 'Forty Acres and a Mule': Louisiana and the Southern Homestead Act," *Louisiana History* 17 (spring 1976): 143–157; Roderick A. McDonald, *The Economy and Material Culture of Slaves: Goods and Chattels on the Sugar Plantations of Jamaica and Louisiana* (Baton Rouge: Louisiana State University Press, 1993); Rodrigue, *Reconstruction,* pp. 154–157; and Dylan C. Penningroth, *The Claims of Kinfolk: African American Property and Community in the Nineteenth-Century South* (Chapel Hill: University of North Carolina Press, 2003).

23. 1867, vol. 2, Diary, box 2, Alexandre E. DeClouet and Family Papers, LLMVC.

24. See Carl A. Brasseaux, "Acadian Life in the Lafourche Basin, 1803–1860," in Ste-

phen S. Michot and John P. Doucet, eds., *The Lafourche Country II: The Heritage and Its Keepers* (Thibodaux, La.: Lafourche Heritage Society, 1996), pp. 21–26.

25. See Appendix Table A.3 and the manuscript returns of the Population Schedules of the Ninth Census of the United States, 1870, reproduced on USNA M593. In Terrebonne Parish (roll 533) black and mulatto heads of household are usually listed as farm laborers, though there are occasional coopers and carpenters, as well as a few farmers. Of the white men listed as farm laborers, some are young men living at home with a father who is a farmer, and may not have worked for wages.

26. See Roger W. Shugg, *Origins of Class Struggle in Louisiana: A Social History of White Farmers and Laborers during Slavery and After, 1840–1875* (1939; Baton Rouge: Louisiana State University Press, 1968), p. 253. On immigrants, see Jean A. Scarpaci, "Italian Immigrants in Louisiana's Sugar Parishes: Recruitment, Labor Conditions, and Community Relations, 1880–1910" (Ph.D. dissertation, Rutgers University, 1972).

27. On the *Tribune,* Louisiana politics, and the question of suffrage, see Eric Foner, *Reconstruction: America's Unfinished Revolution, 1863–1877* (New York: Harper and Row, 1988), pp. 62–67, 262–263. On the "voluntary election," see F. Wayne Binning, "Carpetbaggers Triumph: The Louisiana State Election of 1868," *Louisiana History* 14 (winter 1973): 21–39; and McCrary, *Abraham Lincoln,* pp. 334–338.

28. See Dawson, *Army Generals,* pp. 46–55.

29. "Last Revised Registry List of Lafourche Parish, signed by R. Chandler, Capt. 13th Inf't'y, Ass't Sec. Civil Affairs," in Box 1 of Miscellaneous Records, Executive Department, P1978–143, LSA.

30. Names are all from "Last Revised Registry List." Information on Crozier and Murrell can be found in Eric Foner, *Freedom's Lawmakers: A Directory of Black Officeholders during Reconstruction,* rev. ed. (Baton Rouge: Louisiana State University Press, 1996), pp. 54, 156–157.

31. Identifying information on Lewis and Taylor is discussed in notes 61, 62, and 80.

32. Each of these names appears both on the 1867 voter registration list with a registration number lower than 500, and on the Lafourche Parish lists of the "Schedules Enumerating Union Veterans and Widows of Union Veterans of the Civil War, Louisiana," of the Eleventh Census of the United States (1890), bundles 60 and 61. These have been reproduced as roll 5 of the File Microcopies of Records in the National Archives, no. 123, held in Hill Memorial Library, Louisiana State University.

33. The final 1868 registration figures for the entire state were 78,230 black voters and over 48,000 white. This compares with 1870 population figures of 364,210 black residents and 362,065 white. See Joe Gray Taylor, *Louisiana Reconstructed, 1863–1877* (Baton Rouge: Louisiana State University Press, 1974), p. 139; U.S. Census Office, *Ninth Census of the United States, 1870,* vol. 1, *The Statistics of the Population of the United States* (Washington, D.C.: U.S. Census Office, 1871), p. 34.

34. See Charles Vincent, *Black Legislators in Louisiana during Reconstruction* (Baton Rouge: Louisiana State University Press, 1976); Binning, "Carpetbaggers"; and Ted Tunnell, *Crucible of Reconstruction: War, Radicalism, and Race in Louisiana, 1862–1877* (Baton Rouge: Louisiana State University Press, 1984), chap. 6 and app. 2.

35. The experience of the officers of African descent is examined in Hollandsworth, *Louisiana Native Guards*. The roots of Afro-Creole activism are traced in Rodolphe L. Desdunes, *Nos hommes et notre histoire* (Montreal: Arbour & Dupont, 1911); and in Caryn Cossé Bell, *Revolution, Romanticism, and the Afro-Creole Protest Tradition in Louisiana, 1718–1868* (Baton Rouge: Louisiana State University Press, 1997).

36. Louisiana, *Official Journal of the Proceedings of the Convention for Framing a Constitution for the State of Louisiana* (New Orleans: J. B. Roudanez and Co., 1867–68), pp. 293–294.

37. Ibid. (1868), pp. 117, 276–277, 290–294. Racial identifiers and occupations are from Tunnell, *Crucible*, app. 2.

38. *Official Journal* (1868), pp. 117, 294. The amendment inserting the word "public" after "civil and political" passed 59 to 16. Supporters included Bonseigneur from the *Unión/Tribune* group of Creoles, and Dupart, Murrell, Snaer, Valfroit, and Marie from the bayou parishes, as well as other white and black delegates.

39. Bell, *Revolution;* and Desdunes, *Nos hommes,* pp. 167–177. On 1848 in France, see Maurice Agulhon, *Les Quarante-Huitards* (Paris: Gallimard, 1992). For a more general discussion of the concept of public rights, see Rebecca J. Scott, "Se battre pour ses droits: Écritures, litiges et discrimination raciale en Louisiane (1888–1899)," *Cahiers du Brésil Contemporain* (Paris) 53/54 (2003): 175–209.

40. The rules for disfranchisement for actions under the Confederacy were complex, and included holding office, signing the ordinance of secession, or preaching or publishing in favor of sedition. See Articles 98 and 99, in *Official Journal* (1868), pp. 303–304. On Morris, see Foner, *Freedom's Lawmakers,* p. 155.

41. *Official Journal* (1868), pp. 110, 112, 117. Frederic Marie is something of a mystery figure. Vincent, in *Black Legislators,* pp. 57, 57n, describes him as man of color and a farmer who served as sheriff in Terrebonne; Tunnell, in *Crucible,* p. 235, categorizes him as a white hotelkeeper born in France; Foner, in *Reconstruction,* p. 299, refers to a Frederic Carie, sheriff of Houma, and describes him as a "red Republican" from France. Perhaps Frederick Marie, like his colleague Edouard Tinchant, was a man born in France whose color affiliation shifted depending on the context.

42. *Official Journal* (1868), p. 37.

43. See Taylor, *Louisiana Reconstructed,* p. 158; Tunnell, *Crucible,* p. 134.

44. Desdunes, *Nos hommes,* p. 168, translation mine.

45. Rodrigue makes this argument in *Reconstruction,* chap. 4.

46. See the testimony of John J. Moore, New Orleans, June 8, 1869, in U.S. Congress, House, "Louisiana Contested Elections," 41st Cong., 2d sess., Misc. Doc. 154, pt. 1, pp. 634–642. Moore's testimony is also cited and discussed in Nell Irwin Painter, *Exodusters: Black Migration to Kansas after Reconstruction* (New York: Alfred A. Knopf, 1977), p. 11. For discussions of grassroots mobilization elsewhere in the South, see Foner, *Reconstruction;* Julie Saville, *The Work of Reconstruction: From Slave to Wage Laborer in South Carolina, 1860–1870* (New York: Cambridge University Press, 1994), chap. 5; Steven Hahn, *A Nation under Our Feet: Black Political Struggles in the Rural South from Slavery to the Great Migration* (Cambridge, Mass.: Harvard University

Press, 2003); Leon F. Litwack, *Been in the Storm So Long: The Aftermath of Slavery* (New York: Knopf, 1979); and Michael W. Fitzgerald, *The Union League Movement in the Deep South: Politics and Agricultural Change during Reconstruction* (Baton Rouge: Louisiana State University Press, 1989).

47. See Judgment no. 104 (7 January 1869) and associated cases, pp. 23–30 of the Minute Book, Parish Court of Terrebonne, 17 September 1868–12 April 1876, Office of the Clerk of the Court, Terrebonne Parish, Houma, La. See also Harold Woodman, *New South—New Law: The Legal Foundations of Credit and Labor Relations in the Postbellum Agricultural South* (Baton Rouge: Louisiana State University Press, 1995), pp. 78–79, 79n.

48. Entries for January and February 1869, September, October, and November 1870, Plantation Diary 1869 (Southdown), William J. Minor and Family Papers, LLMVC. The records of the Minor plantation were also studied in detail by Carlyle Sitterson in the early 1940s. See his essay "The Transition from Slave to Free Economy on the William J. Minor Plantations," *Agricultural History* 17 (1943): 216–224. On the Republicans and labor more broadly, see Thomas Holt, *Black over White: Negro Political Leadership in South Carolina during Reconstruction* (Urbana: University of Illinois Press, 1977), chap. 7.

49. See the *Terrebonne Patriot,* 23 and 30 April 1870.

50. Entry for 8 November 1870, Plantation Diary 1869 (Southdown), William J. Minor and Family Papers, LLMVC.

51. See Foner, *Freedom's Lawmakers,* p. 140; Desdunes, *Nos hommes,* pp. 114–116; and David C. Rankin, "The Origins of Black Leadership in New Orleans during Reconstruction," *Journal of Southern History* (August 1974): 417–440.

52. The concept of a "legitimacy crisis" is used by Lawrence Powell in "Southern Republicanism during Reconstruction: The Contradictions of State and Party Formation" (paper delivered at the annual meeting of the Organization of American Historians, 1984) and by Tunnell, *Crucible of Reconstruction,* p. 153.

53. Governor Warmoth claimed to have incorporated "twenty-five hundred young Rebels" into the militia. Henry Clay Warmoth, *War, Politics, and Reconstruction: Stormy Days in Louisiana* (New York: Macmillan Company, 1930), p. 100. See the article from the *Daily Picayune,* 10 November 1870, transcribed in "White League. 1870–77. Supplement. Compiled and edited by P. L. Supas, Archivist. Office of the Adjutant General of Louisiana, Jackson Barracks, 1942," JBL.

54. See *Terrebonne Republican,* 3 June 1871. See the entries for Thomas Cage, William H. Keyes, Frederick Marie, and Frederick R. Wright of Terrebonne Parish in Foner, *Freedom's Lawmakers.* See also Vincent, *Black Legislators.*

55. See Tunnell, *Crucible,* pp. 151–172; Dawson, *Army Generals,* chaps. 6 and 7; and Taylor, *Louisiana Reconstructed.*

56. *Weekly Thibodaux Sentinel,* 31 May 1873.

57. "Usurpation on the Rampage!!!," *Weekly Thibodaux Sentinel,* 24 May 1873.

58. Michele Mitchell coined the term "aspiring class," which seems an apt one to describe the pastors, schoolteachers, and newspaper editors who stand out as activists

in Terrebonne and Lafourche. See Mitchell, " 'The Black Man's Burden': African Americans, Imperialism, and Notions of Racial Manhood, 1890–1910," *International Review of Social History* 44, supp. (1999): 77–99; and Mitchell, *Righteous Propagation: African Americans and the Politics of Racial Destiny after Reconstruction* (Chapel Hill: University of North Carolina Press, 2004), p. xx. On veterans, see the 1890 "Schedules Enumerating Union Veterans and Widows," which found almost 250 surviving veterans in Lafourche Parish.

59. See Transcriptions of Louisiana Police Jury Records, 1811–1940, Historical Records Survey, WPA (Works Progress Administration) Collection, LLMVC, especially those of Terrebonne Parish, 1868–1882, located in box 183.

60. See Louisiana, *Annual Report of the State Superintendent of Public Education, William G. Brown, to the General Assembly of Louisiana for the Year 1873* . . . (New Orleans: The Republican, 1874), pp. 238, 243.

61. See vol. 7, Louisiana, Population Schedules of the Ninth Census of the United States, 1870, reproduced on reel 516, USNA M593.

62. See Louisiana, *Annual Report of the State Superintendent of Public Education, Thomas Conway, to the General Assembly of Louisiana, for the Year 1871* (New Orleans: The Republican, 1872) and *Annual Report of the State Superintendent of Public Education, William G. Brown, to the General Assembly of Louisiana, for the Year 1872* (New Orleans: The Republican, 1873). The supervisor's judgment appears in Louisiana, *Annual Report of the State Superintendent of Public Education, William G. Brown, to the General Assembly of Louisiana for the Year 1875* (New Orleans: The Republican, 1876), p. 262. Earl Lewis has for several years been exploring the role of black schoolteachers in the South, and I am grateful to him for discussions of this topic.

63. *Thibodaux Sentinel,* 29 March, 5 April, and 19 April 1873.

64. Louisina, *Acts Passed by the General Assembly of the State of Louisiana at the First Session of the Third Legislature Begun and Held in New Orleans, January 6, 1873* (New Orleans: The Republican Office, 1873), pp. 53, 134–139, 156–157.

65. See articles in the *New Orleans Republican,* 15 May 1873, transcribed in the typescript "White League. 1870–77. Supplement," JBL.

66. The phrase is from Foner, *Reconstruction,* p. 530. For a description of the events of Easter Sunday, 1873, in Colfax, see Robert M. Goldman, *Reconstruction and Black Suffrage: Losing the Vote in Reese and Cruikshank* (Lawrence: University Press of Kansas, 2001), pp. 42–51.

67. On the breadth of the 1873 crisis, see Peter Gourevitch, *Politics in Hard Times: Comparative Responses to International Economic Crises* (Ithaca, N.Y.: Cornell University Press, 1986).

68. The contraband transatlantic slave trade to Cuba had brought in approximately 30,000 African captives in 1859, 25,000 in 1860, 24,000 in 1861, and 11,000 in 1862. See the semi-official figures cited in David R. Murray, *Odious Commerce: Britain, Spain, and the Abolition of the Cuban Slave Trade* (Cambridge: Cambridge University Press, 1980), p. 244.

69. Export figures can be found in Manuel Moreno Fraginals, *El ingenio: Complejo*

económico social cubano del azúcar, 3 vols. (Havana: Editorial de Ciencias Sociales, 1978), 3:35–44. See also Alan Dye, *Cuban Sugar in the Age of Mass Production: Technology and the Economics of the Sugar Central, 1899–1929* (Stanford: Stanford University Press, 1998), table 2.1, p. 27.

70. See John Heitman, "The Nineteenth and Early Twentieth Century Sugar Industry," in Michot and Doucet, *The Lafourche Country II.* I have converted Heitman's Louisiana short tons to metric tons at a rate of 2,204.6 pounds to the metric ton.

71. The events of 1873–74 are described in Marcus Bruce Christian's manuscript for "A Black History of Louisiana," now held in Special Collections, Earl K. Long Library, UNO; and in Rodrigue, *Reconstruction,* pp. 162–165.

72. W. E. B. Du Bois counted, for the years between 1868 and 1896, some "32 colored state senators and 95 representatives" in Louisiana, though he pointed out that racial categorizations were exceptionally uncertain. Du Bois, *Black Reconstruction in America, 1860–1880* (1935; reprint, New York: Atheneum, 1979), p. 470. See, more recently, Vincent, *Black Legislators,* pp. 232–233, 236–237, who counts 38 state representatives and 12 senators of color in 1872–1874. My count is of legislators listed in Vincent as coming from Lafourche, Terrebonne, Ascension, St. Mary, or St. Martin.

73. *New Orleans Picayune,* 16 and 20 January 1874.

74. See *Picayune,* 14, 15, 16, 18, and 20 January 1874. The Murrell report is in Louisiana, *Journal of the House of Representatives,* pp. 62–63, session of 22 January 1874.

75. See Louisiana, *Annual Report of the Adjutant General of the State of Louisiana for the Year ending December 31st, 1874* (New Orleans: The Republican, 1875), pp. 24, 27, and 47 of the WPA typescript, JBL.

76. See Louisiana, *Annual Report of the State Superintendent of Public Education for 1870* (New Orleans: A. L. Lee, 1871) and *Annual Report of the State Superintendent of Public Education, William G. Brown, to the General Assembly of Louisiana, for the Year 1872* (New Orleans: The Republican, 1873), p. 104. On paper, the salary for a militia captain was $150 per month, but these salaries may have been paid in badly depreciated state warrants. See "Muster and Pay Roll of Louisiana National Guards," in folder titled "January 31, 1877; Aug. 19, 1884" in Executive Department Miscellaneous Records, P1978–143, LSA.

77. On competing recollections of black military service, see David W. Blight, *Race and Reunion: The Civil War in American Memory* (Cambridge, Mass.: Harvard University Press, 2001), chap. 5.

78. Each company had some fifty or sixty privates. See *Annual Report of the Adjutant General, 1874.*

79. See the *Times Democrat* (New Orleans), 3 October 1887, transcribed in *Historical Military Data on Louisiana Militia, July 1–Dec. 31, 1878,* JBL.

80. See household number 135, Third Ward, Parish of Lafourche, State of Louisiana, roll 516, USNA, M593. In "Militia List for Lafourche Militia, 1878" (see discussion in source note for Appendix Table A.3) a Tench Goodin, age twenty-eight, laborer, Colored, appears as residing in Lafourche Crossing. Taylor Nelson, called Nelson

Taylor, appears on the school board in Louisiana, *Annual Report of the State Super-intendant of Public Education, William G. Brown . . . for the Year 1873* (New Orleans: The Republican, 1874), p. 106.

81. Indeed, the 1890 "Schedules Enumerating Union Veterans and Widows" found twenty-seven Union veterans living near Raceland Station.

82. See Taylor, *Louisiana Reconstructed,* pp. 276–296.

83. For the sequence of events of September 1874, see Dawson, *Army Generals,* pp. 155–182; Walter L. Fleming, *Documentary History of Reconstruction,* vol. 2 (Cleveland: Arthur H. Clark Company, 1907), 2:141–150; Lawrence N. Powell, "Reinventing Tradition: Liberty Place, Historical Memory, and Silk-stocking Vigilantism in New Orleans Politics," in Silvia R. Frey and Betty Wood, eds., *From Slavery to Emancipation in the Atlantic World,* a special issue of *Slavery and Abolition* 20 (April 1999): 127–149; and Lawrence N. Powell, "The Battle of Canal Street: An Upper-Class Dream of Power and Preferment" (paper presented at the annual meeting of the Organization of American Historians, Toronto, Canada, April 25, 1999).

84. See Fleming, *Documentary History of Reconstruction,* 2:141–150.

85. See Powell, "Reinventing Tradition"; Dawson, *Army Generals;* and Fleming, *Documentary History of Reconstruction,* 2:141–150.

3. Crisis and Voice

1. See the transcriptions of the Policy Jury Minutes for Terrebonne Parish, 1868–1882 and 1882–1894, box 183, WPA Collection, LLMVC. It is possible that this was the plantation of Taylor Beattie, a Republican and later a judge.

2. F. S. Goode from Terrebonne Parish, quoted in John C. Rodrigue, *Reconstruction in the Cane Fields: From Slavery to Free Labor in Louisiana's Sugar Parishes, 1862–1880* (Baton Rouge: Louisiana State University Press, 2001), p. 167. See Charles Vincent, *Black Legislators in Louisiana during Reconstruction* (Baton Rouge: Louisiana State University Press, 1976), pp. 234–235, on representatives elected.

3. See Lawrence N. Powell, "Southern Republicanism during Reconstruction: The Contradictions of State and Party Formation" (paper presented at the 1984 annual meeting of the Organization of American Historians).

4. See Vincent, *Black Legislators,* pp. 188–189, and Joseph G. Dawson III, *Army Generals and Reconstruction: Louisiana, 1862–1877* (Baton Rouge: Louisiana State University Press, 1982), pp. 218–220, on the workings of the Wheeler Compromise, sometimes called the Wheeler Adjustment.

5. See Dawson, *Army Generals,* p. 220.

6. For discussions of the events in Colfax and in New Orleans, see Joe Gray Taylor, *Louisiana Reconstructed, 1863–1877* (Baton Rouge: Louisiana State University Press, 1974), pp. 267–273; and James K. Hogue, "Bayonet Rule: Five Street Battles in New Orleans and the Rise and Fall of Radical Reconstruction" (Ph.D. diss, Princeton University, 1998).

7. *United States v. Cruikshank,* 92 U.S. 542, 555 (1875).

8. On the impact of the *Cruikshank* decisions, see Eric Foner, *Reconstruction: America's Unfinished Revolution, 1863–1877* (New York: Harper and Row, 1988), pp. 530–531, 569; Lawrence Powell, "The Battle of Canal Street: An Upper-Class Dream of Power and Preferment" (paper presented at the annual meeting of the Organization of American Historians, Toronto, Canada, April 25, 1999); and Robert M. Goldman, *Reconstruction and Black Suffrage: Losing the Vote in Reese and Cruikshank* (Lawrence: University Press of Kansas, 2001). My thinking on the case is much influenced by discussions with Richard Pildes and Ellen Katz. Katz argues that the impact of *Cruikshank* on voting has been overstated, and notes that the *Cruikshank* decision did not assert that state action was necessary for a violation of the Fifteenth Amendment to be alleged. Ellen D. Katz, "Reinforcing Representation: Congressional Power to Enforce the Fourteenth and Fifteenth Amendments in the Rehnquist and Waite Courts," *Michigan Law Review* 101 (June 2003): 2341–2408.

9. *Weekly Thibodaux Sentinel,* 8 January 1876.

10. "Papers in the Case of Acklen vs. Darrall, Third Congressional District of Louisiana, October 31, 1877," in 45th Cong., 1st sess. [1877], House Misc. Docs. 5, pp. 3, 23, 217, 243.

11. See "Papers in the Case of Acklen vs. Darrall," pp. 23, 25, 26.

12. See "Testimony Taken by the Select Committee on the Recent Election in Louisiana," in 44th Cong., 2nd sess., House Misc. Doc. 34, Pt. 5 [1877], for the late 1876 testimony, and "Papers in the Case of Acklen vs. Darrall," for 1877 testimony. As George Rable has noted, such testimony often "reeks of perjury." Rable, *But There Was No Peace: The Role of Violence in the Politics of Reconstruction* (Athens: University of Georgia Press, 1984), p. 141.

13. *Weekly Thibodaux Sentinel,* 18 November 1876.

14. "Papers in the Case of Acklen vs. Darrall," p. 37.

15. Ibid., quotation from Snaer on pp. 241–242. See also pp. 36–37 (on "bullyragging"), 192–193, 203–204, 241–242. On women and elections elsewhere, see Elsa Barkley Brown, "To Catch the Vision of Freedom: Reconstructing Southern Black Women's Political History, 1865–1880," in Ann D. Gordon, ed., *African American Women and the Vote, 1837–1965* (Amherst: University of Massachusetts Press, 1997), pp. 66–99.

16. See *Weekly Thibodaux Sentinel,* 11 November 1876, for the quotation. Every detail about these events is disputed; I am relying in part on the earliest testimony by Frederick Francis, who was a commissioner. See "Testimony on the Recent Election in Louisiana," pp. 121–126. Twelve of the 22 polls are specified as being located at the "plantation-quarters" of different planters, including R. H. Allen's. The opening of the poll in "a room in the quarters once occupied by Buck Payne" is asserted by Lucern Bailes, a fifty-year-old "colored man" and carpenter on the Allen plantation. See "Papers in the Case of Acklen vs. Darrall," p. 8.

17. On black attendance at Democratic meetings, see *Weekly Thibodaux Sentinel,* 28 October 1876. On R. H. Allen's carriage driver, see the testimony of Marcelin Ledet, "Papers in the Case of Acklen vs. Darrall," p. 77.

18. See "Testimony on the Recent Election in Louisiana." Sullivan's initial testimony is on pp. 31–38, Fenstel's on pp. 59–64.

19. See ibid., and "Papers in the Case of Acklen vs. Darrall," pp. 137–138.

20. See "Testimony on the Recent Election in Louisiana," pp. 31–38, 59–64, and "Papers in the Case of Acklen vs. Darrall," pp. 212–213. For the main narrative thread of the paragraphs that follow I have chosen to follow the testimony of the constable Robert Taylor, supplemented by that of Michelet and Ledet. Taylor seems to have refrained from embellishment, and to have had the least at stake.

21. The presence of Lewis was asserted by Michelet in a "Communication" in the *Weekly Thibodaux Sentinel,* 22 October 1887, but not established in the testimony taken at the time.

22. See Michelet's testimony, cited in note 20, and the later "Communication," *Weekly Thibodaux Sentinel,* 22 October 1887.

23. "Papers in the Case of Acklen vs. Darrall," pp. 1, 2. Ledet's testimony from April of 1877 is on pp. 73–78.

24. See Dawson, *Army Generals,* pp. 258–261.

25. See the handwritten drafts of such regulations dated 23 March 1877, in Box 2, Executive Department, Miscellaneous Documents, accession number P1978–143, LSA.

26. On Crozier's political career, see Vincent, *Black Legislators,* p. 193. For his Lafourche Parish landholdings, see the 1875 Assessment Rolls, held in the office of the Clerk of the Court, Thibodaux, Louisiana, and the testimony in "Papers in the Case of Acklen vs. Darrall," pp. 214–219. The *Annual Report of the Adjutant General of the State of Louisiana, for the Year Ending December 31, 1871* (New Orleans: The Republican, 1872), p. 18, lists him as a major in the Fourth Regiment of the Militia in New Orleans. On Crozier's interventions in 1877, see the *Thibodaux Sentinel,* 15 October 1887.

27. *Historical Military Data on Louisiana Militia, July 1–Dec. 31, 1878,* JBL, pp. 87–94.

28. See sheet 38, First Ward, Terrebonne Parish, vol. 16, Louisiana, Tenth Census of the United States, 1880. (Reproduced on roll 472, Microfilm Publication T9, USNA.) B. H. Lewis, mulatto, age forty-two, born in Maine, is listed along with his wife Ester, mulatto, born in Louisiana, and their children Ann Mary (age five) and Ben Philip (age two).

29. On John J. Moore's activities, see Chapter 2.

30. Earl Lewis analyzes a parallel dynamic in *In Their Own Interests: Race, Class, and Power in Twentieth-Century Norfolk, Virginia* (Berkeley: University of California Press, 1991).

31. Albert O. Hirschman has traced the process of "conservation and mutation of social energy" in modern Latin America. In places like Chile during the dictatorship of Augusto Pinochet, men and women who had been activists in now-banned political parties redirected their energies toward specific efforts to defend collective lands. Those engaged in micro-development activities often turned out to have "previously participated in other, generally more 'radical' experiences of collective action, that had generally not achieved their objective, often because of official re-

pression." Albert O. Hirschman, *Getting Ahead Collectively: Grassroots Experiences in Latin America* (New York: Pergamon Press, 1984), pp. 42–43.

32. See the entry for Thomas A. Cage in the manuscript schedules of the Tenth Census of the United States [1880], Agriculture, Louisiana, Terrebonne Parish, held in the Rare Book, Manuscript, and Special Collections Library, Duke University.

33. On Henry Franklin, see the biography of his son Henry O. Franklin, in William Hilary Coston, *The Spanish-American War Volunteer* (1899; reprint, Freeport, N.Y.: Books for Libraries Press, 1971), p. 79. Henry Franklin is located in household 219, sheet 529 of Ward 7, Thibodaux, Lafourche Parish, on roll 516, USNA Microfilm Publication 593, "Population Schedules of the Ninth Census of the United States, 1870." His assets were at this point valued at $500.

34. See John Heitman, "The Nineteenth and Early Twentieth-Century Sugar Industry," in Stephen S. Michot and John P. Doucet, eds., *The Lafourche Country II: The Heritage and Its Keepers* (Thibodaux, La.: Lafourche Heritage Society, 1996), p. 99; and A. Bouchereau, *Statement of the Sugar and Rice Crops Made in Louisiana in 1887–88* (New Orleans: E. A. Brandao and Co., 1888), pp. 32–35.

35. In "Militia List for Lafourche Militia, 1878," PLCC, Leighton plantation (Precinct 2) listed only six white male residents: two planters, one merchant, two young clerks, and one thirty-year-old laborer. The next thirty-seven entries on the assessor's list were of men listed as colored laborers, resident on the plantation. (See source for Appendix Table A.3 for a discussion of this list.) For Upper Ten, see Precinct 22 in the same document.

36. See "Militia List for Lafourche Militia, 1878." On the school, described as "about equally attended by white and colored children," see Louisiana, *Annual Report of the State Superintendent of Public Education, William G. Brown to the General Assembly of Louisiana for the Year 1875* (New Orleans: The Republican, 1876).

37. See entry no. 80, Tenth Ward, Lafourche Parish, Louisiana, population schedules of the Tenth Census of the United States, 1880 (reproduced on roll 472, Microfilm Publication T9, USNA). McEnery is quoted in the *Weekly Pelican* of New Orleans on 15 October 1887.

38. Most of the information on Junius Bailey's career comes from A. E. Perkins, *Who's Who in Colored Louisiana* (Baton Rouge: Douglas Loan Company, 1930), p. 109. For Bailey's place of employment in 1887 I have drawn on Jeffrey Gould, " 'Heroic and Vigorous Action': An Analysis of the Sugar Cane Workers' Strike in Lafourche Parish, November, 1887" (ms.). On the population of Laurel Valley, see "Militia List for Lafourche Militia, 1878."

39. Details of Pierre L. Carmouche's life can be found in his subsequent pension request, held in the U.S. National Archives, file XC2-444-335, and in Coston, *Spanish-American War Volunteer*, pp. 133–135. See the discussion of his grandparents in Chapter 1, and of his father's possible service in the Union Army in Chapter 2.

40. Martinet's notarial records are held in NONARC. On the early political work of Desdunes, see Caryn Cossé Bell, *Revolution, Romanticism, and the Afro-Creole Protest Tradition in Louisiana, 1718–1868* (Baton Rouge: Louisiana State University Press, 1997), pp. 263–264; Lester Sullivan, "The Unknown Rodolphe Desdunes: Writ-

ings in the New Orleans *Crusader*," *Xavier Review* 10 (1990): 1–17; Joseph Logsdon with Lawrence Powell, "Rodolphe Lucien Desdunes: Forgotten Organizer of the *Plessy* Protest," in Sam Hyde, ed., *Sunbelt Revolution: The Historical Progression of the Civil Rights Struggle in the Gulf South, 1866–2000* (Gainesville: University Press of Florida, 2003); and Desdunes's own *Nos hommes et notre histoire*. Many of Desdunes's political writings are held in the Desdunes Family Collection, Xavier University Archives and Special Collections. I thank Lester Sullivan at the Xavier University Archives for bringing these materials to my attention. Desdunes's Masonic writings can be found in the George Longe Papers, held at the Amistad Research Center, Tulane University, New Orleans. See especially folder 5, box 26; and the "Livre d'Or 1e Degré, L'Amitié No. 27," in box 41.

41. Maceo's stays in New Orleans (August–September 1884; January–March 1885; June–July 1885) are described in José L. Franco, *Antonio Maceo: Apuntes para una historia de su vida*, 2 vols. (Havana: Editorial de Ciencias Sociales, 1975), 1:263–283. See also the Maceo correspondence for those months in Sociedad Cubana de Estudios Históricos y Internacionales, *Antonio Maceo. Ideología Política. Cartas y Otros Documentos*, vol. 1 (Havana: Sociedad Cubana de Estudios Históricos y Internacionales, 1950), pp. 249–263. Maceo's wife, María Cabrales, seems to have remained in New Orleans, along with the family of Máximo Gómez, between August of 1884 and July of 1885, while Maceo and Gómez came and went to exile centers in Key West, New York, and Mexico. The addresses of members of the lodge "L'Amitié No. 27" are listed on the back cover of the Livre d'Or 1e Degré, beginning in 1881, held in box 41, George Longe Papers, ARC.

42. The *Daily Crusader* of 22 June 1895 reports on Maceo's military campaign. On the masonic lodges, and their shared meeting space, see *Progrès et Liberté: Bulletin Indépendant de la Franc-Maçonnerie en Louisiane* 2 (February 1886): 34, which provides news of the Loge Amitié No. 27, which included Desdunes, and of the Logia Concordia No. 30, whose "dignatarios" all had Spanish surnames. A copy of this publication is in folder 5, box 26 of the George Longe papers, ARC. I am grateful to Olga Portuondo and María de los Angeles Meriño in Santiago de Cuba for information on Maceo's family history; to Caryn Cossé Bell and Brenda Square for leads on Desdunes and the Scottish Rite Masons; and to Ada Ferrer for searching the archives of the Ministerio de Relaciones Exteriores in Madrid for possible consular reports on Maceo.

43. The report on the meeting is in Louis A. Martinet, ed., *The Violation of a Constitutional Right. Published by Authority of the Citizens' Committee* (New Orleans: The Crusader, 1896). Ramón Pagés is later listed as having been on the steamer *Florida*, escorted by the warship *Osceala*, on 25 May 1898, accompanying some 300 expeditionaries, including the activists of color Martín Morúa Delgado and Generoso Campos Marquetti. See Miguel Varona Guerrero, *La Guerra de Independencia de Cuba 1895–1898*, 3 vols. (Havana: Editorial Lex, 1946), 2:1360–61.

44. *Weekly Pelican* (New Orleans), 8 January 1887.

45. Relatively few of Desdunes's writings from the 1880s have survived, however. He

later laid out his political credo in essays in the *New Orleans Crusader.* See especially the essay from 20–21 December 1895 in folder 1/49/1–6, DFP, ASC, XU.

46. *Louisiana Sugar Bowl,* 15 July 1886, as cited in Gould, "Heroic and Vigorous Action."

47. See Jonathan Garlock, *Guide to the Local Assemblies of the Knights of Labor* (Westport, Conn.: Greenwood Press, 1982), pp. 161–167; Daniel Letwin, *The Challenge of Interracial Unionism: Alabama Coal Miners, 1878–1921* (Chapel Hill: University of North Carolina Press, 1998), esp. pp. 69–71, 77; and Melton Alonza McLaurin, *The Knights of Labor in the South* (Westport, Conn.: Greenwood Press, 1978), pp. 74–76, 131–148.

48. On "marking," see Thomas Holt, "Marking: Race, Race-making, and the Writing of History," *American Historical Review* 100 (February 1995): 1–20. On the Knights, see McLaurin, *Knights.*

49. Details on Pierre Carmouche, including his feats of strength, are from his military pension file, XC 2-444-335, USNA.

50. A valuable source on the Knights in the sugar country is the chapter "Negro Labor" of Marcus Christian's unpublished manuscript, "A Black History of Louisiana," pt. 3, in MCC, UNO. On locals in Donaldsonville, see Garlock, *Guide,* p. 161. On Carmouche's organizing among the Knights, see the *Colored American,* 1 July 1899. On Bailey, see the *New Orleans Daily Picayune,* 30 October 1887 and 2 November 1887. A copy of an account by labor organizer Covington Hall, entitled "Labor Struggles in the Deep South," is held in the Labadie Collection of the University of Michigan Library. Hall's text has also been edited and published with an introduction by David R. Roediger in Covington Hall, *Labor Struggles in the Deep South and Other Writings* (Chicago: Charles H. Kerr Publishing, 1999).

51. *Thibodaux Sentinel,* French-language pages, 22 January 1887. The *Weekly Pelican,* 5 February 1887, added that eight men had been arrested for inciting a riot.

52. See the volume labeled "Criminal Cases, Vol. A, District Court, Parish of Lafourche," pp. 384, 385, in PLCC.

53. See the loose documents titled "Criminal Cases, 1887," PLCC.

54. See "Criminal Cases, Vol. A"; and "Criminal Cases, 1887," both in PLCC.

55. The State of Louisiana v. Peter Young and the State of Louisiana v. Amos Johnson, "Criminal Cases, 1887," PLCC.

56. *Weekly Pelican* (New Orleans), 26 February 1887.

57. *Journal of United Labor,* 30 April 1887.

58. *Weekly Thibodaux Sentinel,* 15 October 1887. The *Sentinel* recalled him as Lewis Benjamin, rather than as Benjamin Lewis.

59. *Daily Picayune* (New Orleans), 30 October 1887.

60. The Republican *Weekly Pelican* (New Orleans) used the figure of 10,000 in its issue of 5 November 1887. On the history of the strike, see Philip S. Foner and Ronald L. Lewis, eds., *The Black Worker: A Documentary History from Colonial Times to the Present* 3 (Philadelphia: Temple University Press, 1978), pp. 143–242, 367–404. William Ivy Hair, in *Bourbonism and Agrarian Protest: Louisiana Politics, 1877–1900* (Baton Rouge: Louisiana State University Press, 1969), pp. 177–185, gives a brief and

vivid narrative. See also Gould, "Heroic and Vigorous Action." I have analyzed the strike in " 'Stubborn and Disposed to Stand Their Ground': Black Militia, Sugar Workers, and the Dynamics of Collective Action in the Louisiana Sugar Bowl, 1863–87," in Silvia R. Frey and Betty Wood, eds., *From Slavery to Emancipation in the Atlantic World,* a special issue of *Slavery and Abolition* 20 (April 1999): 103–126; and "Fault Lines, Color Lines, and Party Lines: Race, Labor, and Collective Action in Louisiana and Cuba, 1862–1912," in Frederick Cooper, Thomas C. Holt, and Rebecca J. Scott, *Beyond Slavery: Explorations of Race, Labor, and Citizenship in Postemancipation Societies* (Chapel Hill: University of North Carolina Press, 2000), pp. 61–106. The most recent analysis is that of John Rodrigue, in *Reconstruction,* pp. 183–191.

61. The visit took place in July of 1887. The firemen formed in line at the depot, marched through the principal streets and then "repaired to Eureka hall, where dancing was indulged in to a late hour." *Weekly Pelican* (New Orleans), 23 July 1887. Emphasis in original. On public space, see Elsa Barkley Brown and Gregg D. Kimball, "Mapping the Terrain of Black Richmond," *Journal of Urban History* 21 (March 1995): 296–346.

62. See Rodrigue, *Reconstruction,* particularly chap. 4.

63. On comparable displays in the 1860s, see Julie Saville, "Rites and Power: Reflections on Slavery, Freedom, and Political Ritual," in Frey and Wood, *From Slavery to Emancipation,* pp. 81–102.

64. See Gould, "Heroic and Vigorous Action"; and the chapter "Negro Labor" of Christian, "A Black History."

65. See *Report of Brig-Gen. William Pierce Commanding State Troops in the Field in District from Berwick's Bay to New Orleans to General G. T. Beauregard, Adjutant General of the State of Louisiana, Nov. 28th, 1887* (Baton Rouge: Leon Jastremski, 1887).

66. Mary W. Pugh to Edward F. Pugh, 25 November 1887, in folder 1, Mary W. Pugh papers, LLMVC. Beattie is quoted in Hair, *Bourbonism,* pp. 182–183. The attack on Franklin and the circumstances of the subsequent massacre are described in *Southwestern Christian Advocate,* 8 December 1887.

67. Hall, "Labor Struggles"; and *Southwestern Christian Advocate,* 8 December 1887.

68. See Gould, "Heroic and Vigorous Action"; Christian, "Negro Labor," in "A Black History"; and the letters of Mary W. Pugh, LLMVC. The editor of the *Star* is quoted in *Southwestern Christian Advocate,* 8 December 1887. On Franklin, see Coston, *Spanish-American War Volunteer,* pp. 79–81; and Foner and Lewis, *Black Worker,* 3:193, in which Franklin is said to have reported an estimated twenty-five dead.

69. See Louisiana, *Constitution of the State of Louisiana Adopted in Convention at the City of New Orleans the Twenty-Third Day of July, A.D., 1879* (Baton Rouge: The Advocate, 1894), pp. 49–50.

70. See Xi Wang, *The Trial of Democracy: Black Suffrage and Northern Republicans, 1860–1910* (Athens: University of Georgia Press, 1997), pp. 210–211. The court ruled that at least in the case of southern states that as of 1870 had attempted to restrict the right to vote to white men, "this fifteenth article of amendment does, *proprio*

vigore, substantially confer on the negro the right to vote, and Congress has the power to protect and enforce that right."

71. These terms are Posey's own, as cited in Perkins, *Who's Who in Colored Louisiana,* pp. 73–74. On registration, see Louisiana, *Report of the Secretary of State to His Excellency W. W. Heard, Governor of the State of Louisiana, May 12th, 1902* (Baton Rouge: Baton Rouge News Pub. Co., 1902), p. 553.

72. T. A. Cage was by the 1880s and 1890s a controversial figure among black Republicans. See R. L. Desdunes, "Chairman Cage as a Leader," *Crusader* 21, 23, 28 September 1895, in folder 1/42/2, DFP, ASC, XU.

73. *Weekly Pelican* (New Orleans), 31 August 1889.

74. See *Weekly Pelican* (New Orleans), 31 August 1889; 21 September 1889; 28 September 1889.

75. *Weekly Pelican* (New Orleans), 7 September 1889.

76. Hall, "Labor Struggles," pt. 2, pp. 14–15.

77. Mary W. Pugh to Edward F. Pugh, 25 November 1887, in folder 1, Mary W. Pugh papers, LLMVC. On the promulgation of white-supremacist ideology, see Powell, "The Battle of Canal Street."

78. Hall, "Labor Struggles," pt. 2, pp. 14–15.

79. For the key documents on the Separate Car Act, see Otto Olsen, ed., *The Thin Disguise: Turning Point in Negro History. Plessy v. Ferguson. A Documentary Presentation (1864–1896)* (New York: Humanities Press, 1967).

80. On mutual-aid associations, see Harry J. Walker, "Negro Benevolent Societies in New Orleans: A Study of Their Structure, Function, and Membership," Department of Social Science, Fisk University, Nashville, Tenn., 1936, typescript in ASC, XU. For the Knights of Reciprocity, see the undated clipping from the *Crusader,* late 1891, in DFC, ASC, XU.

81. Article by R. L. Desdunes, "White Supremacy," in *Crusader,* 19 March 1892. Clipping in DFC, ASC, XU.

82. "Jim Crow Is Dead," *Crusader,* 28 May 1892. The Louisiana Supreme Court case was Abbott v. Hicks Judge et al., 44 La Ann 700. The legal complexities are discussed in Charles A. Lofgren, *The Plessy Case: A Legal Historical Interpretation* (New York: Oxford University Press, 1987). The events are reconstructed in detail in Keith Weldon Medley, *We as Freemen: Plessy vs Ferguson* (Gretna, La.: Pelican Publishing Company, 2003). My own interpretation of the Plessy case is in "Se battre pour ses droits: Écritures, litiges et discrimination raciale en Louisiane (1888–1899)," *Cahiers du Brésil Contemporain* (Paris) 53/54 (2003): 175–209.

83. *Crusader,* ca. October 1894, clipping 1/15, DFC, ASC, XU.

84. *Crusader,* 4 June 1892.

85. For Carmouche's contributions, see *Crusader,* 22 June 1895 and 10 and 27 August 1895. Other contributions from Donaldsonville are recorded in clipping 1/38, all in DFC, ASC, XU.

86. R. L. Desdunes, "Forlorn Hope and Noble Despair," *Crusader,* 15 August 1891; copy held in folder 20, box 2, of the Charles B. Roussève papers, ARC.

87. See the essay by R. L. Desdunes, "Straight from the Shoulder," 11 October 1895.

88. On the failure of the 1896 amendments, see Michael Perman, *Struggle for Mastery: Disfranchisement in the South, 1888–1908* (Chapel Hill: University of North Carolina Press, 2001), pp. 128–132.

4. Finding the Spaces of Freedom

Epigraph: From the article "Freedom in Cuba," in the *New Orleans Republican,* transcribed in the file "Cuba, 1873," in the Marcus Christian Collection, Louisiana and Special Collections Department, Earl K. Long Library, University of New Orleans.

1. See Jorge Ibarra's pathbreaking *Ideología mambisa* (Havana: Instituto Cubano del Libro, 1972); Ada Ferrer, *Insurgent Cuba: Race, Nation, and Revolution, 1868–1898* (Chapel Hill: University of North Carolina Press, 1999); and Paul Estrade, *José Martí: Los fundamentos de la democracia en Latinoamérica* (Aranjuez, Spain: Ediciones Doce Calles, 2000).

2. See Ada Ferrer, "Esclavitud, ciudadanía y los límites de la nacionalidad cubana: La Guerra de los Diez Años, 1868–1878," *Historia Social* (Valencia, Spain) 22 (1995): 101–125; Rebecca J. Scott, *Slave Emancipation in Cuba: The Transition to Free Labor, 1860–1899* (Princeton: Princeton University Press, 1985), chap. 2; Karen Robert, "Slavery and Freedom in the Ten Years' War, Cuba, 1868–1878," *Slavery and Abolition* (London) 13 (December 1992): 181–200; Aline Helg, *Our Rightful Share: The Afro-Cuban Struggle for Equality, 1886–1912* (Chapel Hill: University of North Carolina Press, 1995); Laird Bergad, *Cuban Rural Society in the Nineteenth Century: The Social and Economic History of Monoculture in Matanzas* (Princeton, N.J.: Princeton University Press, 1990), chap. 11. These tensions appear in the 1877 correspondence between Manuel Blanco, owner of the Santa Rosalía plantation in Santa Clara province, and Manuel María de Vivanco, of the Spanish Army, in exps. 42 and 46, CMJL, CC, BNC.

3. Interview with Caridad Quesada, Cienfuegos, June 1999. Rita Lucumí, age thirty-one, appears in a list of estate workers on Santa Rosalía, exp. 178, CMJL, CC, BNC.

4. See David Murray, *Odious Commerce: Britain, Spain, and the Abolition of the Cuban Slave Trade* (Cambridge: Cambridge University Press, 1980); Scott, *Slave Emancipation,* chap. 4.

5. See Josep M. Fradera, *Gobernar colonias* (Barcelona: Ediciones Península, 1999), pp. 71–93; Christopher Schmidt-Nowara, *Empire and Antislavery: Spain, Cuba, and Puerto Rico, 1833–1874* (Pittsburgh: University of Pittsburgh Press, 1999); Orlando García Martínez, "Estudio de la economía cienfueguera," *Islas* (Santa Clara) 55–56 (September 1976–April 1977): 119–145.

6. On the war in Cienfuegos, see Rafael Rodríguez Altunaga, *Las Villas (Biografía de una provincia)* (Havana: El Siglo XX, 1955), pp. 198, 295–298.

7. On slave participation in the Ten Years' War, see Ferrer, *Insurgent Cuba;* Scott, *Slave Emancipation,* chap. 2; and Robert, "Slavery and Freedom." The names of women are from the pardon file, "Expediente promovida por la reclusa morena libre María

Andrea Jiménez en solicitud de indulto (Año de 1877)," leg. 5818, parte 2ª, Ultramar, AHN.

8. For a discussion of the strategy and effects of the Moret Law, see Scott, *Slave Emancipation*, chap. 3.

9. See "Resumen por jurisdicciones del padrón general de asiáticos de la Isla, correspondiente al año de 1872," in "Exp. General, Colonización Asiática," leg. 87, Ultramar, AHN; "Relación de los esclavos comprendidos en el padrón de 1871 clasificados por edades, sexos, ocupaciones y estados," Havana, 30 June 1873, tomo 4, leg. 4882, Ultramar, AHN. See also Scott, *Slave Emancipation*, tables 10 and 13. I have rounded population figures to the nearest hundred. John V. Crawford to A. H. Layard, Havana, 30 November 1873. In Layard Papers, folios 122 and 122v., Additional ms. 39004, Manuscripts, British Library. Manuel Blanco inherited Santa Rosalía after Quesada's death in 1876. See Chapter 8 for a discussion of the transfer.

10. See "Expediente de infidencia de D. Liberato Leiva y Arnau," 1875, in leg. 3901–1, Ultramar, AHN.

11. "Libro Diario del ingenio 'Angelita' de la propiedad de Sr. J. A. Argudín," p. 151, núm. 11536, ML, ANC. In this case the administration of the estate also opposed the auction, which may have made the slaves' challenges somewhat less risky.

12. The classic narrative of the invasion is Ramiro Guerra, *Guerra de los Diez Años,* 2 vols. (Havana: Editorial de Ciencias Sociales, 1972), 2:283–352.

13. See "Padrón general de esclavos . . . Sta. Isabel de las Lajas," exp. B., leg. 3748, ME, ANC; and Carmen Guerra Díaz, Emma S. Morales Rodríguez, and Danilo Iglesias G., "El desarrollo económico-social y político de la antigua jurisdicción de Cienfuegos entre 1877 y 1887," *Islas* (Santa Clara) 80 (January–April 1985): 137.

14. See Guerra, *Guerra de los Diez Años*, vol. 2, chap. 19; Manuel Mª de Vivanco a Sᵒʳ Capitán de la Guerrilla de León, 30 December 1876, and Manuel Mª de Vivanco to Manuel Blanco, 4 June 1877, both in exp. 42, CMJL, CC, BNC.

15. See the telegram of 1 March 1877 from Morales de los Ríos, and the responses to it, in leg. R-427, división 3a, sección 2a, Ultramar, AGM-Segovia.

16. See "Noticia de las fincas azucareras en producción que existían en toda la isla de Cuba al comenzar el presupuesto de 1877–78," *Revista económica*, 7 June 1878, pp. 7–24. The totals are incomplete, because only 77 estates are listed for Cienfuegos, and some filed no returns. The estates that did file counted a total of 5,396 slaves, 1,526 "libres y alquilados" (which could include some freed children and the elderly), and 380 Chinese.

17. See Manuel Mª de Vivanco to Manuel Blanco, Cumanayagua, 7 November 1877, exp. 46, CMJL, CC, BNC.

18. See the correspondence from Santa Rosalía in the 1870s in CMJL, CC, BNC.

19. See Ferrer, *Insurgent Cuba,* chap. 2.

20. See Ada Ferrer, "Social Aspects of Cuban Nationalism: Race, Slavery, and the Guerra Chiquita, 1879–1880," *Cuban Studies* 21 (1991): 37–56.

21. See the *Gaceta de Madrid,* 28 October 1877, included in "Año de 1878, Cuba,

Repartición de terrenos baldíos," exp. 10, leg. 226—Parte 2a, Ultramar, AHN; and "Política, Poblados," February 1877, in leg. R-427, División 3a, Sección 2a, Ultramar, AGM-Segovia.

22. See Guerra, *Guerra*, vol. 2, chaps. 20–21; and Ferrer, *Insurgent Cuba*. On Maceo's subsequent peregrinations, see José Luciano Franco, *Antonio Maceo: Apuntes para una historia de su vida*, 2 vols. (Havana: Editorial de Ciencias Sociales, 1975).

23. Rodríguez Altunaga, *Las Villas*, pp. 197–98.

24. Guerra Díaz, Morales Rodríguez, and Iglesias G., "El desarrollo," p. 158. I am indebted to the late Pedro Deschamps Chapeaux for a typescript list of mutual-aid organizations for this period. His information on these two societies comes from exp. 4424, leg. 97, and exp. 3532, leg. 88, GG, ANC. Deschamps himself studied many of these groups in *El negro en el periodismo cubano en el siglo xix* (Havana: Ediciones R., 1963).

25. See Rodríguez Altunaga, *Las Villas*, pp. 187, 193, 195. On the later stages of this civil rights movement, see Raquel Mendieta Costa, *Cultura, lucha de clases y conflicto racial, 1878–1895* (Havana: Editorial Pueblo y Educación, 1989). On such organizations and their predecessors, see Olga Hevia Lanier, *El Directorio Central de las Sociedades Negras de Cuba, 1886–1894* (Havana: Editorial de Ciencias Sociales, 1996); and Philip A. Howard, *Changing History: Afro-Cuban Cabildos and Societies of Color in the Nineteenth Century* (Baton Rouge: Louisiana State University Press, 1998).

26. On the outbreak of the war, see Francisco Pérez Guzman and Rodolfo Sarracino, *La Guerra Chiquita: Una experiencia necesaria* (Havana: Editorial Letras Cubanas, 1982), pp. 179–193. For a social analysis, see Ferrer, *Insurgent Cuba*, chap. 3.

27. See Captain General to Com. Gen. de Cuba, 9 September 1879, in *Campaña de Cuba. Recopilación de documentos y ordenes dictadas con motivo del movimiento insurreccional . . . del 26 de Agosto de 1879* (Cuba: Sección Tipográfica . . . de la Comandancia General, 1880), pp. 36, 39.

28. See Rodríguez Altunaga, *Las Villas*, p. 308; and "Domingo Stephanopoli, deportado cubano," exp. 368, leg. 4804, Ultramar, AHN.

29. Rosendo Gutiérrez to D. José M. Pérez, 25 July 1879, in exp. 9, CMJL, CC, BNC; "Noticia de las fincas azucareras . . . 1877–78," *Revista económica*, 7 June 1878, pp. 7–24; and J. Mª [Pérez] to D. Manuel Blanco, 26 July 1879, in exp. 10, CMJL, CC, BNC.

30. "Libro Diario del Ingenio Angelita Argudín, 1877," p. 110, núm. 10789, ML, ANC. See Fe Iglesias García, "El censo cubano de 1877 y sus diferentes versiones," *Santiago* (Santiago de Cuba) 34 (June 1979): 167–214.

31. See Carolina Rodríguez to Leandro Rodríguez, [late July 1879?], in *Documentos para servir a la historia de la Guerra Chiquita (Archivo Leandro Rodríguez)* (Havana: Archivo Nacional de Cuba, 1950), 3:208.

32. See Pérez Guzman and Sarracino, *La Guerra Chiquita*, p. 220; and Ferrer, *Insurgent Cuba*, chap. 3.

33. Pérez Guzman and Sarracino, *La Guerra Chiquita*, pp. 194–97.

34. See Ferrer, *Insurgent Cuba*, chap. 3; "D. Belisario Peralta, deportado político de la isla

de Cuba," exp. 351, leg. 4803–pt. 1, Ultramar, AHN; and Rodríguez Altunaga, *Las Villas,* p. 308.

35. For this law, see Fernando Ortiz, *Los negros esclavos* (Havana: Editorial de Ciencias Sociales, 1975), pp. 466–487.

36. "Relación de los individuos á quienes, en virtud de las Reales ordenes de 9 de Febrero de 1883, se ha espedido documentos de libertad por no hallarse empadronados en debida forma; con espresión de sus Patronos," in exp. 289, leg. 4815, Ultramar, AHN. For a further discussion of mechanisms of emancipation in the 1880s, and of this list, see Scott, *Slave Emancipation,* chap. 7.

37. See Franco Oteiza to Manuel Blanco, 25 June and 4, 6 and 13 October 1881, in exp. 13, CMJL, CC, BNC.

38. See Pedro García to Manuel Blanco, 15 March 1885, in exp. 9a, CMJL, CC, BNC. The term "magnetizar" might also be translated as enchant or entrance, and can have overtones of supernatural power. The late Pedro Deschamps Chapeaux clarified the meaning of García's claim that he threatened that he would "romper . . . el bautismo"—crack her head. Pedro García appears in the memoir of Edwin F. Atkins as a Spanish former slave trader and overseer on the Soledad estate: "He was a Gallego . . . the picture of a pirate, with a black beard reaching to his waist." Edwin F. Atkins, *Sixty Years in Cuba: Reminiscences of Edwin G. Atkins* (1926; reprint, New York: Arno Press, 1980), pp. 91–92. See Chapter 8 below for a discussion of Andrea Quesada's later lawsuit against Manuel Blanco's heirs.

39. This document is entitled "Libro No. 1 de los negros, Santa Rosalía," and is held in the Archivo Histórico Provincial de Cienfuegos (AHPC).

40. "Libro No. 1 de los negros, Santa Rosalía," AHPC; and "Cédulas de patrocinado," exp. 158, CMJL, CC, BNC. See also Rebecca J. Scott, "Reclaiming Gregoria's Mule: The Meanings of Freedom in the Arimao and Caunao Valleys, Cienfuegos, Cuba, 1880–1899," *Past and Present* 170 (February 2001): 181–216.

41. Folios 16 and 41, "Libro No. 1 de los negros, Santa Rosalía," AHPC.

42. See folios 15 and 17, "Libro No. 1 de los negros, Santa Rosalía," AHPC. On his service in the rebel army see Scott, "Reclaiming."

43. The entry for Rita Quesada appears on folio 171, "Libro no. 1 de los negros," AHPC. On the workforce in the 1890s, see "Libro Mayor No. 3 perteneciente al Ingenio Sta Rosalía propiedad de Dn Manuel Blanco y Ramos," AHPC.

44. See J. S. Murray to E. F. Atkins, 19 June 1884, in Letterbooks, J. S. Murray, Soledad, to Edwin F. Atkins, Boston, in ser. IV, AFP, MHS.

45. J. S. Murray to E. F. Atkins, 26 May 1885; 2 June 1885; 4 June 1885; ser. IV, AFP, MHS.

46. J. S. Murray to E. F. Atkins, 23 June 1885; 6 August 1885; 11 August 1885; ser. IV, AFP, MHS. Murray reported the current price of freedom to be about $70, scheduled to drop to $50 in May of 1886, and he believed that "a great many will buy their liberty, the price being so low."

47. E. F. Atkins to J. S. Murray, 18 August 1885, in Edwin F. Atkins, Correspondence, Letterbook Jan. 9, 1885 to September 14, 1886, in vol. 2, ser. IV, AFP, MHS.

48. On the general decline of the *patronato,* see Scott, *Slave Emancipation,* chaps. 6–8.

See the letters from J. S. Murray to E. F. Atkins dated 24 May 1886 and 27 May 1886, ser. IV, AFP, MHS. Dollars and pesos seem to have been roughly at par.

49. J. S. Murray to E. F. Atkins, 24 May 1886, ser. IV, AFP, MHS.

50. On Felipe Criollo, see folio 57, "Libro No. 1 de los negros, Santa Rosalía," AHPC.

51. See pp. 148, 194 in Scott, *Slave Emancipation;* J. S. Murray to E. F. Atkins, 2 November 1886, ser. IV, AFP, MHS.

52. See Fe Iglesias García, "La concentración azucarera y la comarca de Cienfuegos," in Fernando Martínez, Rebecca J. Scott, and Orlando García Martínez, eds., *Espacios, silencios y los sentidos de la libertad: Cuba entre 1878 y 1912* (Havana: Editorial Unión, 2000), pp. 85–107.

53. On various categories of workers, see the Statement of Mr. P. M. Beal, Manager of the Guabairo Colonia, in U.S. War Department, *Report on the Census of Cuba, 1899* (Washington, D.C.: Government Printing Office, 1900), pp. 529–530. Several payrolls for Soledad and Santa Rosalía are held in the AHPC.

54. "Lista de la Dotación del Ingenio Santa Rosalía" [18 August 1880], and "Lista de los individuos de color que trabajan en el campo y lo que alcanzaran el 8 del presente que tendran devengados tres meses" [4 January 1887], both in exp. 173, CMJL, CC, BNC.

55. "Lista de los individuos de color" [4 January 1887]; "Lista de la Dotación" [18 August 1880], exp. 173, CMJL, CC, BNC.

56. On population, see Spain, Instituto Geográfico y Estadístico, *Censo de la población de España, segun el empadronamiento hecho en 31 diciembre de 1887,* 2 vols. (Madrid, 1891–92). On farms, see "Ayuntamiento de Cienfuegos. Copia del padrón vigente para la distribucion del impuesto municipal en el año de 1880–81," exp. By, leg. 3097, ME, ANC.

57. J. S. Murray to E. F. Atkins, 14 May 1884, ser. IV, AFP, MHS. On the difficulties of establishing central mills in areas of existing settlement, see Alan Dye, *Cuban Sugar in the Age of Mass Production: Technology and the Economics of the Sugar Central, 1899–1929* (Stanford, Calif.: Stanford University Press, 1998).

58. "The rentals are specified in the contracts so that nobody occupying our land will ever acquire a title. We frequently waive the rents when prices were very low and the colonos were not making enough to pay them for their time." Deposition of Edwin Atkins, p. 138, pt. 1, claim 387, Treaty Claims, RG 76, USNA.

59. P. M. Beal to E. F. Atkins, 16 July 1887. In Letters Sent, Soledad, Dec. 22, 1885–Oct. 17, 1887, libro 974, fondo 51, ICEA, ANC.

60. On abuses, see Juan Bautista Jiménez, *Los esclavos blancos, por un colono de Las Villas* (Havana: Imp. de A. Alvarez y Comp., 1893). See also Alan Dye, "Avoiding Holdup: Asset Specificity and Technical Change in the Cuban Sugar Industry, 1899–1929," *Journal of Economic History* 54 (September 1994): 628–653.

61. See the list of *colonias* in box 169, claim 398 (Francisco J. Terry y Dorticos), Treaty Claims, RG 76, USNA.

62. In the postwar 1899 census, for the province of Santa Clara as a whole, 1,003 colored and 4,350 white owners and renters of sugar farms were enumerated. *Report on the Census of Cuba, 1899,* pp. 553, 560, 448–449.

63. J. S. Murray to E. F. Atkins, 4 June 1885 and 28 May 1888, ser. IV, AFP, MHS.

64. Leonardo Alomá, who lived on the Central Pepito Tey, accompanied Orlando García Martínez, Aims McGuinness, and myself to San Antón in June of 1998. Ramona Quesada and her brothers Gerardo, Francisco, and Humberto Quesada were over the subsequent years extraordinarily generous with their time and their memories. Ramona Quesada's husband, Evelio Castillo, provided crucial additional details. Sadly, Alomá, Castillo, and Ramona Quesada have since died. Michael Zeuske and I have analyzed the history of San Antón and El Palmar in "Property in Writing, Property on the Ground: Pigs, Horses, Land and Citizenship in the Aftermath of Slavery, Cuba, 1880–1909," *Comparative Studies in Society and History* 44 (2002): 669–699.

65. See the "Listas cobratorias de los recibos de fincas rústicas," located in exp. Bh, leg. 1431; exp. B, leg. 872; exp. X, leg. 1370; and the "Fincas Rústicas no destinadas al cultivo del azúcar ni del tabaco," exp. Aj, leg. 3162; all in ME, ANC.

66. "Expediente relativo a la instancia del Pardo Salvador Díaz . . . ," inv. 1, exp. 185, leg. 3, FAL, AHPC. I owe this reference and its interpretation to Michael Zeuske, who is currently completing a study of the political integration of ex-slaves in the region of Lajas.

67. Victor Clark, "Labor Conditions in Cuba," *Bulletin of the Department of Labor* 41 (July 1902): 663–793, p. 671.

68. Interview with Fermín Tellería, Cienfuegos, 1999; J. S. Murray to E. F. Atkins, 24 May 1888, ser. IV, AFP, MHS.

69. See Deposition of Edwin F. Atkins, p. 90, pt. 1, claim 387 (Atkins), Treaty Claims, RG 76, USNA.

70. P. M. Beal to E. F. Atkins, 23 July, 1887. In Letters Sent, Soledad, December 22, 1886–October 17, 1887, libro 974, fondo 51, ICEA, ANC.

71. I thank the family of Marcelino Iznaga Suárez Román, of Vaquería, near Pepito Tey (formerly Soledad) for sharing such photographs. The grandmother in this case was known as Pillita.

72. "Construcción de un ferro-carril para el servicio particular del Ingenio Cieneguita . . . 1890," exp. 5, leg. 201, Ultramar, AHN.

73. Atkins, *Sixty Years,* p. 138. For year-by-year production figures, see Manuel Moreno Fraginals, *El ingenio: Complejo económico social cubano del azúcar,* 3 vols. (Havana: Editorial de Ciencias Sociales, 1978), 3:37–38.

74. Laborers' daily routine is described in Robert P. Porter, *Industrial Cuba* (New York: G. P. Putnam's Sons, 1899), p. 84. On the taxing of land cultivated in *frutos menores* (minor crops) in Cruces, see "Consulta sobre la alzada . . . contra la Junta Provincial de Amillaramiento . . . Cruces, 22 October 1886," exp. 8387, leg. 99, CA, ANC.

75. See Pablo L. Rousseau and Pablo Díaz de Villegas, *Memoria descriptiva, histórica y biográfica de Cienfuegos y las fiestas del primer centenario de la fundación de esta ciudad* (Havana: Siglo XX, 1920), pp. 215–216. On suffrage, see Spain, Ministerio de Ultramar, *Spanish Rule in Cuba. Laws Governing the Island* (New York, 1896).

76. On political life and the Autonomists, see Hugh Thomas, *Cuba: The Pursuit of Free-*

dom (New York: Harper and Row, 1971), pp. 268, 300–304; Fernando Martínez Heredia, "El problemático nacionalismo de la primera república," in José Amador and Fernando Coronil, eds., *Historia y memoria: Sociedad, cultura y vida cotidiana en Cuba, 1878–1917* (Havana: Centro de Investigación y Desarrollo de la Cultura Cubana Juan Marinello and Program in Latin American and Caribbean Studies, University of Michigan, 2003), pp. 281–299; and María del Carmen Barcia Zequiera, *Élites y grupos de presión: Cuba, 1868–1898* (Havana: Editorial de Ciencias Sociales, 1998), pp. 40–85.

77. The description in the paragraphs that follow is based in part on "Reunión autonomista en Cienfuegos," 1886, exp. 174, leg. 4896–pt. I, Ultramar, AHN. I am very grateful to Ada Ferrer for sharing with me her transcription of portions of this file. These events are described with additional details in the standard histories of Cienfuegos: Rousseau and Díaz, *Memoria descriptiva*, pp. 217–218; and Enrique Edo y Llop, *Memoria histórica de Cienfuegos y su jurisdicción,* 2nd ed. (1888; reprint, Cienfuegos: J. Andreu, 1943), pp. 640–642.

78. This account is from Edo y Llop, *Memoria histórica,* pp. 640–642.

79. On the complicated question of the relationship between vote and voice, see Elsa Barkley Brown, "Negotiating and Transforming the Public Sphere: African American Political Life in the Transition from Slavery to Freedom," *Public Culture* 7 (fall 1994): 107–146.

80. Reunión autonomista en Cienfuegos, 1886, exp. 174, leg. 4896–pt. I, Ultramar, AHN. Four years later, in August 1893, yet another proposal for colonial reform was on the table in Spain, and Autonomists and other reformers in the eastern region of Holguín in Oriente tried to rally support for it. An estimated 3,000 men on foot and on horseback gathered to protest the naming of a new mayor known to be opposed to reforms. The organizers protested that official repression had prevented additional supporters located in the countryside from attending. See the exchange of telegrams in August 1893 from Holguín, collected in leg. 3899–pt. I, Ultramar, AHN.

81. See Gabriel Quesada to Juan Gualberto Gómez, 30 December 1893, in exp. 3103, caja 40, Fondo Adquisiciones, ANC.

82. See Maria Poumier-Taquechel, *Contribution a l'étude du banditisme social à Cuba: L'histoire et le mythe de Manuel García "Rey de los Campos de Cuba"(1851–1895)* (Paris: Harmattan, 1986), pp. 74, 75. See also Atkins, *Sixty Years,* p. 151.

83. See Manuel de Paz Sánchez, José Fernández Fernández, and Nelson López Novegil, *El bandolerismo en Cuba (1800–1933): Presencia canaria y protesta rural,* vol. 1. (Santa Cruz de Tenerife: Centro de la Cultura Popular Canaria, 1993); Poumier-Taquechel, *Contribution,* p. 80; Louis A. Pérez, Jr., *Lords of the Mountain: Social Banditry and Peasant Protest in Cuba* (Pittsburgh: University of Pittsburgh Press, 1989); and Rosalie Schwartz, *Lawless Liberators: Political Banditry and Cuban Independence* (Durham, N.C.: Duke University Press, 1989).

84. Atkins, *Sixty Years,* pp. 152–154. It is not clear whether the strikes to which Atkins refers extended beyond the cooks whose work stoppage he mentions.

85. See Jorge Ibarra, "La Guerra del 95: ¿La Guerra de la Voluntad y del Ideal o de la Necesidad y de la Pobreza?," in Amador and Coronil, *Historia y memoria,* pp. 35–53.

86. Estrade, *José Martí,* chap. 6; Louis A. Pérez, Jr., *Cuba between Empires, 1878–1902* (Pittsburgh: University of Pittsburgh Press, 1983), pp. 42–47; Franco, *Antonio Maceo,* 2:87–97.

5. A WARTIME CROSS-RACIAL ALLIANCE

Epigraph: José Miró Argenter, *Cuba: Crónicas de la guerra. Las campañas de invasión y de Occidente, 1895–96,* 2 vols. (1909; reprint, Havana: Editorial Lex, 1945), 1:170. Maceo made the statement just before his forces engaged Spanish troops at Mal Tiempo, in the Cienfuegos district.

1. See Ada Ferrer, *Insurgent Cuba: Race, Nation, and Revolution, 1868–1898* (Chapel Hill: University of North Carolina Press, 1999), chaps. 5 and 6; Louis A. Pérez, Jr., *Cuba between Empires, 1878–1902* (Pittsburgh: University of Pittsburgh Press, 1983), pp. 43–50; Orlando García Martínez, "La Brigada de Cienfuegos: Un análisis social de su formación," in Fernando Martínez Heredia, Rebecca J. Scott, and Orlando García Martínez, eds., *Espacios, silencios y los sentidos de la libertad: Cuba entre 1878 y 1912* (Havana: Editorial Unión, 2000), pp. 163–192; Oilda Hevia Lanier, "1895–1898: Guerra racista o demagogia?" *Debates americanos* 5–6 (January–December 1998): 35–45.

2. See the telegrams in the folder titled "Pinar del Río"; the file "Detenidos y presentados"; and the correspondence in the folder titled "Puerto Príncipe," all in leg. 3899, Ultramar, AHN.

3. Deposition of Lorenzo González, 9 February 1909, claim 475 (Whiting), pt. 2, Treaty Claims, entry 352, RG 76, USNA.

4. See the file of Gaspar Caballero, 1-2-38 Rechazado, Fondo Ejército Libertador, ANC.

5. See Sociedad Cubana de Estudios Históricos e Internacionales, *Antonio Maceo: Ideología política,* vol. 2 (Havana, 1950), pp. 31–33; and Colectivo de autores, *Diccionario enciclopédico de historia militar de Cuba,* pt. 1, vol. 1 (Havana: Ediciones Verde Olivo, 2001).

6. José Miró Argenter, himself from Catalonia, served with Antonio Maceo, and left the memoir *Cuba: Crónicas de la guerra. Las campañas de invasión y de Occidente, 1895–96,* 2 vols. (1909; reprint, Havana: Editorial Lex, 1945). General Carlos Roloff was born in Warsaw, served in an Ohio regiment of the Union Army, and later settled in central Cuba. See Colectivo de autores, *Diccionario,* p. 323.

7. This is the argument of Ferrer, *Insurgent Cuba.* Cf. Jorge Ibarra, *Ideología mambisa* (Havana: Instituto Cubano del Libro, 1972).

8. See the deposition of Humphrey J. Kicley, 21 December 1903, and that of Eduardo Vilar, 12 August 1904, in pt. 1, claim 97 (Central Teresa Sugar Company), Treaty Claims, entry 352, RG 76, USNA. Vilar did not identify either himself or the insurgents using color terms.

9. Enrique Edo y Llop, *Memoria histórica de Cienfuegos y su jurisdicción,* 2nd ed. (1888; reprint, Cienfuegos: J. Andreu, 1943), pp. 221–239; and receipts in envelope 43, exp. 84, CMJL, BNC.

10. Edwin F. Atkins, *Sixty Years in Cuba* (1926; reprint, New York: Arno Press, 1980), chap. 12. For the situation around Cienfuegos, including the alliance of Najarro and Rego, see García Martínez, "La Brigada"; and deposition of Benigno Najarro, 14 May 1906, in claim 387 (Atkins), Treaty Claims, entry 352, RG 76, USNA.

11. For a chronology, see Rafael Rodríguez Altunaga, *Las Villas (Biografía de una provincia)* (Havana: El Siglo XX, 1955), pp. 310ff.

12. E. F. Atkins to Oscar, 9 March 1895, in "Letters Written by E. F. Atkins from Soledad, February 12, 1895 to March 28, 1896," ser. II, AFP, MHS; Atkins, *Sixty Years,* chap. 12, p. 161. See also José S. Llorens y Maceo, *Con Maceo en la invasión* (Havana: Duarte y Iriarte, 1928), p. 39; García Martínez, "La Brigada."

13. See Atkins, *Sixty Years,* p. 162.

14. See *Boletín Oficial de la Provincia de Santa Clara,* 6 August 1895. In the manuscript register at the end of the war he is listed as a shoemaker, born in Bayamo (Oriente). See folio 13, Libro de Relación 52, Fondo Roloff, ANC.

15. Agustín Luque, Governor of Santa Clara, 15 July 1895. In leg. K-7 (2a–4a), Ultramar, Cuba, AGM-Segovia. Ada Ferrer graciously shared her photocopies of this set of documents.

16. Reports and telegrams in leg. K-7 (2a–4a), Ultramar, Cuba, AGM-Segovia.

17. The workers' petition is also in leg. K-7 (2a–4a), Ultramar, Cuba, AGM-Segovia.

18. See Chapter 4 above and J. S. Murray to E. Atkins, 14 September 1886, ser. IV, AFP, MHS.

19. On Claudio Sarría, see the Soledad payroll for January 1890 in Libro 707, Fondo ICEA, ANC; and "Documentos relativos a la Inspección General del Ejército. Expediente que contiene la relación de jefes, oficiales, clases y soldados y el estado de las armas y animales de la Brigada de Cienfuegos, 27 de noviembre de 1896," inventario 1, exp. 60, Colección de Documentos del Ejército Libertador Cubano, Archivo Provincial de Villa Clara, Santa Clara (photocopy courtesy of Michael Zeuske).

20. See the discussion of "el negro Ciriaco" in Chapter 4.

21. These events are recounted in Atkins, *Sixty Years,* chap. 13.

22. See J. S. Murray to E. F. Atkins, 30 November 1886, ser. IV, AFP, MHS; and Atkins, *Sixty Years,* pp. 184–188.

23. Versions of these events vary. See P. M. Beal to Edwin F. Atkins, 9 December 1895, in Edwin F. Atkins Letterbooks, 21 May 1901–29 June 1907, ser. II, AFP, MHS; Deposition of Peter M. Beal, 28 April 1906, p. 4, and Deposition of Benigno Najarro, 14 May 1906, both in claim 387 (Atkins), Treaty Claims, entry 352, RG 76, USNA; García Martínez, "La Brigada"; and Atkins, *Sixty Years.*

24. See García Martínez, "La Brigada"; and Ada Ferrer, "Rustic Men, Civilized Nation: Race, Culture, and Contention on the Eve of Cuban Independence," *Hispanic American Historical Review* 78 (November 1998): 663–686.

25. P. M. Beal to E. Atkins, 17 January 1896, reproduced in Atkins, *Sixty Years,* p. 196.

The text of the letters from Soledad that Atkins reproduced in his published memoir does not always match the manuscript letters, and I generally use the manuscript letter when available. In this case, however, the original letter seems not to be in the Atkins Family Papers at the MHS, so I have relied on the memoir.

26. José Rogelio Castillo, *Autobiografía del General José Rogelio Castillo* (Havana: Editorial de Ciencias Sociales, 1973), p. 149; Atkins, *Sixty Years,* pp. 202, 203.

27. For a discussion of the invasion force in the eyes of western residents, see Ferrer, *Insurgent Cuba,* pp. 147–154.

28. See Michael Zeuske, " 'Los negros hicimos la independencia': Aspectos de la movilización afrocubana en un hinterland cubano. Cienfuegos entre colonia y República," in Martínez Heredia, Scott, and García Martínez, *Espacios, silencios,* pp. 193–234.

29. See "Documentos relativos . . . 27 de noviembre de 1896"; "Pensión interesada por Felipe Santiago Sarría como soldado del Ejército Libertador," Año 1929, exp. 3930, Juzgado, AHPC; and Libro de Relación 52, Fondo Roloff, ANC.

30. Deposition of Emiliano Silva y Placeres, beginning February 15, 1904, in claim 293 (Hormiguero), pt. 3, Treaty Claims, entry 352, RG 76, USNA.

31. Deposition of Miguel Angel Abad, claim 293 (Hormiguero), pt. 1, entry 352, RG 76, USNA.

32. See García Martínez, "La Brigada," p. 174.

33. See Ferrer, *Insurgent Cuba,* pp. 154–169.

34. Reg. 102, sobre 98, caja M-11 (General José Monteagudo and others), Fototeca, ANC; and Colectivo de autores, *Diccionario enciclopédico,* pp. 260–261. Historian Pedro Deschamps Chapeaux once suggested that José de Jesús Monteagudo was nonetheless perceived by some as a *mulato.* Pedro Deschamps Chapeaux, personal communication, spring 1994.

35. See, for example, reg. 104, sobre 100, caja M-11, and reg. 105, sobre 101, caja M-11 (H. Esquerra and others), and reg. 101, sobre 97, caja M-10 (Brigadier José González Planas and others), Fototeca, ANC; and the entries in Colectivo de autores, *Diccionario enciclopédico.* On officers in the Cienfuegos Brigade, see García Martínez, "La Brigada," p. 175. Color attributions and labels could, of course, shift with time and context. See Ferrer, *Insurgent Cuba,* p. 238n50.

36. J. N. S. Williams, cited in Atkins, *Sixty Years,* p. 167.

37. Report of Arsenio Martínez Campos to the Minister of War, June 25, 1895, transcribed in documents from the Spanish military archives, included in claim 293 (Hormiguero), pt. 11, Treaty Claims, entry 352, RG 76, USNA. Considerable energy has been devoted by historians to trying to figure out "the" role of racism and distinctions of color in the war for independence. See Aline Helg, *Our Rightful Share: The Afro-Cuban Struggle for Equality, 1886–1912* (Chapel Hill: University of North Carolina Press, 1995); and the critique by Jorge Ibarra in "Comentarios acerca de 'Mitos de "democracia racial": Cuba, 1900–1912' " in Martínez Heredia, Scott, and García Martínez, *Espacios, silencios,* pp. 332–345. Ada Ferrer's dynamic and dialectical interpretation in *Insurgent Cuba* offers one way out of the impasse.

38. J. N. S. Williams to E. Atkins, November 24, 1895, in Atkins, *Sixty Years,* p. 179.

The testimony of rebel officer Benigno Najarro (cited in note 10) confirms that some insurgents enaged in illegal exactions, but emphasizes that they were court-martialled and punished by the rebel high command.

39. Atkins, *Sixty Years,* p. 202.
40. Deposition of Adolfo Olivera, in case 293 (Hormiguero), pt. 1, Treat Claims, entry 352, RG 76, USNA.
41. Atkins, *Sixty Years,* p. 199.
42. See Pérez, *Cuba between Empires,* pp. 54–55.
43. See Comandancia Militar Cienfuegos, "Zonas de Cultivo, 1896 y 98, las establecidas en Palmira y Cienfuegos." Leg. 20-K, división 3a, sección 2a, Ultramar, AGM-Segovia.
44. Report from the Guerrilla Local of Santa Isabel de las Lajas, to the Commander of the town. Leg. K-7 (2a–4a), Ultramar, Cuba, AGM-Segovia.
45. Pérez, *Cuba between Empires,* p. 54. On the phenomenon of *reconcentración* see Francisco Pérez Guzmán, *Herida profunda* (Havana: Ediciones Unión, 1998). On Hormiguero, see Deposition of Elias Ponvert, 25 January 1904, claim 293 (Homiguero), pt. 1, Treaty Claims, entry 352, RG 76, USNA.
46. Gobernador Civil de la Provincia de Santa Clara to D. Pedro Pin, 12 May 1896. Leg. K-7 (2a–4a), Ultramar, Cuba, AGM-Segovia.
47. See División de las Villas, 1a Brigada, 3a Media Brigada, "Diario de las operaciones practicadas por la columna del Sr Colonel Don Juan Manrique de Lara durante el mes de la fecha," 28 February 1897. Leg. K-1 (2a–4a), Ultramar, Cuba, AGM-Segovia.
48. 1er Batallón del Rgt. Inf. de Bailén no. 24, Mes de Junio 1897, Diario de las operaciones. Leg. K-1 (2a–4a), Ultramar, Cuba, AGM-Segovia.
49. Alcaldía Municipal de Cruces, "Relación de las fincas quemadas en todo ó parte por los insurrectos," 15 September 1897. Leg. K-20, división 3a, sección 2a, Ultramar, AGM-Segovia.
50. See García Martínez, "La Brigada."
51. See Mayra Mena Múgica and Severiano Hernández Vicente, *Fuentes documentales de la administración española en el Archivo Nacional de Cuba: La administración autonómica española de Cuba en 1898* (Salamanca: Ediciones Universidad de Salamanca, 1994); *Suplemento al Boletín Oficial de la Provincia de Santa Clara,* no. 63, 15 March 1898, Ayuntamiento de San Fernando. Men over twenty-five years of age, and in possession of their other civil rights, were permitted to vote.
52. See Helg, *Our Rightful Share,* chap. 1.
53. See *Suplemento al Boletín Oficial de la Provincia de Santa Clara,* no. 63, 15 March 1898, Provincia de Santa Clara.
54. Ibid., Barrio de Arimao, sección única con La Sierra.
55. See Pérez, *Cuba between Empires,* chap. 4.
56. Carlos T. Trujillo, *De la guerra y de la paz* (Havana: Ucar, García y Cia., 1943), pp. 33–34, cited in García Martínez, "La Brigada."
57. See the entry "Sueldos del Mes de Enero de 1898" in libro 712, Fondo ICEA, ANC.

58. I am grateful to Marcelino Iznaga Suárez Román for sharing recollections of the family of his uncle, Rafael Iznaga, during interviews in June and November 1999 and February 2000.

59. Their enlistment appears in "Documentos relativos . . . 27 de noviembre de 1896." Their names do not appear in either vol. 49 or 52 of the discharge lists, Fondo Roloff, ANC. Cayetano Quesada's 1936 pension request is located in leg. 477, Fondo Juzgado de Primera Instancia de Cienfuegos, AHPC. Ciriaco Quesada also settled nearby; see the discussion in Chapter 6 of his participation in an 1899 dispute over a mule.

60. Ramos Quesada's wartime correspondence from Santa Rosalía is in nos. 99–100, CMJL, CC, BNC.

61. These pay lists are in the Soledad volumes, Fondo ICEA, ANC.

62. See the wartime correspondence of Manuel Blanco in nos. 99 and 100, CMJL, CC, BNC. The social composition of the *guerrilla* is the subject of a continuing inquiry by Louis A. Pérez, Jr., and I thank him for several personal communications on this topic.

63. Caridad Quesada was interviewed several times beginning in 1998; Fernando Martínez Heredia recounted the story of his grandmother Faustina Heredia at a conference at the Centro Juan Marinello in June of 2000; Tomás Pérez y Pérez was interviewed in 1998 and 1999. Confirming evidence for Faustina Heredia's dates of birth and marriage is in the possession of Fernando Martínez Heredia.

64. See "Cédulas de Patrocinado, 10 de marzo de 1883," no. 158, CMJL, CC, BNC. Gregoria Quesada appears as a resident of the town of Cienfuegos in 1891 when she gives testimony in a criminal case. See "Juicio de faltas contra el moreno Marcos Rodriguez por golpes y amenazas a la idem Francisca Sarría," Juzgado Municipal de Cienfuegos, Año 1891, AHPC.

65. "Venta de solares por la parda Eleuteria Almoguea a favor de la parda Gregoria Quesada," 24 November 1888, esc. 497; "Venta de finca por la parda Doña Eleuteria Almoguea a favor de la parda Doña Gregoria Quesada," 4 January 1894, esc. 2; and "Venta de finca rústica por la Sᵗᵃ Doña Lutgarda Díaz y Nodal viuda de Rosés, a favor de la morena Dᵃ Gregoria Quesada," 23 October 1897, esc. 617, all in Protocolo Verdaguer, PN, AHPC. Her son is mentioned later in Constantino Pérez to Manuel García Blanco, 28 June 1899, CSR, OGM.

66. Isidro Vera, Sr., Rancho Luna, Cienfuegos, interview, 2000.

67. On the participation of Ramón V. Pagés in the debate in New Orleans, see L. A. Martinet, ed., *The Violation of a Constitutional Right. Published by Authority of the Citizens' Committee* (New Orleans: The Crusader, 1896), p. 16. Pagés is described as "a Spaniard and the President of the Cigar-Makers' Union," but was in fact a Cuban from Matanzas. Ramón Pagés then appears in the list of expeditionaries in Miguel Varona Guerrero, *La Guerra de Independencia de Cuba, 1895–1898*, 3 vols. (Havana: Editorial Lex, 1946), 2:1360–61. On exile cigar workers and the Cuban independence struggle, see Gerald E. Poyo, *"With All, and for the Good of All": The Emergence of Popular Nationalism in the Cuban Communities of the United States, 1848–1898* (Dur-

ham, N.C.: Duke University Press, 1989); and Paul Estrade, *José Martí: Los fundamentos de la democracia en Latinoamerica* (Aranjuez, Spain: Ediciones Doce Calles, 2000), which mentions Pagés on page 693.

68. See Cuba, Archivo Nacional, *Correspondencia diplomática de la delegación cubana en Nueva York durante la Guerra de Independencia de 1895 a 1898,* vol. 5 (Havana: Archivo Nacional de Cuba, 1946), p. 167. The text cited appears there in English translation, dated 4 July 1896: "All lands acquired by the Cuban Republic either by conquest or confiscation, except what is employed for governmental purpose, shall be divided among the defenders of the Cuban Republic against Spain."

69. See U.S. War Department, *Reports of Brigadier-General Leonard Wood, U.S.V. on Civil Affairs in the Provinces of Santiago and Puerto Principe, Cuba* in *Annual Reports of the U.S. War Department,* 1899, vol. 1.

70. Discussions of this phenomenon include Ferrer, *Insurgent Cuba,* and García Martínez, "La Brigada."

6. Democracy and Antidemocracy

Epigraph: Speech of 13 May 1898, in Louisiana, *Official Journal of the Proceedings of the Constitutional Convention of the State of Louisiana, Held in New Orleans, Tuesday, February 8, 1898* (New Orleans: H. J. Hearsey, 1898), p. 380.

1. George P. Marks III, ed., *The Black Press Views American Imperialism (1898–1900)* (New York: Arno Press, 1971), esp. pp. 201–207, and Willard B. Gatewood, Jr., *Black Americans and the White Man's Burden, 1898–1903* (Urbana: University of Illinois Press, 1975).

2. The Fifteenth Amendment holds that "the right of citizens of the United States shall not be denied or abridged by the United States or by any state on acount of race, color, or previous condition of servitude." See J. Morgan Kousser, *The Shaping of Southern Politics: Suffrage Restriction and the Establishment of the One-Party South* (New Haven, Conn.: Yale University Press, 1974), esp. pp. 60–61, 152–165; and Michael Perman, *Struggle for Mastery: Disfranchisement in the South, 1888–1908* (Chapel Hill: University of North Carolina Press, 2001).

3. See William Hilary Coston, *The Spanish-American War Volunteer* (1899; reprint, Freeport, N.Y.: Books for Libraries Press, 1971).

4. See Joseph G. Dawson III, *Army Generals and Reconstruction: Louisiana, 1862–1877* (Baton Rouge: Louisiana State University Press, 1982), pp. 171–175, 226–232. General James H. Wilson, named governor of the Cuban provinces of Matanzas and Santa Clara, had southern experience dating back to 1865, when troops under his command had captured Confederate president Jefferson Davis. See Dumas Malone, ed., *Dictionary of American Biography* (New York: Charles Scribner's Sons, 1936), pp. 334–336.

5. Louisiana, Department of State, *Report of the Secretary of State to His Excellency W. W. Heard, Governor of the State of Louisiana, May 12th, 1902* (Baton Rouge: Baton Rouge News Pub. Co., 1902).

6. See William Ivy Hair, *Bourbonism and Agrarian Protest: Louisiana Politics, 1877–1900* (Baton Rouge: Louisiana State University Press, 1969); Eric Arnesen, *Waterfront Workers of New Orleans: Race, Class, and Politics, 1863–1923* (New York: Oxford University Press, 1991); and David R. Roediger, "Gaining a Hearing for Black-White Unity: Covington Hall and the Complexities of Race, Gender, and Class," in Roediger, *Toward the Abolition of Whiteness: Essays on Race, Politics, and Working Class History* (London: Verso, 1994).

7. See the biography of Brown in Coston, *Spanish-American War Volunteer,* pp. 83–85; and also Arnesen, *Waterfront Workers,* pp. 128–134, 140.

8. Hair, *Bourbonism,* chaps. 9, 10.

9. The 1894 Wilson-Gorman Tariff, whose duties Louisiana producers complained were too low, struck Cuban producers as damagingly high. The tariff also triggered protectionist retaliation by Spain, further damaging Cuban trade with the United States. See Hugh Thomas, *Cuba: The Pursuit of Freedom* (New York: Harper and Row, 1971), pp. 290–291; and Alan Dye, *Cuban Sugar in the Age of Mass Production: Technology and the Economics of the Sugar Central, 1899–1929* (Stanford, Calif.: Stanford University Press, 1998), pp. 50–51. On Louisiana, see John Alfred Heitmann, *The Modernization of the Louisiana Sugar Industry, 1830–1910* (Baton Rouge: Louisiana State University Press, 1987), pp. 166–167, 245; Hair, *Bourbonism,* chap. 10.

10. Quoted in Heitmann, *Modernization,* p. 246.

11. As quoted in Perry H. Howard, *Political Tendencies in Louisiana, 1812–1952* (Baton Rouge: Louisiana State University Press, 1957), p. 98. On Pharr's wealth and his actions in 1887, see Hair, *Bourbonism,* pp. 252, 256.

12. For research in educational psychology that suggests the importance of collaboration as opposed to simple contact, see Rupert Brown, *Prejudice: Its Social Psychology* (Oxford: Blackwell, 1995), pp. 254–256.

13. On the social geography of sugar plantations, see John B. Rehder, *Delta Sugar: Louisiana's Vanishing Plantation Landscape* (Baltimore: Johns Hopkins University Press, 1999), chap. 2. On Italian seasonal migrants, see Jean Ann Scarpaci, "Italian Immigrants in Louisiana's Sugar Parishes: Recruitment, Labor Conditions, and Community Relations, 1880–1910" (Ph.D. diss., Rutgers University, 1972).

14. On the divergence of interests among croppers, tenants, and laborers, see Harold Woodman, *New South, New Law: The Legal Foundations of Credit and Labor Relations in the Postbellum Agricultural South* (Baton Rouge: Louisiana State University Press, 1995); and Neil Foley, *The White Scourge: Mexicans, Blacks, and Poor Whites in Texas Cotton Culture* (Berkeley: University of California Press, 1997). On color and occupation in Louisiana, see Hair, *Bourbonism;* John C. Rodrigue, *Reconstruction in the Cane Fields: From Slavery to Free Labor in Louisiana's Sugar Parishes, 1862–1880* (Baton Rouge: Louisiana State University Press, 2001); and U.S. Bureau of the Census, *Thirteenth Census of the United States Taken in the Year 1910,* vol. 6, *Agriculture 1909 and 1910* (Washington, D.C.: Government Printing Office, 1913), pp. 678–679. Lafourche Parish, for example, counted 1,140 native white farmers and only 71 "Negro and other nonwhite."

15. The quotation is from the *Terrebonne Times*, 17 July 1887.
16. On rhetorical weapons and cognitive framing, see chap. 7, "Framing the Issue: Elite Discourse and Popular Understanding," in Donald Kinder and Lynn M. Saunders, *Divided by Color: Racial Politics and Democratic Ideals* (Chicago: University of Chicago Press, 1996).
17. See the quotation from the *Baton Rouge Daily Advocate*, 27 January 1892, in Hair, *Bourbonism*, p. 234.
18. Indeed, the National Republicans themselves came to be known as the Lily Whites, in contrast to the "Regular Republicans," who included former governor Warmoth. Hair, *Bourbonism*, pp. 247–248.
19. Hair, *Bourbonism*, chap. 10; Kousser, *Shaping*, pp. 152–165; and Perman, *Struggle*, chap. 7.
20. See Kousser, *Shaping*, p. 161; Howard, *Political Tendencies*, p. 103; Perman, *Struggle*, p. 136.
21. See the table opposite p. 42 in Louisiana, *Official Journal of the Proceedings of the Constitutional Convention of the State of Louisiana, Held in New Orleans, Tuesday, February 8, 1898* (New Orleans: H. J. Hearsey, 1898). The number of white voters fell from 164,088 to 74,133.
22. On rule-making, lockup, and electoral practice, see Samuel Issacharoff, Pamela S. Karlan, and Richard Pildes, *The Law of Democracy*, rev. 2nd ed. (New York: Foundation Press, 2002), chap. 1. For delegates, see *Official Journal of the Proceedings, 1898.*
23. See Rodolphe L. Desdunes, *Nos hommes et notre histoire* (Montreal: Arbour & Dupont, 1911), pp. 183–194; and act 1, vol. 3, 1898; act 20, vol. 1, 1891; and act 6, vol. 1, 1890, Notarial Acts of Louis A. Martinet, NONARC.
24. See Coston, *Spanish-American War Volunteer*, pp. 133–134, 218; "When the Victory's Won," *Colored American*, 1 July 1899; and *Daily Crusader*, 22 June 1895, in DFC, ASC, XU.
25. Coston, *Spanish-American War Volunteer*, p. 218.
26. On the process by which the G.A.R. in Louisiana became a largely African American organization, see James G. Hollandsworth, *The Louisiana Native Guards: The Black Military Experience during the Civil War* (Baton Rouge: Louisiana State University Press, 1995), pp. 112–113. On race and the national G.A.R., see David Blight, *Race and Reunion: The Civil War in American Memory* (Cambridge, Mass.: Harvard University Press, 2001), pp. 194–195. The "Faith Cadets" are profiled in Coston, *Spanish-American War Volunteer*, pp. 77–78.
27. See, in particular, the *Washington Bee* for these months. The paper moved over a period of weeks from anger at the selective concern for Cuban human rights to vigorous support of the war effort. See also Gatewood, *Black Americans.*
28. See *Official Journal of the Proceedings, 1898*, p. 9, and passim. On Kruttschnitt's White League past, see *The Orleans Parish Blue Book* (New Orleans: Southern Manufacturer, 1896), p. 32. On the convention, see also Kousser, *Shaping;* and Perman, *Struggle*, pp. 136–147.
29. Thomas J. Kernan, "The Constitutional Convention of 1898 and Its Work," *Proceedings of the Louisiana Bar Association, 1898–1899* (New Orleans: Graham Press, 1899),

pp. 55–73, phrase cited on p. 57. Kernan candidly explains that the educational and property limitations "had to be fixed sufficiently high to bar the negro effectively."

30. See Perman, *Struggle,* p. 139. For the text of Article 197, see *Report of the Secretary of State, 1902,* pp. 271–273.

31. McEnery's initial judgment is quoted in a letter by Jesse Lawson to the *Washington Post,* 13 May 1901, referred to in Jesse Lawson to Booker T. Washington, 13 May 1901, in Louis R. Harlan and Raymond W. Smock, eds., Barbara S. Kraft, asst. ed., *The Booker T. Washington Papers,* vol. 6 (Urbana: University of Illinois Press, 1977), pp. 108–109; Kernan, "The Constitutional Convention," p. 61.

32. *Official Journal of the Proceedings, 1898,* p. 139.

33. Quoted in Howard, *Political Tendencies,* p. 102.

34. Kernan, "The Constitutional Convention," pp. 55–73.

35. See *Official Journal of the Proceedings, 1898,* p. 380.

36. *Washington Bee,* 16 April 1898.

37. See Jesse Lawson to Booker T. Washington, 3 October 1900, in Louis R. Harlan and Raymond W. Smock, eds., Barbara S. Kraft, asst. ed., *The Booker T. Washington Papers,* vol. 5 (Urbana: University of Illinois Press, 1976), pp. 647–648. See also James McPherson, *The Abolitionist Legacy: From Reconstruction to the NAACP* (Princeton: Princeton University Press, 1975).

38. See *Report of the Secretary of State, 1902,* pp. 556–557.

39. See Gatewood, *Black Americans,* chap. 3; and Nancy A. Hewitt, *Southern Discomfort: Women's Activism in Tampa, Florida, 1880s–1920s* (Urbana: University of Illinois Press, 2001), chap. 4.

40. See Gatewood, *Black Americans,* pp. 71–72, 96; and Willard B. Gatewood, *"Smoked Yankees" and the Struggle for Empire: Letters from Negro Soldiers, 1898–1902* (Urbana: University of Illinois Press, 1971), pp. 181–183. On North Carolina, see Piero Gleijeses, "African Americans and the War against Spain," *North Carolina Historical Review* 73 (April 1996): 184–214. On Illinois, see W. T. Goode, *The "Eighth Illinois"* (Chicago: Blakely Printing Company, 1899), p. 42.

41. On meetings in New Orleans, see the *Washington Bee,* 30 April and 14 May 1898.

42. See coverage of the "immune bill" in the *New Orleans Picayune,* 17, 18 May 1898.

43. Biographies and transcripts of the muster rolls can be found in Coston, *Spanish-American War Volunteer.* The original muster-in and muster-out rolls are in the records of the Ninth Regiment of U.S. Volunteers, AGO, RG 94, USNA. Tharp (or Tharpe) appears in Coston's regimental history (p. 103) and as a labor leader in Arnesen, *Waterfront Workers* (pp. 129 and 151). Coston describes Tharp as president of a 12,000-member "C.M.L.'s Alliance," and a physician's affidavit in Tharp's pension file refers to the Longshoremen's Benevolent Association. See medical affidavit of Dr. James I. Newman, 5 April 1900, in Lafayette Tharp's pension file, C-2483201, USNA.

44. Coston, *Spanish-American War Volunteer; New Orleans Picayune,* 17 May 1898.

45. Coston, *Spanish-American War Volunteer,* p. 81.

46. Caryn Cossé Bell, *Revolution, Romanticism, and the Afro-Creole Protest Tradition in Louisiana, 1718–1868* (Baton Rouge: Louisiana State University Press, 1997).

47. See *Washington Bee*, 25 June 1898. The African American chaplain of the Ninth Volunteers, William H. Coston, wrote warmly of the white colonel who supervised recruitment and of the white major who commanded one of the battalions, but his regimental history never mentioned the white captains who were imposed on the companies, except to include their names on the muster roll. Coston, *Spanish-American War Volunteer,* pp. 135–136.

48. See the Muster-Out Roll of Company L, Ninth U.S. Volunteer Infantry, AGO, RG 94, USNA. On the incident between Captain Coleman and the private, see the exchanges dated 28 September 1898 in Letters and Telegrams Received, San Luis, Entry 2004, RG 395, USNA. The quotation is from the sworn statement of Private Lucius Knight of the Eighth Illinois. Captain Coleman, for his part, recalled himself as having ordered the private back and "used only such violence as necessary to compel the execution of the order, advising him, if he were not in the habit of respecting the orders of commissioned officers of his own regiment, he would have to respect the orders of officers of this regiment."

49. See the Court Martial record, U.S. vs. Private Thomas Bazile, San Luis, 25 November 1898, no. 9317, RG 153, USNA. The physical description of Tharp is from his pension file, C-2483201, USNA.

50. See Bazile court-martial record cited in note 49; and "Lafayette Tharp. Procuration to Rev. Isaac H. Hall," 2 August 1898, act 14, 1898, vol. 3 of the notarial books of Louis A. Martinet, NONARC. For the children's ages, see Tharp's deposition of 15 March 1900 in his pension file, C-2483201, USNA.

51. On yellow fever, see A. B. Feuer, *The Santiago Campaign of 1898: A Soldier's View of the Spanish-American War* (Westport, Conn.: Praeger, 1993). The *Times-Picayune* of 18 August 1898 described the departure of the Ninth Volunteers. The description of Haiti is from Bridget Fernández Carmouche, Donaldsonville, to Pierre L. Carmouche, 12 March 1899, from the Carmouche/Conway family papers, courtesy of Leroy Soles of Detroit, Michigan.

52. Emilio Bacardí y Moreau, *Crónicas de Santiago de Cuba,* 2nd ed. (Santiago de Cuba: Tipografía Arroyo Hermano, 1924), 9:109. See the *Times of Cuba: Diario Independiente y de Información,* especially the issue of 18 August 1898.

53. See the Muster-Out Roll of Company L, Ninth U.S. Volunteer Infantry, AGO, RG 94, USNA; and Coston, *Spanish-American War Volunteer.*

54. The 1899 census counted 4,621 residents of San Luis as "mixed," 3,621 as Negro, 2,967 as native white, and 465 as foreign white. See U.S. War Department, *Report on the Census of Cuba, 1899* (Washington, D.C.: Government Printing Office, 1900), pp. 198–199. The soldiers' letters are cited in Gatewood, *"Smoked Yankees,"* pp. 193–194. Coston, *Spanish-American War Volunteer,* pp. 191–193.

55. Gatewood, *"Smoked Yankees,"* pp. 233–234. Other black soldiers, particularly as time wore on, did express scorn for the customs of the Cubans, mocking the palm-leaf houses and the nakedness of the children. See the letters on pp. 186–207.

56. Gatewood, *"Smoked Yankees,"* pp. 203–205.

57. Coston, *Spanish-American War Volunteer,* p. 193.

58. See Agustín Cebreco to Máximo Gómez, 6 September 1898, exp. 1842, leg. 13, Fondo Máximo Gómez, ANC.

59. On the Asamblea de Santa Cruz, see *La Lucha: Diario Republicano,* 5 November 1898; 14 November 1898; 17 November 1898. See the letter from J. Carbó and forty others to "Ciudadano General Leonardo Wood," 1 November 1898, in exp. 15, leg. 875, Fondo Gobierno Provincial, AHPSdeC.

60. Enrique Badell y Lloperena to General Wood, 25 November 1898, exp. 32, leg. 875, Fondo Gobierno Provincial, AHPSdeC. Rafael Ferrer y Bactor appears in Carlos Roloff y Mialofsky, *Índice alfabético y defunciones del Ejército Libertador de Cuba* (Havana: Rambla y Bouza, 1901), Defunciones, p. 81, with a date of enlistment of 1897.

61. Bacardí, *Crónicas de Santiago de Cuba,* 10:187.

62. In Roloff, *Índice,* Defunciones, p. 81, Ferrer's place of death is listed as San Luis, but the date is shifted to January 1898, perhaps so that his widow could apply for a pension. For details of the episode, see notes 63 and 66 below.

63. The incident can be partially reconstructed from Coston's regimental history and from the manuscript regimental records. See Coston, *Spanish-American War Volunteer,* esp. p. 69; the *Picayune* (New Orleans), the *Washington Bee,* and *La Lucha: Diario Republicano* (Havana), all for 15–30 November 1898; and the records of the Ninth U.S. Volunteer Infantry, AGO, RG 94, USNA. The key military court record should be in the U.S. National Archives, but has as yet proved elusive. Col. John R. Marshall is profiled in Goode, *"Eighth Illinois,"* pp. 65–69.

64. See the *Colored American,* 1 July 1898, on the initial reaction of black recruits to the news that their captains would be mustered in as lieutenants; and the same newspaper on 12 November 1898, on the resignation of seven first and second lieutenants of the Ninth Volunteers. On the replacement captains, see notes 48 and 65.

65. Order to Capt. R. M. Nolan, Officer of the Day, 29 November 1898, Regimental Letters Sent and Endorsements, and records of Company D, both in Ninth U.S. Volunteer Infantry, AGO, RG 94, USNA.

66. See the orders of Col. Crane in Regimental Letters, Ninth U.S. Volunteer Infantry, AGO, RG 94, USNA. General Wood's report, dated 18 November 1898, is in Letters Sent, Department of Santiago, Entry 1479, RG 395, USNA. See Claimant's Affidavit, Lafayette Tharp, 31 December 1901, in the pension file of Lafayette Tharp, C-2483201, USNA.

67. *New Orleans Times-Democrat,* 19 March 1899, as quoted in Coston, *Spanish-American War Volunteer,* pp. 55–56. In the decision in *Plessy,* Justice Brown argued that the Fourteenth Amendment "could not have been intended to abolish distinctions based upon color, or to enforce social, as distinguished from political equality." See Plessy v. Ferguson 163 U.S. 537 (1896).

68. In the 10 September 1898 issue of the *Washington Bee,* the editors had argued that volunteers needed some time to achieve the discipline of regulars, and that serious indiscipline was in fact being shown by white southern soldiers who refused to salute "colored" officers.

69. See Louis A. Pérez, Jr., *Cuba between Empires, 1878–1902* (Pittsburgh: University of Pittsburgh Press, 1983), especially pp. 205–227.

70. See Edwin F. Atkins, *Sixty Years in Cuba: Reminiscences of Edwin F. Atkins* (1926; reprint, New York: Arno Press, 1980), pp. 294–296; Ignacio T. Alomá to Demetrio Castillo, 20 February 1899, in exp. 23, leg. 875, and Dominador del Giraudi to Gbr. del Dpto. de Santiago de Cuba, 5 Aug. 1899, exp. 5, leg. 515, both in Fondo Gobierno Provincial, AHPSdeC.

71. Atkins, *Sixty Years,* pp. 297–301; Pablo L. Rousseau and Pablo Díaz de Villegas, *Memoria descriptiva, histórica y biográfica de Cienfuegos y las fiestas del primer centenario de la fundación de esta ciudad* (Havana: Siglo XX, 1920), pp. 265–266. On public culture, see Marial Iglesias Utset, *Las metáforas del cambio en la vida cotidiana: Cuba, 1898–1902* (Havana: Ediciones Unión, 2003).

72. See U.S. War Department, *Reports of Brigadier-General Leonard Wood, U.S.V., on Civil Affairs in the Provinces of Santiago and Puerto Principe, Cuba,* in *Annual Reports of the U.S. War Department,* 1899, vol. 1; "Reports on the agricultural conditions in the Provinces of Matanzas and Santa Clara," by Acting Inspector General Captain Fred. S. Foltz, 3 February 1900, in File 1900:1670, RG 140, USNA; and Brooke's *Civil Report* of 1 October 1899, quoted in David F. Healy, *The United States in Cuba, 1898–1902: Generals, Politicians, and the Search for Policy* (Madison: University of Wisconsin Press, 1963), p. 104.

73. The text, in the official translation, read as follows: "The horses taken by officers or soldiers of the Cuban army during the late war against Spain shall be inscribed in the 'Registro Pecuario' as the property of the said officers or soldiers, on their request, provided that they establish, by the testimony of two reputable witnesses, the fact that the said horses were in their possession or in that of the Cuban army on or before the 12th day of August, 1898." *Civil Report of Major-General John R. Brooke, U.S. Army, Military Governor, Island of Cuba* (Washington, D.C., 1900), pp. 55, 70. For a local ruling from February of 1899, see folio 8, vol. 43 (1899), Actas Capitulares, Municipio de Cienfuegos, AHPC.

74. See Rafael Martínez Ortíz, *Cuba: Los primeros años de independencia* (Paris: Editorial "Le Livre Libre," 1929), 1:83–84.

75. Reports . . . Foltz, 3 February 1900, in File 1900:1670, RG 140, USNA; Informe del Alcalde de la Municipalidad de San Fernando por el semestre que finaliza en Junio 30 de 1900, in File 1900:3589, RG 140, USNA.

76. The division of the Ravella inheritance is on folio 1941ff., Escritura 283, 27 March 1900, Protocolo Fernández Pellón, PN, AHPC. The sale record is "Venta de finca rústica y promesa de venta de otras," folio 7109ff., Escritura 1035, 22 November 1901, Protocolo Fernández Pellón, PN, AHPC. For further details, see Rebecca J. Scott and Michael Zeuske, "Property in Writing, Property on the Ground: Pigs, Horses, Land, and Citizenship in the Aftermath of Slavery, Cuba, 1880–1909," *Comparative Studies in Society and History* 44 (October 2002): 669–699.

77. See Chapter 5 for discussion of Gregoria Quesada's land purchases. Her appeal for the mule, first referred to as "el mulo del hijo de Gregoria" (Gregoria's son's mule), is recorded in Constantino Pérez to Manuel García, 28 June 1899, CSR, OGM.

78. Constantino Pérez to Manuel García, 17 August, 1899, CSR, OGM.

79. See Constantino Pérez to Manuel García, 18 August 1899, and enclosures, in CSR, OGM. This story is narrated in greater detail in Rebecca J. Scott, "Reclaiming Gregoria's Mule: The Meanings of Freedom in the Arimao and Caunao Valleys, Cienfuegos, Cuba, 1880–1899," *Past and Present* 170 (February 2001): 181–216. I have inferred that Francisco A. Oliva is the same Francisco Álvarez Oliva discussed in Chapter 4, given the matching details of locale and affiliation.

80. Local memory of Cayetano Quesada's claim to the *sitio* in San Antón still reflects this view. An elderly neighbor recalled to interviewers in 2001 that he believed that no one should ever have tried to take the land from Cayetano, because Cayetano had "gone to the hills" to fight. Interview by Orlando García, Michael Zeuske, and Rebecca Scott with Francisco Mena Águila, San Antón, 2001.

81. Scott and Zeuske, "Property in Writing," pp. 677–682.

82. Pérez, *Cuba between Empires,* pp. 309–310.

83. Quoted in ibid., p. 311. I thank Richard Turits for clarifying the double meaning of this reference to Santo Domingo.

84. See U.S. Congress, Senate, "Qualification of Voters at Coming Elections in Cuba," 56th Cong., 2nd sess., Sen. Doc. 243, ser. 3867, 1900.

85. See ibid. Among white male adults born in Cuba, 79,000 could read and write, and 94,000 could do neither. Among those born in Spain whose citizenship was "in suspense," 56,000 could read and write; 17,000 could do neither.

86. The story of Cayetano Quesada's loss of his wartime mount is from interviews with his son-in-law, Evelio Castillo, and a neighbor in 2001.

7. THE RIGHT TO HAVE RIGHTS

Epigraph: Cuba, Convención Constituyente, 1900–1901, *Diario de Sesiones de la Convención Constituyente de la Isla de Cuba,* Havana, 1901. Session of January 30, 1901, p. 274.

1. Louisiana, *Report of the Secretary of State to His Excellency W. W. Heard, Governor of the State of Louisiana, May 12th, 1902* (Baton Rouge: Baton Rouge News Pub. Co., 1902).

2. The case file of the initial appeal, dated 22 January 1900, is A. L. Gusman in behalf of Nathan Wright v. L. H. Marrero, Docket no. 12849, in the General Case Files, entry 121, U.S. Circuit Court, New Orleans, Eastern District of Louisiana, Records of the U.S. District Courts, RG 21, USNA-SW Region, Fort Worth, Texas (hereafter Wright v. Marrero case file, Docket no. 12849).

3. For Lewis's early involvement, see ibid. As of June of 1900, support in New Orleans came from a group defined as "Colonel James Lewis, Dr. Scott, Dr. Henderson, and the Rev. Mr. Reynolds, and two other of the more prominent ministers." See Emmett Jay Scott in Tuskegee to Booker T. Washington, in Louis R. Harlan and Raymond W. Smock, eds., Barbara S. Kraft, asst. ed., *The Booker T. Washington Papers,* vol. 5 (Urbana: University of Illinois Press, 1976), pp. 565–567. See also James McPherson, *The Abolitionist Legacy: From Reconstruction to the NAACP*

(Princeton: Princeton University Press, 1975), pp. 363–364; and Louis Harlan, "The Secret Life of Booker T. Washington," *Journal of Southern History* 37 (August 1971): 393–416.

4. Gusman v. Marrero 180 U.S. 81. Jesse Lawson's copy of the brief for the appellant is held in the Daniel A. P. Murray Collection at the Library of Congress, under the title "A. L. Gusman, in behalf of Samuel Wright, appellant, vs. L. H. Marrero, sheriff &c.: brief for appellant." It is transcribed, with several errors, in the American Memory website at *http://memory.loc.gov.*

5. Gusman v. Marrero 180 U.S. 81.

6. See "Grandfather Suffrage Act," col. 6, p. 10, *Washington Post,* 13 May 1901. The case file of State ex rel. Ryanes v. J. M. Gleason, Docket no. 65432 of the Civil District Court, is held in the District Court Records, Louisiana Collection, New Orleans Public Library (hereafter Ryanes v. Gleason, Docket no. 65432, DCR, NOPL).

7. For the briefs, see Ryanes v. Gleason, Docket no. 65432, DCR, NOPL. For Romain's biography, see Alcée Fortier, *Louisiana: Comprising Sketches of Parishes, Towns, Events, Institutions, and Persons, Arranged in Cyclopedic Form,* vol. 3 ([Madison, Wis.]: Century Historical Association, 1914), pp. 382–383. Pierre L. Carmouche to My Dear Wife [Bridget Carmouche], 26 March 1899, from Songo, Cuba, copy in the possession of Leroy Soles, Detroit, Michigan.

8. See the Opinion of Honorable W. B. Sommerville, Judge, Filed August 19th, 1901, in the case of State ex rel. David Jordan Ryanes vs. Jeremiah M. Gleason, Supervisor of Registration. The second case was Docket no. 67606, DCR, NOPL. The original pleadings and testimony in the lower court are reproduced in the case files of the Louisiana Supreme Court: Ryanes v. Gleason, Docket no. 14651, SCC, UNO.

9. See the petition filed with the District Court by Romain on 30 April 1902, reproduced in Ryanes v. Gleason, Docket no. 14651, SCC, UNO. Romain emphasized that only white persons had been eligible to vote on the cutoff date for the grandfather clause—January 1, 1867—and that the entitlement of such persons and their sons and grandsons to achieve permanent registration under Section 5, Article 197, of the 1898 constitution, when they did not meet the literacy or property requirements, was a racially exclusionary "special privilege." The grandfather clause was, moreover, "co-related, interdependent, and inseparable" from the literacy and property requirements, which were designed to "debar the great body of colored citizens of the United States of the African race in said State from the right to vote."

10. In the entire state, only 111 colored men successfully availed themselves of the Section 5 permanent register, on the basis of immigrant status or the grandfather clause. Another 916 registered through the property qualification, and 4,327 were judged to have met the educational qualification. See pp. 556–558 of *Report of the Secretary of State, Louisiana, 1902.*

11. Case file of Ryanes v. Gleason, Docket no. 14651, SCC, UNO.

12. This testimony is transcribed in the case file at the UNO Supreme Court Collec-

tion, but is apparently missing from the District Court files at the New Orleans Public Library.

13. Case file of Ryanes v. Gleason, Docket no. 14651, SCC, UNO.

14. Faced with the challenge from Ryanes, the supervisor of registration introduced testimony that some men of color had in fact availed themselves of the grandfather clause, and implied that this insulated it from interpretation as a racially exclusionary provision. Romain tried to get the state to admit that these few registrants (seven men in the Parish of Orleans) had white grandfathers, but the supervisor professed to know nothing about this. Case file, Ryanes v. Gleason, Docket no. 14651, SCC, UNO. The formal grounds for dismissal were *res adjudicata* (that is, the court considered the issue to have been definitively judicially decided already).

15. Activists were well aware of the difficulty of confronting this situation. See Albert Enoch Pillsbury to Booker T. Washington, 30 July 1901, in Louis R. Harlan and Raymond W. Smock, eds., Barbara S. Kraft, asst. ed., *The Booker T. Washington Papers,* vol. 6 (Urbana: University of Illinois Press, 1977), p. 182–183, 183n. Pillsbury pointed out that overthrowing the grandfather clause alone would simply "disfranchise the poor and illiterate whites who are voting under it, without opening the suffrage to the negroes. But this is at least a sentimental victory, and may be all that it is possible to accomplish."

16. Giles v. Harris 189 U.S. 475 (1903).

17. Giles v. Teasley 193 U.S. 146 (1904). The Alabama Supreme Court had held, in a breathtaking Catch-22, that "if the provisions of the state constitution were repugnant to the Fifteenth Amendment they were void and that the board of registrars appointed thereunder had no existence and no power to act and would not be liable for a refusal to register him, and could not be compelled by writ of mandamus to do so; that if the provisions were constitutional the registrars had acted properly thereunder and their action was not reviewable by the courts."

18. See the entries for Docket no. 14651 in Supreme Court of Louisiana, Docket Books and Index. (Microfilm held at the Earl K. Long Library, University of New Orleans; original held by the Louisiana Supreme Court.)

19. Giles v. Teasley 193 U.S. 146 (1904); case file Ryanes v. Gleason, Docket no. 14651, SCC, UNO.

20. The final decision was published in State ex rel. Ryanes v. Gleason, Supervisor, 112 La. 612.

21. See the analysis of *Giles* in Richard H. Pildes, "Democracy, Anti-Democracy, and the Canon," *Constitutional Commentary* 17 (2000): 295–319.

22. See Giles v. Harris 189 U.S. 475 (1903), and Pildes, "Democracy."

23. Giles v. Harris 189 U.S. 475 (1903).

24. "Grandfather Suffrage Act," col. 6, p. 10, *Washington Post,* 13 May 1901.

25. See the discussion of Guinn v. United States 238 U.S. 347 (1915) and the Court's ruling against Oklahoma's "grandfather clause" in Samuel Issacharoff, Pamela Karlan, and Richard Pildes, *The Law of Democracy: Legal Structure of the Political Process* (Westbury, N.Y.: Foundation Press, 1998), pp. 75–77.

26. In 1900, local Republicans challenged the Democrats, "are you absolutely sure that your ticket has the name of no man who is in any way tainted with African blood. We know that the Republican Fusion ticket has the name of no man who is an African or in any way blood tainted." *Terrebonne Times,* 7 April 1900.

27. Pierre Carmouche's quest for a position is documented in family papers in the possession of Leroy Soles, Detroit, Michigan.

28. *Report of the Secretary of State, Louisiana, 1902,* p. 564. See William Ivy Hair, in *Bourbonism and Agrarian Protest: Louisiana Politics, 1877–1900* (Baton Rouge: Louisiana State University Press, 1969), chap. 11.

29. J. Bradford Laws, "The Negroes of Cinclare Central Factory and Calumet Plantation, Louisiana," *Bulletin of the Department of Labor* 38 (January 1902): 95–120. On voters, see *Report of the Secretary of State, Louisiana, 1902,* pp. 556–557.

30. Louisiana, *Official Journal of the Proceedings of the Convention for Framing a Constitution for the State of Louisiana* (New Orleans: J. B. Roudanez, 1867–68), pp. 293–294. Article 13 of Title I held explicitly that "All persons shall enjoy equal rights and privileges upon any conveyance of a public character; and all places of business, or of public resort, or for which a license is required by either State, parish, or municipal authority, shall be deemed places of a public character, and shall be opened to the accommodation and patronage of all persons, without distinction or discrimination on account of race or color."

31. See the volumes of Louis A. Martinet's notarial registers in NONARC.

32. Rodolphe L. Desdunes, *Nos hommes et notre histoire* (Montreal: Arbour & Dupont, 1911), pp. 193–194.

33. See Ada Ferrer, *Insurgent Cuba: Race, Nation, and Revolution, 1868–1898* (Chapel Hill: University of North Carolina Press, 1999); Alejandro de la Fuente, *A Nation for All: Race, Inequality, and Politics in Twentieth-Century Cuba* (Chapel Hill: University of North Carolina Press, 2001); Fernando Martínez, Rebecca J. Scott, and Orlando García Martínez, eds., *Espacios, silencios y los sentidos de la libertad: Cuba entre 1878 y 1912* (Havana: Editorial Unión, 2000); and Fernando Martínez Heredia, "Nationalism, Races, and Classes in the Revolution of 1895 and the Cuban First Republic," *Cuban Studies* 33 (2002): 95–123.

34. The Republican Party platform adopted in Philadelphia in June of 1900 read: "It was the plain purpose of the Fifteenth Amendment to the Constitution to prevent discrimination on account of race or color in regulating the elective franchise. Devices of State governments, whether by statutory or Constitutional enactment, to avoid the purpose of this amendment, are revolutionary and should be condemned." See also J. Morgan Kousser, *The Shaping of Southern Politics: Suffrage Restriction and the Establishment of the One-Party South* (New Haven, Conn.: Yale University Press, 1974), pp. 22–23; Alexander Keyssar, *The Right to Vote: The Contested History of Democracy in the United States* (New York: Basic Books, 2000), p. 118; and David W. Blight, *Race and Reunion: The Civil War in American Memory* (Cambridge, Mass.: Harvard University Press, 2001). The 1901 Greeting from "The Colored Citizens of Donaldsonville, Louisiana," is reproduced in the microfilm edition of the Papers of President William McKinley (indexed under Carmouche).

35. The typescript introduction added to the copy of Carlos Roloff y Mialofsky, *Índice alfabético y defunciones del Ejército Libertador de Cuba* (Havana: Rambla y Bouza, 1901), held by Widener Library, Harvard University, suggests some of the dynamics of this process. The copy belonged to Leonard Wood, and had been given to him by Carlos Roloff, who seems to have written the typescript.

36. On Gregoria Quesada's purchases, see Chapter 5. For the description of the rumors of bundles of cash, I am grateful to Marial Iglesias, pers. comm., 2001. On the symbolism of Cuban nationality, see Marial Iglesias Utset, *Las metáforas del cambio en la vida cotidiana: Cuba, 1898–1902* (Havana: Ediciones Unión, 2003).

37. For the 1900 electoral lists, see the May 1900 issues of the *Suplemento al Boletín Oficial Provincia de Santa Clara;* and "Documentos sobre elecciones de Cienfuegos. Año 1900," caja 237, Fondo Secretaría de Gobernación, ANC.

38. Louis A. Pérez, Jr., *Cuba between Empires, 1878–1902* (Pittsburgh: University of Pittsburgh Press, 1983), chaps. 16, 17. On Wood's personal motives, see David F. Healy, *The United States in Cuba, 1898–1902: Generals, Politicians, and the Search for Policy* (Madison: University of Wisconsin Press, 1963), chap. 12. The President declined to permit Wood to exit to China.

39. See Sergio López Rivero and Francisco Ibarra, "Sobre Transigentes e Intransigentes en la Cuba Ocupada, 1898–1902"; and Michael Zeuske, "Clientelas Regionales, Alianzas Interraciales y Poder Nacional en Torno a la 'Guerrita de Agosto,' " both in *Illes i Imperis* (Barcelona) 2 (Spring 1999): 111–125 and 127–156. A list of delegates and alternates appears in Cuba, Senado, *Mención histórica. Documentación relacionada con los acontecimientos que dieron, como resultado definitivo, la independencia y el establecimiento en república de Cuba, 1892–1902* (Havana: Rambla, Bouza y Ca., 1918), pp. 169–173. Some of the manuscript election returns are held in the Cuban National Archives. Those for the Barrio of Arimao, for example, are in "Elecciones para delegados a la Convención Constituyente Verificadas el 15 de Septiembre de 1900," libro 1110, inv. 1, leg. 299, Fondo Secretaría de Estado y Gobernación, ANC.

40. See Cuba, Convención Constituyente, 1900–1901, *Diario de Sesiones de la Convención Constituyente de la Isla de Cuba* (Havana, 1901). The Fifteenth Amendment to the U.S. Constitution is framed as a prohibition on specified abridgments of the right to vote, not as an affirmative right to vote.

41. For an example of such a document, see the discharge papers of Jesús Pérez, in sig. núm 1, caja 124, Fondo Secretaría de la Presidencia, ANC. For the phrase "right to have rights," see Abdelmalek Sayad, *La double absence: Des illusions de l'émigré aux souffrances de l'immigré* (Paris: Éditions du Seuil, 1999), p. 324. It echoes concepts developed in Hannah Arendt, *The Origins of Totalitarianism* (New York: Harcourt, Brace and World, 1966), pp. 296–297.

42. See Ada Ferrer, "Rustic Men, Civilized Nation: Race, Culture, and Contention on the Eve of Cuban Independence," *Hispanic American Historical Review* 78 (November 1998): 663–686; and Orlando García Martínez, "La Brigada de Cienfuegos: Un análisis social de su formación," in Martínez Heredia, Scott, and García Martínez, *Espacios, silencios,* pp. 163–192.

43. See Rafael Serra y Montalvo, *Para blancos y negros: Ensayos políticos, sociales y económicos* (Havana: Imprenta "El Score," 1907), especially his writings in the newspaper *La Discusión*. See also Alejandra Bronfman, *Measures of Equality: Social Science, Citizenship, and Race in Cuba, 1902–1940* (Chapel Hill: University of North Carolina Press, 2004), chap. 3.

44. The conspicuous exception, of course, was on the question of women's rights, raised on the floor of the convention by Representative Gener, but quickly buried in procedural discussion. See *Diario de Sesiones,* session of 29 January 1901, pp. 283–285.

45. See the debates and votes in *Diario de Sesiones,* session of 29 January 1901, pp. 272–286.

46. On the earlier revolutionary constitutions, see Julio A. Carreras, *Historia del estado y el derecho en Cuba* (Havana: Ministerio de Educación Superior, 1981).

47. This humiliation, part of the twentieth-century "national narrative" of Cuba, is captured in Pérez, *Cuba between Empires,* chap. 17.

48. Some of the largest central sugar mills in the world were to be found in central Cuba, particularly in the zone of Cienfuegos, including the immense Constancia and the huge Caracas. Cuba, Gobierno Civil de Santa Clara, *Memoria Año 1901* (Villaclara: Imp. El Iris, 1902). For payroll lists, see the volumes of the Fondo Centrales Azucareros de Cienfuegos, AHPC. On exports and the evolution of the sugar industry, see Oscar Zanetti Lecuona, *Los cautivos de la reciprocidad* (Havana: Ministerio de Educación Superior, 1989), chap. 2.

49. See Pablo L. Rousseau and Pablo Díaz de Villegas, *Memoria descriptiva, histórica y biográfica de Cienfuegos y las fiestas del primer centenario de la fundación de esta ciudad* (Havana: Siglo XX, 1920), p. 286, and Iglesias, *Las metáforas del cambio.*

50. See the English- and Spanish-language pages of *La Lucha* (Havana) for 13, 19, 20, and 26 November 1902.

51. *La Lucha,* 28 November 1902.

52. See *La Lucha,* 28 November 1902. See also the telegrams of Baehr to Squiers, 29 and 30 November 1902; and the draft despatch of Squiers to Hays, 2 December 1902, in Despatches from U.S. Ministers to Cuba, RG 59, USNA (available as USNA Microfilm Publication T158, roll 4).

53. See *El Imparcial* (Cienfuegos), 29 November, 1 December, 5 December 1902.

54. On Cruces and Lajas, see Rebecca J. Scott and Michael Zeuske, "Property in Writing, Property on the Ground: Pigs, Horses, Land, and Citizenship in the Aftermath of Slavery, Cuba, 1880–1909," *Comparative Studies in Society and History* 44 (October 2002): 669–699; and John Dumoulin, "El primer desarrollo del movimiento obrero y la formación del proletariado en el sector azucarero: Cruces 1886–1902," *Islas: Revista de la Universidad de las Villas* 48 (May–August 1974): 3–66.

55. On anarchism in the late colony, see Joan Casanovas, *Bread, or Bullets! Urban Labor and Spanish Colonialism in Cuba, 1850–1898* (Pittsburgh: University of Pittsburgh Press, 1998), especially chap. 8.

56. Quoted in Dumoulin, "El primer desarrollo," pp. 15–16. For a witty portrait of the

crew of vegetarian anarchists associated with the Havana newspaper *Tierra!* see Carlos Loveira, *De los 26 a los 35 (Lecciones de la experiencia en la lucha obrera)* (Washington, D.C.: Law Reporter Printing Company, 1917), pp. 78–83.

57. See Dumoulin, "El primer desarrollo" and entry 470 of the 1907 voter registration list for Barrio Centro, Santa Isabel de las Lajas, in exp. 14590, leg. 265, Fondo Secretaría de Estado y Gobernación, ANC. The electoral register designates Landa as black and able to read and write; other sources describe him as *mulato*.

58. For the names of members, see *El Imparcial* (Cienfuegos), 1 December 1902. For a list of plantations and their owners, see Gobierno Civil de Santa Clara, *Memoria Año 1901*. The telegram is reproduced in Dumoulin, "El primer desarrollo," p. 21.

59. On José Miguel Gómez, see Dumoulin, "El primer desarrollo." For the draft despatch, see Squiers to Hay, 2 December 1902, in Despatches from U.S. Ministers to Cuba, RG 59, USNA (available as T158, roll 4). Squiers seems to have thought better of this blunt statement, and pencilled "omit" over the last phrase.

60. See Angel C. Betancourt, *Código Penal* (Havana: Rambla, Bouza, y Ca., 1922), Article 567.

61. *El Imparcial* (Cienfuegos), 2, 3, 5 December 1902. Local activists later referred to the danger for workers in the cane of being thus *ausentados* (disappeared). Throughout 1903 anarchists organized protests against the killings. See Dumoulin, "El primer desarrollo," pp. 22–27, 40.

62. *El Imparcial* (Cienfuegos), 5 December 1902.

63. See Dumoulin, "El primer desarrollo," pp. 18–20, 39–40.

64. Dumoulin, "El primer desarrollo." On the composition of the Rural Guard in later years, see Edwin F. Atkins to General Leonard Wood, War Department, 22 May 1912, in vol. 38, series II, AFP, MHS. By 1912 Atkins believed that in his area of Santa Clara, "nearly half the force is composed of negroes."

65. See Fernando Martínez Heredia, "Nationalism, Races, and Classes," also published in somewhat different form as "Nacionalismo, Razas y Clases en la Revolución del 95 y la Primera República Cubana," in Olga Portuondo Zúñiga and Michael Zeuske, eds., *Ciudadanos en la nación* (Santiago de Cuba: Oficina del Conservador de la Ciudad and Fritz Thyssen Stiftung, 2002), pp. 118–147.

66. See *El Imparcial* (Cienfuegos), December, 1902; and Manuel Moreno Fraginals, *El ingenio: Complejo económico social cubano del azúcar,* 3 vols. (Havana: Editorial de Ciencias Sociales, 1978), 3:38, 61.

67. See Michael Zeuske, "Clientelas regionales, alianzas interraciales y poder nacional en torno a la 'Guerrita de Agosto,'" *Illes i Imperis: Estudis d'història de les societats en el món colonial i post-colonial* (Barcelona) 2 (Spring 1999): 127–156; and de la Fuente, *A Nation for All,* pp. 60–63.

68. This description draws on Louis A. Pérez, Jr., *Cuba under the Platt Amendment, 1902–1934* (Pittsburgh: University of Pittsburgh Press, 1986), pp. 91–95.

69. The notion of 1906 as a carnivalesque reenactment of 1895 comes from Zeuske, "Clientelas," building on the work of Jorge Ibarra.

70. See Pérez, *Cuba under the Platt Amendment,* chap. 4.

71. On the second occupation in the countryside, see Rebecca J. Scott, " 'The Lower Class of Whites' and 'the Negro Element': Race, Social Identity, and Politics in Central Cuba, 1899–1909," in Consuelo Naranjo Orovio, Miguel Ángel Puig-Samper, and Luis Miguel García Mora, eds., *La nación soñada: Cuba, Puerto Rico y Filipinas ante el 98* (Aranjuez: Doce Calles, 1995).

72. The electoral lists were printed. See, for example, the *Lista Electoral* in exp. 14476, leg. 261, Fondo Secretaría de Estado y Gobernación, ANC.

8. The Search for Property and Standing

Epigraph: González was protesting the exclusion of men of color from preparations for the Conferencias Nacionales de Beneficencia y Corrección (National Conferences on Charity and Correction). A copy of the handbill is in item 150, file 58, Correspondence, Military Information Division, Army of Cuban Pacification, entry 1008, Record Group 395, U.S. National Archives, Washington, D.C.

1. The original notarized copy of José Quesada's will is "Testamento," 1870, escr. 338, Notario Verdaguer, PN, AHPC. For the names of Quesada's slaves, see "Registro de Esclavos de la Isla de Cuba (Rural). Jurisdicción de Cienfuegos. Pueblo de Cumanayagua," in exp. 157, CMJL, CC, BNC. Our window into the 1906–1907 rediscovery of Article 11 is a subsequent case titled "Martín e Isidora Cabrera de Ávila, contra Cándida Blanco Ramos, Manuel García Blanco, Cándida García Blanco, Socorro García Blanco de Teijero, María García Blanco de Soto, como herederos de Manuel Blanco Ramos . . . ," in leg. 459, Secretaría a Cargo de Rafael Roses y Hernández, Civil, Juzgado de Primera Instancia de Cienfuegos, 1927, AHPC. The summary of the 1907 case is transcribed on folios 118–129. I shall refer to this set of folios, which includes the sentence, the pleadings, and the decision of the appeals court, as "Demanda, Andrea Quesada," 12 April 1907, in "Demanda, Martín e Isidora Cabrera," 1927, AHPC.

2. See the documents concerning the inheritance in exp. 34, and the file "Cédulas de patrocinado, 10 de marzo de 1883, Alcaldía del barrio de Arimao," exp. 158, both in CMJL, CC, BNC. Edwin Atkins's memoir also discusses, in somewhat garbled form, the Quesada will. Edwin F. Atkins, *Sixty Years in Cuba: Reminiscences of Edwin F. Atkins* (1926; reprint, New York: Arno Press, 1980), pp. 59–60. The records of freedom are in "Libro No. 1 de los negros, Santa Rosalía," AHPC. Some immigrant workers may have been kinsmen of Blanco's from the Canary Islands; others were from Spain itself. See, for example, the 1891–92 entries for José Gómez Teijero and José Ferreira Fernández, on folios 158 and 159 of "Libro Mayor No. 3 perteneciente al Ingenio Sta Rosalía propiedad de Dn Manuel Blanco y Ramos," AHPC.

3. On the torching of cane, see José Villares to Manuel Blanco, 27 February 1898, in exp. 9A, CMJL, CC, BNC. On the difficult postwar relations with employees, see the 1899 exchanges between the adminstrator, Constantino Pérez, and Blanco's representative, Manuel García Blanco, in CSR, CP, OGM, especially the letters

from Pérez on 9 July, 7 August, 19 August, 23 August, 5 September, and 27 December 1899.

4. "Demanda, Andrea Quesada, 12 April 1907," in "Demanda, Martín e Isidora Cabrera," 1927, AHPC. I infer Blanco's personality from the legal record and from the Atkins memoir. Atkins, *Sixty Years,* p. 60.

5. See "Poder," 23 May 1906, esc. 120, Notario Felipe Silva Gil, PN, APC; and "Demanda, Andrea Quesada, 12 April 1907," in "Demanda, Martín e Isidora Cabrera," 1927, AHPC.

6. Caridad Quesada, now in her eighties, recalls that Andrea Quesada was said to be a strong-minded woman to whom other parents would send children for disciplining when they could not control them. Interview with Caridad Quesada, Cienfuegos, 2001. The 1885 episode is discussed in Chapter 4 above. The overseer's letter of resignation is [P.?] García to Manuel Blanco, 15 March 1885, in exp. 9A, CMJL, CC, BNC. ". . . yo le pido á U. me relevo pues yo no he venido á esta Finca para estar sapateado por negras y de semejante clase menos. . . ." The phrase "estar sapateado" is somewhat ambiguous, indicating something between a literal kicking and a more metaphorical "being kicked around."

7. "Demanda, Andrea Quesada, 12 April 1907," in "Demanda, Martín e Isidora Cabrera," 1927, AHPC.

8. Ibid.

9. Folio 119, "Demanda, Andrea Quesada," 12 April 1907, in "Demanda, Martín e Isidora Cabrera," 1927, AHPC.

10. See "Poder," 22 May 1906, esc. 120; "Poder para pleitos," 26 July 1906, esc. 174; and "Poder para pleitos," 31 July 1906, esc. 184, all in Notario Felipe Silva y Gil, PN, AHPC.

11. The use of "sin otro apellido" is discussed in Michael Zeuske, "Hidden Markers, Open Secrets: On Naming, Race-Marking, and Race-Making in Cuba," *New West Indian Guide* 76 (2002): 211–241. See "Poder general," 28 May 1906, esc. 122, and "Poder para pleitos," 2 August 1906, esc. 174, both in Notario Pedro Fuxá y Seuret, PN, AHPC.

12. Interviews with Caridad Quesada, Cienfuegos, 1999 and 2000; with Marcelino Iznaga Suárez Román, 2002.

13. For a discussion of Asunción Quesada's remark and the dynamics of postwar relations on Santa Rosalía, see Rebecca J. Scott, "Reclaiming Gregoria's Mule: The Meanings of Freedom in the Arimao and Caunao Valleys, Cienfuegos, Cuba, 1880–1899," *Past and Present* 170 (February 2001): 181–216.

14. On similar phenomena in Europe, see Armando Petrucci, "Escribir para otros," in Petrucci, *Alfabetismo, escritura, sociedad* (Barcelona: Gedisa, 1999), pp. 105–116. Petrucci uses the term "afín-popular," emphasizing popular-group membership, to describe figures who are closely linked to those for whom they serve as delegated writers.

15. On clientelism, see Michael Zeuske, " 'Los negros hicimos la independencia': aspectos de la movilización afrocubana en un hinterland cubano. Cienfuegos entre

colonia y República," in Fernando Martínez Heredia, Rebecca J. Scott, and Orlando García Martínez, eds., *Espacios, silencios y los sentidos de la libertad: Cuba entre 1878 y 1912* (Havana: Editorial Unión, 2000), pp. 193–234.

16. Mariano Averoff Puron, *Los primeros partidos políticos* (Havana: Instituto Cubano del Libro, 1971), pp. 38, 57–58.

17. "Demanda, Andrea Quesada," 12 April 1907, in "Demanda, Martín e Isidora Cabrera," 1927, AHPC.

18. Interviews with Marcelino Iznaga Suárez Román, Vaquería (Pepito Tey), Cienfuegos, 2001 and 2002.

19. Folios 126–129, "Demanda, Andrea Quesada, 12 April 1907," in "Demanda, Martín e Isidora Cabrera," 1927, AHPC.

20. In 1997, I interviewed a white former employee on the Santa Rosalía plantation. The old planter José Quesada, he said, had meant to leave all of the land on the plantation to his slaves, but Manuel Blanco had cheated them out of it. When, in 2001, archivist Orlando García Martínez discovered the record of Andrea Quesada's lawsuit, the origins of these lingering stories became clearer. Interview with Sebastián Asla Cires, Rancho Luna, Cienfuegos, 1997.

21. On the occupation, see Louis A. Pérez, Jr., *Cuba under the Platt Amendment, 1902–1934* (Pittsburgh: University of Pittsburgh Press, 1986), pp. 94–107. The correspondence files of the Military Information Division of the U.S. Army of Cuban Pacification for the province of Santa Clara are in entry 1008, RG 395, USNA.

22. See Rebecca Scott, " 'The Lower Class of Whites' and 'the Negro Element': Race, Social Identity, and Politics in Central Cuba, 1899–1909," in Consuelo Naranjo Orovio, Miguel Ángel Puig-Samper, and Luis Miguel García Mora, eds., *La nación soñada: Cuba, Puerto Rico y Filipinas ante el 98* (Aranjuez, Spain: Ediciones Doce Calles, 1996) pp. 179–191. See also Enid Lynette Logan, "Conspirators, Pawns, Patriots and Brothers: Race and Politics in Western Cuba, 1906–1909," *Political Power and Social Theory* 14 (2000): 3–51.

23. Cuban citizens of electoral age included roughly 260,000 white men born in Cuba, 138,000 men of color, and 31,000 white men born in Spain. The census takers grouped under the rubric *de color* those whom they categorized as *negros, mestizos,* and of the *razas amarillas* (yellow races). See Cuba, Oficina del Censo, *Censo de la República de Cuba bajo la Adminstración Provisional de los Estados Unidos, 1907* (Washington, D.C.: U.S. Census Office, 1908), p. 233.

24. "Report No. 15. Confidential. W. D. Beach," 23 August 1907, item 12, file 88, Correspondence, MID, ACP, entry 1008, RG 395, USNA. For the flavor of these evaluations, see "Report no. 245," on Pedro Valdés Fuentes, of Sagua la Grande, item 299, file 37, MID, ACP, entry 1008, RG 395, USNA: "Mulatto. Liberal-National. Redactor jefe del Periódico 'La Protesta.' About thirty-three years old. Served during war of '95–'98 with grade of Captain; joined the government forces '96 ['06?] having grade of Major. This man is never satisfied unless he is talking politics, a red hot Liberal and opposed to American occupancy of Cuba. Takes prominent part in all political gatherings and is a staunch supporter of General Robau. He enjoys the

reputation here as being a grafter of the first class. Believe he would do his best to stir up trouble should he have the slightest excuse for same."

25. See the article "A mis amigos," in *El Nuevo Criollo,* 30 September 1905, as excerpted in Tomás Fernández Robaina, *El negro en Cuba, 1902–1958: Apuntes para la historia de la lucha contra la discriminación racial* (Havana: Editorial de Ciencias Sociales, 1990), pp. 52–53. On Estenoz's earlier activism, see Lillian Guerra, "From Revolution to Involution in the Early Cuban Republic: Conflicts over Race, Class, and Nation, 1902–1906," in Nancy P. Appelbaum, Anne S. Macpherson, and Karin Alejandra Rosemblatt, eds., *Race and Nation in Modern Latin America* (Chapel Hill: University of North Carolina Press, 2003), p. 143; and Thomas T. Orum, "The Politics of Color: The Racial Dimension of Cuba Politics during the Early Republican Years, 1900–1912" (Ph.D. diss., New York University, 1975), chap. 4.

26. See "Report of W. D. Beach, Major 15th Cavalry," 5 April 1907, and enclosure, in item 150, file 58, Correspondence, MID, ACP, entry 1008, RG 395, USNA.

27. Item 150, file 58, Correspondence, MID, ACP, entry 1008, RG 395, USNA.

28. See Fernández, *El negro,* pp. 55–56.

29. "Confidential Report No. 15, W. D. Beach," 16 September 1907, item 16, file 88, Correspondence, MID, ACP, entry 1008, RG 395, USNA.

30. Fernández, *El negro,* pp. 60–62. Serafín Portuondo Linares, *Los independientes de color: Historia del Partido Independiente de Color* (1950; reprint, Havana: Editorial Caminos, 2002), p. 136.

31. Fernández, *El negro,* pp. 62–67.

32. "Confidential Report no. 11," 2 May 1907, Cienfuegos, item 244, file 58, Correspondence, MID, ACP, entry 1008, RG 395, USNA.

33. Information on this tract is recorded in "Venta de finca rústica y promesa de venta de otras," 22 November 1901, esc. 1035, Protocolo Fernández Pellón, PN, AHPC. For the history of this settlement, see Chapter 6, above, and Rebecca J. Scott and Michael Zeuske, "Property in Writing, Property on the Ground: Pigs, Horses, Land, and Citizenship in the Aftermath of Slavery, Cuba, 1880–1909," *Comparative Studies in Society and History* 44 (October 2002): 669–699. On cane suppliers and laborers, see fols. 174, 176, and 178 of "Soledad Sugar Co. Diario de Operaciones, 1908–09," and the 1906–1911 payrolls from Belmonte, both in Fondo Centrales Azucareros de Cienfuegos, AHPC.

34. See "Cesión de derechos y acciones," 17 September 1913, esc. 366, vol. 4, Protocolos Dr. Antonio J. Font, PN, AHPC. In this document Señor Teodoro Quesada *sin segundo apellido* cedes to his brother Señor Amelio Quesada his proportional rights over the rural plot measuring one-half *caballería* called La Sierra, as well as eleven other pieces of land in the hamlet of the same name, all of which have been inherited from their mother, Gregoria Quesada. In return, Teodoro Quesada receives 75 pesos in gold. Amelio Quesada specifies that he is receiving these lands as equal partner with his siblings Doña Juana and Don Manuel Quesada, the first living in Santiago and the second in Abreus, who have contributed to the purchase price. Neither party to the contract is able to sign his name.

330 Notes to Pages 228–232

35. Gabriel Quesada appears on the 1900 electoral list for the Barrio de Aduana, published in *Suplemento al Boletín Oficial,* in leg. 1343, Fondo Secretaría de Estado y Gobernación, ANC; and as voter number 986 in Barrio de Aduana in *Lista electoral. Municipio de Cienfuegos. Provincia de Santa Clara. Censo de Septiembre 30 de 1907,* in exp. 14476, leg. 261, Fondo Secretaría de Estado y Gobernación, ANC. The other Quesadas listed are also from the Barrio de Aduana.

36. A report for the U.S. Army includes Gabriel Quesada's name on a list of "negros of this vicinity . . . considered to be very bad agitators and citizens." See the "Report of 23 September 1907" by the Intelligence Officer with the 15th Cavalry, item 147, file 79, Correspondence, MID, ACP, entry 1008, RG 395, USNA.

37. On the responses of the various national parties to the Agrupación, see Jorge Ibarra, *Cuba: 1898–1921. Partidos políticos y clases sociales* (Havana: Editorial de Ciencias Sociales, 1992), pp. 319–330.

38. Alejandro de la Fuente, *A Nation for All: Race, Inequality, and Politics in Twentieth-Century Cuba* (Chapel Hill: University of North Carolina Press, 2001), p. 66.

39. The key text is Rafael Serra y Montalvo, *Para blancos y negros: Ensayos políticos, sociales y económicos* (Havana: Imprenta "El Score," 1907). The classic appreciation is Pedro Deschamps Chapeaux, *Rafael Serra y Montalvo, obrero incansable de nuestra independencia* (Havana: UNEAC, 1975). See also Alejandra Bronfman, *Measures of Equality: Social Science, Citizenship, and Race in Cuba, 1902–1940* (Chapel Hill: University of North Carolina Press, 2004), chap. 3. Serra died before the Partido Independiente de Color moved to armed protest.

40. The papers of Juan Gualberto Gómez, with their massive files of letters from local activists, convey something of the breadth of his appeal. See Fondo Adquisiciones, ANC. On the idea of the "aspiring classes," see Michele Mitchell, " 'The Black Man's Burden': African Americans, Imperialism, and Notions of Racial Manhood, 1890–1910," *International Review of Social History* 44, supp. (1999): 77–99; and Mitchell, *Righteous Propagation: African Americans and the Politics of Racial Destiny after Reconstruction* (Chapel Hill: University of North Carolina Press, 2004), chap. 2.

41. See Fernando Martínez Heredia, "Ricardo Batrell Empuña la Pluma," in Martínez, Scott, and García, *Espacios, silencios,* pp. 295–313.

42. The distinction between racial equality as myth and as ideal is explored in Ada Ferrer, *Insurgent Cuba: Race, Nation, and Revolution, 1868–1898* (Chapel Hill: University of North Carolina Press, 1999) and de la Fuente, *A Nation for All.* Gabriel Quesada's letter is in "Cartas dirigidas a Juan Gualberto Gómez por Gabriel Quesada fechadas en Cienfuegos a 30 diciembre 1893, 6 febrero 1908, 5 junio 1922," exp. 3103, caja 40, Fondo Adquisiciones, ANC.

43. See Pablo L. Rousseau and Pablo Díaz de Villegas, *Memoria descriptiva, histórica y biográfica de Cienfuegos y las fiestas del primer centenario de la fundación de esta ciudad* (Havana: Siglo XX, 1920), pp. 315–321.

44. For Ivonet's February 1910 proposal to Gómez, see Michael Zeuske, *Insel der Extreme: Kuba im 20. Jahrhundert* (Zurich: Rotpunktverlag, 2000), pp. 39–40, 188n57.

45. Analyses of *Previsión* appear in Aline Helg, *Our Rightful Share: The Afro-Cuban Struggle*

for Equality, 1886–1912 (Chapel Hill: University of North Carolina Press, 1995), pp. 146–156, and Fernández, *El negro,* pp. 63–81.

46. Aline Helg quotes these numbers, expresses appropriate reservations, and then suggests that they nonetheless show that the party was "growing steadily" and able to count between 10,000 and 20,000 of what she refers to as "potential supporters." She cites documents from the evidence submitted during the legal prosecution of the party in 1910, but does not indicate how these could independently support estimates on the order of 10,000 and 20,000. It is difficult to see how, absent sources other than the party newspaper and statements attributed to its leaders, such figures could be made convincing to a skeptic. Helg, *Our Rightful Share,* pp. 155–156, 290nn64–66. Serafín Portuondo Linares enumerates 23, not 53, committees in Santa Clara, and 98 in the country as a whole. Portuondo Linares, *Los independientes de color,* pp. 25–28.

47. Quoted and analyzed in Portuondo Linares, *Los independientes de color,* pp. 31–33.

48. See Helg, *Our Rightful Share,* pp. 40–41, on Morúa's rivalry with Juan Gualberto Gómez in the 1890s, and pp. 165–167 on Morúa's proposed amendment. The amendment was passed by the Senate on 14 February 1910, and then passed by the House and signed by the president in May of 1910. The final text was "No se considerarán como partidos políticos o grupos independientes, a los efectos de esta Ley, a las agrupaciones constituidas exclusivamente por individuos de una sola raza o color, que persigan fines racistas." Portuondo Linares, *Los independientes de color,* p. 85.

49. On Hermenegildo Portuondo Río, see Fernando Martínez Heredia, prologue to the reprint edition of Portuondo Linares, *Los independientes de color,* pp. vii–xxiii.

50. On the response to Estenoz in different districts, see the correspondence gathered in leg. 1790, Fondo Gobierno Provincial, AHPSdeC.

51. In 1899 Demetrio Castillo, the newly named civil governor of the province, cited the U.S. General Order no. 3 of 1898, which permitted land claims, and placed a time limit on claims brought under it. *Boletín Oficial del Departamento de Santiago de Cuba,* 15 March 1899.

52. This framing of the dilemma owes much to Sidney W. Mintz, *Caribbean Transformations* (Chicago: Aldine, 1974), and to Thomas C. Holt, *The Problem of Freedom: Race, Labor, and Politics in Jamaica and Britain* (Baltimore: Johns Hopkins University Press, 1992). On the expansion of commercial agriculture in Oriente, see Louis A. Pérez, Jr., "Politics, Peasants, and People of Color: The 1912 'Race War' in Cuba Reconsidered," *Hispanic American Historical Review* 66 (August 1986): 509–539.

53. Alan Dye, *Cuban Sugar in the Age of Mass Production: Technology and the Economics of the Sugar Central, 1899–1929* (Stanford, Calif.: Stanford University Press, 1998), pp. 14–19, highlights the contrast between central Cuba and eastern Cuba. An analysis of Oriente that emphasizes dispossession is Pérez, "Politics, Peasants, and People of Color."

54. See *Censo de la República de Cuba, 1907,* pp. 316–317, 358. The category "white men born in other countries" included 319 men of electoral age.

55. On the 1908 elections, see Orum, "The Politics of Color," chaps. 6 and 7; and de la Fuente, *A Nation for All,* p. 65. Serra was affiliated with the Conservative Party. On Lino D'Ou, whom Nicolás Guillén characterized as electorally a Conservative, but affectively a Liberal, see *Papeles del Tte. Coronel Lino D'Ou* (Havana: Cuadernos de la Revista Unión, Unión de Escritores y Artistas de Cuba, 1977).

56. See leg. 1790, Fondo Gobierno Provincial, AHPSdeC; and María de los Ángeles Meriño Fuentes, *Gobierno municipal y partidos políticos en Santiago de Cuba (1898–1912)* (Santiago de Cuba: Ediciones Santiago, 2001).

57. These exchanges are documented in exp. 2, leg. 1790, Fondo Gobierno Provincial, AHPSdeC.

58. See exp. 3, leg. 1790, Fondo Gobierno Provincial, AHPSdeC.

59. Fernández, *El negro,* pp. 71–72, 198.

60. "Causa seguida . . . contra Abdón Raspall, Rafael Zayas. . . . (Comisión del Partido Independiente de Color) [1910]," exp. 12, leg. 6, Audiencia de Santiago de Cuba [1959], ANC.

61. Helg, *Our Rightful Share,* pp. 170–171, portrays the tendency of other groups to dissociate from the Independent Party of Color as evidence of their unwillingness to "confront racism." Portuondo Linares, *Los independientes de color,* pp. 53–107, traces the events of 1910 in detail.

62. See Portuondo Linares, *Los independientes de color,* chap. 18. Portuondo argues that Estenoz himself opposed the decision to undertake an armed protest.

63. See Portuondo Linares, *Los independientes de color,* p. 150; and telegram, [Pastor] Alech, Alcalde Municipal to Provincial Governor, 10:10 P.M., 19 May [1912], in exp. 4, leg. 1790, Fondo Gobierno Provincial, AHPSdeC.

64. See telegram, Alech, Alcalde Municipal to Provincial Governor, 10:30 P.M., 20 May 1912, in exp. 4, leg. 1790, Fondo Gobierno Provincial, AHPSdeC; and Portuondo Linares, *Los independientes de color,* p. 151.

65. See *La Correspondencia* (Cienfuegos), 21 May 1912.

66. Telegram, Alech to the Provincial Governor, 23 May 1912, in exp. 4, leg. 1790, Fondo Gobierno Provincial, AHPSdeC.

67. See telegram, Alech to the Provincial Governor, 23 May 1912, in exp. 4, leg. 1790, Fondo Gobierno Provincial, AHPSdeC.

68. On the president's statements and actions, see the narrative in Helg, *Our Rightful Share,* pp. 203–205, and the coverage in *La Correspondencia* (Cienfuegos), during late May of 1912. On rumors of landings of U.S. troops, see telegram, Provincial Governor to Alcalde, San Luis, 11 June 1912, in exp. 4, leg. 1790, Fondo Gobierno Provincial, AHPSdeC. See also Portuondo Linares, *Los independientes de color,* p. 152.

69. See, for example, "Blancos Conspiradores," in *La Correspondencia,* 30 May 1912.

70. See *El Cubano Libre* (Santiago de Cuba), Edición extraordinario, 27 May 1912. For early statements by Conservatives in support of the Partido Independiente de Color (PIC), see Gobernador Santiago de Cuba to Secretario Gobernación, 21 May 1912, exp. 6, leg. 1790, Fondo Gobierno Provincial, AHPSdeC.

71. This analysis of the 626 volunteers was carried out by the late José Ramón Miyares Puig in an unpublished essay titled "Approximación a un estudio del alzamiento de

los Independientes de Color en Santiago de Cuba (Mayo–Julio de 1912)," copy in possession of María de los Ángeles Meriño, and cited with her permission. Miyares notes that at least 44 members of the volunteers had served in the Liberation Army, and 16 in the Spanish Army.

72. On Miró Argenter, see *La Correspondencia* (Cienfuegos), 25 May 1912. Cebreco's role was debated and disputed in the pages of *El Mundo* in late May and early June 1912.

73. For a vivid account reflecting this conviction, see Horacio Ferrer, *Con el rifle al hombro* (Havana: Imp. "El Siglo XX," 1950).

74. Complex conspiracy theories also flourished, according to which other actors (José Miguel Gómez, according to some) had led the PIC into a trap. These theories seem to reflect a general incredulity that so much killing could have resulted simply from a protest organized by the PIC. For family memories of the killings, see Daisy Rubiera Castillo, *Reyita, sencillamente (Testimonio de una negra cubana nonagenaria)* (Havana: Instituto Cubano de Libro, 1997), pp. 47–49.

75. Aline Helg assesses some of the attempts to estimate the casualties in *Our Rightful Share*, pp. 225, 311n187. She also provides a description of the stories that circulated about the actions of the army. Orum uses U.S. sources systematically in "The Politics of Color," as does Pérez in "Politics, Peasants, and People of Color." A full analysis of the movement and of the magnitude of the repression itself, however, will need to be built on research in local archives and in oral history. This task has been begun by María de los Ángeles Meriño, in "El alzamiento de los Independientes de Color: Una vuelta necesaria a mayo de 1912," ms., 2005, cited with permission of the author, and by historian Julio Corebea, of Cobre. An important recent discussion to emerge from Cuba itself is Martinez Heredia's introduction to the 2002 reprint edition of Portuondo Linares, *Los independientes de color.*

76. Pérez, "Politics, Peasants, and People of Color," emphasizes the social dimension of rebel violence. On repression more generally, see the masterful analysis of the 1938 massacre in the Dominican Republic in Richard Lee Turits, *Foundations of Despotism: Peasants, the Trujillo Regime, and Modernity in Dominican History* (Stanford, Calif.: Stanford University Press, 2003), chap. 5. Cebreco was quoted in an article in *La Discusión,* 14 October 1916.

77. *La Correspondencia* (Cienfuegos), 21, 22, 23, 28 May 1912, 1 June 1912; *El Comercio,* for the same period. See also Alejandra Bronfman, "Mas Allá del Color: Clientelismo y Conflicto en Cienfuegos, 1912," in Martínez, Scott, and García, *Espacios, silencios,* pp. 285–294.

78. The wording of the report suggests that it could have been written with or without evidence: "Los ánimos en este pueblo se encuentran muy excitados, por notarse movmientos sospechosos entre el elemento de color, que hacen suponer que se medita algún golpe de rebelión." *La Correspondencia* (Cienfuegos), 22 May 1912.

79. *La Correspondencia* (Cienfuegos), 22 May 1912.

80. *La Correspondencia* (Cienfuegos), 28, 31 May 1912. *El Comercio,* 23 May 1912, made reference to a Spaniard *(un gallego)* among the rebels. Miguel Barnet, *Biografía de un cimarrón* (Havana: Academic de Ciencias de Cuba, Instituto de Etnología y Folklore,

1966). Barnet has explained that he consciously omitted discussion of 1912 in his biography of Montejo. See Michael Zeuske, "The Real Esteban Montejo?: A Rereading of Miguel Barnet's *Cimarrón*," *New West Indian Guide/Nieuwe West-Indische Gids* 71 (1997): 265–279; and reply by Barnet in the same issue.

81. *La Correspondencia* (Cienfuegos), 3 and 4 June 1912.

82. Bronfman describes the surrender in "Mas Allá del Color," p. 291.

83. See *La Correspondencia* (Cienfuegos), 2 July 1912. On Oriente, see the report of Florentino Más, 20 Jefe de la Policía Gubernativa, that more than 1,500 "personas, negras, de distintas edades" were "reconcentradas" in the town of Cobre. Many had apparently brought food with them when they came in from the countryside. See exp. 12, leg. 1790, Fondo Gobierno Provincial, AHPSdeC.

84. Aline Helg is harsh in her judgment of men of color who endorsed what she sees as "the myth of racial equality." See *Our Rightful Share,* pp. 245–247.

85. On the deaths of Estenoz and Ivonet, see Portuondo Linares, *Los independientes de color,* chap. 26. E. F. Atkins to General Leonard Wood, War Department, 22 May 1912, and E. F. Atkins to Leonard Wood, 7 June 1912, both in vol. 38, ser. II, AFP, MHS.

86. The petition and a later letter from Cebreco appear in *El Mundo,* June 1912. See also Bronfman, *Measures of Equality,* chap. 3; and Portuondo, *Los independientes de color,* pp. 172–174.

87. "Tribuna Libre," *La Correspondencia* (Cienfuegos), 2 July 1912.

88. See the article "Conflicto en Puerta," *La Correspondencia* (Cienfuegos), 19 July 1912. The government stepped in to negotiate.

89. See Portuondo Linares, *Los independientes de color,* chap. 28.

90. On the political aftermath of 1912, see de la Fuente, *A Nation for All,* pp. 82–89, and María de los Ángeles Meriño, "Libertad bajo fianza," in Meriño, "El alzamiento."

91. As late as the 1990s, one black resident of Cienfuegos was reluctant to speak of the events of 1912 when white Cubans were present, but later recalled family stories of an uncle who was arrested after a search of his house turned up PIC literature.

92. See Ricardo Batrell Oviedo, *Para la historia: Apuntes autobiográficos de la vida de Ricardo Batrell Oviedo* (Havana: Seone y Álvarez, 1912). The document is "Promesa de reparación de una casa," 31 October 1912, escr. 233, Notario Domingo Losada, PN, APC.

93. See, for example, Jesús Masdeu, *La raza triste* (Havana: Rambla, Bouza y Ca., 1924); and the writings discussed in Bronfman, *Measures of Equality,* chap. 4.

9. DIVERGING PATHS AND DEGREES OF FREEDOM

1. On Cebreco and Rabí, see Colectivo de autores, *Diccionario Enciclopédico de Historia Militar de Cuba,* vol. 1, *Biografías* (Havana: Ediciones Verde Olivo, 2001), pp. 84–85, 331–332. Aline Helg, *Our Rightful Share: The Afro-Cuban Struggle for Equality, 1886–1912* (Chapel Hill: University of North Carolina Press, 1995), contains information on the careers of Ivonet (spelled in some sources as Ivonnet) and Estenoz.

2. On the movement for amnesty, see the chapter "Libertad bajo fianza," in María de los Ángeles Meriño, "El alzamiento de los Independientes de Color: Una vuelta necesaria a mayo de 1912," ms., cited with permission of the author. On mutual-aid associations, see Alejandra Bronfman, *Measures of Equality: Social Science, Citizenship, and Race in Cuba, 1902–1940* (Chapel Hill: University of North Carolina Press, 2004), chap. 4.

3. See *Memoria de los trabajos presentados al Congreso Nacional Obrero 15 de Marzo de 1915* (Havana: Imprenta y Papelería "La Universal," 1915).

4. See Olga Portuondo Zúniga, *La Virgen de la Caridad del Cobre: Símbolo de cubanía* (Santiago de Cuba: Editorial Oriente, 2001), pp. 244–245. Depictions of the Virgin's skin color range from palest white to brown.

5. See Alejandro de la Fuente, *A Nation for All: Race, Inequality, and Politics in Twentieth-Century Cuba* (Chapel Hill: University of North Carolina Press, 2001), pp. 83–91.

6. On the 1907 census as an electoral list, see Cuba, *Report of Provisional Administration from October 13th, 1906 to December 1st, 1907 by Charles E. Magoon, Provisional Governor* (Havana: Rambla y Bouza, 1908). On the cédulas and a later census, see Cuba, Dirección General del Censo, *Censo de la República de Cuba. Año de 1919* (Havana: Maza, Arroyo y Caso, 1920), pp. 770–772, 798, 940.

7. Yick Wo v. Hopkins 118 U.S. 370 (1886).

8. On these linkages elsewhere in Latin America, see Hilda Sábato, "Citizenship, Political Participation, and the Formation of the Public Sphere in Buenos Aires, 1850s–1880s," *Past and Present* 136 (August 1992): 139–163.

9. "Louisiana Sugar News," in *Louisiana Planter and Sugar Manufacturer,* 9 August 1919, p. 86.

10. U.S. Bureau of the Census, *Thirteenth Census of the United States Taken in the Year 1910,* vol. 6, *Agriculture 1909 and 1910* (Washington, D.C.: Government Printing Office, 1913), pp. 680–681.

11. Ambiguity and change over time in the census categories make it impossible to compare Louisiana with Cuba with any statistical precision, but there is no mistaking the overall contrast. For Cuba, see the printed nominal lists from the 1907 electoral census, which include color and occupation, titled *Lista Electoral . . . Provincia de Santa Clara. Censo de Septiembre 30 de 1907* (Havana: Imprenta y Libreria "La Moderna Poesía," 1907), and found in legs. 261 and 265, in the Fondo Secretaría de Estado y Gobernación, ANC.

12. An excellent overview of this period is Barry Carr, " 'Omnipotent and Omnipresent'?: Labor Shortages, Worker Mobility, and Employer Control in the Cuban Sugar Industry, 1910–1934," in Aviva Chomsky and Aldo Lauria-Santiago, eds., *Identity and Struggle at the Margins of the Nation-State: The Laboring Peoples of Central America and the Hispanic Caribbean* (Durham, N.C.: Duke University Press, 1998), pp. 260–291. On the strike, see *La Correspondencia* (Cienfuegos), 18 July 1912.

13. For recent discussions of the long-debated question of racism and color categories, see Martha Hodes, "The Mercurial Nature and Abiding Power of Race: A Transnational Family Story," *American Historical Review* 108 (February 2003): 84–118; and Robin Sheriff, *Dreaming Equality: Color, Race, and Racism in Urban Brazil* (New Bruns-

wick, N.J.: Rutgers University Press, 2001). Several political scientists have grappled with the structural correlates of divisions by ascribed color. See, most recently, Anthony W. Marx, *Making Race and Nation: A Comparison of South Africa, the United States, and Brazil* (Cambridge: Cambridge University Press, 1998); and Philip A. Klinkner with Rogers M. Smith, *The Unsteady March: The Rise and Decline of Racial Equality in America* (Chicago: University of Chicago Press, 1999).

14. Sidney J. Romero, *"My Fellow Citizens . . .": The Inaugural Addresses of Louisiana's Governors* (Lafayette, La.: Center for Louisiana Studies, University of Southwestern Louisiana, 1980), pp. 245–246. Emphasis added.

15. See David R. Roediger's edition of Covington Hall, *Labor Struggles in the Deep South and Other Writings* (Chicago: Charles H. Kerr Pub., 1999); and David R. Roediger, *Towards the Abolition of Whiteness: Essays on Race, Politics, and Working-Class History* (London: Verso, 1994), pp. 127–180. See also Steven Hahn, *A Nation under Our Feet: Black Political Struggles in the Rural South from Slavery to the Great Migration* (Cambridge, Mass.: Harvard University Press, 2003), especially chap. 9 and the epilogue.

16. See Carr, " 'Omnipotent and Omnipresent'?"; Bronfman, *Measures of Equality;* and de la Fuente, *A Nation for All.*

17. Tomás Pérez y Pérez recalled that the social club at Soledad would allow him to enter, but barred his darker-skinned daughters. He described the scenes as double-edged, because the president of the social club tried to have it both ways, admitting a respected fellow workman who was known to be descended from a former-slave mother, but excluding his family. Interviews with Tomás Pérez y Pérez, 1998 and 1999.

18. Cayetano Quesada's funeral was announced in the local press, and recalled by his daughter Ramona Quesada in interviews in 1998. Faustina Heredia's funeral was described by her grandson, Fernando Martínez Heredia, in conversations in 2000 and 2004.

19. In thinking about politics in the Cuban Republic after World War I, I have been much influenced by conversations with Fernando Martínez Heredia, whose family, from Yaguajay, long supported the Liberal Party. For a vivid portrait of the constrained world of Louisiana sugar plantations, as they began to be pried open by the return of African American veterans from World War II, see the short stories and novels of Ernest Gaines, including *Bloodline* (New York: W. W. Norton, 1976).

20. The cane sugar industry in Louisiana would eventually collapse into a mechanized and subsidized relic without most of its workers' ever having known the most basic rights to collective bargaining. By 1974 only 17,000 workers in Louisiana earned their living on sugar plantations. See Thomas Becnel, *Labor, Church, and the Sugar Establishment: Louisiana, 1887–1976* (Baton Rouge: Louisiana State University Press, 1980), p. 205.

21. Carmouche's life history is discussed in Chapters 6 and 7 above. The 1912 letter is transcribed in Louis R. Harlan and Raymond W. Smock, eds., *The Booker T. Washington Papers,* vol. 13 (Urbana: University of Illinois Press, 1982), pp. 61–64.

22. See, in particular, H. Honora to Mr. V. Ware, Commissioner of Pensions, 16 October 1906, in the pension file of Lafayette Tharp, C-2483201, USNA.
23. See the final volumes of the notarial records of Louis Martinet in NONARC.
24. Interviews with Tomás Pérez y Pérez, his daughter Olga Pérez, and her son Daniel Ponvert, Cienfuegos, 1998 and 1999.
25. *Daily Crusader,* June 1895, in DFC, XU.

Select Bibliography
of Primary Sources

GOVERNMENT DOCUMENTS

Cuba. [Comandancia General de la Provincia de Santiago de Cuba.] *Campaña de Cuba. Recopilación de documentos y órdenes dictadas con motivo del movimiento insurreccional . . . del 26 de Agosto de 1879.* [Santiago de] Cuba: Sección Tipográfica del E. M. de la Comandancia General, 1880.

———— Centro de Estadística. *Noticias estadísticas de la Isla de Cuba, en 1862.* Havana: Imprenta del Gobierno, 1864.

———— Convención Constituyente, 1900–1901. *Diario de Sesiones de la Convención Constituyente de la Isla de Cuba.* Havana, 1901.

———— Dirección General del Censo. *Censo de la República de Cuba. Año de 1919.* Havana: Maza, Arroyo y Caso, 1920.

———— Gobierno Civil de Santa Clara. *Memoria Año 1901.* Villaclara: Imp. El Iris, 1902.

———— Military Governor (John R. Brooke). *Civil Orders, Headquarters Division of Cuba, 1899.* Havana, 1899.

———— Military Governor (John R. Brooke). *Civil Report of Major-General John R. Brooke, U.S. Army, Military Governor, Island of Cuba.* Washington, D.C.: Government Printing Office, 1900.

———— Oficina del Censo. *Censo de la República de Cuba bajo la Administración Provisional de los Estados Unidos, 1907.* Washington, D.C.: U.S. Census Office, 1908.

———— Provisional Governor (C. E. Magoon). *Report of Provisional Administration from October 13th, 1906 to December 1st, 1907 by Charles E. Magoon, Provisional Governor.* Havana: Rambla y Bouza, 1908.

———— Senado. *Mención histórica. Documentación relacionada con los acontecimientos que dieron, como resultado definitivo, la independencia y el establecimiento en república de Cuba 1892–1902.* Havana: Rambla, Bouza y Ca., 1918.

Fuqua, James O., ed. *Civil Code of the State of Louisiana.* New Orleans: B. Bloomfield and Co., 1867.

Louisiana. *Constitution of the State of Louisiana Adopted in Convention at the City of New Orleans the Twenty-Third Day of July, A.D. 1879.* Baton Rouge: The Advocate, 1894.

———— *Official Journal of the Proceedings of the Constitutional Convention of the State of Louisiana, Held in New Orleans, Tuesday, February 8, 1898.* New Orleans: J. J. Hearsey, 1898.

———— *Official Journal of the Proceedings of the Convention for Framing a Constitution for the State of Louisiana.* New Orleans: J. B. Roudanez and Co., 1867–68.

———— *Report of Brigadier-General William Pierce Commanding State Troops in the Field in District from Berwick's Bay to New Orleans to General G. T. Beauregard, Adjutant General of the State of Louisiana, Nov. 28th, 1887.* Baton Rouge: Leon Jastremski, 1887.

———— Adjutant General's Office. *Annual Report[s] of the Adjutant General of the State of Louisiana* [for the years 1871 and 1874]. New Orleans: The Republican, 1872 and 1875.

———— Department of Education. *Annual Report of the State Superintendent of Public Education for 1870.* New Orleans: A. L. Lee, 1871.

———— Department of Education. *Annual Report[s] of the State Superintendent of Public Education* [for the years 1871, 1872, 1873, and 1875]. New Orleans: The Republican, 1872, 1873, 1874, and 1876.

———— Department of State. *Report of the Secretary of State to His Excellency W. W. Heard, Governor of the State of Louisiana, May 12th, 1902.* Baton Rouge: Baton Rouge News Pub. Co., 1902.

———— Legislature. *Acts Passed by the General Assembly of the State of Louisiana at the First Session of the Third Legislature Begun and Held in New Orleans, January 6, 1873.* New Orleans: The Republican, 1873.

———— Legislature. *Journal of the House of Representatives.* [Various years, some published in New Orleans, some in Baton Rouge.]

Spain. Instituto Geográfico y Estadístico. *Censo de la población de España, segun el empadronamiento hecho en 31 diciembre de 1887,* 2 vols. Madrid, 1891–92.

———— Ministerio de Ultramar. *Spanish Rule in Cuba. Laws Governing the Island.* New York, 1896.

United States. Bureau of the Census. *Twelfth Census of the United States Taken in the Year 1900. Census Reports, Agriculture.* Washington, D.C.: U.S. Census Office, 1902–1903.

———— Bureau of the Census. *Thirteenth Census of the United States Taken in the Year 1910.* Vol. 6. *Agriculture 1909 and 1910.* Washington, D.C.: Government Printing Office, 1913.

———— Census Office. *Agriculture of the United States in 1860; Compiled from the Original Returns of the Eighth Census.* Washington, D.C.: Government Printing Office, 1864.

———— Census Office. *Ninth Census of the United States, 1870.* Vol. 1. *The Statistics of the Population of the United States.* Washington, D.C.: U.S. Census Office, 1871.

———— Census Office. *Population of the United States in 1860; Compiled from the Original Returns of the Eighth Census.* Washington, D.C.: Government Printing Office, 1864.

———— Congress. House. "Louisiana Contested Elections." 41st Cong., 2nd sess. [1870] Misc. Doc. 154, pt. 1, pp. 634–642.

———— Congress. House. "Testimony Taken by the Select Committee on the Recent Election in Louisiana." 44th Cong. 2nd sess. [1877]. House Misc. Doc. 34, pt. 5.

———— Congress. Senate. "Qualification of Voters at Coming Elections in Cuba." 56th Cong. 2nd sess. Senate Doc. 243. Ser. 3867. 1900.

———— War Department. *Report on the Census of Cuba, 1899.* Washington, D.C.: Government Printing Office, 1900.

———— War Department. *Reports of Brigadier-General Leonard Wood, U.S.V., on Civil Affairs in the Provinces of Santiago and Puerto Principe, Cuba.* In *Annual Reports of the U.S. War Department,* 1899, vol. 1.

———— War Department. *The War of the Rebellion: A Compilation of the Official Records of the Union and Confederate Armies,* ser. I, vol. 15. Washington, D.C.: Government Printing Office, 1886.

OTHER PRIMARY PRINTED SOURCES

Atkins, Edwin F. *Sixty Years in Cuba: Reminiscences of Edwin F. Atkins.* 1926. Reprint. New York: Arno Press, 1980.

Bacardí y Moreau, Emilio. *Crónicas de Santiago de Cuba.* 2nd ed. Santiago de Cuba: Tipografía Arroyo Hermano, 1924.

Bautista Jiménez, Juan. *Los esclavos blancos, por un colono de Las Villas.* Havana: Imp. de A. Alvarez y Comp., 1893.

Berlin, Ira, Barbara J. Fields, Thavolia Glymph, Joseph P. Reidy, Leslie S. Rowland, eds. *Freedom: A Documentary History of Emancipation.* Ser. I, vol. 1, *The Destruction of Slavery.* Cambridge: Cambridge University Press, 1985.

Berlin, Ira, Thavolia Glymph, Steven F. Miller, Joseph P. Reidy, Leslie S. Rowland, Julie Saville, eds. *Freedom: A Documentary History of Emancipation.* Ser. I, vol. 3, *The Wartime Genesis of Free Labor: The Lower South.* Cambridge: Cambridge University Press, 1990.

Berlin, Ira, Joseph P. Reidy, and Leslie S. Rowland, eds. *Freedom: A Documentary History of Emancipation, 1861–1867.* Ser. II, *The Black Military Experience.* Cambridge: Cambridge University Press, 1982.

Betancourt, Angel C. *Código Penal.* Havana: Rambla, Bouza, y Ca., 1922.

Cantero, Justo. *Los ingenios: Colección de vistas de los principales ingenios de azúcar de la isla de Cuba.* Havana: L. Marquier, 1857.

Castillo, José Rogelio. *Autobiografía del General José Rogelio Castillo.* 1910. Reprint. Havana: Editorial de Ciencias Sociales, 1973.

Champonier, P. A. *Statement of the Sugar Crop Made in Louisiana in 1861–62.* New Orleans: Cook, Young, and Co., 1862.

Clark, Victor. "Labor Conditions in Cuba." *Bulletin of the Department of Labor* 41 (July 1902): 663–793.

Coston, William Hilary. *The Spanish-American War Volunteer.* 1899. Reprint. Freeport, N.Y.: Books for Libraries Press, 1971.

Cuba. Archivo Nacional. *Correspondencia diplomática de la delegación cubana en Nueva York durante la Guerra de Independencia de 1895 a 1898.* Vol. 5. Havana: Archivo Nacional de Cuba, 1946.

———— *Documentos para servir a la historia de la Guerra Chiquita (Archivo Leandro Rodríguez).* Havana: Archivo Nacional de Cuba, 1950.

Desdunes, Rodolphe Lucien. *Nos hommes et notre histoire.* Montreal: Arbour & Dupont, 1911.

Edo y Llop, Enrique. *Memoria histórica de Cienfuegos y su jurisdicción.* 1888. Reprint. Havana: Imprenta Ucar, García y Cía, 1943.

Feuer, A. B. *The Santiago Campaign of 1898: A Soldier's View of the Spanish-American War.* Westport, Conn.: Praeger, 1993.

Fleming, Walter L. *Documentary History of Reconstruction.* Vol. 2. Cleveland: Arthur H. Clark Company, 1907.

Foner, Philip S., and Ronald L. Lewis, eds. *The Black Worker: A Documentary History from Colonial Times to the Present.* Vol. 3. Philadelphia: Temple University Press, 1978.

Fortier, Alcée. *Louisiana: Comprising Sketches of Parishes, Towns, Events, Institutions, and Persons, Arranged in Cyclopedic Form.* Vol. 3. [Madison, Wis.]: Century Historical Association, 1914.

Gatewood, Willard B. *"Smoked Yankees" and the Struggle for Empire: Letters from Negro Soldiers, 1898–1902.* Urbana: University of Illinois Press, 1971.

Goode, W. T. *The "Eighth Illinois."* Chicago: Blakely Printing Company, 1899.

Harlan, Louis R., and Raymond W. Smock, eds., Barbara S. Kraft, asst. ed. *The Booker T. Washington Papers.* Vols. 5, 6, 13. Urbana: University of Illinois Press, 1976, 1977, 1982.

Hall, Covington. *Labor Struggles in the Deep South and Other Writings.* Edited by David Roediger. Chicago: Charles H. Kerr Pub., 1999.

Jiménez, Juan Bautista. *Los esclavos blancos, por un colono de Las Villas.* Havana: Imp. de A. Álvarez y Comp., 1893.

Kernan, Thomas J. "The Constitutional Convention of 1898 and Its Work." *Proceedings of the Louisiana Bar Association, 1898–1899.* New Orleans: Graham Press, 1899.

Laws, J. Bradford. "The Negroes of Cinclare Central Factory and Calumet Plantation, Louisiana." *Bulletin of the Department of Labor* 38 (January 1902): 95–120.

Llorens y Maceo, José S. *Con Maceo en la invasión.* Havana: Duarte y Iriarte, 1928.

Loveira, Carlos. *De los 26 a los 36 (Lecciones de la experiencia en la lucha obrera).* Washington, D.C.: Law Reporter Printing Company, 1917.

Marks, George P., III, ed. *The Black Press Views American Imperialism (1898–1900).* New York: Arno Press, 1971.

Martinet, Louis A. *The Violation of a Constitutional Right. Published by Authority of the Citizens' Committee.* New Orleans: Crusader Print, 1896.

Martínez Ortíz, Rafael. *Cuba: Los primeros años de independencia.* Paris: Editorial "Le Livre Libre," 1929.

Masdeu, Jesús. *La raza triste.* Havana: Rambla, Bouza y Ca., 1924.

Memoria de los trabajos presentados al Congreso Nacional Obrero 15 de Marzo de 1915. Havana: Imprenta y Papelería "La Universal," 1915.

Miró Argenter, José. *Cuba: Crónicas de la guerra. Las campañas de invasión y de Occidente, 1895–96.* 2 vols. 1909. Reprint. Havana: Editorial Lex, 1945.

Northup, Solomon. *Twelve Years a Slave.* Edited by Sue Eakin and Joseph Logsdon. 1853. Reprint. Baton Rouge: Louisiana State University Press, 1968.

Olsen, Otto, ed. *The Thin Disguise: Turning Point in Negro History. Plessy v. Ferguson. A Documentary Presentation (1864–1896).* New York: Humanities Press, 1967.

The Orleans Parish Blue Book. New Orleans: Southern Manufacturer, 1896.

Perkins, A. E. *Who's Who in Colored Louisiana.* Baton Rouge: Douglas Loan Company, 1930.

Porter, Robert P. *Industrial Cuba*. New York: G. P. Putnam's Sons, 1899.

Rebello, Carlos. *Estados relativos a la producción azucarera de la Isla de Cuba*. Havana, 1860.

Reid, Whitelaw. *After the War: A Southern Tour, May 1, 1865, to May 1, 1866*. Cincinnati: Moore, Wilstach and Baldwin, 1866.

Roloff y Mialofsky, Carlos. *Índice alfabético y defunciones del Ejército Libertador de Cuba*. Havana, 1901.

Romero, Sidney J. *"My Fellow Citizens . . .": The Inaugural Addresses of Louisiana's Governors*. Lafayette, La.: Center for Louisiana Studies, University of Southwestern Louisiana, 1980.

Rousseau, Pablo L., and Pablo Díaz de Villegas. *Memoria descriptiva, histórica y biográfica de Cienfuegos y las fiestas del primer centenario de la fundación de esta ciudad*. Havana: El Siglo XX, 1920.

Serra y Montalvo, Rafael. *Para blancos y negros: Ensayos políticos, sociales y económicos*. Havana: Imprenta "El Score," 1907.

Sociedad Cubana de Estudios Históricos y Internacionales. *Antonio Maceo. Ideología política. Cartas y otros documentos*. Havana: Sociedad Cubana de Estudios Históricos y Internacionales, 1950.

Warmoth, Henry Clay. *War, Politics, and Reconstruction: Stormy Days in Louisiana*. New York: Macmillan Company, 1930.

LEGAL CASES

Papers in the Case of Acklen vs. Darrall, Third Congressional District of Louisiana, October 31, 1877. 45th Cong. 1st sess. [1877]. House Misc. Doc. 5.

Giles v. Harris 189 U.S. 475 (1903).

Giles v. Teasley 193 U.S. 146 (1904).

Gusman, A. L. in behalf of Nathan Wright v. L. H. Marrero. Docket no. 12849. General Case Files, entry 121, U.S. Circuit Court, New Orleans, Eastern District of Louisiana. RG 21, USNA-SW Region, Fort Worth, Texas.

Gusman v. Marrero 180 U.S. 81 (1901).

Macarty, Nicolas Theodore & autres, appelants v. Eulalie Mandeville, F.C.L. intimée (1847). Docket no. 626, N.O., 1846–1861, SCC, UNO.

Plessy v. Ferguson 163 U.S. 537 (1896).

Quesada, Andrea. Demanda. 12 April 1907. Partial transcription in Demanda, Martín e Isidora Cabrera de Ávila, contra Cándida Blanco Ramos, Manuel García Blanco, Cándida García Blanco, Socorro García Blanco de Teijero, María García Blanco de Soto, como herederos de Manuel Blanco Ramos. Filed in leg. 459, Secretaría de Rafael Roses y Hernández, Civil, Juzgado de Primera Instancia de Cienfuegos, 1927, AHPC.

Ryanes v. Gleason. Docket no. 65432, Civil District Court. DCR, NOPL.

Ryanes v. Gleason. Docket no. 67606, Civil District Court. DCR, NOPL.

Ryanes v. Gleason. Docket no. 14651, Louisiana Supreme Court. SCC, UNO.

Ryanes v. Gleason, Supervisor 112 La. 612.

State of Louisiana vs. Amos Johnson. Criminal Cases 1887. PLCC.

State of Louisiana v. Peter Young. Criminal Cases 1887. PLCC.

U.S. v. Cruikshank, 92 U.S. 542 (1875).

U.S. v. Private Thomas Bazile, San Luis, 25 November 1898, no. 9317. JAG, RG 153, USNA.
Williams v. Mississippi, 170 U.S. 213 (1898).
Yick Wo v. Hopkins 118 U.S. 370 (1886).

NEWSPAPERS AND OTHER PERIODICALS

Bee (Washington, D.C.)
Boletín Oficial del Departamento de Santiago de Cuba (Santiago de Cuba)
Boletín Oficial de la Provincia de Santa Clara (Santa Clara)
Colored American (Washington, D.C.)
La Correspondencia (Cienfuegos)
Crescent (New Orleans)
Crusader (New Orleans)
Daily Advocate (Baton Rouge)
Gaceta de Madrid
La Igualdad (Havana)
El Imparcial (Cienfuegos)
Journal of United Labor (Philadelphia)
Louisiana Planter and Sugar Manufacturer
La Lucha: Diario Republicano (Havana)
Pelican (New Orleans)
Picayune (New Orleans)
Post (Washington, D.C.)
Progrès et Liberté: Bulletin Indépendant de la Franc-Maçonnerie en Louisiane (New Orleans)
Republican (New Orleans)
Revista económica (Havana)
Southwestern Christian Advocate (New Orleans)
Terrebonne Patriot (Houma, La.)
Terrebonne Republican (Houma, La.)
Terrebonne Times (Houma, La.)
Thibodaux Sentinel / La Sentinelle de Thibodaux (Thibodaux, La.)
Times of Cuba: Diario Independiente y de Información (Santiago de Cuba)
Times Democrat (New Orleans)

ARCHIVES AND MANUSCRIPT COLLECTIONS

Cuba, Spain, and Great Britain
Archivo Histórico Provincial de Cienfuegos, Cienfuegos
    Fondo Ayuntamiento de Lajas
    Protocolos Notariales

Archivo Histórico Provincial de Santiago de Cuba
    Fondo Gobierno Provincial

Archivo Nacional de Cuba, Havana
   Fondo Consejo de Administración
   Fondo Gobierno General
   Fondo Instituto Cubano de Estabilización del Azúcar
   Fondo Miscelánea de Expedientes
   Fondo Miscelánea de Libros

Biblioteca Nacional "José Martí," Havana
   Colección Cubana, Colección Manuscrita Julio Lobo

Personal collection of Orlando García Martínez, Cienfuegos
   Colección Santa Rosalía

Archivo General Militar, Segovia
   Sección de Ultramar

Archivo Histórico Nacional, Madrid
   Sección de Ultramar

British Library, London
   Manuscripts, Layard Papers

United States
Amistad Research Center, Tulane University, New Orleans

Jackson Barracks (New Orleans), Library

Louisiana State Archives, Baton Rouge

Louisiana State University, Hill Memorial Library, Baton Rouge
   Special Collections, Louisiana and Lower Mississippi Valley Collection

Massachusetts Historical Society, Boston
   Adams Family Papers
   Atkins Family Papers

New Orleans Notarial Archives Research Center

New Orleans Public Library
   District Court Records

Parish of Lafourche, Office of the Clerk of the Court, Thibodaux, Louisiana

Parish of Terrebone, Office of the Clerk of the Court, Houma, Louisiana

United States National Archives, Washington, D.C.
   Army of Cuban Pacification, in Record Group 395

United States National Archives (continued)
   Adjutant General's Office, Record Group 94 (War with Spain)
   Records of the Bureau of Refugees, Freedmen, and Abandoned Lands, Record
      Group 105
         Records of the Assistant Commissioner, Louisiana (Microfilm Publication 1027)
      Records of the Judge Advocate General, Record Group 153
      U.S./Spain Treaty Claims, in Record Group 76

University of New Orleans, Earl K. Long Library, Department of Archives and Manu-
   scripts
   Marcus Christian Collection
   Supreme Court of Louisiana Collection

Xavier University, University Library, New Orleans
   Archives and Special Collections, Desdunes Family Collection

Illustration and Map Credits

Acknowledgments

A COMPARATIVE PROJECT OF THIS SORT IS INEVITABLY A GAMBLE. A scholar trained as a historian of one part of the world imagines that it will be possible, in a finite period of time, to move into other areas, acquire the necessary linguistic and bibliographic competence, carry out primary research, and come to reasonable conclusions, all without making a complete fool of herself. Over the past years I have more than once thought that I might suffer the fate normally reserved in Greek tragedy for those who display such hubris.

There is, however, a provisional protection from that fate. It comes in the form of generous colleagues who are themselves specialists on the component regions of the study. Instead of shooing you off their territory, they give advice on sources. And instead of dismissing your outsider's hypotheses, they suggest ways of testing them. Lawrence Powell, Joseph Reidy, and John Rodrigue were just such hosts in the field of Louisiana history, sharing ideas, encouragement, and important unpublished work. While studying Louisiana, I also benefited from the generosity of Ira Berlin, Leslie Rowland, and other members of the Freedmen and Southern Society Project at the University of Maryland; the good advice of Caryn Cossé Bell, Eric Foner, and Harold Woodman; and the encouragement of Ernest and Dianne Gaines. In 1986 Sidney Chalhoub, the late Peter Eisenberg, Peter Fry, Michael Hall, Silvia Lara, Hebe Mattos, Nancy Naro, João José Reis, and Robert Slenes welcomed me into the field of Brazilian history, which in the initial conception of this book was to have constituted a third comparative element. In subsequent years, Sueann Caulfield, Walter Fraga Filho, Keila Grinberg, and Katia Mattoso extended the welcome. In the end, it proved impossible to integrate the Brazilian portion of the project into this book while still keeping the narrative readable and relatively balanced. The ideas developed during the research in

Brazil, however, do inform my overall interpretation, and the Brazilian material will appear elsewhere.

A comparative study also carries the risk that in the eagerness to give each case its due one will inadvertently produce multiple monographs in a single binding, histories juxtaposed but not truly compared. Thomas C. Holt, at crucial moments, warned of this danger and provided comments and criticism that enabled me to develop more explicitly comparative questions. Louis A. Pérez, Jr., would in turn remind me that Cuban history is much more than a "case study." Ed Barber, Sidney Mintz, and Sarah Hirschman urged me to write about people with names and voices, and showed why it was important to do so.

Sylvia Frey, Martha Jones, Mary Niall Mitchell, and Diana and Larry Powell made fieldwork in Louisiana a real pleasure. The staffs of the New Orleans Notarial Archives Research Center, the Tulane University Library, the Louisiana and Lower Mississippi Valley Collection at Louisiana State University, the Archives Division of the Ellender Memorial Library of Nicholls State University, the Louisiana State Archives, the Louisiana State Library, the Louisiana Collection of the New Orleans Public Library, the Xavier University Library, and the Southern Historical Collection at the University of North Carolina were helpful and patient, as were archivists at various branches of the U.S. National Archives, particularly Mitchell Yockelson. Marie Windell of the Louisiana Supreme Court Collection at the Earl K. Long Library, University of New Orleans, was both archivist and guardian angel. The Clerks of the Court of Lafourche and Terrebonne Parishes kindly offered me access to their nineteenth-century records. Leroy Soles generously shared genealogical data and family papers related to Pierre Lacroix Carmouche. Jeffrey Gould shared photocopies from his own research on the 1887 sugar strike in Louisiana.

Within Cuba, numerous historians have provided guidance and advice, foremost among them the other two members of the "Cienfuegos trio": Orlando García Martínez and Michael Zeuske. We embarked in 1996 on a set of adventures in collaborative microhistorical research that would a few years earlier have seemed impossible. I am also grateful to the scholars at the Instituto de Historia in Havana, including the members of the LASA/CEA Working Group on Cuban History and its co-chairs, Oscar Zanetti and Louis A. Pérez, Jr. Over many years, Alejandro de la Fuente, John Dumoulin, Tomás Fernández Robaina, Ada Ferrer, Reinaldo Funes, Gladys Marel García, Alejandro García, Fe Iglesias, Marial Iglesias, Julio LeRiverend, Enrique López, María de los Ángeles Meriño, Olga Montalván, Manuel Moreno Fraginals, Pablo Pacheco, Olga Portuondo, Sixto Valón, and Carlos Venegas have provided valuable suggestions and moral support. Fernando Martínez Heredia and Esther Pérez have accompanied me nearly every step of the way. Eliades Acosta, director of the Biblioteca Nacional "José Martí," shared ideas and granted access to the valuable papers of the Colección Julio Lobo. Under difficult circumstances, Pedro Deschamps Chapeaux courteously received Ada Ferrer and myself in Havana in the summer of 1994. His death a few months later was an immense loss to the community of scholars.

As director of the Archivo Histórico Provincial de Cienfuegos, Orlando García Martínez and his staff often kept the doors open for long hours to accommodate the needs of a researcher pressed for time. In Havana, the director of the Archivo Nacional de Cuba, Dra. Berarda Salabarría, and the staff, including Alberto Arcos, Bárbara Danzie, Diana Ferrer, Jorge Macle, Mayra Mena, Julio López, and others, were generous with their time and effort. As always, the greatest debt of the researcher in that ancient building at the corner of San Isidro and Compostela is to Julio Vargas, the man who best knows the long dark corridors in which the documents are kept. He succeeded in bringing up to the daylight a mass of records from the Ingenio Soledad that were thought nearly unretrievable, opening the way for scholars to complement Edwin Atkins's own account in *Sixty Years in Cuba* with the correspondence and account books of the estate. Peter Drummey and William Fowler, in Boston, then arranged for the cataloguing of the complementary materials in the Atkins Family Papers in the Massachusetts Historical Society. Chester and Corinne Atkins graciously offered time and resources to support the Boston-Cienfuegos reconnection. Some of the results will appear in a pamphlet from the Massachusetts Historical Society.

In a first major research project one characteristically owes an immense debt to one's thesis advisor, and I owed just such a debt to Stanley J. Stein when I was writing *Slave Emancipation in Cuba*. In subsequent projects one owes a comparably large debt to one's own students and colleagues. I thank my fellow co-organizers of the graduate seminars of the University of Michigan Postemancipation Societies Project, Thomas Holt and Frederick Cooper, and the successive groups of students who participated in them, as well as the Center for Afroamerican and African Studies, which provided a home for that project. The volume *Societies after Slavery: A Select Annotated Bibliography of Printed Sources on Cuba, Brazil, British Colonial Africa, South Africa, and the British West Indies* (University of Pittsburgh Press, 2002) reflects the depth and breadth of the work of the project students and faculty.

In gathering and indexing evidence from the National Archives in Washington I enjoyed the collaboration of Kristine Komives and Tim Scarnecchia. Aims McGuinness helped me navigate the parish archives of Louisiana and participated in fieldwork in Cuba in 1998. Evelyn Baltodano, Alejandra Bronfman, Shannon Dawdy, Paul Eiss, Larry Gutman, Sherri Harper, Kathleen López, Rebekah Pite, Alice Ritscherle, and David Sartorius provided insights and assistance as they developed their own research projects. Catherine LeGrand, Michele Mitchell, Robert Paquette, John Shy, and J. Mills Thornton shared leads and references. The staff of the University of Michigan Law Library, particularly Beatrice Tice, Aimée Mangan, and Barbara Snow, were generous with their time and skills.

Portions of this manuscript were drafted while I was at the École des Hautes Études en Sciences Sociales in Paris, where I benefited from the collegiality of a far-flung European community of scholars and writers. I thank in particular Luiz Felipe de Alencastro, Anne-Marie Chartier, Myriam Cottias, Paul Estrade, Afrânio Garcia, Françoise Grard, Jean Hébrard, Sara LeMenestrel, Katia Mattoso, Anne-Marie Pathé, Maria Poumier, Jacques Revel, Jean-Frédéric Schaub, and François Weil in Paris; Astrid Cubano, Josep María Fradera, Albert García, Jordi Maluquer de Motes, and Martin Rodrigo in Barcelona; James Amelang, Luis Miguel García Mora, and Consuelo Naranjo in Madrid; and Alf Lüdtke, Hans Medick, and Michael Zeuske in Germany.

Back in the United States I turned to Louis A. Pérez for comments on large portions of successive drafts, and I have imposed the whole manuscript on Ada Ferrer, Jean Hébrard, Fernando Martínez Heredia, Aims McGuinness, Lawrence Powell, Peter Railton, Anne F. Scott, Joyce Seltzer, and Michael Zeuske. John Rodrigue and a second, anonymous reader for Harvard University Press provided valuable comments. Sections of the text were also read by Caryn Cossé Bell, Sueann Caulfield, Shannon Dawdy, Alejandro de la Fuente, Orlando García Martínez, Thomas Holt, Martha Jones, Ellen Katz, J. Morgan Kousser, Earl Lewis, Sidney Mintz, Richard Pildes, Lara Putnam, Hannah Rosen, Andrew M. Scott, Richard Turits, and Hernán Venegas. I thank all of these readers for their suggestions and their patience. The greatest patience was that shown by Elizabeth Gilbert, manuscript editor extraordinaire.

In 2001, as I was writing what I thought was the end of the manuscript, Dean Jeffrey Lehman welcomed me to the University of Michigan Law School, first as a Sunderland Fellow and then as a joint faculty member. Teaching there, and studying constitutional law, changed my perspective on the intertwined histories of suffrage in Cuba and the United States, expanding and transforming the final chapters of the book. I have benefited in particular from conversations with my Law School colleagues Susanna Blumenthal, Hanoch Dagan, Bruce Frier, Thomas A. Green, Daniel Halberstam, Donald Herzog, Rick Hills, Ellen Katz, William Miller, Sallyanne Payton, Richard Pildes (now of New York University), Richard Primus, Peter Westen, and James Boyd White. At other institutions, Robert Gordon, Hendrik Hartog, Daría Roithmayr, Carol Rose, and John Witt have also provided valuable advice on matters of law and history. I am grateful to the present Dean of the University of Michigan Law School, Evan Caminker, for continuing support.

Financial assistance has come from several sources, including the French and Brazilian Fulbright Programs, the John D. and Catherine T. MacArthur Foundation, the Huetwell and Edman Funds of the College of Literature, Science, and the Arts of the University of Michigan, and the Cook and Wolfson Funds of the University of Michigan Law School. The larger Postemancipation Societies Project of which my work is a part also received support at the University of Michigan from the Center for Afroamerican and African Studies, the International Institute, the Office of the Vice President for Research, the Rackham Graduate School, the Kellogg Foundation through the Presidential Initiatives Fund, the Latin American and Caribbean Studies Program, and the Department of History. I wish to convey particular thanks to Jeanette Diuble, who enabled me to interweave the drafting of portions of this manuscript with the fulfillment of my responsibilities as chair of the Department of History. Remarkably, she was willing to continue her commitment after the end of my term as chair, for which I am enormously grateful. I thank Robert Forget for drawing such splendid maps.

Some of the interpretations in the present book were first developed in preliminary essays. For permission to draw on these essays in revised form, I thank Duke University Press for material from "Race, Labor and Citizenship in Cuba: A View from the Sugar District of Cienfuegos, 1886–1909," *Hispanic American Historical Review* 78 (1998): 687–728; the Past and Present Society for material from "Reclaiming Gregoria's Mule: The Meanings of Freedom in the Arimao and Caunao Valleys, Cienfuegos, Cuba, 1880–1899," *Past and Present* 170 (February 2001): 181–216; and the University of North Carolina Press for material from Frederick Cooper, Thomas C. Holt, and Rebecca J. Scott, *Beyond Slavery: Explorations of Race, Labor and Citizenship in Postemancipation Societies,* published in 2000.

I can only hope that Peter Railton, Arthur Railton, Anne Scott, and Andrew Scott realize just how much I have learned from them over the years. Along with the late Marjorie Railton, they have shown limitless patience and affection, and I thank them warmly. I would also like to thank my sons John and Thomas Scott-Railton for their good cheer, good ideas, and good company.

This book is dedicated to the memory of Tomás Pérez y Pérez. He was ninety-six years old when we began our conversations about land and labor in rural Cuba, during which he recalled work routines, baseball games, political showdowns, and personal crises. Equally important, he recounted the life history of his mother, Bárbara Pérez, born into slavery on the Santa Teresa plantation. Tomás Pérez wished to show me each of the places where he and his family had worked and lived, but blindness and his physical fragility made this impossible. So with his blessing but with other companions, I went into the countryside to meet his friends and co-workers. Most of these conversations were carried out in the context of the project Rescate de la Memoria Viva, organized through the Provincial Archive of Cienfuegos. Rather than list all of the participants by name here, I have cited them one by one in the notes to specific interviews. I shall always be deeply grateful to Tomás Pérez and to his former neighbors in Cienfuegos, Rosario, San Antón, Pepito Tey, Arimao, and La Sierra for sharing with me their visions of the world that was built with freedom.

Index

Blanco, Manuel, 97, 101, 106; nonregistration
of slaves by, 109; during 1895–1898 war,
132, 148; and inheritance from José
Quesada, 216–223
Bohíos, defined, 18
Borrell de Águila, Flora, 105
Brazley, Stella A. E., 168
Bringier, M. S., 27
Brooke, John R.: in Louisiana, 59–60, 155; in
Cuba, 155, 178, 180, 186
Brown, Scott, 57
Brown, Sterling Price, 156, 167, 177
Bulldozers. *See* Vigilantes
Bureau of Refugees, Freedmen and Abandoned
Lands. *See* Freedmen's Bureau
Butler, Benjamin, 30, 31

Caballería defined, 23
Cabrera y Cao, Julián, 218
Caffery, Donelson, 198
Cage, Thomas A., 50, 86; elected to office, 52,
55, 69; as cane farmer, 72
Caillou Grove plantation, 48
Calleja y Capote, Andrés, 251–252
Calumet plantation, 199
Camagüey, province. *See* Puerto Príncipe
Campos Marquetti, Generoso, 248
Canary Islands: immigrants from, 115
Caonao, 245
Caracas plantation, 115
Caridad de Juraguá plantation, 23
Carmouche, Pierre Lacroix, 9, 27, 75, *170,*
173, 266–267; and recruitment to U.S.
Army (1898), 3–4, 6, 162, 166–170, 172;
and Knights of Labor, 78; and *Plessy* chal-
lenge, 90–91; in Cuba, 192, 199, 234; after
1898 war, 198, 201
Carmouche et Dupart, Pierre (Pierre
Carmouche, Sr.), 15, 27, 36
Carrier, Noël, 15
Casañas, Joaquín, 210
Casinos Españoles, 97, 104, 232
Castaño, Nicolás, 209
Caste: opposition to, 44–47, 88–93, 226, 247;
legislation, 88–89, 91
Castillo, José Rogelio, 141
Cebreco, Agustín, 3, 4, *249,* 253–254, 256; in
exile in Central America, *127,* 128; and

1895–1898 war, 130, 139, 151; ideas of,
131; after 1895–1898 war, 174, 203, 234,
236; and events of 1912, 243, 244
Cédulas (identity papers/voter registration
cards), 113
Censuses: 1877, of Cuba, 102, 116; 1899, of
Cuba, 187; 1907, of Cuba, 214–215, 236,
261; 1910, of Louisiana, 261; categories in,
261n11
Central mills *(centrales),* 117
Central Narcisa, 134–135
Centro Africano (Casino Africano), 251
Chandler, R., 40
Chinese, in Cuba, 25, 27, 97; during Ten Years'
War, 101–102; in the 1870s, 106; in the
1880s and 1890s, 112, 115, 116, 122; as
voters, 146
Chinese, in Louisiana, 49
Christian, Nelson, 58, 79
Cienfuegos (city and district), 5, 17, 20, 101,
121; population of, 97, 102, 116; effects of
Ten Years' War in, 97–100; sugar produc-
tion in, 115; newspapers in, 123; and 1895–
1898 war, 133–150; after 1895–1898 war,
208, 228, 232; and events of 1912, 245–
246
Cienfuegos Brigade, 134, 140, 141, 147
Cinclare plantation, 199
Ciriaco Criollo, 109, 111. *See also* Quesada,
Ciriaco
Citizens' Committee (also called the Citizens'
Committee to Test the Constitutionality of
the Separate Car Act), 3, 88–93, 199
Citizenship, 7, 39, 56, 62, 115, 119, 147, 155,
159, 195, 252, 253; Spanish, for residents of
Cuba, 145; Cuban, 178, 183, 188
Civil rights. *See* Rights *entries;* Suffrage
Civil War (U.S.), 28–29, 30–36, 94
Clark, Victor, 120
Clark, Willie, 175, 176
Cleveland, George, 47
Cleveland, Grover, 156
Cobre, 236; Virgin of, 237, 256
Cohen, Walter L., 200
Coleman, Willis Prague, 169
Colfax massacre, 53, 63, 66
Colomb, Adèle, 16, 27, 266
Colonos (cane farmers), 117, 118, 152

Liberation Army, Cuban (Ejército Libertador): recruitment to, 132–147; strategies of, 136, 140; divisions within, 141, 142; desertions from, 145; access to officer status in, 152. *See also* Cuban wars for independence; Veterans

Libertos (freedpeople), 112, 118

Lincoln, Abraham, 31, 36

Lodge Elections Bill, 87

Lombano Blanco, Manuel, 135

Lombillo, Ramona, 105

Longstreet, James, 50; and militia, 56, 57

López Zapata, Tomás, 240

Los Guaos, 133, 245

Lottery: in Louisiana, 87; in law of Cuban abolition, 108–114

Louverture, Toussaint, 76, 168, 172

Lucas (Lucust), Israel, 73, 78–79

Luis (resident of Santa Rosalía plantation), 102

Luna Peralta, Rafael, 245

Macarty, Eugène (immigrant from France), 15, 21

Macarty, Eugène V. (Creole activist), 49

Maceo, Antonio, 2–4, 173; in exile in New Orleans, 2–3, 76; in Ten Years' War, 103; Protest of Baraguá, 104; in exile in Central America, 127, 127–128; and 1895–1898 war, 129, 130, 131, 137–139; ideas of, 131, 224, 226, 264; death of, 145; remembered, 168, 234

Maceo, José, 3, 234; in Ten Years' War, 103; in Guerra Chiquita, 105; in 1895–1898 war, 139

Machado, Damián, 112

Madison, James, 57

Magoon, Charles Edward, 214

Mal Tiempo, battle of, 138

Mambí/mambisa (Cuban rebel soldier). *See* Liberation Army, Cuban

Mandeville, Eulalie, 15, 21

Manduley, Rafael, 237

Manifesto of Montecristi, 131

Manrique de Lara, Juan, 144

María (daughter of Carlos Dupart and Carlota Belair), 15

Marie, Frederick, 42, 45, 46; elected to office, 55, 62

Marigny, Bernard, 15

Marking, by class or color, 78, 219, 250

Marrero, Lucien, 190–191

Marshall, John R., 176

Martí, José, 127, 128, 129, 130; ideas of, 131, 139, 224, 264

Martinet, Louis A.: elected to office, 55, 62; in the 1880s and 1890s, 88, 151; as notary, 161, 172, 200, 267

Martínez Campos, Arsenio, 101, 141

Martínez Ortiz, Rafael, 180, 184

Mary plantation, 78–79

Masó, Bartolomé, 212

Masonic lodges, 75, 76, 192

Matanzas (town and province), 16, 17, 140

McCall, Henry, 157

McEnery, Samuel D., 74, 160, 164

McKinley, William, 154, 155, 160; and 1898 war, 163, 166, 167; and U.S. occupation of Cuba, 178

Metropolitan Police (New Orleans), 51, 59

Michelet, H. H., 40; and militia, 57, 70, 71; and elections, 64–65, 67, 69

Microhistory, as method, 5–6

Militia, in Louisiana, 50, 52–53, 56–57, 63, 64, 69, 83, 162

Millán Ferrez, Lieutenant Colonel, 135

Minor, Henry C., 55, 86

Minor, William H., 22, 48–49

Miró Argenter, José, 243

Mitchell, Michele, 51n58

Moderate Party, 212–213, 236

Moncada, Guillermo, 103, 108, 234

Monroe, Frank A., 196

Montalvo, Canuto, 251

Monte, Rafael ("Tata"), 137–138

Monteagudo, José de Jesús ("Chucho"), 140, 210; and events of 1912, 241–244, 247, 250, 257

Montejo, Esteban, 245

Montero, Amado, 210

Moore, John J., 47–49, 71, 165

Mora, Tomás, 119

Moret Law, 97, 100, 102, 116

Morgan City, 77, 80

Morris, Milton, 42, 45, 49, 55

Morúa Amendment (Ley Morúa), 233, 237, 238, 239, 240, 242